4.95

The Great EB

Encyclopædia Britannica;

OR, A

DICTIONARY

OF

ARTS and SCIENCES,

COMPILED UPON A NEW PLAN.

IN WHICH

The different SCIENCES and ARTS are digested into
distinct Treatises or Systems;

AND

The various TECHNICAL TERMS, &c. are explained as they occur
in the order of the Alphabet.

ILLUSTRATED WITH ONE HUNDRED AND SIXTY COPPERPLATES.

By a SOCIETY of GENTLEMEN in SCOTLAND.

IN THREE VOLUMES.

VOL. I.

EDINBURGH:

Printed for A. BELL and C. MACFARQUHAR;
And sold by COLIN MACFARQUHAR, at his Printing-office, Nicolson-street.

M.DCC.LXXI.

Title page of Volume I of the first edition, 1768-71

Library of Congress Catalog Number: 58–8379

THE UNIVERSITY OF CHICAGO PRESS, CHICAGO 37
Cambridge University Press, London, N.W. 1, England
The University of Toronto Press, Toronto 5, Canada

The Great EB

THE STORY OF THE ENCYCLOPÆDIA BRITANNICA

By Herman Kogan

THE UNIVERSITY OF CHICAGO PRESS

Some Prefatory Notes

This book, in which I have sought primarily to fill the assignment of chronicler, is not intended to be the definitive history of the *Encyclopaedia Britannica* but is essentially an informal narrative designed to tell the general reader of the origins, development, trials, and triumphs of the great reference work. As such, it also relates the experiences of many individuals—publishers, editors, scholars, and contributors, printers, critics, promoters, and salesmen—who have been part of the encyclopaedia's long and often exciting life.

I hasten to express the hope that the intellectual and scholarly aspects of the *Encyclopaedia Britannica* have been competently treated here. The discussion of each edition against its specific historical era may not be as extensive or as analytical as some may wish, but I have sought to extract and synthesize from those editions and from those eras articles and events of significance which typified the prevailing spirit and intellectual atmosphere, whether hostile or friendly. Additional material pertaining to the encyclopaedia's editorial history, principally in its first 125 years, remains to be mined, and I hope that those qualified to do so will be stimulated to engage in this task and offer the results of their inquiries. It is a venture worthy of the efforts of the best of scholars, and one that presents many provocative possibilities—suggested, I feel, in the pages that follow.

There is as much emphasis here on the *Encyclopaedia Britannica* as a publishing enterprise—a business—as on its intellectual and scholarly elements. Justification for such emphasis is apparent to anyone familiar with the history of encyclopaedias. Walter Yust, editor of the *Encyclopaedia Britannica* since 1938, once told a convention of librarians, "The business of revising books needs the businessman even before it needs the editor and the scholar." He was referring to the financial requirements of the system of continuous revision now used by the *Encyclopaedia Britannica*. But his statement applies with equal importance to the broader endeavor of encyclopaedia-making itself.

As this narrative shows, the *Encyclopaedia Britannica* has had individuals associated with it as publishers who were chiefly businessmen eager to maintain its physical and intellectual continuity. Some were thwarted scholars or had bold streaks of vanity or were interested, above all, in profits. And some were concerned seriously with stimulating learning and with furnishing to a vast number of persons a means of acquiring knowledge.

Without these men, the notable editors and the distinguished contributors might well have had no *Encyclopaedia Britannica* in which to present the intellectual products of their erudition and experience. With these men to finance publication, to work out plans for promoting the sale of the work, and to gamble on their business acumen and ingenuity for the financial success of various editions, the continued existence of the *Encyclopaedia Britannica* was assured.

A full listing of reference materials and other sources appears at the end of this volume, but I wish at this point to thank various individuals for their indispensable help. They are, among myriad officials of Encyclopaedia Britannica, Inc., the publisher and chairman, William Benton; its editor-in-chief, Walter Yust; its president, Robert C. Preble; its managing editor, John V. Dodge; and the chairman of its Board of Editors, Robert Maynard Hutchins. In Great Britain, John Armitage, London editor of the *Encyclopaedia Britannica,* and Miss Christine L. Turner, for many years the London company's secretary, supplied data elsewhere unavailable. Stanley Morison, scholar and wit, one of the world's prime authorities on typography, and the official historian of the *Times* of London, offered vital counsel. J. S. Maywood, chief of the intelligence division of the *Times,* and former officials and employees of the *Encyclopaedia Britannica,* including A. E. Dolphin, Miss Ellen Snoxall, and M. D. Law, now editor of *Chambers's Encyclopaedia,* granted interviews yielding information that expanded my knowledge of the subject and clarified obscurities.

The responsibility for all that follows is, despite all aid and assistance, fully my own.

HERMAN KOGAN

Contents

Contents

Part One

I

Three Men of Edinburgh

On a dismal February day in 1898 a man sat brooding in his dimly lit office in London's Printing House Square, home of the *Times*. For eight years Charles Frederick Moberly Bell, managing director of "The Thunderer," had struggled with the problem of keeping the newspaper great—and solvent. Sometimes the task seemed forlorn. Sometimes a faint hope of success was aroused. In the years since he had been summoned from his correspondent's post in Egypt, Bell, stolidly and almost desperately, had prevented his newspaper from sinking into a financial morass. Excessive costs, falling circulation, and wasteful expenditures, together with the complicated arrangement by which the heirs of the founder, the first John Walter, demanded immediate payment for printing the newspaper that persisted in growing economically ill year after year, continued to be burdensome, almost disastrous.

Bell had worked hard. He had maintained the journalistic prestige of the *Times* and built an illustrious staff, especially of foreign correspondents. He had established a publications department and issued a *Times Gazetteer* which produced extra revenue. And yet more money was now needed, and more subscribers. The paper simply was unable to support itself, certainly not with the competition from the popular halfpenny newspapers and magazines designed principally for the hundreds of thousands of newly educated readers.

To Bell had come scores of ideas and suggestions: the paper must be made livelier in appearance and its grayness erased, its editorial costs must be slashed and its high-priced foreign staff reduced. Although he punctiliously scrawled earnest replies to such proposals, Bell rejected them, for he considered them no proper solutions for basic problems; moreover, they would require a lowering of standards and lead to a decline in the newspaper's prestige and importance.

Now he slouched in a chair at his big oaken desk covered with unanswered letters, galley proofs and page proofs, messages and memorandums. Musing on the present and the future, he glanced at his appointment book and stirred himself. On his schedule was a meeting with a pair of visitors to London—two Americans—prepared to offer yet another proposition. Perhaps they were worth listening to. Perhaps their plan would have some merit. Yet, Americans?

Soon the men arrived. One was sharp-eyed, dartingly quick in his movements and talking swiftly and choppily, a daring fellow named James Clarke, already prospering in the book business in the United States. The other was stocky, his eyes glistening beneath heavy brows; he was Horace Everett Hooper, one of Clarke's partners in a firm that specialized in bargain sales of reprints and sets of Dickens, Thackeray, and George Eliot to settlers on the American prairies and in the new cities of the Midwest, in sales of books publishers found it difficult to ged rid of, and in mammoth auctions of "cheap books."

The callers wasted no time. They had come, they quickly informed the weary Bell, with a letter of introduction from Adam W. Black of the venerable publishing firm of A. & C. Black, in Soho Square. Bell scanned the brief note, then lifted his shaggy head to listen.

"We have a contract with the Blacks," said Clarke, "for the reprint rights to the ninth edition of the *Encyclopaedia Britannica*. We propose to reissue it at a very low price, much lower than it has ever sold for. Now, we know the *Times* needs money and . . ."

"I've been here for a year or more, sir. I have found this out," interrupted Hooper.

Bell shrugged and motioned for Clarke to continue.

"Well, we know the value of the *Times*'s name. We can do each other great good. Now here's our proposition. We propose that the *Times* advertise that anyone can have a set of the *EB* by paying only a guinea down and thirteen more guineas—yes, fourteen in all, much less than the regular price—in monthly instalments, not before the set is delivered but after. We, Mr. Bell, will take the risk of collecting the payments. We will pay for the advertisements in the *Times* and even in other papers. We'll take at least a hundred columns of advertising space. And all we want is the name of the *Times* behind us—and we'll pay the *Times* a good royalty. What say?"

Bell stared at the men. "But the edition is old. It's out of date. Surely, gentlemen, everybody who wants it already owns it."

"That's not true," replied Hooper quickly. "There is a public—a new public—that cannot pay cash and will buy it. This is a public that cannot persuade a bookseller to give credit."

"But surely that public doesn't want an encyclopaedia at any price, however low," Bell said.

"Leave it to me," replied Hooper. "We'll create a public that will want it."

Despite the self-assurance of the Americans, Bell asked for time to consider their proposition. When they left, he wrote a letter to Black, seeking verification of the details they had given him:

"I have had much pleasure in seeing Mr. James Clarke, who presented your letter of introduction, and discussing with him and another gentleman, whose name I must apologize for forgetting, the proposal as to the reissue of the *Encyclopaedia Britannica*. The proposal is somewhat a novel one and from several points of view deserves very careful consideration. . . ." Was the arrangement a valid one, Bell wanted to know. And was it safe to place the general proposition before Arthur Walter, governing proprietor of the *Times?*

Black's reply reassured Bell, and soon he was in conference with Walter, who was coldly unresponsive to any idea of affiliation with Americans. But Bell drove hard. He emphasized the financial advantages that might accrue to the *Times*. "We stand to lose nothing, not even if only a single set is sold. Perhaps we will gain no revenue at all. I understand the Civil Service Supply Association and the Army and Navy stores are taking orders for the same set at eighteen guineas, only four more than these Americans propose selling it for. Perhaps the prospects of a big sale aren't very good, but I believe it is a plan worth trying."

Within a week, Clarke and Hooper were back. The *Times*, Bell informed them, accepted their proposition. But, as ever, it must remain conservative. In this unusual venture, the initial printing order would be for only eight hundred sets.

2

With this pact, Bell instituted an extremely significant development in the lives of the *Times* and the *Encyclopaedia Britannica*. The events that followed upset tradition and precedent, created excitement, fury, and controversy in the worlds of journalism, scholarship, bookselling, and advertising, and helped to rescue from disaster both the newspaper and the encyclopaedia.

At the time of this vital transaction, the *Encyclopaedia Britannica* had been in existence for 130 years, its life marked by some chaos and much calm, its appeal, especially in its home country, limited mainly to those few capable of affording it. Its progenitors had been numerous and varied. One of the earliest works designed to present information within the circle of human knowledge was the *Naturalis historia* of Pliny the Elder in A.D. 77, which contained some twenty thousand extracts from two thousand works by more than four hundred writers of his own and preceding ages. And through ensuing centuries there appeared scores of other works encyclopaedic in nature: compilations of philosophical or informational essays and treatises on the arts and sciences. The Chinese are commonly accorded the distinction of having published the first modern-style encyclopaedia, *T'ai P'ing Yu Tan,* in the tenth century. Most remarkable in the thirteenth century was the colossal *Imagi mundi* of Vincent of Beauvais, a Dominican friar and librarian to France's Louis IX, who gathered together the knowledge of the Middle Ages, working for twenty-four years, from 1240 to his death in 1264. First to actually use the title of "Cyclopaedia"—from the Greek words meaning "learning within the circle"—was a compiler named Ringelberg in Basel in 1541; this work and others in the last half of the sixteenth century and early part of the next were intended to comprise, within moderate compass, a series of systematic digests applicable to certain major departments of man's knowledge and art or to the entire body of human learning.

The first important encyclopaedia in English—most of its predecessors were in Latin—was the *Lexicon Technicum,* issued in 1704 by a London clergyman named John Harris. Because, unlike its predecessors, its contents were arranged in alphabetical order, Harris' work was acclaimed an estimable advance toward a general encyclopaedia of value. Actually, though it professed to be universal, the work was limited almost entirely to mathematics and the physical sciences; one of its contributors was Sir Isaac Newton. But its success in scholarly circles encouraged Ephraim Chambers, a London globe-maker, to bring forth in 1728 his impressive *Cyclopaedia,* or *Universal Dictionary of Arts and Sciences,* in two large folio volumes. He included such innovations as an elaborate system of cross-references by which the material, alphabetically arranged, was correlated.

Chambers' volumes were the direct inspiration for the famed and influential French *Encyclopédie*—Denis Diderot's *Encyclopédie, ou Dictionnaire raisonné des sciences, des arts et des métiers*—for which the first prospectus appeared in 1750. Originally this work was intended as a translation of Chambers' encyclopaedia and an expansion of it to eight volumes with some six hundred plates. But the project developed far beyond this innocent plan. Ostensibly the *Encyclopédie* was a reference work; but its main purpose, from the very first volumes in 1751 and 1752, was to bend its readers to rational and scientific points of view rather than merely to impart knowledge and information. Rousseau and Voltaire were among its contributors, and throughout the thousands of pages in the twenty-eight volumes into which the encyclopaedia finally grew there were strong notes of skepticism, firm emphasis on subjects of positive knowledge, science, and technology rather than on theology and religion, and sly criticism of existing conditions in France and other parts of Europe.

The first two volumes were suppressed as injurious to royal authority and to religion, and the police tried to seize all copies and the manuscript of the next volumes. Governmental permission was eventually secured to continue the work, and five more volumes appeared by late 1757. Within a year, however, Diderot was harassed by official interference, this time by a decree stopping the sale and an order to burn all copies. From this point on until completion of the massive work in 1765, Diderot was forced to work in secret, but he succeeded in completing his tremendous undertaking with the occasional connivance of friendly French authorities. For his important work, Diderot was said to have received a meager sum, while the publishers of the *Encyclopédie* amassed fortunes.

3

Publication of the French *Encyclopédie*, discussed and fought over, praised and criticized and evaluated everywhere as sections and then whole volumes became available in western Europe, directly stimulated the creation of the *Encyclopaedia Britannica*. Three Scots, all men of Edinburgh, were responsible, two of them, Andrew Bell and Colin Macfarquhar, for the central idea and for obtaining subscribers and the third, William Smellie, a scholar brilliant and bibulous, for the editing, writing, and arrangement of articles. Until this venture, Bell was known in Edinburgh primarily for his skill in engraving names, crests, or initials on dog collars. He was a spry fellow of unusual appearance; he stood four and a half feet tall and had an enormous nose and crooked legs. At parties, when guests stared or pointed to his nose, he would disappear, then return with an even larger nose of papier-mâché. And, instead of riding a small horse through the streets of Edinburgh, he chose the largest he could find, always mounting the beast with a ladder while loungers cheered. Macfarquhar was a hard-headed printer with a bent for learning. He soberly concentrated on his business and possible profits. Evidently he engaged in what was then and later called "ethical piracy," for he was twice brought into court, once for reprinting without permission an edition of the Bible and again for the same offense with Lord Chesterfield's *Letters to His Son*. Each time he was compelled to pay small fines.

This pair considered the year 1768 a good one for bringing out an encyclopaedia. Agitation and controversy over the French *Encyclopédie* was still rife. Edinburgh was a city on the verge of a golden age, a center of learning and a home of writers, thinkers, and philosophers, wags, wits, and teachers. Bell and Macfarquhar intended to profit from what they considered the errors of Diderot and other encyclopaedists. Their production, they agreed, would differ in its basic nature: it would have an orderly arrangement of the arts and sciences, and, although it might be subtitled a "dictionary," it would contain not merely brief definitions but, wherever feasible, lengthy essays and treatises. Each art, each science, would be treated completely and definitively in a systematic form and under its proper denomination, with technical terms and subordinate topics also listed alphabetically. And they were emphatic in their avowals that their *Encyclopaedia Britannica* would, in intent and purpose, be as utilitarian as it would be philosophical.

Their choice for editor was only twenty-eight years old, but William

Smellie was already adjudged "a veteran in wit, genius and bawdry" among Edinburgh's literary men and intellectuals. As a boy of twelve Smellie had been apprenticed by his father, Alexander Smellie, an architect and stonemason in an Edinburgh suburb, to a maker of whalebone stays for ladies' corsets. But such work was not for this boy, and he shifted to Messrs. Hamilton, Balfour and Neal, official printers for Edinburgh University. During his years there, Smellie was permitted to attend whatever classes at the university he wished; he concentrated on Latin, English, and the natural sciences. He won a prize offered by the Edinburgh Philosophical Society for setting up a special edition of Terence, and, by the time he was nineteen, he was editing a literary weekly called the *Scot's Journal*. At twenty-four he was a master printer, publishing with two other men a compilation of news and philosophical discussion, the *Weekly Journal*. Eager and intellectually curious, he was one of the founders of the Newtonian Society "for young men desirous of mental improvement." He assisted Dr. William Buchan in preparing his scientific classic, *Domestic Medicine*, and, after intensive botanical studies, published a series of dissertations on the sexes of plants, in which he took strong issue with some of the basic theories of Linnaeus and other orthodoxists.

As devoted to whiskey as to scholarship, Smellie, when roistering, delighted in reciting tedious poems written in Latin by his father. But Bell and Macfarquhar, appreciating his intellectual abilities, chose him after only fleeting consideration of other possible editors. After Smellie had agreed with the general plan of arrangement and publication, Bell wrote him a formal letter to bind the pact:

"Sir, as we are engaged in publishing a Dictionary of the Arts and Sciences; and as you have informed us that there are fifteen capital sciences which you will undertake for, and write up the subdivisions and detached parts of these conform to your plan, and likewise to prepare the whole work for the press etc. etc.; we hereby agree to allow you £200 for your trouble."[1]

Once hired, Smellie temporarily abandoned his drinking and devoted himself to his tasks. Bell and Macfarquhar bustled about Edinburgh with a prospectus of the forthcoming work, rounding up enough interested Scots to be included in the "Society of Gentlemen" under whose financial auspices the single sections, the individual volumes, and then the entire work would be published. This kind of subscription

[1] Throughout this book, the rate of exchange for the British pound is approximately $5 in American currency.

plan had evolved from the mode of individual patronage. As far back as 1552 John Coxe's *Tables of Grammar* printed a subscription roster of eight lords of the Privy Council. A surge in Great Britain's subscription book publishing had come at the end of the seventeenth century with Dryden's translation of Virgil, followed by long lists of subscribers for Milton's *Paradise Lost* and for various works of Pope and Steele, though Pope, in his "Epistle to Dr. Arbuthnot," railed against those "who roar aloud, 'Subscribe! Subscribe!'" Samuel Johnson's every enterprise had required subscribers before publication could be contemplated, and it was he who had written, "He that asks subscribers soon finds that he has enemies. All who do not encourage him, defame him."

Bell and Macfarquhar managed to obtain the money they needed, and, although Smellie insisted that he required time to turn out a more comprehensive work, they and the subscribers pressed him. So, for three years, sections of the encyclopaedia were issued periodically. The first two numbers came in December, 1768, costing sixpence a copy on plain paper and twopence more on finer paper. The first volume ("Aa" to "Bzo") was completed and bound in 1769, the second ("Caaba" to "Lythrum") a year later and the third ("Macao" to "Zyglophyllum") in 1771. The price for the full set was £12, and scattered through the volumes' 2,659 quarto pages were superb copperplate engravings by Bell of 160 illustrations ranging from a detailed sketch of Noah's Ark to a contemporary map of North America.

4

Purpose, method, and aim were crisply clear in Smellie's Preface. "Utility ought to be the principal intention of every publication. Wherever this intention does not plainly appear, neither the books nor their authors have the smallest claim to the approbation of mankind." The departure from usual encyclopaedic method was cogently stated: "To diffuse the knowledge of Science, is the professed design of the following work. What methods, it may be asked, have the compilers employed to accomplish this design? Not to mention original articles, they have had recourse to the best books upon almost every subject, extracted the useful parts, and rejected whatever appeared trifling or less interesting. Instead of dismembering the Sciences, by attempting to treat them intelligibly under a multitude of technical terms, they have digested the principles of every Science in the form of systems or distinct treatises, and explained the terms as they occur in the order of the alphabet, with references to the Sciences to which they belong."

Smellie stressed his hope that this new kind of encyclopaedia would benefit the greatest number of persons rather than merely please or educate a limited group. "It is well if a man be capable of comprehending the principles and relations of the different parts of science, when laid before him in one uninterrupted chain. But where is the man who can learn the principles of any science from a Dictionary compiled upon the plan hitherto adopted? We will, however, venture to affirm, that any man of ordinary parts, may, if he chuses, learn the principles of Agriculture, of Astronomy, of Botany, of Chemistry, etc., etc., from the ENCYCLOPAEDIA BRITANNICA." As for the "principal authors made use of in the compilation," Smellie listed more than 150 sources, including Francis Bacon's essays, John Balfour's philosophical writings, Chambers' *Universal Dictionary of Arts and Sciences*, and other similar encyclopaedias, Hume's essays, Locke's essays on human understanding and Voltaire's on taste, and varied gazettes, pamphlets, magazines, newspapers, and textbooks.

5

How much of this first three-volume set Smellie wrote has never been determined, but many of his own tastes, inclinations, and interests were reflected in the pages. Certainly the article "Abridgement" was Smellie's, for he was critical of windy rhetoric in writing and discourse. "Abridgement," he wrote, "is a term signifying the reduction of a book into smaller compass. . . . This talent is peculiarly necessary to the present state of literature; for many writers have acquired the dexterity of spreading a few critical thoughts over several hundred pages. When an author hits upon a thought that pleases him he is apt to dwell upon it, to view it in different lights, to force it in improperly, or upon the slightest relations. Though this may be pleasant to the writer, it tires and vexes the reader."

Smellie's essay on "Language" was timely. He concluded his long treatise on the language of the British: "Like a healthy oak planted in rich and fertile soil, it has sprung up with vigour; and although neglected, and suffered to be run over with weeds; although exposed to every blast, and unprotected from every violence; it still beareth up under all these inconveniences, and shoots up with a robust healthiness and wild luxuriance of growth. Should this plant, so sound and vigorous, be now cleared from those weeds with which it has been so encumbered; should every obstacle which now buries it under thick shades, and hides it from the view of every passenger, be cleared away; should the soil be cultivated with care, and a strong fence be placed around it, to prevent the idle or the wicked from breaking or distorting its branches; who can tell with what additional vigour it would flourish; or what amazing magnitude and perfection it might at last attain!—How would the astonished world behold, with reverential awe, the majestic gracefulness of that object which they so lately despised!"

Although poetry was discussed in a mere five hundred words and drama in seven lines, Samuel Johnson's dictionary, published little more than a decade before, received six pages. And not all of them were laudatory: "Dr. Johnson, with great labour, has collected the various meanings of every word, and quoted the authorities. But, would it not have been an improvement if he had given an accurate definition of the precise meaning of every word; pointed out the way in which it ought to be employed with the greatest propriety; shewed the various deviations from the original meaning, which custom had so far established as to render allowable; and fixed the precise limits beyond which it could not be employed without becoming a vicious expression?"

On "Woman," the encyclopaedia was at its most succinct: "The female of man. See HOMO." California was described as "a large country of the West Indies"; Nigeria was called "Nigroland"; the Sahara Desert "Sara"; Arabia "Felix"; and the mid-Atlantic referred to as the "Ethiopic Ocean." India was described as the "Mogul Empire," and South Africans were characterized as "Hottentots." Even a prescription for toothache was included: "Laxatives dissolved in asses' milk." Cold baths were prescribed for melancholy madness and the bites of mad dogs. And in the article on "Tobacco," readers were solemnly advised that its excessive use was capable of "drying up the brain to a little black lump consisting of mere membranes." With these oddities were others deemed of interest at that time. No less than thirty-nine pages were devoted to a comprehensive discussion of "Farriery," the art of curing the diseases of horses, treated so fully, explained Smellie, because most of the men engaged in this profession were universally illiterate, and "the practice of this useful art has been hitherto almost entirely confined to a set of men who are totally ignorant of anatomy." On biblical matters, the articles reflected the current acceptance of much legend as certain fact. Only an inch of space was devoted to a simple but serious account of Jonah's encounter with the whale, but the section on Noah's Ark, illustrated with Bell's engravings, was longer and quite explicit. A portion of it, referring to the drawing of the Ark "floating on the waters of the deluge," read: "It must be observed that besides the place requisite for the beasts and birds, and their provisions, there was room required for Noah to lock up household utensils, the instruments of husbandry, grain and seeds, to sow the earth with after the deluge; for which purpose it was thought that he might spare room in the upper storey for six and thirty cabbins, besides a kitchen, a hall, four chambers, and a space about eight and forty cubits in length to walk in."

6

Financially, the three volumes brought no great riches to the men most closely affiliated with the set, but the three thousand purchased by others than subscribers constituted a reasonably good sale. Intellectually, the new encyclopaedia evidently created no stir either in this "Athens of the North" or elsewhere in the British Isles; James Boswell, who followed almost all that went on in Edinburgh, nowhere in his writings mentioned this initial edition.

Even the ubiquitous Boswell evidently was not aware of the angry reaction among some buyers of the encyclopaedia to the inclusion in the third volume not only of an unusually instructive article on "Midwifery" but of the three accompanying full pages of copperplate engravings that showed, in clinical detail, the exact processes involved in normal and abnormal deliveries of babies. Many who considered the illustrations obscene ripped the offending pages from the volume and some, especially parents with children in school, threatened in addition to start legal action against Bell and Macfarquhar. No qualms of any kind, however, affected two brothers, Edward and Charles Dilly, well known in London as booksellers and exporters of books to the American colonies; they thought well enough of this first edition of the *Encyclopaedia Britannica* to issue in 1773 a reprint, omitting the names of Bell, Macfarquhar, and Smellie but retaining on the title page the dignified appellation of "Society of Gentlemen."

Bell and Macfarquhar pondered the possibility of establishing continuity with another edition, but for a time they did nothing about it. Periodically both men discussed the idea with Smellie. But he proffered no definite answer. He had turned to other editorial pursuits and resumed his boisterous sessions with tavern cronies. In 1773 he started the *Edinburgh Magazine and Review* with Gilbert Stuart, but the project expired after little more than a year, primarily because the cantankerous Stuart's slashing satires on the figures of his day, his intemperate drinking, and his erratic ways led to bickering and quarrels. Smellie also engaged in the study of French, the better to translate Buffon's *Natural History of the Earth and of Men and Quadrupeds,* a task on which he was engaged when Bell and Macfarquhar, early in 1776, approached him with a definite offer to be editor of the second edition of the *Encyclopaedia Britannica.*

Smellie listened, but he was unenthusiastic about their proposition, although instead of a flat fee they now offered him one-third of the profits. Smellie's refusal was based not on financial considerations but on the fact that the Duke of Buccleuch, enlisted by Bell and Macfarquhar as one of their major subscribers, insisted that biographies of living persons be included in the contemplated new edition. Angrily, Smellie balked at this suggestion, maintaining that only the perspective of time could safely evaluate who was worthy of inclusion in a contemporary encyclopaedia. When Bell and Macfarquhar sided with their patron, Smellie declined the proposition, and his former associates were obliged to look elsewhere for an editor.

Smellie proceeded with his translation of Buffon's classic work and in 1780 was elected superintendent of natural history in the Society of Antiquarians of Scotland. He also began to write his own *General System of Natural History,* and his reputation as an elder in the coteries of Edinburgh's literary set grew. With other lighthearted Scots he organized the Crochallan Fencibles. They met periodically in the tavern of Downey Douglas in the Anchor Close and invited politicians, artists, writers, philosophers, and professors to speak at their gatherings, afterward subjecting them to the most merciless verbal assaults. Smellie held court at these sessions, often bellowing, when asked by a newcomer about his editorship of the *Encyclopaedia Britannica,* "I wrote most of it, my lad, and snipped out from books enough material for the printer. With pastepot and scissors I composed it!"

A rather grotesque figure in his later years, carelessly dressed, with hair long and bushy, black clothes wrinkled and covered with snuff, cocked hat rusty with wear, Smellie became a close friend of Robert Burns when the poet came to Edinburgh. They were good companions, drinking and talking far into many nights. Burns considered Smellie, as he later wrote to Peter Hill, an Edinburgh bookseller, a man "positively of the first abilities and greatest strength of mind, as well as one of the best hearts and keenest wits," commenting that when he was in bad circumstances "if you add a tankard of brown stout and super-add a magnum of right Oporto, you will see his sorrows vanish like the morning mist before the summer sun." This buoyant poet, Smellie's "Rabbie," left, in a few lines, a vivid portrait of Smellie in those days after his editorship of the *Encyclopaedia Britannica:*

> To Crochallan came
> The old cock'd hat, the grey surtout, the same;
> His bristling beard just rising in its might,
> 'Twas four long nights and days to shaving night;
> His uncomb'd grizzly locks, wild staring, thatch'd
> A head for thought profound and clear, unmatch'd;
> Yet tho! his caustic wit was biting, rude,
> His heart was warm, benevolent, and good.

2

"Balloon Tytler" and Others

Rebuffed by Smellie, Bell and Macfarquhar searched among the talented men of Edinburgh and decided upon a brilliant eccentric named James Tytler to edit the second edition. Born twenty-nine years earlier in Fearn, Tytler had once inclined toward the ministry, planning to follow the example of his father, a clergyman in the established church of Scotland. But, unable to accept the strict doctrines, he had then turned to medicine. To pay part of his expenses at Edinburgh University, he had shipped out for a year to Greenland as a ship's surgeon. Once graduated, Tytler promptly abandoned medicine to open a small pharmacy in Leith, two miles out of Edinburgh. When this enterprise failed because Tytler spent most of his working hours reading obscure medical books, he took on literary hack work and dabbled in scientific writing, toiling at meager fees for booksellers who employed him to abridge, rewrite, or compile various volumes.

Tytler lived miserably and dressed carelessly. He was a slender little man, a pathetic figure shuffling from bookseller to bookseller as he sought work. As a family provider, he was abominable. It was not uncommon to see one of his children trudging through the Edinburgh streets with a packet of copy for a printer, on whom the family's next meal depended. Tytler's first wife deserted him and their children; his second wife nagged and scolded him incessantly, and not without cause.

He drank heavily, but he had phenomenal recuperative powers. Once a Scottish gentleman requiring a brief treatise on some historical matter tracked Tytler to a grimy garret where he was temporarily hiding from family and creditors. Tytler, snoring heavily, lay on a rickety bed. Roused and informed what was wanted, Tytler mumbled to his landlady to bring paper, pen, and ink, scribbled away atop the upturned washtub he used for a desk, and within two hours had completed the assignment "as completely," an admiring biographer, Robert Meek, recorded later, "as if it had been the result of the most mature deliberation, previous notice and a mind undisturbed by the fumes of any liquid capable of deranging its ideas."

When Bell and Macfarquhar decided on Tytler as editor, he was ensconced in Holyrood Palace, a debtors' sanctuary. Relieved of family and financial responsibilities, Tytler had devoted himself there almost entirely to his writing. He produced a volume titled *Essays on the Most Important Subjects of Natural and Revealed Religion,* a compilation underscored with a strong note of religious skepticism. Unable to afford a printer, he had built his own press and set the essays by hand. He had also written a great number of medical treatises, edited a short-lived periodical called *A Gentleman's and Ladies' Magazine,* and undertaken an abridgment of a *Universal History,* which he abandoned after turning out a single volume.

It was this gift for varied literary enterprise that prompted Bell and Macfarquhar to overlook the many defects of Tytler's character. They paid his debts, took him out of Holyrood Palace and installed him in Macfarquhar's office on Nicolson Street. Not only did they know Tytler to be a many-talented man; they also were aware of his constant state of penury. Tytler could be had without great expense. He agreed to work for only seventeen shillings a week, and, in his seven years with Bell and Macfarquhar, Tytler's salary never increased; on this and related matters his biographer had cause to lament: "To supply the exigencies of the present moment always set bounds to his pursuits, and he was certainly happier in the possession of a few shillings than an ignorant money-maker can possibly be with all the treasures of India. . . . Like many of the sons of literature, he knew not how to appreciate his own merit, and would have furnished more valuable materials for the contemptible sum of a few shillings than a man of inferior abilities would have given for as many pounds."

2

But Tytler's encyclopaedia, for all his low pay, was a success, within the limits of his time and place. Like the first edition of the *Encyclopaedia Britannica*, this one also was issued in separate parts, the first appearing on June 21, 1777, the last on September 18, 1784—101 in all, making up ten volumes totaling 8,595 pages. This time Bell contributed 340 plates, with a number of excellent maps placed together in the 195-page article "Geography." A great many articles were taken over from the first edition; Tytler wrote dozens of new ones. On the title page of the first bound volume of the "greatly Improved and Enlarged" edition were indications of the advanced steps taken. For it not only emphasized the inclusion of biographies "of the most Eminent Persons in every Nation from the Earliest Ages down to the Present Times" but boasted that the whole had been "COMPILED FROM THE WRITINGS OF THE BEST AUTHORS, IN SEVERAL LANGUAGES; THE MOST APPROVED DICTIONARIES, AS WELL OF GENERAL SCIENCE AS OF PARTICULAR BRANCHES; THE TRANSACTIONS, JOURNALS, AND MEMOIRS, OF LEARNED SOCIETIES, BOTH AT HOME AND ABROAD; THE MS LECTURES OF EMINENT PROFESSORS ON DIFFERENT SCIENCES; AND A VARIETY OF ORIGINAL MATERIALS, FURNISHED BY AN EXTENSIVE CORRESPONDENCE."

Yet, for all the self-praise, there were important omissions. Although the individual parts were issued during and after the American Revolution, there was no mention of that event. Only in the article on Boston—there were none on Philadelphia or New York—did an oblique reference creep in: "The following is a description of this capital before the commencement of the present American war." America was not completely neglected, however. In discussing New England, for instance, Tytler laid emphasis on the "blind fanaticism" with which the Puritan communities established legal codes ("a singular mixture of good and evil, wisdom and folly") and offered this explanation for the witchcraft frenzy of Salem: "Posterity will, probably, never know exactly what was the cause or remedy of this dreadful disorder. It had, perhaps, its first origin in the melancholy which those persecuted enthusiasts had brought with them from their own country, which had increased with the scurvy they had contracted at sea, from a change of climate and manner of living. The contagion, however, ceased like all other epidemical distempers, exhausted by its very communication. A perfect calm succeeded this agitation; and the Puritans of New England have never since been seized with so gloomy a fit of enthusiasm."

The highly touted biographies—"A new department which has not been found in any other collection of the same kind, except in the French Encyclopedists"—included an interesting assortment, subject and space considered. A full page was given to Chaucer, a little over a page to Jesus Christ, a page and a half to Shakespeare, a page and a quarter to John Milton, and two pages to the essayist Joseph Addison, "one of the brightest geniuses that this or any other country has produced." Among the longest articles was that on war; it ran to 132 pages, enlarging in detail on the opening theme, "War is a great evil but it is inevitable and oftentimes necessary." In "Chronology," the date of the world's creation—based on Archbishop Ussher's reckoning, first added to the English Bible in 1701—was given with firm decisiveness as 4004 B.C. Cain's birth, appropriately enough, was set at 4003, and in 2348 B.C., read the article, "The old world is destroyed by a deluge which continued 777 days." This event was referred to again in the section placing the building of the Tower of Babel in 2247 B.C.—"About the same time Noah is with great probability supposed to have parted from his rebellious offspring and have led a colony of some of the more tractable into the east and therefore either he or one of his successors to have founded the ancient Chinese monarchy."

An indication of methods of the age in treating diseases little understood then was reflected in an article recording the cure devised by Solano de Luque for tuberculosis. "He chose," wrote Tytler, "a spot of ground on which no plants had been sown, and there he made a hole large and deep enough to admit the patient up to the chin. The interstices of the pit were then carefully filled up with the fresh mould, so that the earth might everywhere come in contact with the patient's body. In this situation the patient was suffered to remain till he began to shiver or felt himself uneasy. . . . The patient was then taken out, and, after being wrapped in a linen cloth, was placed upon a mattress, and two hours afterwards his whole body was rubbed with the ointment composed of the leaves of the *solanum nigrum* and hog's lard."

3

One article undoubtedly written by Tytler was "Flying," for he was fanatically interested in the possibility of man's flight. After relating how birds propelled themselves through air, Tytler told of the experiments of Friar Bacon, who, five hundred years before, had affirmed that the art of flying was possible. "He assures us, that he himself knew how to make an engine wherein a man sitting might be able to convey himself through the air like a bird; and further adds, that there was then one who had tried it with success. The secret consisted in a couple of large, thin, hollow copper globes, exhausted of air; which being much lighter than air, would sustain a chair, wherein a person might sit."

Tytler's devotion to these and other theories of flight was not limited to writing about them. He devoutly believed that "in future ages, it will be as usual to hear a man call for his wings, when he is going on a journey, as it is now to call for his boots." Early in 1784, after completing his work for the final volume of the edition and having contracted with Bell and Macfarquhar to edit the next, Tytler set out to test some of his theories of flight.

Spurred by the successful ascensions the previous year at Annonay, France, of the Montgolfier brothers, Joseph and Jacques, in their newly invented balloon, Tytler secured financial backing for his experiment. He built a fire balloon in which hot air from a bucket of burning coals or a small stove was introduced into the balloon, thereby presumably making the balloon lighter than air. And on August 27, 1784, he and a crowd of cronies and backers, including a well-known golf caddie nicknamed Lord North, the caricaturist John Kay, and businessmen and merchants, gathered at Comely Gardens, near King's Park in Edinburgh. His balloon, 40 feet high and 30 feet in diameter, rose to 350 feet. But, after sailing jerkily for half a mile at that height, it suddenly plummeted down upon a refuse pile along a road leading out of the city.

Two other attempts in the next few months were equally unsuccessful. In the first, the men hired to build the stove designed to furnish hot air deceived Tytler by making it smaller than he had directed them to, and the flight failed, a calamity that caused several gazettes, inspired by Tytler's disgruntled backers, to vilify him and suggest he be placed under magisterial surveillance. But he made a final effort one dawn in King's Park. This time, however, the stove engendered so much heat that the balloon swiftly floated, before Tytler could control its course, into a towering tree. The stove itself exploded and shattered, and Tytler barely escaped with his life.

There were no further balloon ascensions, but his efforts won him the mocking appellation of "Balloon Tytler." Robert Burns knew him thus, writing in *Notes on Scottish Song:* "An obscure, tippling, but extraordinary body of the name of Tytler, commonly known by the name of Balloon Tytler, from his having projected a balloon—a mortal who, though he trudges about Edinburgh as a common printer, with leaky shoes, a skylighted hat and knee buckles as unlike as 'George-by-the-Grace-of-God and Solomon-the-Son-of-David,' yet that same unknown drunken mortal is author and compiler of three-fourths of Elliott's pompous 'Encyclopaedia Britannica,' which he composed at half a guinea a week." On another occasion, when Tytler wrote a pamphlet in defense of Mary, Queen of Scots, Burns was more friendly. He sent his picture and "A Poetical Address to Mr. James Tytler," one stanza of which read:

> I send you a trifle, a head of a bard,
> A trifle scarcely worthy your care;
> But accept it, good sir, as a mark of regard,
> Sincere as a saint's dying prayer.

The Elliott in Burns's verbal caricature was Charles Elliott, in whose Edinburgh bookshop sets of the *Encyclopaedia Britannica* could be purchased unbound for ten pounds. Elliott disposed of more than fifteen hundred sets in less than a year, a sale that convinced Bell and Macfarquhar that a third edition would yield even bigger profits.

But this edition was destined to do without the services of Tytler, although he did write a dozen articles for it before disaster befell him. After the failure of his balloon experiments, he devoted himself primarily to literary work. His only extracurricular activity involved tests with a perpetual motion machine, which proved unsuccessful, and the concoction of a bleach for linen, which was effective but was promptly purloined from him by unscrupulous clothing merchants to whom he made his discovery known.

His non-encyclopaedic writings led to disaster. In 1792 he was importuned by a group calling itself "Friends of the People" to prepare a pamphlet advocating more equal representation of all citizens in Parliament. In the slim booklet he called on all the citizenry to address the throne directly and scored the usual custom of petitioning Parliament itself for reforms. For such suggestions more important men had been tried for high treason. When Tytler heard that official inquiries were being made about the writer of the pamphlet, he left Scotland. He took refuge first in a friend's house on the desolate Salisbury Crags, then continued on to Belfast, where he waited for the fury to die down by completing a three-volume *System of Surgery*, on which he had labored intermittently for many years.

But Tytler never again returned to Scotland. When he failed to appear before the High Court of the Justiciary early in 1793, he was banished from his native land. He sailed then for America, composing at sea a long, banal poem titled, "The Rising of the Sun in the West, or The Origin and Progress of Liberty." He settled in Salem, Massachusetts, where he resumed the kind of life he had led in Scotland, interspersing periods of great conviviality with literary hack duties or newspaper work. The periods of conviviality soon surpassed the periods of industry. On a freezing January day in 1805, having celebrated vigorously with drinking companions, Tytler staggered into a deep ditch at the edge of a country road and caught a severe cold. He died within a week, a failure in one sense, yet, considering the *Encyclopaedia Britannica*, a man of accomplishment, a man of whom his sorrowing but perceptive biographer offered apt estimate: "The world was his country and the whole human race his brethren and sisters. . . . He was a real friend to the whole human race, and if he was an enemy to one human being, it was to himself."

4

At the time of Tytler's banishment, a number of single volumes of the third edition had already been issued. Weekly numbers had started to appear in 1787. Tytler made his editorial contributions, but Macfarquhar, self-educated and intellectually inquisitive, had as much to do with the editing as Tytler. When Tytler fled the country, Macfarquhar took over the editorship. He intended to recruit notable contributors, for he had great plans for expanding each edition of the *Encyclopaedia Britannica*, as the limits of knowledge themselves were constantly expanding, to make his set truly a compendium of all the world's information and knowledge. But before he could put this plan into action, Macfarquhar died in 1793, worn out, it was recorded, "by fatigue and anxiety of mind."

Bell, a more sanguine and hardy man, now assumed full ownership and responsibility. He pushed publication, and the weekly numbers at ten shillings each kept issuing from the printers, arousing more interest, attracting more subscribers. Shortly after Macfarquhar died, Bell hired George Gleig of Stirling to be editor. Gleig was a formidable scholar, specializing in the moral and physical sciences. Earlier he had been recruited as a contributor, and eventually his writings in this edition totaled eighteen articles, varying from "Episcopacy" to "Passion" to "Love and Marriage" to "Mathematics," the latter running to 229 double-column pages. In contrast to Smellie and Tytler, Gleig, destined in later years to be appointed a bishop of the Episcopal Church of Scotland, worked steadily and soberly. He carried through Macfarquhar's idea of recruiting notable contributors, inducing, among others, Professor John Robinson, secretary of the Royal Society of Edinburgh, to revise the article on "Optics" and to write a series of articles on natural philosophy that attracted considerable attention from the contemporary philosophers and intellectuals. William Smellie himself was also a contributor. He composed a biography of Lord Kames to supplant a scheduled sketch which the noted jurist's son, Hugh Drummond, considered a "miserable tissue of falsehood and malignity."

Steadily the numbers kept coming out, regularly the bound volumes appeared, and by 1797 the third edition was deemed complete, in eighteen volumes instead of a planned fifteen. It was a handsome set with close to 15,000 pages, 542 engravings, and well-wrought maps in a special section. An elaborate frontispiece showed a library with huge Corinthian columns, in front of which men and women were practicing the various arts and sciences described in the work; a background disclosed a man and woman in a field with an elephant and lion; and atop it all floated a balloon, which some wagsters reckoned was a tribute to "Balloon Tytler." For the first time, the set was officially dedicated. The honor was bestowed on King George III, "Father of Your People, and enlightened Patron of Arts, Sciences and Literature." Taking note of the war with the French, the dedication expressed the wish that "by the Wisdom of Your Councils, and the Vigour of Your Fleets and Armies, Your MAJESTY may be enabled soon to restore Peace to Europe; that You may again have leisure to extend Your Royal Care to the Improvement of Arts, and the Advancement of Knowledge; that You May Reign long over a Free, Happy and a Loyal People. . . ."

Gleig used the Preface to take note of a prime competitor—Chambers' *Cyclopaedia*—and though he cited it as a valuable work he also referred to it as one of the "mere dictionaries." A distinguished feature of the new edition, Gleig wrote, was that it gave "short, though luminous detail of the progress of each particular nation which from the remotest period to the present time has acted a conspicuous part on the theatre of the world." As if to stress this aim, "America," which had covered eighteen pages in the second edition, now filled eighty. Many articles were reprinted from the earlier editions. The one on "Adam" informed the reader that he was "the first of the human race" and "was formed by the Almighty on the sixth day of the Creation. His body was made of the dust of the earth." The article concluded: "Some are of the opinion that he died on the very spot where Jerusalem was afterwards built; and was buried on the place where Christ suffered, that so his bones might be sprinkled with the Savior's blood!" In this edition, one exclamation mark was sufficient; there had been three in the second edition.

In the Edinburgh community of scholars and savants, the edition was a popular one, the best-received yet. This had been presaged almost from the first volume. "The patronage of a liberal subscription made it necessary," wrote Gleig, "to double the number originally intended." Eventually thirteen thousand sets were printed and the sale of this edition and its predecessor together yielded £42,000 for Bell, who had acquired all copyrights and sole ownership, and the heirs of Macfarquhar. As editor, Gleig received £500 and Bell, as engraver, received £1,000. James Hunter, an Edinburgh bookseller who acted as a wholesaler, parceling out copies to other booksellers to dispose of to subscribers, also profited, as did John Brown, who served as "corrector of the press."

5

Popular in Scotland, its renown spreading to other sections of the British Isles, this edition of the *Encyclopaedia Britannica* was the first of many to fall prey to the "ethical pirates" in the United States. Although the new nation's copyright laws protected Americans in America, the act of 1790 also protected any American publisher who wanted to reprint any British work by a special clause limiting benefits to American citizens.

First to take advantage of this largess was an energetic Philadelphia printer named Thomas Dobson. He imported each number of the new *Encyclopaedia Britannica* as it emerged from the printing presses and began to issue his own by 1790. He hired such American writers as Jedidiah Morse to rewrite sections he considered either British-biased or inaccurate, and he kept pace with the original edition, his eighteenth volume appearing only a month or two after the one in Edinburgh. Dobson called his set simply the *Encyclopaedia;* on his title page appeared "THE FIRST AMERICAN EDITION, IN EIGHTEEN VOLUMES, GREATLY IMPROVED." He eliminated, of course, the dedication to King George. His price was only six dollars for the entire set, less than one-third the price of the original. His customers included George Washington, who had tried to win a set in a lottery and had failed; Thomas Jefferson, who wrote Dobson to tell him of his delight with the articles on architecture; and Alexander Hamilton, who made the purchase shortly before his fatal duel with Aaron Burr.

Dobson hired a number of skilled young engravers to make plates for his edition, but all they did was to alter some of the details in Bell's drawings. Each engraver scratched out Bell's name and substituted his own—whether Scot, Thackara, Akin, Allerdice, Barker, Ballance, Seymour, Lawrence, Smither, Lawson, or Trenchard—and it is ironic that, although some of these men gained considerable fame as artists and engravers in later years, their biographers invariably indicated that their renown stemmed from the plates in Dobson's *Encyclopaedia.*

A case of literary piracy closer to home was in Dublin, where James Moore, a bookseller who also operated a lottery brokerage on College Green, published a reprint of the third edition in 1791. It bore the full title of *Moore's Dublin Edition, Encyclopaedia Britannica,* and word for word, plate for plate, was a precise reproduction of the Edinburgh publication.

But neither Dobson's nor Moore's depredations appear to have aroused any protest from Bell. Dobson did not halt his activities with the third edition itself. In 1800, Gleig edited and Bell and his son-in-law, Thomson Bonar, published a two-volume supplement to the edition, and Dobson appropriated this, too, noting blandly in his prospectus to potential buyers that Gleig intended to update various important subjects that had been treated in the first volumes of the third edition; "Chemistry" was one of these, and "Astronomy" and "Electricity" were others. In "Chemistry," chemical symbols were used for the first time in an article written by the great Dr. Thomas Thomson, who later based his notable *System of Chemistry* on his encyclopaedia article.

The supplement itself was of considerable value in correcting errors of earlier editions, although Gleig, for all his praise of its "beautiful articles," was honest enough to acknowledge that imperfections still existed: "For perfection seems to be incompatible with the nature of works constructed on such a plan, and embracing such a variety of subjects." But the supplement is remembered because of several less important but more picturesque details.

In the dedication to his monarch, Gleig took harsh notice of the French *Encyclopédie*, hitting directly on the basic difference between it and his own. His was a conveyer of information, the other a shaper of ideas and morals. "The French Encyclopédie," he wrote, "has been accused, and justly accused, of having disseminated far and wide the seeds of anarchy and atheism. If the *Encyclopaedia Britannica* shall in any degree counteract the tendency of that pestiferous work, even these two volumes will not be wholly unworthy of Your Majesty's attention."

And it surely must have been pleasing to Gleig and Bell to hear the story, one that has been retained in *Encyclopaedia Britannica* folklore, of how the ruler of Persia, Futteh Ali, responded when the British ambassador carried a set with him all the way from London through months of weary traveling by land and sea. Overwhelmed by the gift, the Shah decreed that his full title would be, after he had read all of the volumes, "Most Exalted and Generous Prince; Brilliant as the Moon, Resplendent as the Sun; the Jewel of the World; the Center of Beauty, of Musselmen and of the True Faith; Shadow of God; Mirrow of Justice; Most Generous King of Kings; Master of the Constellations Whose Throne is the Stirrup Cup of Heaven; and Most Formidable Lord and Master of the *Encyclopaedia Britannica*."

6

Despite the satisfactory sale of this edition, strife and quarrels speckled the final years of Andrew Bell's life. Over a disagreement about whether to limit sales to subscribers or to attempt wider distribution through bookstores, he and his son-in-law parted company so bitterly that Bell vowed never to speak to Bonar again, a pledge he kept to the day of his death in 1809. Also, after decreeing a new edition of the *Encyclopaedia Britannica*, Bell found considerable fault with the man he had hired as editor, Dr. James Millar, a classical scholar and fellow of Edinburgh's Royal College of Physicians. Bell considered Dr. Millar too slow and dilatory. Dr. Millar, probably with justification, insisted his salary was too meager, and for nearly a year the two dour men refused to talk to each other and conducted their editorial conferences through intermediaries.

In this strange arrangement, Dr. Millar's representative was Macvey Napier, a bright young literary man and a member of the Society of Writers to the Signet. Bell's representative was the man soon to be called in Edinburgh "The Napoleon of Publishing," bold and aggressive Archibald Constable. Apprenticed when a boy of twelve to a bookseller, Constable had spent a few years in London, then had returned to Edinburgh's High Street to open a store bearing the sign, "Scarce Old Books." His first attempts at publishing, in 1795, were quickly triumphant; he printed an account of bloody riots in Granada by a man who had escaped. Then he sped on to more solid ventures. In 1802 he was twenty-eight, a round-faced man, with no great learning but a fiery ambition. He was friendly with the leading literary Scots who gathered regularly in his High Street bookshop. Even while he was serving as Bell's intermediary with Millar, he was publishing the new *Edinburgh Review and Critical Journal*, a savage, smart, and witty journal which featured the writings of Francis Jeffrey, the lawyer-critic, and Sydney Smith, the Anglican clergyman with the acid-tipped pen. Constable smashed traditions and broke in on the London literary monopoly by offering unprecedented sums to his contributors—£20 for a single-page book review and as much as £1,000 for a philosophical dissertation or a long epic poem. Despite the strong Whig tone of this journal and Constable's own political leanings, he was strengthening relations with Sir Walter Scott, an exponent of anti-Whiggism who was nevertheless willing to deal with Constable in publishing matters.

Through the efforts of Constable and Napier, a dubious peace between Bell and Millar was established. At Bell's urging, Constable began to take considerable interest in the publication. Harassed by relatives demanding that he give Bonar a greater share in the enterprise and irritated by quarrels with Millar, Bell turned increasingly to the ruddy-faced High Street publisher. "Indeed," Constable recalled later, "his calls upon my time were frequently a little inconvenient. I gave him a great deal of advice, and if he had not had grandchildren and two or three writers as agents, besides other interested persons about him, the trouble I took in his service might have been beneficial to us both."

By 1804, Bell proposed that Constable buy all the rights to the *Encyclopaedia Britannica,* plus the parts of the fourth edition being issued, for £20,000. But Constable declined. The work on the fourth edition proceeded. Most of the volumes contained little more than reprints of the third edition, except for several articles on mathematics which won some acclaim, and a rather comprehensive account of Dr. Edward Jenner's successful introduction of vaccination for cowpox in 1796. When the edition was finally complete in 1810, it ran to twenty volumes of 16,033 pages and 581 engravings, and about four thousand sets, at £36 each, were sold. By this time Bell had been dead a year, and Constable actively re-entered negotiations for possession of the publication.

To begin with, he purchased from Bonar the copyright to the supplement to the third edition for only £100. Within three years, Bell's heirs had so mismanaged the affairs of the firm and its finances were so snarled that its stock was put up for sale. All manner of legal muddles had to be cleared, but now Constable was persistent in his zeal to become the owner. He saw it as a property with a great future, "a first-rate property," and his nimble mind, contemplating the advances in knowledge, especially in scientific fields, bustled with ideas for its improvement. So he put in his bid to purchase it all—copyrights, copies of the fifth edition that had been started in 1810 as a reprint of the fourth, heirs' shares—for £14,000. For a time Bonar delayed negotiations; he had friends with money, and he threatened to buy the publication himself. Eager to avoid further complications and delay, Constable compromised by allowing Bonar a third interest and finally came into possession of the property. In 1814, when Bonar died, Constable bought his share from his heirs for a generous £4,500.

7

The transaction was derided by Constable's fellow publishers. They pointed to articles already outdated. They predicted Constable would bring ruin on himself and all connected with him by paying so large a sum for ownership of the *Encyclopaedia Britannica,* especially since he had acquired eighteen hundred copies of each of the first five volumes of the fifth edition along with all the rest. But Constable shrugged off the jeers. "The Encyclopaedia is no doubt the greatest speculation we ever made," he wrote to Robert Cathcart, one of his partners, "and will require a great command of money; but should any doubt be entertained of the safety of it, we could have no difficulty in selling it in shares for a very great premium."

Freed of the encumbrances of lawyers and Bell's relatives, Constable proceeded with spirit. He hired Dr. Millar to edit the remaining volumes of the fifth edition. When the work neared completion in 1813, he arranged for wider distribution than any of the earlier editions had had, for he was determined that the fame of the *Encyclopaedia Britannica*—and of Archibald Constable—should spread beyond the smoky limits of Edinburgh. He printed elaborate brochures describing the virtues of the volumes; *Blackwood's Magazine*, started in 1809 as a rival to Constable's *Edinburgh Review*, scoffed at "the pomp of the announcement." And he became the first of the publishers of the *Encyclopaedia Britannica* to place advertisements in the newspapers—small, dignified, and discreet, in the mode of the day —offering the set for £36. Moreover, Constable determined to issue a supplement to the fifth edition. This venture was to bring new prestige to the *Encyclopaedia Britannica,* offer important contributions to knowledge, and confound those who scoffed.

3

Constable's Famous Supplement

For good reason was Archibald Constable known in his trade as "The Crafty." Shrewd in business affairs, he was also aware of new trends in science and philosophy. He readily realized the importance of keeping high the standards of the *Encyclopaedia Britannica* and making it an authoritative record of such developments. He realized, too, that unless his *Encyclopaedia Britannica* kept pace with rising competitors, it might easily be outdistanced. Chambers' *Cyclopaedia,* now published by Abraham Rees, was still thriving. In 1808, Dr. David Brewster, a physicist of wide learning, had begun his *Edinburgh Encyclopaedia.* A group of scholars was preparing an *Encyclopaedia Metropolitana,* abandoning the alphabetical arrangement and grouping subjects under headings of science—pure, mixed, and applied—history and biography, geography, and lexicography.

Of first importance to Constable was the recruiting of authorities to write about the subjects they knew best. In his brochure announcing his proposed supplement to the fifth edition, he made it clear how vital he considered such contributors. "The last four volumes of this edition," he wrote, "will be composed entirely of original *Articles, written by persons of the first literary eminence,* purposely that all of the most important Discoveries and Improvements in the Sciences, Arts and Manufactures, may be brought down to the latest date; an advantage which similar undertakings, published progressively during a period of ten or twelve years, cannot possibly possess." No man of modesty when his publishing projects were involved, Constable declared that these volumes would "thus render the *Encyclopaedia Britannica* the most complete repertory of human knowledge that has yet been given to the public."

Even before selecting an editor, Constable engaged several outstanding scholars to write special dissertations to be published separately, then to be placed in the front of each volume of the supplement. Dugald Stewart, the Scottish savant especially noted for his application of common sense to the problems of philosophy, was his guide in this venture. Stewart suggested that four major discourses be written, one for each proposed volume, to form a general map of the various departments of human knowledge, in much the same way that D'Alembert's discourses served the French *Encyclopédie.* Each writer would describe intellectual progress since Bacon's time.

The most distinguished of the dissertations—all were long enough for a full-sized book—was Stewart's. Titled "A General View of the Progress of Metaphysical, Ethical and Political Philosophy Since the Revival of Letters in Europe," it ran to 423 pages of elegant rhetoric studded with anecdote and analogy and ideas slightly tinged with the sentiments of revolutionary France. To most readers, it imparted, as one critic wrote, "a belief in progress—the real progress which practical and human improvement are steadily, even when most imperceptibly, making." Constable himself was so full of admiration that he increased his original payment of £1,000 to the philosopher by £700.

John Playfair, another Edinburgh scholar, not only received £500 for consenting to write the dissertation on advances in mathematics and physics—he died before completing it—but also profited in another way. As a move toward setting up the supplement, Constable asked half a dozen literary men to examine previous editions of the *Encyclopaedia Britannica* and to prepare reports on their defects and how they might be remedied or eliminated. Each received from £100 to £200 for recommendations on which Constable based his plan for the supplement. He turned his prospectus over to Stewart for an expert opinion, but Stewart passed it on to Playfair. That diligent scholar examined the prospectus and returned it to Constable within a week, greatly improved. So pleased was Constable with Playfair's revised plan that he sent him six bottles of his finest sherry, later writing, "It was not to everybody I would have parted with such wine! But the only regret which I felt upon this occasion was that I had nothing better to offer."

With prospectus in hand, Constable sought his editor—two editors, at first, for he intended to use one for literary articles and another for scientific essays. He considered Robert Cadell, his son-in-law and another of his partners, and Dr. Thomas Brown, professor of moral philosophy at Edinburgh University. Cadell was quickly rejected as not sufficiently learned, and Dr. Brown refused the offer, an insult which later led Constable to comment testily, "He preferred writing trash or poetry to useful lucrative employment. It is fortunate all of us are not equally fond of money, or the scramble would be greater and hard blows more frequent."

Then Constable remembered the man who had been James Millar's alter ego in the squabbles with Andrew Bell. In the decade since, Macvey Napier had risen in stature as a contributor to magazines and editor of the works of Sir Walter Raleigh. Constable had always admired in Napier "a dash of gentility and aspiring consequence." Napier accepted the assignment as sole editor. His contract, signed on June 11, 1813, guaranteed him a fee, substantial for that period, of £1,575, with an extra £735 if the supplement were reprinted or if the first printing sold beyond 7,000 copies, and an additional £300 for expenses. Napier promptly set out to line up contributors who would fulfil Constable's requirement of "first literary eminence." Furnished with letters of introduction from Stewart, Napier went to London. "Constable has prevailed upon him, after much solicitation," wrote Stewart to Francis Horner, the political economist, "to undertake the laborious task of being the Editor of this work; and I really know of no person more likely to execute it with judgment and ability."

2

Even when he left for London, Napier had promises of contributions from notables besides Playfair and Stewart. Francis Jeffrey was one, Sydney Smith another, and a third was Sir Walter Scott.

Scott had been affiliated with Constable since 1802, when "The Crafty" had published his two-volume collection of folk songs, *Minstrelsy of the Scottish Border*. In 1808, responding to Constable's offer of one thousand guineas for a new poem, Scott produced *Marmion*, that vast romantic epic; its critical reception was cool, but popular approval was so overwhelming that Constable happily printed eight editions of the work. Although he had good reason to be grateful, Sir Walter quarreled with Constable because of an adverse review of *Marmion* in the *Edinburgh Review* and the magazine's strong Whiggism. The poet also fought with another of Constable's partners, Alexander Gibson Hunter, who insisted that Scott complete a biography of Jonathan Swift he had agreed to write for the firm. For a few years Scott shunned Constable, except to send a messenger for his share of the profits from *Marmion*, and wrote for the brothers Ballantyne— James, the fat, irresponsible one, whom the poet labeled "Aldibotontiphoscophornio," and John, the lean one Scott called "Rigdumfunnidos"—who were notably inept at the publishing business. The War of 1812, the final months of the Napoleonic War, soaring prices, economic distress, and starvation piled external chaos on the internal chaos of the Ballantyne enterprise and led them toward the abyss of bankruptcy. As they teetered there, Constable came to their rescue. Because he realized how awkward it would be for Scott to be exposed as an associate of wildcat publishers, Constable advanced the poet and the brothers enough money for them to avoid ruin, then formed a business alliance with Scott.

When Napier approached him to write for the supplement, Scott was in the midst of the first of his Waverley novels. But he felt he owed Constable a favor. He was not fond of the portly little publisher; yet he respected him for his ability, for his role in transforming Edinburgh into a thriving publishing center, and for his influence in diffusing knowledge and encouraging the impulse to self-education. Although he called Constable "The Emperor" and grumbled about his aggressive ways, Scott agreed to be a contributor, promising to write on "Chivalry."

He turned in the first half of his article in the spring of 1814, complaining that he did not have at his Abbotsford estate a sufficient number of reference books on the subject, suggesting that illustrations be used to achieve a richer effect, and proposing that the article be set in type as fast as possible to determine whether it were of the required length. When Napier told him more was needed, Scott responded with enough material to fill thirty pages. After tracing the history of "this curious and important subject" colorfully and eloquently to its origins, Scott noted that "the total decay of the chivalrous principle is evident. As the progress of knowledge advanced, men learned to despise its fantastic refinements; the really enlightened, as belonging to a system inapplicable to the modern state of the world; the licentious, fierce and subtile, as throwing the barriers of affected punctilio betwixt them and the safe, ready and unceremonious gratification of their lust or their vengeance."

When Napier called at Abbotsford to thank Scott for his article and to present him with £100, the poet snorted.

"Now, tell me frankly," he asked, "if I don't take this money, does it go into your pocket or the publisher's? It is impossible for me to accept a penny for it from a literary brother."

Napier replied that he had nothing to gain if Scott refused the money.

With a shrug, Scott pocketed the £100. "I have trees to plant and no conscience as to the purse of my fat friend Constable."

Subsequently, at the height of his new success as a historical novelist, Scott contributed two other articles to later volumes of the supplement. For each he received £100, with no inquiries about who would profit if he refused the payment. "Romance," which he defined as "a fictitious narrative in prose and verse, the interest of which turns upon marvellous and uncommon incidents," was twenty-one pages long. But "Drama" ran for forty-three pages and was considerably more contentious. It included not only an able historical survey of the subject but a sharp and pertinent critique of the British theater of Scott's day. He lamented the strong influences of lesser German dramatists on the national stage; he complained that "the wretched pieces of Kotzebue have found a readier acceptance, or more willing translators, than the sublimity of Goethe, the romantic strength of Schiller, or the deep tragic pathos of Lessing." London, he wrote, was cursed with a monopolistic set of theatrical entrepreneurs and a sordid collection of theatergoers—"a corrupted metropolis" catering to an awful class of people and allowing vice and indecency to present a bold and audacious front. He pleaded for the restoration of high standards and good entertainment, although he had scorned the puritanical who deemed all theater evil. "To those abstracted and enrapt spirits, who feel, or suppose themselves capable of remaining constantly involved in heavenly thoughts, any sublunary amusement may justly seem frivolous," Scott wrote. "But the mass of mankind are not so framed. . . . When the necessity of daily labour is removed, and the call of social duty fulfilled, that of moderate and timely amusement claims its place, as a want inherent in our nature."

In writing "Drama" Scott was substituting for William Hazlitt, for when that critic-essayist was approached as an expert on the subject, he had begged off with the excuse, "I know something about Congreve, but nothing at all of Aristophanes, and yet I conceive that a writer of an article on the Drama ought to be as well acquainted with the one as the other." Eventually Hazlitt did write "Fine Arts," which was considered by various critics, notably those of *Blackwood's Magazine*, to be incomplete and inaccurate in important details. With characteristic honesty, Hazlitt admitted that the criticism was valid and promised to do better in future assignments.

3

Extremely conscientious, Macvey Napier kept hard after prospective contributors he had encountered in London, engaging in constant correspondence with all who had promised articles.

His most prolific writer and his best proselytizer of talent for the supplement was the historian and philosopher James Mill. A contributor to scores of magazines and an East India House official, he was famous for his massive *History of India* and equally renowned as leader of the philosophic radicals, who derived their basic tenets from the Utilitarian teachings of Jeremy Bentham: "It is the greatest happiness of the greatest number that is the measure of right and wrong." Mill was a precise and lucid writer, energetic and enthusiastic. He was eventually responsible for more major articles than any other man—twelve in all, from "Beggar" to "Prison Discipline," written while serving as tutor and companion to his brilliant young son, John Stuart Mill, who worked and studied in the same room and was encouraged to interrupt his father for long discussions on political economy.

James Mill also shot a fusillade of letters to Napier. In the six years during which he sent in his erudite articles, Mill preceded, accompanied, or followed each with a letter elucidating various points, personal and philosophical. He kept Napier informed on the state of his health—he was compelled to decline to write an additional number of articles because of periodic attacks of gout—and on the progress of his son in his philosophical and linguistic studies. To his treatise on "Law of Nations" he appended a note: "My principal object will be to show that there is hardly any such thing as a Law of Nations;

that hardly anything deserving the name of Law between Nation and Nation has existed or ever can exist." He sent detailed assurances with potentially controversial contributions: "You need be under no alarm about my article, 'Government'. I shall say nothing capable of alarming even a Whig, and he is more terrified at the principles of good government than the worst of the Tories."

Actually, Mill's theories of government were considered quite bold, so much so that he had not been permitted to write about them for the *Edinburgh Review*. And his article on the subject for the *Encyclopaedia Britannica*, embodying some of the basic theories of Utilitarianism—one that seemed to especially displease its opponents was that good government could best be obtained by an extension of the rights of franchise—aroused great discussion and controversy. Although many considered the treatise a masterpiece of political wisdom, it provoked a number of articles by Thomas Babington Macaulay in the *Edinburgh Review* defending Whiggism, which, despite its principles of toleration, its theory of emancipation, and its philosophy of resistance to the arbitrary powers of government, feared what its leaders considered the extremism of Philosophical Radicalism. And Macaulay in turn elicited a reply by John Stuart Mill in the *Westminster Review* enlarging on his father's theories. All the discussion had a marked effect on the agitation for governmental renovation that culminated in the Reform Bill of 1832. The elder Mill was so important a contributor to the supplement that eventually all his articles were published in a single volume that served as a guidebook for a new generation of philosophic radicals at the University of Cambridge, a group vividly described years later by John Stuart Mill in his autobiography.

4

As a recruiter of contributors for Napier, James Mill was especially assiduous. He suggested names; he nagged those whom he suggested to accept assignments; he harassed those who had accepted to meet their deadlines. He proposed that David Ricardo, the economist, write the article on Great Britain's funding system. A diffident man, Ricardo at first declined because he felt he was not qualified, although he had spoken often on the subject in the House of Commons. But Mill, in Napier's behalf, persisted. Ricardo finally completed a paper in which he repeated his frequent charges that the system was a delusion to the citizens, who fancied that the government's sinking fund was paying off their national debt, and a snare to the government, which was consequently tempted to divert it to other purposes. All nations, Ricardo urged, should defray their expenses, ordinary or extraordinary, at the time incurred instead of providing for them by loans.

Ricardo refused payment for the article. As Mill informed Napier, the economist had moral objections to taking money for such work: "Ricardo adds that his scruples are of two kinds—first on account of the article, which he says is not worth payment; secondly, because, payment having formed no part of the motive which forced him to write the article, he reckons himself not entitled to payment." Ricardo thus joined Francis Jeffrey as one of the only two contributors to the supplement who steadfastly refused payment. Though a pungent and harsh critic in the *Edinburgh Review,* Jeffrey was mild and gentle when offered compensation for his article on "Beauty." To Napier he wrote, "I really have scruples about taking so much more than I can possibly persuade myself I have earned, and seriously beg you to consider whether you are not throwing work on me that would otherwise be bestowed upon more variable contributions."

Despite his diffidence, Ricardo firmly defended his views when Thomas Robert Malthus, importuned to write the article on "Population," opposed inclusion of his essay in the same supplement with Ricardo's. "I am not disposed to be offended at differences of opinion," Malthus wrote to Napier, "but I confess to you that I think the general adoption of the new theories of my excellent friend Mr. Ricardo into an Encyclopaedia . . . was rather premature." To this Ricardo promptly replied, "I think the supplement will gain credit by being among the first publications which has embodied and given circulation to the new, and notwithstanding Mr. Malthus' opinions I will add correct, theories of political economy. Your publication was not intended merely to give a view of the sciences that stood 45 years ago, but to improve it, and to extend its boundaries." Napier agreed with Ricardo, allowing the economist's article to stand as he had written it. Malthus' article also appeared in the supplement.

Another contributor whose modesty vanished once he began to write was Thomas Young, a many-sided scholar, a physicist who discovered the law of the interference of light, a philosopher, a physician, and an Egyptologist. When he was first approached by Napier, Dr. Young refused to write on any subject but medicine, explaining that he did not consider himself competent to discuss any of the others suggested by the editor. But once he completed the medical dissertation, he grew more pliable. Agreeing to submit others if he could remain anonymous, he ultimately wrote, between 1816 and 1823, no less than sixty-three articles, many of them brief biographies, half a dozen of major proportions. His most notable was "Egypt," in which appeared the first written account and partial interpretation of the Rosetta stone and its hieroglyphics. The Rosetta stone had been discovered in 1799, and Dr. Young's analysis of the writings contained a number of flaws, as later scholars discovered. But for its time his account was a remarkable one, still hailed a generation later as "the greatest effort of scholarship and ingenuity of which modern literature can boast." Young also contributed the article "Bridge," stimulated by the current controversy about whether to replace old London Bridge with a single-span iron bridge six hundred feet long: Young was in favor of the new bridge and sought, in his writing, to dispel prevailing ignorance and prejudice about its construction. His other contributions varied greatly: they included "Carpentry," "Chromatics," "Cohesion," "Languages," "Life Preservers," "Road-making," "Steam Engine," "Tides," and "Weights and Measures."

For the first time in the history of the *Encyclopaedia Britannica*, foreign experts contributed to its pages. One was the great French physicist, Dominique François Jean Arago, whose article on "Polarization" was translated by Dr. Young and whose treatment of "Double Refraction" also appeared in a translation by an anonymous scholar. Arago's contemporary, Jean Baptiste Biot, was represented by translations of his writings on "Electricity" and "Pendulum." Another innovation in the supplement was that contributors, except for those like Dr. Young who preferred anonymity, were identifiable by assigned letters at the end of their writings which were keyed to a table of contributors printed elsewhere in the volumes.

5

From the beginning the supplement, as Constable had hoped, was a remarkable success. He printed 7,000 copies of the first volume at twenty-five shillings each; all were disposed of within six months. Copies of the second volume, at the same price, totaled 10,500, and these, too, were sold rapidly not only in Great Britain but on a contract basis in Philadelphia by a bookseller named Thomas Wardle.

Simultaneously with the publication of the individual volumes of the supplement, Constable printed a sixth edition that was mostly a reprint of the fifth edition, with corrections of errors and a handful of new articles. Some of Constable's associates opposed this as unduly costly and unnecessary, but the pugnacious publisher emphasized the need for keeping the encyclopaedia as current as possible, no matter what the expense. As editor of this edition, he chose Charles Maclaren, a staunch Whig literary man who owned and edited the *Scotsman,* and paid him £500 "to keep the press going and have the whole finished in three years." This edition appeared in twenty volumes from 1820 to 1823, at thirty-two shillings a volume.

When the supplement was finally completed in 1824, it ran not to the contemplated four volumes but to six. It comprised 4,933 pages, crammed with 699 principal articles—informational and philosophical, argumentative and disputative—125 plates, and 9 maps.

Constable was pleased, especially so because during the time it took to produce the supplement, he had been vexed by business worries. The Ballantynes, with whom he was still affiliated, conducted their affairs carelessly, and Constable was frequently compelled to pay their debts. Scott himself drew heavy overdrafts on the firm. He insisted that his lands and estates were good security for these withdrawals and sold to Constable batches of copyrights of poems and novels. Occasionally business woes so plagued Constable that he fell ill and was compelled to rest in the south of England for months at a time. But always he was alert with comment and ideas for the *Encyclopaedia Britannica.* "The value of the Encyclopaedia as a property must always be great," he now wrote to his London agent, Joseph Ogle Robinson. Estimating that the gross sales revenue from the encyclopaedia since he had taken it over in 1812 was £60,000, he added: "We cannot have had less than a profit of 20,000 on these sales; we shall not, I think, under any circumstances, get less than 10,000 at the final close of the present impression; and we have the copyright free." Noting that a new edition of Chambers' *Cyclopaedia* had put a crimp in sales of his encyclopaedia, he nevertheless remained firm in his intentions. "The state of the book has been kept pure. . . . The Supplement has surely a present value—that is, for the volumes yet to come out—and it will supply materials for at least an equal number of volumes of a new edition. . . . We shall make from 20,000 to 30,-000 by the first edition of the Supplement, and this we owe to being the proprietors of the greatest work. . . ."

The supplement must be sold wherever possible, he later advised Robinson when the volumes were completed. He himself made a number of trips to London to visit booksellers and expound on its sales value. His imagination spurred by his own enthusiasm, he talked happily of publishing an *Encyclopaedia for Youth* and an *Encyclopaedia for Mechanics,* both to be compiled from special sections of the *Encyclopaedia Britannica.* He contemplated a completely new edition, the seventh, and signed Macvey Napier to be its editor at the munificent fee of £7,000. And always he urged larger appropriations for promoting the sale of the supplement and the sixth edition. "This book," he wrote to Robinson, "must have the most vigorous advertising. It is worthy of the best consideration all of us can give to the subject, and must have it. The sale will then, I hope, be what the most sanguine of us could wish it. . . . It is the most valuable collection of treatises ever combined in one work."

6

Unhappily for Constable and his glowing plans for his *Encyclopaedia Britannica,* there could not have been a less opportune time than this January of 1825 to write to Robinson about "vigorous advertising." For Robinson and his partner, Thomas Hurst, were momentarily uninterested in the mundane business of selling books. With many thousands of others they had indulged in an orgy of speculation raging throughout the British Isles. They were pouring their money—and thereby Constable's and Scott's and the Ballantynes'—into the wildest of schemes, gambling in South American mines, railways, and gas companies, existent and non-existent alike, investing most recklessly in hops and malt.

By midsummer a recession started and in October a panic was on. Bankers restricted credit. Hurst and Robinson found themselves close to ruin. They appealed for help to Constable, who scraped up all his personal and business funds and sent large sums to London. Yet by December disaster overtook them. Again Hurst and Robinson, unable to meet current obligations, turned to Constable. But he had exhausted most of his available cash. All sources of credit were stopped. The Ballantyne firm collapsed with a floating debt of £46,000. Constable found that his debts totaled some £200,000. Scott's obligations, when all the complexities of his tangled agreements and loosely drawn contracts with the Ballantynes and Constable were smoothed out, came to £130,000. One more effort Constable made to save himself and the others. Suffering from gout and dropsy, he painfully made his way to the Bank of England and begged its officers for a loan of

£200,000, offering as security the copyrights he owned of Scott's works. He was turned down.

Scott blamed Constable for his woes, charging that the publisher had been too rash in his expenditures and his general business conduct. With a noble air, the poet-novelist announced he would seek to pay all his debts and set out grimly with his pen to make good his vow. He signed a contract with Constable's son-in-law, Robert Cadell, whose prudence had saved him from the fate that had befallen other publishers. As Constable and Scott came to the end of their long association, the publisher was by turn humble and arrogant. At one meeting in Scott's paneled library at Abbotsford, he tried to show some cheer.

"Come, come, Sir Walter," rumbled Constable, "matters may yet come round, and I trust that you and I may yet crack a cheerful bottle of port together."

Scott replied frigidly, "Mr. Constable, whether we ever meet again in these conditions must depend upon circumstances which yet remain to be cleared up."

On a second visit, Constable rode back from the mansion to London with young Benjamin Disraeli, another visitor at Abbotsford. The publisher boasted about his publishing exploits, Disraeli later recalled, and acted as if he himself had written all the Waverley novels. When the coach stalled on a muddy patch of highway, Constable leaped out. Commanding the coachman to continue the journey, Constable yelled, "Do you not know who I am? My man, look at me! I am Archibald Constable!"

Constable managed to secure enough money to publish a cheap edition of Scott's *Miscellany,* but the new volumes soon to be produced with such labor and such speed at Abbotsford were no longer to be issued under his imprint. And the great plans he had for the *Encyclopaedia Britannica,* for the advertising and promotion of the supplement, lay in his desk in his office, gathering dust as the office itself gathered gloom and dust, and there they remained when Constable, to the end desperately striving to repay his debts, died in July, 1827.

7

Despite his dismal final years, Constable had made enduring contributions to the development of the *Encyclopaedia Britannica,* for the editions he published had added significantly to its original character.

Since the first edition in 1768, a major asset stressed by the various publishers and editors had been inclusiveness—the presentation of an orderly system of knowledge as comprehensive as the physical limits of the books would permit. Smellie's idea of an encyclopaedia that would digest the principles of every science in the form of systems or distinct treatises had been something of a revolution in encyclopaedia making. The second edition, with its biographies and history, and the next, principally with Professor Robinson's treatises and those of Dr. Thomson on chemistry, had taken strides toward establishing other vital qualities of the *Encyclopaedia Britannica*—authority and authenticity.

With Constable, these concepts received massive impetus. Increasingly, he and Napier had insisted on contributors who were established authorities in their fields, who were more aware than anyone else of the fresh advances in their specialties and could adequately and accurately record these advances for readers. Throughout the final volumes of the fourth edition, in the fifth, sixth, and the brilliant supplement to the fifth, these authorities had their say—even if some contemporary critics disagreed with their theories and views. And by recruiting authorities outside Great Britain, Constable had set a notable precedent for international orientation that would subordinate national pride to editorial excellence.

Financially, Constable had shown the skeptics that such a work as the *Encyclopaedia Britannica* could be profitable when sold at twenty or thirty pounds. The profits from the sales were not large enough, when calamity came, to offset the tremendous debts incurred in other ventures, but the showing had been respectable. To his last sad days Constable knew he had an important property in the *Encyclopaedia Britannica,* and he had faith in its future. But, sick and bankrupt, he had neither energy nor funds to carry through any of the grand plans he had made for it, and he regretted this failure more than any other part of his debacle.

There were others in the book business who also realized the importance of keeping the encyclopaedia alive as an instrument of knowledge and as a money-making device. Being canny, they sniffed about, once Constable had died, and made discreet inquiry about where and when and how the remaining copies of the *Encyclopaedia Britannica* and its copyright might be secured. Being thrifty, they pondered the price for this potentially valuable publication.

8

One such man was Adam Black, owner of a bookshop at North Bridge, confident in his methods, ambitious in his aspirations. Born in Edinburgh in 1784, Black, after a stint as apprentice to a bookseller and a term of military service, had gone to London, where one of his first —and briefest—positions had been with Thomas Sheraton, that moody, solemn genius in furniture design, then preparing *The Cabinet-Maker and Artist's Encyclopaedia*. Black worked for Sheraton only a week, writing a few articles for him. Then he left, unable to keep up with Sheraton's erratic working habits. He was twenty-four when he came back to Edinburgh to open his bookshop and to make tentative advances into publishing.

Black was thriving comfortably when the opportunity arose, upon Constable's death, to acquire the *Encyclopaedia Britannica*. The price at auction was only £6,150. This was a fraction of its real and potential value, yet Black needed financial aid to make the purchase. He persuaded three other men—Thomas Allan and Alexander Wight, bankers and publishers of the *Caledonian Mercury,* and a bookbinder named Abram Thompson—to join him. As he enlarged the firm, he took a relative, Charles Black, in with him and renamed the company A. & C. Black. Once in possession of the encyclopaedia, Black subordinated his other interests to it and set about to produce the seventh edition, establishing 1830, three years away, as the time of publication.

4

A Generation Spanned

With Macvey Napier, Black started placidly. Napier's reputation had flourished. He was now an editor of the *Edinburgh Review,* a professor of real estate and law at Edinburgh University, and chief clerk at the Court of Sessions. Black assented to having him continue as editor, agreeing without question to pay what Constable had proposed in his contract, although Napier himself, eager to assure enough money for good contributors, suggested that he receive £6,500 instead of the £7,000, with the difference being given to writers. Black also hired a subeditor, James Browne, to handle the burden of the editorial work, thereby setting a pattern for future editions.

But a conflict sprang up. The nub of the argument between editor and publisher was the number of volumes in the seventh edition. Black directed that the set have twenty volumes, to be issued, as always, in monthly parts and then in single books. Napier insisted that only in twenty-five volumes could justice be done the full scope of the enterprise. In the correspondence with Black, Napier, sometimes acrimonious, sometimes patiently tolerant, had much to say on subjects that have remained the unending dilemmas of encyclopaedists —how much to put into their books, how much money to spend on editorial material, how deeply or how superficially to treat a subject.

One of Napier's arguments involved the sizes of competitors' works; the new edition of the revised Chambers' *Cyclopaedia* under Abraham Rees would run to thirty-five volumes, the *Encyclopaedia Metropolitana* to at least twenty-five. He noted, too, the shifting character not only of the *Encyclopaedia Britannica* but of similar works: "Encyclopaedias have risen into consequence with an important and influential class, for whose use they were not originally designed. As they have been found to furnish the best means yet devised for diffusing knowledge in a systematic form, and have been largely used for that purpose, both in this and other countries they are now regularly perused or consulted by men of science, and the whole body of the learned. To limit the Encyclopaedia in such a way as to render it necessary, either to diminish the quantity of miscellaneous matter more particularly adapted to the wants and tastes of ordinary readers, or to treat important subjects in a way too curt and superficial to satisfy those of a higher class, would lower its popularity and reputation, and enable its rivals to gain an ascendancy at its expense. . . . It seems pretty clear, therefore, that the *Encyclopaedia Britannica* would take a lower station than it holds were it limited, in its renovated form, to the same number of volumes that was so long ago judged necessary to its completeness."

This last comment was in support of Napier's claim that if the growth of the set from ten to twenty volumes thirty years earlier had been judged necessary, more were now needed to cover the advances in knowledge since then. Pressed by Black to make a compromise, he wrote that with judicious editing the twenty-five volumes might be reduced to twenty-four. Finally, after more letters were exchanged, an interesting solution was achieved. When the seventh edition was finished in 1842, it filled twenty-two volumes. Evidently as able a bargainer as he was an editor, Napier really was the victor, for the 17,801 pages were larger and there were more pages in each volume than in the preceding edition. The final volume served as an index to the other twenty-one, the first index in the history of the *Ency-*

clopaedia Britannica. Its 187 pages, prepared by a Robert Cox, contained numerous errors and defective references. But the index was popular with purchasers and established another precedent for future editions.

The full set retained a large number of the best articles from the supplement to the fifth and sixth editions, especially Scott's contributions and the dissertations by Professors Stewart and Playfair. There were notable newcomers. Thomas de Quincey wrote "Schiller," "Shakespeare," and "Pope," all three "much admired," according to the *Quarterly Review,* "as specimens of critical biography." Another new contributor was Sir James Mackintosh, a brilliant but querulous philosopher. For his lengthy dissertation on the progress of ethical philosophy in the seventeenth and eighteenth centuries he insisted on being paid £600 instead of the £500 offered him. He also asked for as many as one hundred pages, a demand not granted by Napier. *Meliora* and other critical quarterlies found the article too skimpy and devoid of information on the history of ethical philosophy on the Continent but acknowledged that it was lucidly written. Another important article was by Sir John Leslie, a professor of natural philosophy at Edinburgh University, who took up the progress of the mathematical and physical sciences where the Playfair article in the supplement had concluded. This difficult section was unusually well conceived by Leslie and described in *Meliora* as "an animated and instructive sequel."

One article prompted heated reaction even before it was completed. Influential Catholics denounced the apostate priest Joseph Blanco White, an authority on Spanish subjects, and expressed concern that he would be assigned articles on Catholic doctrine. Black was quick to assure them that all articles on Catholic matters would be written by a respected member of that faith. His reply promptly embroiled the publisher with rabid members of antipapist cliques. In 1836, at a public meeting of the Edinburgh Protestant association, Rev. William Cunningham, a raucous anti-Catholic, cried out to his audience that Black was being coerced by officials of the Catholic hierarchy.

"The Papists, ever alive to the advancement of their own purposes," declared the minister, "have sent a communication to the publisher of the *Encyclopaedia Britannica* to the effect that unless he would allow them to revise and superintend the articles in the work in connection with or having reference to Popery, they would use their influence to prevent its circulation." He also inveighed against what he called "Popish influences" in the reference work.

Black acted swiftly. He filed a suit for libel to the amount of £10,000. Just as promptly, Mr. Cuningham backed down and paid to have his public apology printed in the newspapers.

2

During the twelve years in which monthly numbers, half-volumes, and full volumes came from the presses, Adam Black prospered and bought out his partners. Throughout the period, he carefully watched this most important of his expanding publishing interests. He advertised frequently, regularly inserting in the columns of the London *Times* small, one-column ads sandwiched between other advertisements, such as those for Josiah Conder's thirty-volume *The Modern Traveller: A Description, Geographical, Historical and Topographical, of the Various Countries of the Globe* and for *A Comparative Statement of the Emoluments of the Lord Chancellor, and Some of His Officers in the Year 1797*. In all, £5,354 were spent in advertising this edition, not only in London and Edinburgh, but in key newspapers all over the British Isles.

To acquaint more booksellers with his encyclopaedia, Black himself went on the road, as Constable had done before him. He visited new territories never invaded by Constable, seeking agents to handle the sale of the completed edition, though in Ireland, he reported, virtually everyone except Dubliners seemed uninterested in reading anything but their prayer books. He also sent out a number of travelers to sound out booksellers in every city and hamlet where potential customers might be found. Black himself covered fourteen hundred miles in three months by coach, gig, and foot and left a record that told of the receptions and rebuffs he received and the idiosyncrasies of some of the sellers. Black and his colleagues sought subscribers, for without an estimate of the number of possible buyers, it was, of course, impossible to proceed from single part to volume to full edition.

When the edition was finished, it went on sale for £24. Later Black reported to his associates that he had spent £108,766 on the entire project. Besides the allotment for advertising, others included £8,755 for editing, £13,887 to 167 contributors, £13,159 for plates, £29,279 for paper, £19,813 for printing. Five thousand sets of the seventh edition were sold, plus uncounted individual sections, half-volumes, and single volumes. Black's profit from the sale was modest, but he derived great satisfaction from the intellectual prestige it brought him. The *Athenaeum*, commenting carefully on each part as it emerged, concluded that the entire edition was "the most valuable digest of human knowledge that has yet appeared in Britain," and *Gentleman's Magazine* intoned: "Unlike all other works of the same class, it seems destined to maintain its place among the standard works of our national literature."

3

For the next decade Black was content to rest on this prestige, printing only as many copies as were requested by scholars or the well-to-do. There was no continuing sales campaign, no program of editorial revision.

He became involved in a lawsuit when Colonel Matthew Stewart demanded £2,000 in damages because the seventh edition had reprinted the dissertation of his father, Dugald Stewart. The colonel claimed that copyright of the article belonged to him as the professor's heir. In a hearing before Lord Patrick Robertson two days before Christmas, a jury took merely an hour to declare Black guiltless, a verdict greeted by applause in the courtroom and in the newspapers. "It appears to us," editorialized the *Caledonian Mercury*, remarking on Black's expenditures and the risk involved in publishing the edition, "that if the verdict of the jury had been in favor of the pursuer, the effect would have been to extinguish publications of this class altogether, and thus deprive the public of those most useful and instructive repertories of literary and scientific information. Such a result would have been most injurious."

Black expanded his other publishing interests and became prominent in civic and political affairs. Excessively devout in his religious ways, Black was also a deeply tolerant man who could say at a church meeting, "Every man who discharges the duties of a good citizen, whether he is Papist or Protestant, Jew or Gentile, Mohammedan or Hindoo, is entitled to the same civil privileges, and the State has no right to give a preference to one man over another, or to lay a burden upon one man rather than another because he thinks differently from you on some religious question." He was elected chief magistrate of Edinburgh and developed a reputation as a fair and liberal man. As he rose in eminence, he received a letter from the Queen's representative offering him a knighthood. He read it at the breakfast table to his wife and family. They discussed the letter, as was customary with the Blacks. Then he replied that he could not accept. "The title would only be an encumbrance," he wrote. "My wife has no desire to be called 'My Lady' and it would only foster vanity in my children."

In 1851 there occurred two important events in his publishing career. From the trustees of Robert Cadell he bought all the remaining copyrights of Scott's Waverley novels for £27,000, and he bestirred himself to publish a new edition of the *Encyclopaedia Britannica*. The decade since the seventh edition had been one marked by progress in scientific, industrial, literary, and philosophic fields. Besides, sales of the seventh edition were dwindling.

Macvey Napier had died in 1847, his final literary production a massive *History of the World,* and as his successor Black chose Dr. Thomas Stewart Traill, professor of medical jurisprudence at Edinburgh University and a versatile scholar who, most importantly, held Black's liberal principles. Half a dozen subeditors also were hired to handle the details of editorial production, among them Traill's son Thomas, and several bright young instructors and professors from the university were recruited along with a number of young ministers. They did their work—pasting up articles from earlier editions to be sent to experts for rewriting, reading manuscripts, checking proofs, preparing corrected copy for final publication—in a large room at Black's expanded North Bridge establishment. When Dr. Traill fell ill, a young philosopher, John Downes, did most of the editing, besides writing articles on "Pantheism," "Spinoza," and "Skepticism."

Black was especially active in the physical phase of the enterprise, for he was eager to keep costs down. Contributors were startled to have proofs of their writings returned to them with the admonition, "Seventy-nine lines to strike out" or "Forty-two lines to fill." These notations were always Black's. Dr. Traill, an amiable man, did not protest this invasion of the editorial sanctum.

Black's methods did cut costs. Instead of the £108,766 spent for the seventh edition, the new one of equal size was published for £75,655. And this was done without great harm to the work, although complaints were heard that some of the articles—especially those dealing with scientific subjects—had been drastically reduced, that not enough revisions had been made, that the tone was antiquated. *Meliora* added its plaint: "There is no account given of the temperance movement. Literary men must have heard of this Cause. Its advocates and adherents have long been collected into societies which have a good position in the country and ought to have been known to literary men."

Yet *Meliora,* which prided itself on being "A Quarterly Review of Social Science in its Ethical, Economical, Political and Ameliorative Aspects," fittingly took a larger view. "It is the greatest collection of literary wealth ever compiled," stated the same article, "and the greatest investment of wealth in literature ever made." Reporting on a statement issued by Black that of both the seventh and the new eighth editions a total of ten thousand copies had been sold, the reviewer added, "It is gratifying to be able to record the success which the spirited publishers have obtained by the sale of copies which, considering their great outlay and liberal conduct throughout, is eminently deserved. Such publishers do much for their country, and enshrine by their words their names among the memorable."

Enthusiastically, the journal continued: "Three hundred and forty writers . . . have united their learning to make this gigantic storehouse of knowledge. The possession of such a work is a library, for its matter is equal to one hundred ordinary octavo volumes. No library of English literature is complete without this Encyclopaedia."

Again, such classics, or purported classics, as Scott's treatise on "Drama" were reprinted. "Drama" carried an ingenuous footnote affirming that this was the same article that had been published in the supplement: "We have deemed this homage due to the fame and genius of this illustrious author, whose splendid view of the origin and progress of the dramatic art we have accordingly presented to the reader exactly as it proceeded from his own hand, leaving every contemporaneous allusion and illustration untouched." But this also was the edition which included some important writing by Thomas Babington Macaulay, notably his biographies of Samuel Johnson, John Bunyan, Oliver Goldsmith, and William Pitt. All were adjudged literary gems, and Macaulay was pleased with them, although slightly disparaging about the article on Pitt. He worked on it from November, 1857, to August, 1858, stating to Black when finally he submitted it, "What a time to have been dawdling over such a trifle!" He did them all as a favor to his good friend Black, refusing to accept a single shilling for the work.

There were other new contributors of consequence. They included Charles Kingsley, the tall, spare, and sinewy clergyman, poet, and novelist; Robert Chambers, a biologist and geologist who, in 1859, would start a new *Chambers's Encyclopaedia* with his brother, William; Baron Karl Josias von Bunsen, the Prussian diplomat and scholar; and Sir John Herschel, a kindly and serene astronomer and chemist. Dugald Stewart's article was reprinted from the previous editions, and John Leslie's was continued by Professor David Forbes, who spent three years on it. A new treatise by Archbishop Richard Whately of Dublin was an account of the "Rise, Progress and Corruptions of Christianity." Archbishop Whately's and Forbes's writing filled 1,000 pages, constituting a compendium of information on religion, philosophy, and science nowhere else available. An American contributor appeared for the first time: Edward Everett, whose career as orator and statesman included terms as governor of Massachusetts, president of Harvard College, ambassador to Great Britain, Secretary of State, and senator from Massachusetts, composed a 40,000-word biographical eulogy of George Washington, concluding, "In the possession of that mysterious quality of character manifested in a long life of meritorious service . . . and [in being] a living proof that pure patriotism is not a delusion, or virtue an empty name, no one of the sons of man has equalled George Washington."

A representative number of contributors and editors gathered at a gala dinner arranged by Black on June 5, 1861, to celebrate completion of the eighth edition. Held in the Trafalgar Hotel at Greenwich, it set a tradition for future publishers. The contributors listened comfortably to inevitable tributes to themselves and drank toasts to the success of the *Encyclopaedia Britannica*. "A gay troop of authors," reported the correspondent for the *Inverness Courier*, "might be seen eating whitebait and drinking champagne and claret supplied in profusion by their publishers," and, he added, "the long-tried integrity and independent public character of Mr. Adam Black were cordially acknowledged."

4

But all this—indeed, all the editions from the very first through the recently acclaimed eighth—was the prelude to the next edition, the famous ninth.

Aging and increasingly economy-minded in spite of his accumulation of wealth, Black was content to halt with the eighth edition. He realized the vast expenses involved in issuing new editions, the difficulties of gathering new editorial and sales staffs, the delays in publication. But he was hard-pressed by the three of his four sons whom he had taken into the firm in the 1860's to prepare a new edition. They —James T., Francis, and Adam W.—considered it sound business, and yet they were equally stimulated by the basic motives that had stirred the wisest of their predecessors: they wanted to include in their encyclopaedia as much up-to-date information as was physically possible. They were sharply aware of the massive changes in thinking and philosophies and meanings that had developed since the publication of Charles Darwin's *Origin of Species* in 1859, and they argued incessantly with their father in behalf of an edition that would reflect modern trends not only in England but in many parts of the world. By 1870 their collective persuasion had its effect. The elder Black sanctioned the venture, turned the publishing firm over to his sons, and toward the end of that year, just as the preliminary plans for the ninth edition were being mapped, he retired to spend four quiet years, before his death at the age of ninety, in placid contemplation of a life well spent.

For the first time, the man chosen to be editor was not a Scot but an English-born scholar, Professor Thomas Spencer Baynes. He had spent much time in Scotland, however, as editor of the *Edinburgh Guardian* and as professor of logic at St. Andrews University. Originally trained for the ministry, he had turned to philosophy while studying at the Philosophical Institute of Edinburgh. He was a very tense man; twice in his career before his appointment as editor he had suffered nervous breakdowns. But he was cognizant of the Darwinian concepts of man's origins and the importance of such concepts, of shifting ideas in the biological and physical sciences, and of revolutionary tendencies and methods of comparative study in history, religion, philosophy, and literature. The great objects of inquiry in this exciting age, in Baynes's view, were human nature and human life, and his general mission was to record in the pages of the planned edition of the *Encyclopaedia Britannica* all new findings and all new theories with a steady eye and an impartial mind. Baynes wrote:

This is the more necessary as the prolific activity of modern science has naturally stimulated speculation, and given birth to a number of somewhat crude conjectures and hypotheses. The air is full of novel and extreme opinions, arising often from a hasty or one-sided interpretation of the newer aspects and results of modern inquiry. The higher problems of philosophy and religion, too, are being investigated afresh from opposite sides in a thorough earnest spirit, as well as with a directness and intellectual power, which is certainly one of the most striking signs of the times. This fresh outbreak of the inevitable contest between the old and the new is a fruitful source of exaggerated hopes and fears, and of excited denunciation and appeal. In this conflict a work like the *Encyclopaedia Britannica* is not called upon to take any direct part. It has to do with knowledge, rather than opinion, and to deal with all subjects from a critical and historical, rather than a dogmatic, point of view. It cannot be the organ of any sect or party in science, religion or philosophy. Its main duty is to give an accurate account of the facts and an impartial summary of results in every department of inquiry and research.

As yet the rich materials thus supplied for throwing light on the central problems of human life and history have only been very partially turned to account. It may be said indeed that their real significance is perceived and appreciated almost for the first time in our own day. But under the influence of the modern spirit they are now being dealt with in a strictly scientific manner.

This "modern spirit" reflected itself in the men Dr. Baynes approached to be contributors. The first volume showed the wisdom of his choices. When it was issued in 1875, after four years of work, *Nature* extolled it above all other encyclopaedias, predicting that the entire edition would be "regarded as indicating the highest tidemark of the science, literature and arts of the time. Baynes has already justified the choice made of him as editor, and shown himself in all respects competent to be the leader of such a splendid undertaking." Such a reception—other journals duplicated the praise—pleased Baynes and his associates, and they worked diligently to produce each volume on schedule. As in the past, the timing and publication of each new volume depended on the revenue from the preceding volume. Each volume of the ninth sold for thirty to thirty-six shillings, depending on the quality of the binding. Sometimes the sale was slow, sometimes the books went well. It took fourteen years, from 1875 to 1889, to complete all twenty-four volumes and the index.

In true modernist tradition, an important contributor was Thomas Henry Huxley, the most stalwart proponent of the Darwinian theories of evolution. He was prolific but sometimes tardy in sending his articles. "I will do what I can if you like," he assured Baynes, "but if you trust me it is at your proper peril." His own almost illegible handwriting gave Huxley quaint amusement: "Why people can't write a plain legible hand I can't imagine." But Huxley was an extremely valuable man. He helped to classify the biological subjects, suggested the best men to write on them, and proposed changes in format and in individual articles. Among his treatises were "Actinozoa," "Amphibia," "Animal Kingdom," and, of course, "Biology" and "Evolution." The latter two synthesized the findings of Darwin. At first Huxley was reluctant to write on evolution, but eventually he agreed to do it. "Don't see how it is practicable to do justice to it with the time at my disposal," he told Baynes, "though I should really like to do it and I am at my wit's end to think of anybody who can be trusted with it."

Huxley complained often. "Your printers," he once wrote peevishly, "are the worst species of that diabolic genus I know of. It is at least a month since I sent them a revise of 'Evolution' by no means finished, and from that time to this I have had nothing from them. I shall forget all about the subject and then at the last moment they will send me a revise in a great hurry, and expect it back by return post. But if they get it, may I go to their Father!" But the complaints about punctuality were more often turned against him. He had a good sense of humor about his own tardiness, writing when he sent in his article on "Amphibia" in August, 1875, "Considering it was to be done in May, I think I am pretty punctual."

Baynes had difficulties with other contributors. The historian Edward Augustus Freeman was commissioned to write on "England." Once he begged that he could not submit his article on time because of a severe cold. Weeks later, while cruising in the Mediterranean, he suddenly sent a note to his wife: "A thing has flashed across my mind which may hasten my steps homeward. I had well nigh forgotten that I have to finish—which I have barely begun—the article on England for the *Encyclopaedia Britannica* by September. 'Tis a matter of 315 pounds so I cannot afford to let it slip." This fee was among the highest, amounting to almost four pounds a page for an eighty-page article covering the history of England up to the reign of James I.

John William Strutt Rayleigh, later the Lord Rayleigh who won the Nobel Prize for physics in 1904, was another procrastinator. Asked to write the article "Light," intended for Volume XIV, he was not ready at the designated time. The article was scheduled for a later volume under "Optics." Again Rayleigh's article was not finished. So Baynes set it forward to another volume, retitling the treatise "Undulating Theory of Light." Once more Rayleigh was not finished. When finally the article did appear, it was in the next to the last volume, under "Wave Theory of Light."

One writer whose article was not used at all was Robert Louis Stevenson, then twenty-five and with no great reputation. He was paid five pounds, five shillings for an article on Robert Burns, but Baynes rejected the finished product because it showed "want of enthusiasm." With this opinion Stevenson reflectively agreed, writing later, "To say truth, I had, I fancy, an exaggerated idea of the gravity of an encyclopaedia and wished to give mere bones, and to make no statement that should seem even warm. . . . I believe you are right in saying that I had not said enough of what is highest and best in him. Such a topic is disenheartening; the clay feet are easier dealt with than the golden head."

Some of the young British literary writers were contributors. Algernon Charles Swinburne wrote "Keats" and "Mary, Queen of Scots." When Baynes asked him to do a historical sketch of the latter, the great lyric poet was delighted. To Edmund Clarence Stedman, he expressed his pleasure that Baynes had written to "me, a mere poet, proposing that I should contribute to that great repository of erudition the biography of Mary, Queen of Scots. I doubt if the like compliment was ever paid before to one of our 'idle trade.'" William Rossetti, of the Pre-Raphaelite group of poets, painters, and essayists, proved an asset for Baynes, penning a large number of biographies of painters, revising earlier ones, and writing a major biographical study of Percy Bysshe Shelley. "My function," he told friends, "is that of the utility man rather than of the desiderated expert bespeaking his own subjects."

The article "Anarchism" was by an expert, Prince Pëtr Alekseevich Kropotkin, geographer and revolutionary. Exiled from his native Russia, he had settled in Switzerland but was ousted from his home there after the assassination of Alexander II in Russia. In 1883, tried for various acts of revolutionary agitation and for his role in arousing strikes among the silkworkers at Lyons, he was removed to prison at Clairvaux, France, where he was permitted a desk, ink, and pen. His trial had caused a sensation among the intellectuals of Europe, and Swinburne, Herbert Spencer, and others had signed petitions demanding his release. He was not freed, but authorities at Clairvaux fitted out a special room for him, and he was permitted to continue writing for the *Encyclopaedia Britannica* and other publications.

5

Of all the distinguished contributors, none aroused so much strife and controversy—and none so typified the conflicts between the old and the new—as William Robertson Smith, a short-statured, dark-haired, and dark-eyed man with a swarthy complexion and a taste for fine wines and tobacco, a scholar of profound learning and wisdom, yet "lively and merry as a grig," and at twenty-eight one of the most brilliant theologians in the British Isles.

Born in 1846 at Keig in Aberdeenshire, where his father, William Pirie Smith, was a Free Church minister, Smith had entered Aberdeen

University as an intellectual prodigy of fifteen. Later, after specializing in theology at the Free Church College in Edinburgh, he had become an assistant professor of natural philosophy at Edinburgh University. In his two years there, from 1868 to 1870, he was popular with colleagues and students. He composed much original work in experimental and mathematical phases of electricity and produced complex, erudite treatises such as *Electrical Steam Lines* and *Hegel and the Metaphysics of the Fluxional Calculus*. Always an intense student of religion, he had often interrupted his scientific lectures to engage in long philosophical discussions with his eager students, among them the young Robert Louis Stevenson. At twenty-four, Smith had been appointed professor of oriental languages and Old Testament exegesis at the Free Church College in Aberdeen, and it was here that Smith, happy in his studious research, was approached by Baynes to join his contributors as an expert on Old Testament history.

Baynes commissioned Smith to furnish five articles for Volume II— "Angel," "Apostle," "Aramaic Languages," "Ark of the Covenant," and "Assideans"—and two for Volume III—"Baal" and "Bible." Duly written and printed, the first group aroused little comment, except from a reviewer or two who noted very slight inaccuracies.

Then on December 7, 1875, appeared the volume with the writings on "Baal" and "Bible." Before submitting the second of these two contributions, Smith had asked several of his friends among the clergy to read it. All, orthodoxists and modernists alike, had judged it sound in concept and execution. Its major thesis was that the Bible could be considered not only as theology but as literature and that it had historical links with other religions. Smith's theory was that the Semitic religious concepts were common to all primitive peoples and could be deduced from the data of known popular religions.

These ideas of historical interpretation of the Bible were then widely accepted by the more enlightened theologians on the Continent. Yet in this field more than in any other, sharp changes had taken place since the founding of the *Encyclopaedia Britannica* and, in point of fact, since the preceding edition; in no portion of the encyclopaedia had the interval between the eighth and ninth editions been more fruitful in new queries and new replies. Smith's article on "Bible" reflected these changes and queries.

Among those steadfast in refusing to consider either questions or answers were the elders of the Free Church of Scotland, narrow in their dogmatism, rigid in their doctrines. Some of the younger churchmen had turned to the "new" kind of historical inquiry, but the church hierarchy and many ministers held strictly to the orthodox interpretations, to the unswerving belief that every word of the Bible, and especially of the Old Testament, was divinely inspired. Still, Smith's fifteen-page treatise raised no immediate hubbub.

Then the *Edinburgh Courant* sent the volume for review to Dr. A. H. Charteris, professor of biblical criticism at Edinburgh University, a divine of the Free Church and the embodiment of the pietism of the orthodox. He was shocked by Smith's article. It was close to heresy, he wrote, to insist that there might be errors in the Bible. Smith's article stated theories contrary to those of the established church; it imperiled the fundamental doctrines of Christianity; it brought discredit upon the theological professoriate of Scotland. Charteris' critique, appearing on April 16, 1876, demanded to know of the elders of the Free Church precisely what they intended to do about Smith's statements.

For a month quiet prevailed. But in May, Dr. James Begg, leader of the church's most conservative branch and minister of the Newington Free Church, cried out against Smith in the tones of a loud and truculent traditionalist. A special committee was named to investigate the article—and the others Smith had written for the *Encyclopaedia Britannica*—and while this group deliberated, the church split between the orthodoxists and the Smith adherents. The church's leader, Robert Rainy, principal of the New College of Edinburgh and professor of church history, tried to bring about a reconciliation, shuddering at the prospect and notoriety of a heresy hearing. A man who always shied away from real controversy, preferring to arbitrate and negotiate differences—he was later described as having "a mind that wormed like a corkscrew through material soft enough to be perforated in a chisel thrust"—Rainy asked Smith to write an open letter, gentle and full of atonement, disavowing what he had written.

Angrily, Smith refused. But he was forced to heed the growing discord when a pamphlet, "Infidelity in the Aberdeen Free Church College," directly charged him with expressing dangerous, heretical ideas. Smith responded with a slashing reply which appeared in all Edinburgh newspapers. Immediately the orthodoxists clamored for his neck and preachers harangued their congregations. "Have we a Bible or haven't we?" they chorused.

For two years the Smith case raged. A special Free Church College committee was named to examine the facts of the case, and for these ministers Smith wrote a paper explaining his views. Early in 1877 the committee ruled that, while there were no grounds for a heresy proceeding against Smith, certain statements in the *Encyclopaedia Britannica* article were "fitted to create apprehension" and the full treatise was of "a dangerous and unsettling tendency." The argument was referred to the Higher Assembly of Aberdeen for action, while Smith was temporarily deprived of his teaching post at the Free Church College. Insisting that this action constituted a libel against him, Smith demanded that all charges be itemized before the assembly's meeting. What he requested was promptly granted, and the way was open for a final showdown.

He was accused, in the indictment, of a number of theological sins as determined by officials of the Free Church. He had, they stated, rejected the Mosaic authorship of Deuteronomy, thereby implying that the Scriptures were not divinely inspired. He had contradicted orthodox doctrine by "neutrality of attitude and rashness of statement tending to disparage" the divine authority and inspired character of the Scriptures. He had taught that the Levitical system was not a Mosaic institution; that Deuteronomy was not the historical record it professed to be; that the sacred writers were liable to error in questions of fact and occasionally sacrificed accuracy to party spirit; that some parts of the Scriptures had the character of fiction; that the Song of Solomon was a love poem and devoid of spiritual significance; that the prophets were merely men of spiritual insight and had no supernatural revelations of the future.

The assembly delegates gathered at Edinburgh in an atmosphere of excitement. Thousands of pamphlets by as many as twenty-five different writers were distributed by opponents and defenders of Smith. The orthodoxists yelled "Heretic!" and the adherents of the man they admiringly called "Smith o'Aiberdeen" replied, "A second Galileo!" At the meeting, Dr. Begg warned that the eyes of all Scotland were upon the assembly: "The righteous are trembling before the Ark of God!" But Smith, eloquently and at length, made a point-by-point defense of his article and his teachings and at the meeting's end was cleared of all charges but one—that he had rejected the Mosaic authorship of Deuteronomy. Did a professor of the Free Church College, the assembly asked, have a right to hold such a view?

Smith declared that he had made no irreligious statements either in the article in the *Encyclopaedia Britannica* or in his teachings, and the assembly put off a decision until its next meeting in 1880. Smith went off to the Orient, where he visited the Abdullah Effendi of Jeddah and lived with the Richard Burtons in Arabia for several months. He returned to face the assembly on a motion to deprive him of his teaching job because of his allegedly unorthodox views.

At a meeting on May 27, 1880, before an overflowing crowd in the assembly hall, with theological students thronging the balconies and shouting for or against Smith or Begg, Smith began by denouncing the assembly's action as irregular. Then he strode out. For fourteen hours debate surged in the low-ceilinged hall. Finally Gilbert Beith, a conciliatory elder of the church, offered a motion to admonish Smith rather than eject him from his teaching position and to warn him against publishing "unguarded and incomplete statements." This motion carried by a vote of 299 to 292, and Smith returned to accept the verdict.

"I hope that I am not out of place," he declared, "when I say that while I thank God for the issue of this evening—an issue which I trust will be for His glory and for the maintenance of His truth—I have never been more sensible than on the present occasion of the blame that rests upon men for statements which have proved so incomplete that, even at the end of three years, the opinion of this House has been so divided upon them. I feel that, in the providence of God, this is a very weighty lesson to one placed, as I am, in the position of a teacher, and I hope that by His grace I shall not fail to learn by it."

This seemingly abject yet tactful statement brought cheers from every corner of the crowded hall. And the rancorous dispute appeared to have ended.

Ten days later, however, it was renewed, violently and decisively. For there now appeared a new volume of the *Encyclopaedia Britannica*, the "H" volume. It was to have been issued earlier in the spring but had been delayed because the article "Heat" by William Thomson, Lord Kelvin, had been late in arriving. In this book was an article, "Hebrew Language and Literature," with the initials W. R. S. at its end. And in it the church elders found new faults. They charged that the article contained "unguarded statements" of the sort that had appeared in "Bible" and other Smith writings, and they denounced Smith as a man without honor. Smith argued that the article had been written months before and that, in line with the assembly's admonition to use greater care in stating his views, he had actually refused to contribute articles on "Isaiah" and "Israel." New accusations that he had broken faith and made flimsy promises now thudded against him. On

May 24, 1881, he was ordered removed from his job at the Free Church College.

6

The ultimate effect of this battle between traditional orthodoxy and modernist theology of the Victorian age was to vindicate the right of free historial inquiry. The immediate effect of Smith's dismissal was that he was hired, within a month, to serve with Baynes as joint editor of the ninth edition. He accepted the post with the understanding that he could continue to give attention to the biblical and philological studies by which he had made his reputation. Thirteen more volumes remained to be issued. Because Baynes was ill and beset with the weaknesses of advancing age, Smith assumed much of the burden of putting them out. For eighteen months he toiled at the job, not enjoying it—"Anyone can edit," he would grumble—and often acting the autocrat with his staff. He made his presence felt, and his personality and his gifts. To the first eleven volumes he had contributed some twenty articles; for the final thirteen he wrote more than two hundred.

Moreover, Smith broadened the *Encyclopaedia Britannica's* international aspect by including the work of the eminent European scholar Julius Wellhausen, the German theologian whose ideas had formed the basis of Smith's thinking in comparative religion. Another contributor closer to home was a young don at Christ College at Cambridge, James G. Frazer, to whom Smith assigned "Totemism" and "Taboo." Smith considered these subjects important and saw an opportunity, by printing good articles on them—especially on the first—of being ahead of all other encyclopaedists then probing new findings in the science of anthropology. Both of Frazer's articles constituted an important development in the career of the future author of *The Golden Bough*, for the seven months' research for them were, as Frazer recalled in later years, "the beginning of a systematic application to anthropology and especially to the study of the backward races of men whom we call savages and barbarians."

In 1883 Smith was named professor of Arabic at Cambridge, and he rejoiced at being once again in academic work with a chance of escaping "the treadmill of the encyclopaedia." Actually he remained as editor until the final volume was issued in 1888, a year after Baynes's death, although for the five final years much of the editorial labor was carried on by J. Sutherland Black, subsequently Smith's official biographer. When the edition was finished, another huge dinner was held for contributors, after which Smith went off to Cambridge to teach and work on plans for an *Encyclopaedia Biblica*. The final uproar in his life, and a very mild one compared with what had gone before, came shortly after the gala dinner, when an article appeared in the *Scot's Observer*, commenting on the affair and making sour remarks about Smith—"All Scotland held him in flattering respect, or still more in flattering horror." The writer was believed to be W. E. Henley, once employed by A. & C. Black, a fact that prompted Adam W. Black to write to Smith deploring any association with anyone who would make so derogatory a comment about him.

By the time Smith died in 1894 at forty-seven, this insulting incident was forgotten, and what remained was the memory of an earnest thinker who had advanced the cause of truth in dark and shadowed places. For, largely as a result of Smith's articles in the *Encyclopaedia Britannica* and subsequent writings, the movement for a more liberal and rational tone in theological matters was begun in Scotland and elsewhere where rigidity of thought had held command. Writing of the Smith case two decades after the turmoil, James Bryce saw its effect clearly:

The trial proved a turning point for the Scottish churches. . . . Opinions formerly proscribed were thereafter freely expressed. Nearly all the doctrinal prosecutions subsequently attempted in the Scottish Presbyterian Churches have failed. Much feeling has been excited, but the result has been to secure a greater latitude than was dreamt of forty years ago. . . . It may be conjectured that as the process of adjusting the letter of Scripture to the conclusions of science which Galileo was not permitted to apply in the field of astronomy has now been generally applied in the fields of geology and biology, so the churches will presently reconcile themselves to the conclusions of historic and linguistic criticism, now that such criticism has become truly scientific in its methods.[1]

[1] *Studies in Contemporary Biography* (New York: Macmillan Co., 1902).

5

The Ninth Edition—And Horace Hooper

Besides the comments on the Smith case in newspapers and magazines everywhere, the completed ninth edition spurred much additional discussion about its virtues and defects. Many called this the "scholars' edition," pointing out the authenticity of the work, the originality of the thought, and the contributions to the intellectual thinking of the time. Its eleven hundred contributors had been chosen with infinite care, and they came not only from the British Isles but in greater numbers than ever before from Germany, France, the Netherlands, Sweden, Norway, Belgium, and the United States.

Interspersed among the 16,000 articles stretching over 25 volumes and 20,504 pages were superb woodcuts, colored plates, and special colored maps of London, Rome, Paris, New York, and Philadelphia. Dates of a person's birth and death were used for the first time, a device quickly copied by other encyclopaedias. All the long, important articles had individual indexes and bibliographies—also innovations— and the final volume of the entire set was a complete index. And for all its lofty intellectual nature, the ninth edition had its utilitarian side. It gave detailed instructions and advice on how to make liquid glue, how to tie knots, how to make gold lacquer, how to fashion snowshoes, how to perform sleight-of-hand tricks, how to collect butterflies, how to construct cheap farm bridges, how to make putty, how to build an icehouse, how to shoe a horse, how to devise flies for trout fishing.

All the wonders, philosophical and practical, were duly noted by the critics. The general reception of the entire work was highly favorable, best exemplified by the closing comment of a nine-page critique in the discriminating *Edinburgh Review:* "Thoroughly well executed, both in point of style and matter. . . . There never was a time when the results of science and the results of history have been more ably presented and preserved, although, as is inevitable, it exhibits and provokes diversities of opinion on many subjects." Yet there were persistent complaints that it had taken so long to produce the full set that many of the early volumes were out of date by the time the later volumes became available. This was inevitable under the system by which the *Encyclopaedia Britannica* and other encyclopaedias of that era were published, because publication of each volume always depended on the success of the sale of the one preceding it. In the ninth edition there had been frequent delays between volumes, since some sold better than others.

Perhaps the most irate of all critics was an American, Thaddeus K. Oglesby, a journalist of Montgomery, Alabama. The edition was published in the United States through an arrangement A. and C. Black had with Charles Scribner's publishing firm. So far as is known, Oglesby may never have read beyond the first volume. But on page 719 he came upon a single paragraph that propelled him on a one-man crusade against the *Encyclopaedia Britannica.* Under "American Literature" he read:

Since the Revolution days . . . the few thinkers of American born south of Mason and Dixon's line—outnumbered by those belonging to the single State of Massachusetts—have commonly migrated to New York or Boston in search of a university training. In the world of letters, at least, the Southern States have shone by reflected light; nor is it too much to say, that mainly by their connection with the North the Carolinas have been saved from sinking to the level of Mexico or the Antilles. . . . Like the Spartan marshalling his helots, the planter lounging among his slaves was made dead to Art. . . . It has only flourished freely in a free soil; and for almost all its vitality and aspirations . . . we must turn to New England.

In his fury at such scurrilous sentiments, Oglesby dashed off paragraph after paragraph in the *Montgomery Advertiser,* finally collecting all his flaring prose in a book he titled *Some Truths of History: A Vindication of the South against the Encyclopaedia Britannica and Other Maligners.* He roared out against the "lies and calumnies" and presented a historical summary to prove that the South had given more presidents, soldiers, poets, painters, and musicians to the nation than any other part of the country. As for Massachusetts, whither the erudite encyclopaedist had insisted the cultured sons of the South invariably fled, Oglesby ranted: "Where was there such bloody and violent anti-Quakerism, religious intolerance, bigotry? Where were so-called witches prosecuted, hanged, tortured, innocents murdered? Where were skins of persons who died in almshouses tanned and made into articles of merchandise? Where were people banished for being Quakers? To each and all of these questions, History with its inexorable, unerring pen, answers—'MASSACHUSETTS!' "

2

Notwithstanding blasts from such impassioned critics as Oglesby, the ninth edition gained overwhelming popularity in the United States. With Scribner's firm and Little, Brown and Company acting as distributors, A. & C. Black had been selling single volumes since 1875. Of complete sets, Adam W. Black reported later that while only ten thousand were sold in Great Britain, five times that number were purchased in the United States.

These, of course, were the authorized copies of the *Encyclopaedia Britannica.* Their sale was a fraction of total sales that included pirated editions. Hundreds of thousands of direct, condensed, mutilated, or revised reprints were issued by large and small American publishers in the decade after 1888. Laws preventing such practices were no stronger than they had been in those days when Thomas Dobson of Philadelphia had appropriated the third edition. Again it was a Philadelphian who led the "ethical pirates," a Joseph M. Stoddart. Stoddart's volumes appeared almost simultaneously with the originals, a feat made possible by the theft of proof sheets by a young man who worked in the Neill and Company printing plant in Edinburgh, one of several printers to whom the task of setting type for the large edition had been allotted. As fast as sheets were turned over to proofreaders, the thief succeeded in getting extra copies and sending them on the fastest boat to the United States. This kind of activity fazed Stoddart not at all—he later issued a curt denial that he had obtained material for his volumes through thievery—and he continued to issue his books for $5.00 each, while the authentic volumes were sold for $9.00.

As in previous cases of piracy, the American courts actually protected Stoddart. When the Blacks and Scribner's sought to enjoin him from publishing his reprint, he received a favorable ruling in 1879, literally condoning what he was doing. Justice Arthur Butler declared: "To reproduce a foreign publication is not wrong. There may be differences of opinion about the morality of republishing a work here that is copyrighted abroad; but the public policy of this country, as respects the subject, is in favor of such republication. . . . It is supposed to have an influence upon the advance of learning and intelligence." Stoddart did more than steal the contents. He went so far as to publish a newspaper, *Stoddart's Weekly,* upholding his depredations. He claimed—as did most of his imitators—that he was bringing the original *Encyclopaedia Britannica* up to date by issuing supplements containing biographies of living persons.

Stoddart's closest competitor in piracy was Henry G. Allen of New York, who had developed a special photographic process by which the original pages could be copied. Allen's set, which he sanctimoniously announced he had published "to answer the popular demand for a work of moderate dimensions," sold for only $2.50 a volume, and, although he claimed that the physical quality of the edition matched the excellence of the original, the fact was that it was printed on rough paper and the type was dim and difficult to read.

Adding to the din of the literary pirates, publishers of rival encyclopaedias raised a clamor of their own against the *Encyclopaedia Britannica.* One of the most vociferous was Alvin J. Johnson, a former Yankee schoolmaster who had started his book career in the sixties by selling cheap atlases. He soon succeeded so well that he organized a firm to compete with his employer; in the same year that the first volume of the *Encyclopaedia Britannica's* ninth edition was published he started his *Universal Encyclopaedia*—"A Scientific and Popular Treasury of Useful Knowledge"—edited by F. A. P. Barnard, president of Columbia University, and Professor Arnold Guyot of Princeton. An irrepressibly unorthodox promoter, Johnson created vigorous sales campaigns. "Never let your prospect say 'No.' Answer all questions and be courageous," he told his solicitors. "It you are ejected by the front door, get back into the house by the basement and start all over again."

His blatant ads against the *Encyclopaedia Britannica* were equally unrestrained. "THE BIG BLUNDERING BRITANNICA. . . . An Expensive, Cumbersome, and Almost Useless Work for Practical People," began one of his typical broadsides. He cited purported errors. He assailed Thomas Henry Huxley's treatise on "Evolution." Huxley, he declaimed, had dogmatically stated that everything in the Bible was false. "If evolution is true, the Bible is false. The Bible *is* true, and evolution is a malicious, diabolical lie!"

The publishers of *Appleton's American Cyclopaedia* were less strident but no less bitter. They dispatched thousands of pamphlets through the nation, especially in the newly settled farmlands of the West, and each of these booklets, extolling the Appleton publication, demanded to know: "The Encyclopaedia Britannica: Is it adapted for American Circulation?" Comments were sprinkled throughout the booklets alleging that the Huxley articles and the rationalistic approach of William Robertson Smith in his theological contributions veered close to godlessness. The *Encyclopaedia Britannica* was attacked by the Appleton firm for too much indifference toward American subjects, for including "long essays on dry subjects," for scoffing at American culture. "Is this caricature of American character an edifying sort of reading for American families?" the pamphlets asked, before offering on their final pages this advice: "Buy the American Cyclopaedia at $5 to $10 a volume—The Best Encyclopaedia ever Published—A SAVING OF TEN CENTS PER DAY, the price of a cigar or many other expenditures for luxuries or frivolities of a like amount, would pay for a complete set of the Cyclopaedia by a bimonthly subscription."

Neither the Blacks nor their American agents took the literary thievery and the criticisms mildly. They responded with advertisements: "Beware of Mutilated and Spurious Reprints! All alleged 'Reprints' of the Encyclopaedia Britannica issued in this country are to a large extent incomplete, inaccurate, and, by reason of serious mutilations of the text, unreliable for purposes of reference." Adverse reviews of rival products were reprinted. Indorsements of the *Encyclopaedia Britannica* from important readers, ministers, educators, authors, and government officials were scattered through the advertisements. Although these advertisements rarely replied directly to the outcry of the competitors, occasionally notice was taken of one specifically; *Appleton's American Cyclopaedia*, for example, was characterized as "An Unsafe Guide."

Booksellers joined in the general uproar. One of those most active was a Chicagoan, J. W. Dickinson, who wrote long and colorful letters to editors of the nation's leading newspapers inveighing against the pirates and sent postal cards to prominent educators warning of the attempts to sell pirated copies. "Some of these 'Reprint' hyenas are prowling round in my territory, snarling at the houses of Adam and Chas. Black of Edinburgh and Scribner's Sons of New York, as well as at our own Chicago house," read a typical Dickinson communiqué. "They are lying. . . . Should they appear in your vicinity, you will do me a personal favor either to write or telegraph me. All their lies can be exploded with ease, anything they may say to the contrary notwithstanding."

Occasionally the newspapers in which the advertisements appeared joined the battle. In 1890, the high-minded editor of the *New York Evening Post*, E. L. Godkin, denounced two would-be pirates of the *Encyclopaedia Britannica*. One of those whom he accused was no less a personage than John Wanamaker, the wealthy merchant, postmaster-general of the United States, and advocate of an extended Sunday School system, and the other was Rev. Isaac Funk, head of the firm of Funk and Wagnalls. Wanamaker had advertised that, by a special photographic process similar to that used by Henry G. Allen, he intended to issue a reprint of the *Encyclopaedia Britannica* and sell it through his stores at only $38, as compared with the $225 for the authentic *Encyclopaedia Britannica*. Funk and his partner also trumpeted their intention of issuing a cheap reprint for only $40.

Godkin exploded. He headed his editorials on the subject "The Black Robbery," denounced the plans of Wanamaker and of Funk as "Plunder!" and "Theft!" and characterized both as "Parasites of the Trade!" Wanamaker replied that what he intended to do was simply good business, a practice engaged in by scores of others. Funk answered with long diatribes against the *Post*. For six months both sides exchanged angry statements, but on June 26, 1890, an important decision by Judge William D. Shipman in the New York Supreme Court stilled the clangor and brought an end to the plans of Wanamaker and the clergyman-publisher.

Judge Shipman's ruling involved the ingenious complaint of Henry G. Allen that A. & C. Black had sought to entrap potential pirates by copyrighting in the United States articles in the authentic publication written by Americans. Allen's lawyers, while acknowledging that if these articles were reprinted by the expropriators they were liable to action under the American copyright laws, claimed that the British publishers had copyrighted the Americans' articles merely for the "immoral purpose" of legally ensnaring the pirates. But Judge Shipman refused to sustain this demurrer and ruled that Allen had indeed violated the current copyright law by including the articles in his reprint.

This case was still pending in the courts when Congress, where agitation for a new act had long been brewing, passed the International Copyright Law of 1891, which, while it did not afford complete protection for foreign publishers, made depredations somewhat more difficult for the pirates. Despite this law, bogus sets continued to come from the presses and Americans by the many thousands continued to buy.

3

In the thick of literary buccaneering was James Clarke, operating in Chicago as one of the country's largest producers of cut-rate books.

Clarke was a Canadian who had joined the three Belford brothers, Alexander, Charles, and Robert, in their Toronto bookselling business early in 1875. Four years later, having evidently exhausted all sales possibilities there, Clarke and Alexander Belford moved to Chicago, where they formed the Belford-Clarke Company. In a town already noted for energetic hustlers as well as unethical ones, Clarke and Belford carried on a profitable enterprise as "Cheap Johns," as the publishers and distributors of inexpensive books were scornfully labeled by their more dignified contemporaries. Their system exemplified prevailing customs in a feverish book industry. They would publish a brace of books—usually a cheaply printed set of the complete works of Dickens, Scott, Thackeray, or George Eliot—at artificially high prices and send as many as they could to jobbers. Then they dispatched traveling salesmen on the road to stock up booksellers. After a few months, prices were slashed and local dry-goods stores and small department stores were supplied with the same sets at lower prices. Often the "Cheap Johns" clapped up makeshift bookstores in small towns. In larger cities, if established booksellers refused to deal with them, Belford and Clarke simply sent their representatives to the nearest department store or furniture emporium and opened a book department on commission.

In addition to this kind of operation, Belford and Clarke issued a pirated edition of the *Encyclopaedia Britannica* in 1890, calling it the *Americanized Encyclopaedia Britannica Revised and Amended*. It ran to only ten volumes and purported to condense the material in the original so that their edition would "contain all that is important to know, in a nutshell—compact, reliable and intelligible." Each volume bore Christopher Marlowe's quotation "Infinite riches in a little room" atop its pages. This publication sold so well for the pair that in a few years they issued another, calling it the *Home Encyclopaedia* and admitting that it was largely derived from the ninth edition ("this magnificent monument of Genius").

Clarke was active in another phase of bookselling. As head of James Clarke and Company, he held exclusive rights to the distribution and sale in the Midwest and West of the six-volume *Century Dictionary*. This impressive encyclopaedic lexicon of the English language had been compiled during a period of seven years under the editorship of Dr. William D. Whitney, a Yale University philosopher. It appeared in sections from 1889 to 1891 with scores of illustrations and, for the first time in the history of American dictionaries, dialect terms, colloquialisms, provincialisms, and slang. For wide sales, Clarke avoided the ordinary bookstores, concentrating instead on advertisements in newspapers which offered the work, for a limited time, at a reduced price ranging from $60 to $125. For an even more limited period, the ads announced, an instalment-buying plan was available.

In the mid-1890's, the treasurer of James Clarke and Company was a man teeming with sales ideas and promotional devices. In the book business since his teens, Horace Everett Hooper had come to Chicago from the West at the time of the World's Columbian Exposition of 1893. A sturdy young man of thirty-five, he had a proven talent for knowing how to sell books and, more importantly, how to persuade people they really needed the books he offered for sale.

4

Hooper was descended from a Colonial family of Massachusetts whose beginnings in this country went back to 1650. One of his ancestors was nicknamed "King Hooper" and in the late 1700's controlled nearly all the fishing interests and real estate in Marblehead. Horace's father, William, was a Marblehead lawyer who dabbled in journalism. For a brief time he was an editor of the *Worcester Spy*, the newspaper famous in the days of the American Revolution for its report of the Battle of Lexington headed "Americans! Liberty or Death! Join or Die!" and for the rebellious writings of its first editor, Isaiah Thomas. Hooper's mother was also of an old American family, descended from John Leverett, one of Massachusetts' first governors.

Horace Hooper was born in Worcester in 1859, the sixth of eight children, but when he was still a small boy the family moved to Washington, where the elder Hooper had acquired a civil service job. Horace attended elementary schools there and also went to a special school to prepare for Princeton University; he spent one term at prep school, where he was interested only in playing shortstop on the freshman baseball team. At sixteen his formal schooling was at an end. For a year or more he clerked in a bookstore in the capital; then he took his savings and ran off to the new West, settling in Denver, Colorado, where he quickly secured work as a book agent for a number of eastern companies.

America was experiencing a boom in the sale of books by subscription. The origins of this upsurge were rooted in the western migrations, for in the wake of the covered wagons and the new settlers had come circuit riders, district schoolmasters and, inevitably, book agents ready to accept down payments for almost any kind of reading matter, from Bibles to compendiums of cookery, from collections of legal treatises to Civil War reminiscences. Indeed, the first affluent era for the traveling book salesman came immediately in the decades after the Civil War; Mark Twain, for one, had helped publish on a subscription basis the *Memoirs of General Grant*, which netted the general and his heirs $450,000 in royalties. Many of Mark Twain's own books were sold by subscription, and his American Publishing Company, centered in Hartford, Connecticut, was typical of those calling for salesmen and canvassers: "The sale of our works is an honorable and praiseworthy employment, and is particularly adapted to disabled Soldiers, aged and other Clergymen having leisure hours, Teachers and Students during Vacation, etc., Invalids unable to endure hard physical labor, Young Men who wish to travel, and gather knowledge and experience by contact with the world, and all who can bring industry, perseverance, and a determined will to work."

Many who responded to such advertisements engaged in high-pressure selling methods that made book agents unpopular for years in the new territories. Some were unscrupulous and never sent on the giant volumes or sets for which subscribers had handed over their initial payments. But there were also scores of eager young men to whom this kind of enterprise was an introduction to wider, deeper pathways of the book world. Hooper fit neatly into the ranks of these younger book agents, for he was a facile speaker, bursting with sincerity and a genuine love for books. He read widely, shunning fiction but memorizing whole pages of histories, biographies, and scientific books. He joined the salesmen swarming into the West.

Before he was thirty, Hooper had established in Denver the Western Book and Stationery Company, a distributing agent for books throughout Colorado and adjoining states. Through friendship with George Clarke, brother of the Chicago entrepreneur, he helped to organize the sale of the *Century Dictionary* throughout that territory, mapping out plans for his salesmen that brought results so pleasing to James Clarke that he persuaded Hooper to move his firm to Chicago. There Hooper's Western Book and Stationery Company became the entire book section of The Fair, a State Street department store founded by an ingenious merchant, Edward J. Lehmann, who parceled out, for suitable commissions, parts of his emporium to various businesses. Associated with Hooper as a partner in this venture was George Clarke, and, soon enough, associated with both Clarkes in James Clarke and Company, was Horace Hooper.

Hooper quickly showed how adept he was. By 1895, the sale of the *Century Dictionary* had slowed down, and James Clarke was left with many hundreds of sets on his hands. Hooper waited until a few weeks before that year's Christmas season. Then he filled the local newspaper with ebullient prose written by the firm's young advertising man, Henry Haxton, offering the multivolumed dictionaries at special holiday rates. For a down payment of only fifteen dollars the entire set would be delivered, with the balance to be paid monthly. "An ideal Christmas present! Take advantage of this never-again offer! BUY NOW! A GREAT BOON!" read the ads in the Chicago newspapers. In a month all the leftovers were sold.

With the holidays over and the firm looking ahead to a new year—Clarke's other company, Belford and Clarke, was then issuing its pirated *Home Encyclopaedia*—Hooper decided that he had earned a vacation. When Haxton, who spent part of every year abroad, left for England, Hooper followed.

5

It was a vacation trip, this maiden voyage of Hooper's, that would result in a tremendous change in his fortunes and his future.

Haxton met Hooper at Plymouth when his ship landed. Flamboyant characters both—Haxton with his elegant clothes, his spade beard, and his flashing rings, Hooper with a full, curled mustache, a snappish style of speech, and eyes darting everywhere. No railroad would do for them. Instead, they hired horses and rode to London over moors and through country towns, arriving flushed and excited.

It was inevitable that Hooper, although he had come to London for pleasure, would soon be involved with business. He went to places where there was talk of books and printing and newspapers and publishing. Already aware of the sales figures of the *Encyclopaedia Britannica* in the British Isles and in the United States—the meager amount in the first country and the overwhelming one, of both genuine and pirated copies, in the second—he learned that a new printing of the *Encyclopaedia Britannica's* ninth edition had fared poorly. The perennial complaint of out-of-dateness had balked a satisfactory sale, and the price of £37 was too high for the mass of the population.

Hooper was aware, too, of the swift development of a new kind of newspaper in England for a new kind of reader. The many thousands who had benefited from the Education Act of 1870 and the thousands more who followed them were eager for almost any kind of reading matter they could afford, and in this very year of 1896 there were smart and bold men to fill part of that need. The energetic Alfred Harmsworth was one. Although only in his thirties, he was already a success in newspaper publishing. His latest project was a halfpenny newspaper, the *Daily Mail,* an eight-page gazette with special appeal for the large and growing white-collar class through full treatment of scandal as well as governmental news. In tone and form of advertising, it was alert and colorful, shattering a century-old tradition by the use of display type, broken column rules, and illustrations. There was also George Newnes's sprightly weekly, *Tit-Bits,* which printed news and oddments from many newspapers and was bright in style, jammed with ads, and imitated by scores of other weeklies. Newnes's *Strand Magazine* often carried as many as a hundred pages of advertisements.

Hooper heard and retained much of what was happening in journalism and in advertising. He met another American, Paul E. Derrick, who a few years earlier had opened an advertising office and was a pioneer in using illustrated ads in periodicals. He read and leafed through dozens of magazines in which he saw advertisements using drawings and engravings especially created by noted artists for firms selling everything from soap to cigarettes. All this had begun in the middle of the 1880's, when Sir John Millais had painted his grandson blowing bubbles. Eventually Thomas A. Barratt, managing director of A. and F. Pears, had purchased the canvas from its first owner, the *London Illustrated News*, for £2,300 and used it as an advertisement for Pears soap. Some of the flashier halfpenny newspapers were splattered with advertising sketches—Sunlight Soap was touted by drawings of a wife bending over a washtub, with a pouting husband in the background, and the admonition, "Don't let steam and suds be your husband's welcome on wash days!" Poster advertising was rampant all over London, with ballyhoo for pills and nostrums, cereals and cigarettes. And to act as a watchdog over all this there had been formed the Society for the Checking of Abuses in Public Advertising.

But in the advertisements for books staid Victorianism persisted. Most publishers simply inserted small ads containing the name of the firm, the title of the book, and its author, occasionally adding a favorable comment from a reviewer. It was considered bad taste to engage in this new kind of advertising puffery for cultural products, although, interestingly enough, one of the biggest advertisements— and, it must be added, one of the few of this kind—carried up to that time by the *Times* had been for a book. As far back as 1829, Edmund Lodge's *Portraits and Memories of the Most Illustrious Personages of British History* had been given a full-page ad. But this had indeed been a rarity. Now the *Times*, although faced with the growing competition of the new gazettes, weekly and daily, symbolized the stolidity of the passing generation. Its dull gray columns rarely were broken by attention-attracting advertisements; its reputation was for solemnity, its future uncertain.

All this Hooper was quick to notice and consider. And he was soon outlining a plan to Haxton in their rooms at the Savoy or at a mutton dinner in Simpson's in the Strand. Question after question he hurled at Haxton: Why was the sale of the *Encyclopaedia Britannica* so low here? "Because the price is too high and they don't know how to sell it," Hooper would reply to his own query. Who owned the copyright? Who were the printers?

Aware of the growing effect of advertising on the London public,

Hooper was certain that what was selling soaps and oatmeal and pills could sell the *Encyclopaedia Britannica*. Never one to show indifference when an advertising campaign was in prospect, Haxton matched Hooper's excitement with action. Within a week he and Hooper were on their way to Edinburgh to confer with Edward Clark, head of R. and R. Clark, chief printers of the ninth edition.

"Do you think it would be possible to lease the plates of the edition from the owners and give them a royalty on the sets we sell or give them cash?" Hooper asked.

Clark demanded more details.

"I don't know exactly what we'll do, I only have it generally in mind," said Hooper. "But I know that with the right kind of advertising and the right kind of approach, our sale can be a great success."

Carefully, Clark estimated that an arrangement with A. & C. Black was not outside the realm of possibility. Only two years earlier the Blacks had moved from Edinburgh to new quarters in London's Soho Square. The youngest and most enterprising of the brothers, Adam W. Black, was the one most active in the firm. He contemplated expansion of other publishing plans and, disappointed in the company's inability to sell the *Encyclopaedia Britannica*, would be receptive, Clark told Hooper, to any sound proposal.

Hooper wasted no time in speeding back to the United States. Excitedly he outlined the project to James and George Clarke. He and the Clarkes would secure the copyright or the plates from the Blacks, then market the *Encyclopaedia Britannica* on the widest scale. "We'll turn them topsy-turvy," Hoover cried, "and we'll all make money."

Readily the Clarkes agreed, James informing Hooper of an interesting coincidence. He had recently discussed, he said, with Walter Montgomery Jackson, head of the Grolier Society, a similar idea, and he now proposed that Jackson be invited to join the project. "This will take money," he said, "and Jackson's got it."

Hooper offered no objections, for he was aware that Jackson was one of the most astute bookmen in the country. And the way was clear for the affiliation of the two men who would mean so much to the future of the *Encyclopaedia Britannica*.

6

Like Hooper, Walter Montgomery Jackson had been involved in the making and selling of books since boyhood. His first job had been to tidy up the bookshop and offices of Estes and Lauriat in Boston, ten miles from Newton Lower Falls, Massachusetts, where Jackson had been born in 1863. An agile worker, young Jackson had swiftly come to the attention of Dana Estes when, after each clean-up session in the stockroom, the youth urged the publisher to come to the room to see the results of his labors and then, after receiving routine approval, asked, "What's next for me, sir?" At twenty-two, Jackson was a partner in charge of the Estes and Lauriat manufacturing and publishing department. He helped greatly in expanding the company's business and building a distribution system that covered the country. Within a few years he was so eager to branch out that he made a pact to spend half his time with the Estes and Lauriat firm and the rest with his own non-competing enterprises.

By this time Jackson was part owner or director of half a dozen publishing and distribution houses. His prime interest was in the Grolier Society, which he had organized the previous year to publish high-grade books for a limited clientele able and eager to pay top prices for richly bound, specially illustrated editions of rare literature and of standard classics. Jackson had derived both the name and the idea for his firm from the Grolier Club, organized in 1884 by a group of New York editors, publishers, bibliophiles, and art collectors for "the literary study and promotion of the arts entering into the production of books." Club and company were named for Jean Grolier de Servières, a former treasurer-general of France who loved fine books and had employed the most skilful French binders to prepare beautiful volumes for his library. Jackson's Grolier Society was prospering, as were his other companies, and in the book trade he was known as a man of active imagination and sound business sense.

7

Early in the summer of 1897, a conference was held in the New York offices of James Clarke and company. Present were the Clarke brothers, Hooper, and Jackson. The time was ready for their invasion of Great Britain.

All agreed that if they succeeded in persuading the Blacks to assent to Hooper's plan, a British corporation would be organized to sell the *Encyclopaedia Britannica* at reduced rates through an energetic advertising campaign under the direction of Hooper and Haxton. Each of the four men was to put into such a corporation an equal amount of money; each would share equally in any profits.

Because James Clarke had other business to tend to in London, he was designated to present the joint proposition to the Blacks. He sailed later that summer but, before approaching the publishers, carried through negotiations to acquire a company owned by another American, Carlyle Norwood Greig, who had created a successful business by printing a shiny picture booklet called *Beautiful Britain* and selling it to thousands of grocers who gave copies to customers purchasing a specified amount of groceries. Greig's offices were on Ludgate Hill, and there Clarke prepared for his assault on the publishers of the *Encyclopaedia Britannica*.

His conquest was swift and simple. Adam W. Black and his brothers actually were as eager as Hooper had heard they were to rid themselves, under proper financial terms, of the edition they were having such trouble selling to their countrymen. They accepted Clarke's proposals quite readily, and on September 17 a contract was signed yielding to James Clarke and Company the right to print five thousand copies of the ninth edition for sale in the United Kingdom. For this privilege, the Blacks were to receive a flat £6,500—£1,000 on the signing of the contract, the rest when the books were available.

Contract in hand, Clarke hurried back to the United States. Now it was Hooper's turn. He went to London that November, taking over the Ludgate Hill offices—for many months his door would still bear the name of Greig and Company, Limited—and began the tasks of ordering stock for the five thousand copies, of conferring with printers, and, most important of all, of planning an advertising campaign with Haxton.

By February, 1898, all was ready. And Hooper, writing to Clarke, suggested, almost offhandedly, an interesting proposition. Always on the alert for the best advertising medium, Hooper had persistently had in mind the *Times,* despite that newspaper's reputed aversion to hullabaloo in either its news or advertising columns. Haxton was not easily upset by daring suggestions of any sort, but even he was skeptical of any success in this, and so was every British publisher or bookdealer with whom Hooper talked. But Hooper insisted that he sensed a possibility of acceptance. To Clarke he wrote, "I am nearly ready to begin selling operations. I suggest that you come to England and that the two of us secure, if possible, *The Times* of London as the medium through which the sales of the *Encyclopaedia Britannica* should be made. I believe it likely that this can be done."

Clarke was aware of the element of daring in the entire venture, and, like Haxton, he was not too enthusiastic about Hooper's proposal to sell the encyclopaedia with American-style advertisements in the *Times*. Before arranging to sail for England he conveyed his doubts in a letter to Hooper, but by return mail Hooper replied, "I've found out a few important things since I've been here. We need someone big in this project and we can use *The Times*. But I think *The Times* needs us as much as we need *The Times*."

6

An Amazing Alliance

All the information Horace Hooper had collected about the *Times* pointed to the fact that "The Thunderer" had reached a dangerous financial plateau. Never in its long history had the newspaper been so sorely in need of funds. This condition stemmed from many factors, old and new. Back in 1789, when the first John Walter had transformed his *Daily Universal Register* into the *Times,* he had created a perpetual contract providing that his printing business possess sole rights for printing the newspaper. In its first years, the *Times* was merely an adjunct to the prospering printing firm. Walter had also given a number of persons shares and half-shares in perpetuity, providing that under no circumstances were any but these specified shareowners and their heirs to own the *Times.* John Walter II, forceful and despotic, had built the newspaper into a profitable institution, and a vastly respected one. He had given part interests in the paper to friends and employees, so that now there were at least eighty so-called proprietors with varying degrees of power. The printing business was still thriving, and not only were the Walters as publishers of the newspaper required to pay the cost of printing to the Walters as printers, but there was rent to be derived from Printing House Square and its environs, also owned by the Walter family. After the death of the second Walter, when John Walter III was well into his term as governing proprietor, the *Times*'s profits dwindled. But in spite of this, costs and rents had to be paid by the terms of the perpetual contract.

By the 1880's, this arrangement was responsible for complex litigation, with the result that a huge reserve fund established by the Walters was dissipated. The *Times* was lagging editorially, too, and much of its vigor and reputation had diminished. An especially heavy blow damaged its prestige in 1887. On March 7, the *Times* initiated a series of articles, "Parnellism and Crime," contending that Charles Stewart Parnell, the fiery exponent of Irish home rule, was behind a movement to cause the revolutionary overthrow of British authority in Ireland. In the final article, on April 18, a letter was printed, purportedly the facsimile of one written by Parnell to Patrick Egan, secretary of the Land League, condoning the murder of Permanent Undersecretary Burke and Lord Frederick Cavendish, chief secretary for Ireland, in Dublin's Phoenix Park five years earlier. This letter had been obtained from a Richard Piggott, a shady journalist, and in the heat of the fight over home rule, George Edward Buckle, the *Times*'s editor, had decided to print it. Charging that the letter was a forgery, Parnell sued for libel in the sum of £100,000. In the ensuing trial, Piggott admitted the letter was spurious, then fled to Madrid where he hanged himself. Although Parnell settled for £5,000, the total costs of the suit to the *Times* and, worse, the injuries to its reputation were serious.

Although John Walter III was still alive, his son, Arthur Fraser Walter, served as the newspaper's managing director. A leisured country gentleman, distrustful of intellectual persons, gentle and courteous, he cared more for landscape gardening than for newspaper management. To aid him in running the newspaper, he sent in 1890 for Charles Frederick Moberly Bell, who for twenty years had been the paper's chief correspondent in Egypt. Bell had been born in Alexandria, where his father, Thomas Bell, was an English merchant trading in wheat and cotton. While a clerk for his father's firm, he had started to send long dispatches to the *Times*'s financial columns, and from 1870, when he was only twenty-three, he had been a steady correspondent, authoritative and dullish, but reliable.

When Arthur Walter summoned him, Bell believed that he would assume his job as assistant to the managing director for only a few months, then return to the comparative ease of his post in Alexandria. But he was in his Printing House Square office only a week before he realized that his return would be long delayed, if not impossible. The *Times*, he quickly and sadly learned, was virtually insolvent, with assets of £61,000 and liabilities of nearly twice that amount. Revenues, the books showed, had fallen steadily at the rate of £9,000 a year in the preceding fifteen years. The accounting system was in a woeful state; one foreign correspondent claimed he had not received any expense money for six years, while another, who had been allotted £1,-850 in 1885 and £1,770 in 1889, could not furnish any evidence of having spent more than £800 in either year. Circulation in fifteen years had dropped from 65,000 to 40,000. Advertisements—principally the small want ads on which the *Times* a decade before had had a monopoly—had decreased considerably. A passionate believer in serving the public, Bell found to his great displeasure that many of the newspaper's ad takers sulkily refused to tell customers when their notices would appear. Staff morale was weak, and there was grumbling and dissatisfaction with the way the Walters concentrated only on taking profits from the printing business and permitted the editorial side of the newspaper to languish.

Surveying all this, Bell set assiduously to work. He often remained in his office eighteen hours a day, seeking to bring order out of financial and editorial chaos. He was powerless, of course, to break up the complex arrangement of Walters-the-printers versus Walters-the-proprietors, but wherever this hulking, swarthy man—his associates called him "The Assyrian"—sensed a chance for improvement, he moved ahead energetically. He hired as foreign reporters a number of distinguished writers and several who would later become famous. Donald Mackenzie Wallace, formerly correspondent at Constantinople and St. Petersburg, was appointed head of the foreign service. Valentine Chirol, whom Bell had known in Egypt, was dispatched to the Near East. The first woman ever to work on the *Times*, Flora Shaw, was made a foreign correspondent, and still another new reporter was G. E. Morrison, later to gain renown as "Morrison of Pekin." Although Bell enlarged his foreign staff, he cut down on cable costs and expense accounts. "The merit of a correspondent," he wrote to one of his foreign reporters, "depends on the quality, not the quantity of his dispatches. Remember that telegrams are for facts; appreciation and political comment can come by post."

He sought advertisements, but always with an eye toward the vaunted conservatism of the *Times*. When subscribers complained about advertisements of certain stockbrokers, Bell explained in personal letters: "It is extremely probable that many advertisements are misleading, and I am afraid that if we were to refuse all advertisements which had this tendency none would remain. . . . We are extremely careful to exclude from our advertisements anything of an immoral character, and daily refuse advertisements on this ground."

In 1895, after the death of John Walter III and the accession of Arthur Walter as governing proprietor, Bell was named managing director and given some additional powers. To the Thursday edition he added the *Literary Supplement*, its first number carrying a poem written by Rudyard Kipling, its subsequent issues devoted to reviews of books without prejudice of politics or nationality. That same year Bell opened a publications department by issuing a *Times Gazetteer;* its sale yielded a profit of nearly £2,000, but its success was limited because it was printed on poor paper and was cheaply made. A biography of Bismarck had an inferior sale, primarily because of insufficient promotion and advertising.

2

For a time Bell appeared to be clearing away the deadwood. A debt of £41,000 was converted, through economies instituted by him, to a profit of £24,000. But this was not enough. Costs rose anew. Circulation and advertising revenue continued to fall. On the February morning in 1898 when Clarke and Hooper laid before Bell their proposition to reissue the ninth edition of the *Encyclopaedia Britannica* under sponsorship of the *Times*—to the paper's possible financial advantage —circulation stood at a new low of thirty-six thousand, and money was needed, and needed quite desperately.

Still, before signing any agreement with Clarke and Hooper, Bell was wary about the plan. He sent letter after letter to the Blacks, making certain that all would go as the two Americans promised. "Before we publish advertisements inducing people to send one guinea to this office," he wrote, "we must have some guarantee that the E.B. *will be delivered as promised.* This guarantee must be given by you or some responsible firm in this country." And again, when Adam W. Black's reply was not satisfactory: "I do not think you quite see my point. By inserting an advertisement that the E.B. shall be sent to anyone who subscribes a guinea we guarantee that anyone who subscribes shall receive an E.B. But we have no control over the *Encyclopaedia Britannica*. Who guarantees us that the *Encyclopaedia Britannica* will be delivered? If your firm does so, we know where we are—but we know nothing of Messrs. Clarke and Hooper or of the printer, binder or others through whose hands the book will pass. Before we put in Advertisements that may result in 10,000 people having a claim on us for a book which may be valued at 20 pounds—before, that is, we enter into a contract which may involve a liability of 200,000 pounds we must be covered by some responsible, well known signature."

Bell's qualms finally were eased. On March 14, 1898, an agreement, terse and pointed, was drawn in his office and duly signed. "We must have a contract," said Hooper, looking ahead to any crisis, "that we can drive a cart through in case of need. We can never provide for all the ruts we shall meet on the road, and we've got to get through." The terms were plain: the *Times* would take orders for this special reprint of the ninth edition, deliver the orders to the Clarkes, Hooper, and Jackson—operating as James Clarke and Company, Limited—and retain as its commission one guinea on each order.

3

Within a week, the campaign was ready. And on March 23 the advertisement for the reprint of the ninth edition covered page 15 of the *Times*, an advertisement that exhorted, persuaded, lectured, and, most startling, offered the set for only fourteen guineas—fourteen pounds, a bit less, if cash were paid—with delivery promised not when this total amount was received but immediately upon a down payment of a single guinea. For the first time in England that anyone could recall, the instalment plan—the so-called hire-purchase system—was applied to book-buying. It had been used for some other commodities but never for books and, above all, never for the *Encyclopaedia Britannica*.

"THE ENCYCLOPAEDIA BRITANNICA is not a mere aid to memory to be hastily consulted in moments of emergency," trumpeted Henry Haxton's first ad. "It is not only the greatest of works of reference, but it is a Library in Itself, a collection of admirable treatises upon all conceivable subjects. Even the most recondite branches of learning are treated without a trace of pedantry. The volumes are EMINENTLY READABLE."

In another section of the announcement, potential purchasers were warned that the offer was for a limited time, that this was the prime opportunity to enrol in the plan before actual publication of the reprint. "The *Times* does not guarantee that all orders will be filled, but provision is made for the expected quotum of PROMPT APPLICATIONS." For readers with more expensive tastes, a set bound in half morocco was available at eighteen guineas, and for twenty-five guineas one might acquire a still richer one bound in dark green leather with the royal arms stamped in gold on the side covers. "Although this set of 25 volumes weighs 175 pounds, terms provide for free delivery within the London postal district."

This *Encyclopaedia Britannica* was no mere rehash of mundane writing; it was, boasted the advertisement, dramatic and personal. "THE ENCYCLOPAEDIA BRITANNICA gives no hospitality to the sort of 'harmless' drudge who used to compile works of reference when the world was younger. . . . The ENCYCLOPAEDIA BRITANNICA is essentially the production of men who wrote out of the fullness of knowledge. The wonderful story of the 19th Century is told by the men who made its greatness; the history of modern progress in the arts, sciences and industries has the glow that only a soldier can give to the tale of a campaign; for the men who fought against ignorance, and brought enlightenment to their generation, themselves tell how the light was spread."

There were admonitions that only through this ninth edition—although the last volume had been printed a decade earlier—could the intelligent person be aware of modern trends and current events. There were quoted opinions, including Gladstone's: "To own a set of the Encyclopaedia Britannica is to acknowledge one's self as recognizing the best there is in literature." There was a list of some of the eleven hundred distinguished contributors. And again, emphatic and bold, there was the fact that a down payment brought the encyclopaedia to one's doorstep at a 60 per cent reduction in the previous price— an "UNPRECEDENTED PRICE!"

4

Day after day the barrage continued; week by week public interest expanded. August 6 was set as the "Absolutely Final Day," after which the bargain offer would be withdrawn—forever. Each advertisement stressed the limited number available, the need for swift action by all eager for "learning, scholarship and general information." Together with these exhortations appeared specialized ads. Throughout April, for example, readers of the *Times* were treated to tempting sections from articles on "Birds" and "Easter," and, when the Spanish-American War broke out in the last week of the month, a specimen page from the article on "Cuba" plus parts of others on the American and Spanish armies, albeit from the 1875 printing, were quoted. In May another inducement was put forward: two hundred revolving bookcases of quartered oak, available to the first readers who applied, "without favor of privilege," for only three pounds and delivered without extra charge inside the London postal district. And through every ad, large and small, echoed the theme: "HURRY! HURRY! HURRY!"

And hurry they did, with almost as many customers willing to pay cash as buy on the instalment plan. By the end of the campaign's second month the results were joyously good. Old-timers at Printing House Square deplored the bustle of the Americans, notably Hooper and Jackson, as they came and went to Bell's office, or clucked unhappily about the uses to which the columns of the *Times* were being put. But Bell, as he saw the orders pouring in, was not among these. By the end of May the number sold stood at forty-three hundred—five times and more the amount Bell had hoped might be sold in a year. For the first time in many months, the hard-working managing director was jubilant over immediate and future prospects. The *Times* had found a staunch ally, and his name was Horace Hooper. To Hooper had fallen most of the organizational work of the campaign, both Clarkes having been occupied with other publishing interests and Jackson not having even arrived in England until the advertising was about to begin. From this point on, as Hooper and Bell drew closer, there was not much Hooper would propose in which Bell would not concur. It was obvious that the Americans' plan, which had seemed so unpromising to Bell at first, was the medium by which the *Times* might be immeasurably aided. Henceforth Bell would keep an ear eagerly cocked for other proposals from these uninhibited newcomers.

Part Two

7

"We've Done It! We've Done It!"

The lure of the advertisements endured. Rarely had there been such a response to any campaign in Great Britain in or out of publishing, and so sustained was the popular reaction that it was soon announced that individual inquiries could no longer be answered and all further particulars of the offer would be found in the columns of the *Times*.

In August, the low price was withdrawn, but the new offer at sixteen guineas was still considerably below the amount charged originally by A. & C. Black. Not only was the announcement of this price carried in the *Times*, but advertisements of the set for seventeen guineas appeared in the *Daily Mail*. Bell offered no objection to the use of columns in the Harmsworth paper, for he was elated with the progress of his own venture. Besides, Hooper explained that the *Daily Mail* plan, while selling the volumes at a higher price, was actually designed for lower-income groups, presumably non-readers of the *Times,* who were required to make an initial instalment of only five shillings with the rest payable in as many as thirty months. Bell felt that any other profits Hooper and his associates could honestly make were no concern of his. Moreover, the figures at the end of 1898 disclosed that, by carrying through this plan with Hooper and Clarke and the others, no less than £ 11,830 had been added to the coffers of the *Times.*

2

But one irritating complaint, enough to irk a man of Bell's sensitive morality and touchy temperament, had been provoked. Although every advertisement had prominently mentioned that the *Times* edition of the *Encyclopaedia Britannica* was a reprint of the old ninth and by no means a new one, there were grumblings. Some of the complainants had evidently been so dazzled by Haxton's rhetoric that they had disregarded the information about the reprint. Other criticisms undoubtedly were spurred by jealous rivals of the *Times,* and a witticism was circulated among other journalists: "The *Times* is behind the *Encyclopaedia* and the *Encyclopaedia* is behind the times."

Patiently Bell scrawled detailed answers to those who wrote to him about this matter. And he also authorized and helped write an advertisement emphasizing the value of the *Encyclopaedia Britannica* as a kind of permanent library, with immense advantages over competing publications: "The various almanacs and Year Books supply to the public the sort of ephemeral information which is in its way convenient and useful, just as the minute hand of a clock is serviceable when one has a train to catch, but for the broader purpose of life it is necessary that men and events should be regarded from a point of view neither too shifting nor in too point-blank a proximity. In the distance it is interesting to know that Socrates loved better to stroll through the streets than to stride over the fields, but the fact that a man of our day —whose house is just around the corner—prefers billiards to golf hardly fits the scholarly atmosphere of such a work as the *Encyclopaedia Britannica.* It has none of the perishability of a directory, because its editors were wise enough not to attempt to give it the advantages and disadvantages of an annual."

Any who felt cheated were invited to return their copies at the *Times's* expense. Evidently Bell's sincere letters dissuaded many complainants from asking for refunds, for he later reported that in the first two months of the sale, when such objections were most frequent, only eleven of the forty-three hundred who ordered asked to be freed from their contracts.

But these developments persuaded Bell that a new edition needed to be prepared—and, certainly, under the aegis of the *Times*. The same advertising methods might well be employed, he reflected, and the same hire-purchase system. He was noticing with some satisfaction that instalment buying, once frowned on by all but low-wage earners, had taken on a kind of respectability, obviously the result of the sale of the reprint. One publisher of novels established a system of selling a batch of half a dozen of his current books, to be delivered on payment of the price for only one. And a firm of furniture-makers proclaimed itself, in the midst of the campaign, "The Times Furnishing Company, Limited," printing its title in the old English type of the *Times*.

3

Hooper was in full agreement with Bell's suggestion that a new edition be published. But he amended the plan. "We must get out a new version in the shortest time possible, and it will be impossible to make it an entirely new one," he said. "My idea is to put out a supplement, maybe six, seven volumes, bringing everything as up to date as possible, and bring these out all at once. We'll do a lot of advertising and we'll hit it right again. Later, we can think about a completely new edition."

Both Hooper and Jackson agreed that Bell should be placed in over-all editorial charge. He could name the editor, pick a staff, and commit the *Times* to full editorial responsibility. Clarke and Company would pay all expenses. Bell also proposed that special editions of the *Century Dictionary* and the *Gazetteer* be issued, both under auspices of the *Times*, to be sold on the instalment plan. This latter project, when carried through during 1899, eventually yielded some £8,000 for the paper.

Donald Mackenzie Wallace, the *Times*'s foreign editor, was named by Bell to edit the supplement. Hugh Chisholm, editor-in-chief of the *St. James's Gazette*, was named his associate. At Hooper's suggestion, an American office was established in New York. His brother, Franklin H. Hooper, left his post as associate editor of the *Century Dictionary* to become American editor, and Arthur T. Hadley, president of Yale University, was major consulting editor.

Throughout 1899 various announcements appeared in the *Times* relating to this supplement. The first, on February 23, thanked the thousands who had purchased the reprint, then went on to disclose that because it had been so well received a new edition, to consist of the twenty-five volumes of the ninth and ten additional volumes to bring information up to date, would be prepared and issued before the end of the century. Contracts legalizing this venture were signed with A. and C. Black; taking another step toward eventual liquidation of their ownership of the *Encyclopaedia Britannica,* the Blacks received £40,-000 for various rights.

When Wallace was summoned by royal command to accompany the Prince of Wales on a trip around the world, Chisholm stepped into his place. One of the most brilliant men in his class at Oxford, Chisholm, still in his early thirties, had been extremely independent as editor of the *St. James's Gazette,* achieving a certain fame when he among all others, friend or foe, refused to praise William Gladstone upon that statesman's death in 1898. Instead he had written, "The *St. James's Gazette* had always seen in Gladstone a national danger. The danger had been none the less because it was now removed. Therefore why gloss over the past?"

Now, he and his staff of writers, rewriters, and subeditors—who did little more than paste up long articles from the ninth edition before sending them off to experts for revision—were housed in a top floor of Printing House Square, there to be regularly visited by Hooper or Jackson, the first talking rapidly, the second silently puffing on a big cigar.

In the American office, Franklin Hooper prepared a long list of articles he thought Americans might want in the supplement and, with Hadley's aid, secured qualified contributors. Ultimately, 43 of the contributors were professors from Harvard and 39 from Yale, with 212 from Cambridge and 178 from Oxford, and others from universities in Athens, Lisbon, Montreal, Florence, and Paris.

An extremely conscientious worker, Franklin Hooper read proofs of all articles, whether by Americans or Europeans. One, "Algebraic Forms," was so complicated and difficult that he assigned an assistant, Edward S. Holden, a leading astronomer, to read and report on it. Holden studied it for three days, then returned it. "It's beyond me," he said. He suggested taking it to Simon Newcomb, professor of mathematics at the Johns Hopkins University, the only man in America who might understand it. Newcomb, after reading the article, wrote, "It's magnificent, although I am not sure it is all clear to me. But it's really magnificent." Hooper rejected the article as being "too magnificent."

4

While this tenth edition was in editorial preparation, a number of vital changes occurred in the business organization of the Anglo-American venture. Far more than the Clarke brothers, Hooper and Jackson saw in the *Encyclopaedia Britannica* a glowing future—or, more precisely, one that might be made to glow. All four partners had gained profit from the reprint of the ninth edition, although because of their extremely free and easy accounting methods, the precise amounts accruing to each could never be reckoned. Hooper netted enough, however, to bring his bride, the former Harriett Meeker Cox—whom he had met on a business trip in her home town of Ames, Iowa, and had married early in 1900—to an imposing country house named Pendell Court, in Redhill, Surrey. This was a large manorial structure built in 1620, fronted by two yews Hooper called Adam and Eve, and graced with rose gardens and a private lake with swans. Jackson also purchased a country place, somewhat less impressive than Hooper's. But the Clarkes were not happy with British life and customs and shunned any prospect of settling more or less permanently in Great Britain; they far preferred to spend most of their time in New York and Chicago.

This cleavage of interests, plus the extensive interests of the Clarkes in other book properties in America—notably the "Peck's Bad Boy" series written by George Peck, a Wisconsin judge—led to a dissolution of the partnership. Early in 1900 the Clarkes sold their interests in Clarke and Company, Limited, to Hooper and Jackson. In a complex transaction, Hooper gave the Clarkes five hundred shares of his stock in the Western Book and Stationery Company and Jackson gave them five hundred shares of stock in one of his several enterprises, the Standard American Publishing Company. For these shares and a cash payment of $425,000, Hooper and Jackson took over the entire British firm which controlled the *Encyclopaedia Britannica*.

No formal partnership papers were ever signed between Hooper and Jackson, so alike in some respects, so radically different in others. They agreed to a general policy. For the time being, they retained the name of Clarke and Company, Limited. Whenever possible, major action was to be taken only with mutual consent, but in most cases either was empowered to carry on the business without the other. They had respect for each other's abilities. Hooper was the master promoter, quick to realize public susceptibility to strategic advertising and persuasive promotion. Jackson was the solid businessman, wise in the ways of developing a sound organization, skeptical about promotional excesses. They conducted their business then, and would continue to do so during the unruffled years of their association, in an unusually informal, almost slipshod way. Neither drew a salary; each had the privilege of taking what he needed for personal or business expenses from drawing accounts established at several banks in the firm's name.

In their attitude toward the *Encyclopaedia Britannica* they differed. Jackson was aware of its educational and commercial values and of how to increase both, but he was not imbued with Hooper's fanaticism. Hooper, emotionally devoted to the publication, had read nearly all the ninth edition, starting in the years when he was hawking books in Colorado. He believed deeply that, profits aside, the *Encyclopaedia Britannica* was an educational heritage that needed to be brought within reach of every person able to read English. He often spoke of the *Encyclopaedia Britannica* as "a thorough library of knowledge." He respected its editors and contributors, both past and present. He felt that the surest way of democratizing the means of self-education was to introduce the *Encyclopaedia Britannica* into the homes of those who, he was confident, yearned for instruction and information but had never believed it possible that they might one day own "the best of all encyclopaedias." In this sense, Hooper was an important pioneer in adult education, although to those who were becoming increasingly annoyed by his kinetic presence in Printing House Square and in the London habitats of bookdealers and publishers, he seemed brash, overeager, and grasping, and some staid British gentlemen considered him "much too American."

Within six months after Hooper and Jackson bought out the Clarkes, they established business offices in the High Holborn section of London, at No. 125, meanwhile maintaining the editorial staff in quarters at Printing House Square. And in May, 1901, they acquired full ownership of the *Encyclopaedia Britannica* from A. & C. Black with a contract that guaranteed a maximum final payment—in addition to the earlier ones of £6,500 and £40,000—of £5,000 through royalties to the publishers of five shillings for every set of the tenth edition sold.

When Hooper went to the Soho Square offices of the Blacks to sign the agreement, Mrs. Hooper accompanied him. They rode in a handsome carriage. After the contract was signed, the aged James Black invited Hooper to his basement to sample his favorite whisky from huge casks stored there. Hooper did so and emptied two glasses. When he emerged into the cool air he became so suddenly exhilarated that he dismissed the coachman, mounted the driver's seat, and gaily whisked his startled wife back to their hotel, crying as the carriage clattered along the streets, "We've done it! We've done it!"

5

One further business adjustment took place before Hooper and Jackson could concentrate on methods of interesting the public in their tenth edition. In 1902, they liquidated Clarke and Company, Limited, and formed two new firms. A British company named Hooper and Jackson, Limited, was established solely for business to be conducted in the United Kingdom, and for its operating expenses they transferred $100,-000 from the old firm. The Encyclopaedia Britannica Company was established in New York for business in America; all the remaining assets of Clarke and Company were transferred there for the issuance of its capital stock of $500,000 and bonds for $1 million. In the British firm the capitalization was for twenty thousand shares at one pound each; Hooper and Jackson each held 9,997, with 6 remaining shares, and in New York, each man had 2,498 shares, with 4 remaining shares. The individual shares remaining were placed in the names of various associates of Hooper and Jackson, including Hooper's brother, Franklin; his brother-in-law, William J. Cox, who worked for the American company as a clerk; and Harris B. Burrows, a book publisher in Cleveland. These men understood that they were merely dummy directors and had no voice in the management of the companies. Haphazard as this all seemed, no one could then foresee any time when such an arrangement might be used to personal advantage by either Hooper or Jackson in case of dissension. Profits were high, the immediate past had been successful, and in this bright April of 1902 there was the next edition of the *Encyclopaedia Britannica* to look forward to, and a new and spirited campaign to persuade the populace to come forward with down payments.

8

Devices Novel, Devices Picturesque

Hooper had hoped to bring out all ten volumes of the supplement simultaneously, but the financial arrangements still made the issue of one volume dependent upon the successful sale of its predecessor. With the reorganization of the firms and the accompanying expense, it was deemed wise to adhere to the old method.

So in May, 1902—with an astonishing lack of hullabaloo, considering the events that subsequently revolved around this tenth edition—the first volume appeared. It was greeted by the *Encyclopaedia Britannica*'s sternest watchdog, the *Athenaeum*, with a full measure of praise, principally for the high degree of proficiency in proofreading: "The accuracy attained in a mass of matter which only experts can correct is most creditable. We only hope it may encourage others who would produce books of permanent importance to attain a like standard."

The rest of the year, as each volume appeared, this periodical systematically evaluated it. It found that the most worthwhile article in the third volume was "Charity and Charities." It frowned on the biographies of living persons because "there is a school of wordy compliment not unrepresented here." It complained of windy rhetoric, writing of one contributor that "learning seems cast about his shoulders with the elegance and decorum of a toga about those of a Roman senator." While stating that William Archer brought a wide knowledge to his article on "Drama," the *Athenaeum* felt that he allowed "his prejudices and convictions to colour his work, and [was] oblivious to the fact that a man of taste should have preferences, but no exclusions." It praised the great lucidity of the scientific articles and hailed the bibliographies at the end of major sections as "a highly important feature."

The third volume was delayed because Bell, in checking one of the first of the bound copies, found an error in the date on which Edward VII was crowned. He had all copies called back, the offending page taken out, and a new page, with the correct date, tipped back into the books.

During the summer the ads promoted the encyclopaedia more intensely. This tenth edition, comprising the ten new volumes and the twenty-five of the ninth, would be a "bargain of bargains," although no specific price had yet been decided upon. "Biography since Dickens, Statistics since the census of '71, Philosophy since Mill, Surgery since Ascepticism, Politics since Peel, Sports since The Safety Bicycle, Electricity since Incandescent Lighting, Agriculture since English Wheat Stood at 56/9 a quarter!"

By November, it was time to announce that the entire set would soon be on sale. Taking as his example the dinners held by the Blacks in earlier years, but enlarging on the basic idea, Hooper officially declared the advertising campaign open with a lavish banquet for as many of the one thousand contributors as could come. It was held at the Hotel Cecil, with Donald Mackenzie Wallace presiding. Hooper and Haxton worked to make it memorable. On the first page of each menu a portrait of the *Encyclopaedia Britannica*'s first editor, William Smellie, stared out at the diners, and on the final page were portraits of notable contributors to earlier editions, including Scott, De Quincey, and Macaulay, with brief quotations beneath the list of toasts from some of the first edition articles, such as "Rhetoric," "Wine," and "Banquet." Especially eloquent was Wallace, who in his remarks touched on the history of the *Encyclopaedia Britannica* and evoked applause with his announcement that the final volume would be an index of six hundred thousand references. Guests at the dinner included not only contributors but other notables as well. The political opponents Arthur Balfour and James Bryce both attended, a circumstance that prompted the *Times* in its lengthy report next morning to comment that the "two are not only able to meet on friendly terms on the neutral ground of literature and science, but they rejoice to recognize the fact that, however different the points of view, they are working for the same high and noble objects."

More ads soon began to appear, urging all who had bought the *Times* edition of the ninth to write for terms in purchasing the supplement. These ads were not startling; they stated simply that the price of the new edition would be twenty pounds, a figure determined by Hooper, Haxton, Jackson, and Franklin Hooper early that summer at a meeting in Paris. There was a reason for this approach. Haxton had worked all year to devise, with Hooper's counsel, an ingenious plan for arousing interest in the tenth edition, and he wanted to reveal it only when the finished product was ready the following spring.

2

"A TOURNAMENT FOR READERS!" In the *Times* of March 31, 1903, this announcement touched off Haxton's campaign. Spread above a full page, it was an invitation to readers to engage in an intellectual contest. By answering correctly three series of twenty questions on general knowledge, contestants were eligible to win one of a number of prizes, the total cash value of which came to nearly £4,000. There was a prize of a scholarship to Oxford or Cambridge or, for female winners, Girton. There was another of £1,000, and dozens of other awards were possible for any man, woman, or child who sent in an entry blank which appeared on the bottom of the page. No entrance fee was required. And, insisted the ad, there was no motive in this joust of knowledge except to make fortunate readers richer or to send a worthy student to college. In arranging the competition, said the ad, "*The Times* has attached special value in one form of mental activity—the searching for what may be described as convertible information, knowledge that is gathered for instant use. Each competitor will gain increased power of mental concentration, will receive an admirable mental exercise in following a train of reasoning, will learn exactly where to look for a particular fact, will find a new form of recreation and will gain a fund of general information."

Near the bottom of the page appeared the only clue to future events that were to stem from this initial announcement: "No one need be deterred from entering the competition by the fact that he does not enjoy convenient access to a large collection of miscellaneous books; a standard work of reference so widely distributed that everyone can easily use it, the *Encyclopaedia Britannica*, will yield all the information required for the answers, nor is it necessary that the competitor should even own that one book."

For the next three days the advertisements made no further mention of the *Encyclopaedia Britannica*; instead each was keynoted by such slogans as "A Novel Pastime," "A Test of Wits," and "A New Influence." Readers were invited to join and delight in "a new form of recreation and a source of pleasure." Then a three-column advertisement headed "Urgent Notice" mentioned the set again. It was not necessary, this ad emphasized, to own the *Encyclopaedia Britannica*. It was futile to inquire how many sets one had to buy in order to win a prize. On April 6 appeared another full-page ad, replying to a number of contestants who presumably had written to ask for further details. No, it was not necessary to subscribe to the *Times*. No, two persons could not use a single group of questions. No, purchase of a set of the *Encyclopaedia Britannica* was not mandatory. Prospective competitors were duly informed now that those from whom inquiries and entry blanks had been received included members of the House of Commons, a professor of mathematics, an assistant manager of a hotel, a justice of the peace, a clergyman, a clothier, a pawnbroker, a king's counsel, a War Office clerk, a tailor, a glass manufacturer, a retired rear admiral, a lodginghouse keeper, a solicitor, a timber importer, an accountant, a wine-merchant.

Another two weeks passed, with intermittent ads, before the new *Encyclopaedia Britannica* appeared. Then, on April 16, after the tenth edition officially went on sale, the approach was made bolder. The tournament, all were now informed, had really been organized to give a novel and wholesome form of entertainment to owners of the *Encyclopaedia Britannica*, to help develop "the encyclopaedia habit." True enough, all others were eligible to join the competition, but it was made quite clear that set owners had an advantage over all others. The *Encyclopaedia Britannica*, exhorted the ad, was the best place to find the answers to questions. If the reader had none, perhaps he could use a friend's. If the friend had none, fortunately the *Times* possessed a small number: "If you hurry you can get a loan set of 35 volumes for

100 days at less than 3 shillings a week. When you see what a wonderful book this is you will understand the purpose which animated the *Times* in arranging this competition. . . . No other book in the world could stand such an ordeal as that to which the competition subjects the ENCYCLOPAEDIA BRITANNICA, because no other book in the world contains all human knowledge from the time when the Temple of El-lil was built at Niffer." Then followed an all-important suggestion: "Remember that if you have any idea of buying the ENCYCLOPAEDIA BRITANNICA (and here is a practical point which will come home to every man who hates to throw away money) that the *Times* is now offering this newly-completed book, just a fortnight old today, at an introductory price which is half the catalogue price." With this ad was a new entry blank including a request for specimen pages of the tenth edition.

The approach had now been made directly. Each day the appeal grew stronger. On April 17, users of the *Encyclopaedia Britannica* were quoted as "expressing surprise at the ease with which they find their way in the volumes . . . to any information they desire." On April 20, an offer was made of a 220-page pamphlet illustrating the wonders to be found in the new edition. Next day appeared a portion of an article in the *Bristol Mercury* praising the contest and declaring "it is unnecessary to go beyond the ENCYCLOPAEDIA BRITANNICA for the answer to the most formidable questions on the list." On April 22, the news of publication of the tenth edition was again reprinted, urging readers to buy this "great inducement to study."

By May, the contest was relegated to the background and the qualities of the encyclopaedia were loudly acclaimed. The ads made comparisons with prices of other kinds of reading material: "When you pay six shillings for a novel, middlemen add 71 per cent profit to the sum they pay the publisher. When you buy the *Encyclopaedia Britannica,* you get it at first hand; the process is as direct as that of eating an apple when you pluck it from a tree." Not only was the new edition "the most authoritative, the most complete and the most useful work of reference," it also, "at its present temporary price," was the cheapest. Clothbound, it cost twenty-seven guineas and would be delivered on a down payment of a single guinea; in half morocco, it was thirty-three guineas; in three-quarter, thirty-six guineas; in full morocco, forty-seven guineas. Again, the device of timeliness was used; when the *Times* of June 12, 1903, announced the assassination of King Alexander and Queen Draga of Serbia, there appeared on the opposite page a large ad with extracts from the encyclopaedia's article on "Serbia." Similar extracts were printed in conjunction with important news about discussions in Parliament on free trade and protection, about eccentric weather, about financial activities in the City of London, about cricket, and about important litigation.

3

Thousands of eager competitors sent in their entry blanks; other thousands responded to invitations for pamphlets about the *Encyclopaedia Britannica,* and from these many names the clerks at High Holborn drew up long lists of prospects. The winners of scholarships were less important now than the rate of sales.

All the rest of the year, Haxton continued to create new advertisements and new devices for keeping interest high. He was a man who worked at a feverish pace and in eccentric ways. While in London, he occupied a suite at the Savoy Hotel and often went without sleep for three days and nights, using stenographers in shifts as he paced about his rooms dictating, in a loud and shrill voice, his ads and prospectuses. In regular conversation he stuttered badly, but when he embarked on one of his dictating marathons he spoke easily and without hesitation, the purple prose issuing from him quickly and exuberantly. Sometimes his excitement with what he had just dictated got the better of him, and he rushed to the lobby and ordered the head porter to fetch a horse. This done, he leaped astride and galloped through the London streets for hours until the horse grew weary. Then he returned to his suite to continue his dictation to a bewildered stenographer. Once, after a series of full-page ads appeared, he ripped them from the newspaper and plastered the wall of one of his rooms with them, compelling the management to demand that he leave. But Hooper brought calm by paying for the cost of repapering the wall. "Haxton's too good a man to lose," he told Jackson, who protested that the advertising director's eccentricities would damage their reputation. "We have to take care of him when he goes off this way. We need him."

During the summer months, the tall, spade-bearded Haxton lived in the country, moving from one rural hotel to another as the mood pleased him. There, too, he wore out shifts of secretaries hired from adjoining villages or driven in by carriage and train from London. He preferred to dictate most of his verbiage while seated in a rowboat on the lake nearest whatever inn was his temporary home, his eyes flashing and his arms waving wildly while he composed long sentences extolling the virtues of the *Encyclopaedia Britannica*. Frequently he frightened a secretary sitting primly at the other end of the boat when he stripped to his underwear and, with a wild yell, leaped into the lake for a few minutes' swimming. Soon he would clamber back into the boat, explaining, "I was carried away, I had to cool off," and continue from the point at which he had been so aroused by his own prose. But this strange man did produce effective and highly readable ads, and the pace of the selling campaign quickened in the final months of the year.

To the numerous prospects gleaned from the various lists went special letters warning that the last days of the special sale of the tenth edition were swiftly approaching. Not only in the columns of the *Times* but in newspapers in the farthest reaches of the British Isles announcements appeared. Any innocent inquiry brought to the information-seeker a flurry of leaflets, pamphlets, an illustrated booklet or two, even prepaid telegrams which prospects needed but to sign and return. "Flight was useless," a *Times* editor later recalled. "The whole country from Land's End to John o'Groats and from Yarmouth to Dunmore Head was pervaded by the *Encyclopaedia Britannica*. It loaded the British breakfast table with the morning coffee, and lay, hard and knobby, under British pillows throughout uneasy nights. There was no escape from the torrent of 'follow ups' save by the despatch of a firm order to purchase accompanied by an installment of one guinea."[1]

In this persistent drive for purchasers, Haxton hammered on the theme of taking advantage of an opportunity never again to be realized. When the bargain offer had but eight more days to run, he composed ads that appealed to every aspect of a reader's personality. He warned that, after December 19, no one could buy the tenth edition for less than fifty-seven pounds, twice the bargain rate. "This does not mean that the price will be increased for a short time only. It means that the book will never again be sold for one penny less than the full catalogue price. . . ." Nor was this, suggested the ads, something to be regarded fleetingly and as of slight importance. "If you had determined to insure your life and the premium was to be more than doubled unless you made your application before a certain day, how great an effort you would make to be in time. This is a parallel case. You are asked to choose between being one of the men who are on time

[1] F. Harcourt Kitchin, *Moberly Bell and His Times* (London: Phillip Allan and Co., 1925).

and being one of the men who are too late, between ranking yourself on one side of the actors in the world's drama who have succeeded because they have been prompt, and those who have failed because they have let the moment that never comes back slip past them beyond recall."

His advertisements based on this idea cited anecdotes—drawn, of course, from the pages of the *Encyclopaedia Britannica*—of "A Man Who Missed His Moment" against "A Man Who Took Time by the Forelock." A moment-misser was Boulanger, who, in January, 1899, could have become dictator of France had he acted in time, and a forelock-grabber was Nathan Mayer Rothschild, who had used advance information of the results at Waterloo to make tremendous profits in stock transactions. Placing these cases side by side, the ads thundered: "UNDER WHICH OF THE ABOVE TWO COLUMNS WOULD YOU CHOOSE TO FIGURE—THE COLUMN OF SUCCESS OR THE COLUMN OF FAILURE?"

The ads proclaiming "Going! Going! Gone!" continued. The tributes grew to dithyrambs. Most books in a library, they scoffed, were "no more than ephemeral phonograph records of obiter dicta by persons of no authority." But the *Encyclopaedia Britannica?* "It represents an accumulation of the permanent facts acquired by the light of science of ages in every quarter of the globe. The *Encyclopaedia Britannica* can reveal all the kingdoms of the world in a moment of time. Railway communication, the telegraph, the motor car are slow vehicles in comparison with the rapid course of a thought that with the aid of these volumes can fly from Thibet to Korea, from Korea to the Congo!"

Did a man work as a banker and did his sister, perhaps, spend her time in embroidery or in the study of Browning? "The *Encyclopaedia Britannica* makes the pursuit of the one intelligible to the other." Did the goggle-eyed reader of Haxton's prose wish to save a part of his household bills, those paid to his doctor, carpenter, or lawyer? "The doctor, the carpenter, the lawyer have all gone to the *Encyclopaedia Britannica* to learn. WHY NOT GO DIRECT and save the expense of an intermediary?" Was the reader embarrassed when called on to explain what he knew about any household object—a clock, telephone, furniture, piano? "When once his curiosity is aroused, even at the expense of some humiliation, he will want a book to help him. The only book in the English language that can be relied on to help him over an innumerable list of inquiries is the *Encyclopaedia Britannica!!*"

4

Naturally, such appeals were designed to bring results. Just as naturally, the entire advertising campaign, from the first days of the now-neglected scholarship competition to the frenzy of the final appeals, evoked considerable criticism.

Chief among the fault-finders were those in the British publishing world who increasingly resented these aggressive Americans and their methods of promotion. There were unpleasant references to "that American syndicate" and "those alien Americans," and there was, of course, a general deploring of the affiliation of the *Times* with the schemes devised by Hooper and Haxton and with their ostentatious pronunciamentos about their *Encyclopaedia Britannica*. One reproof from the editors of the *Saturday Review,* expressing the views of these nettled publishers, read: "Tempora mutantur; the *'Times'* has changed; and the satirist's wail for the first time finds its full force: O Tempora O Mores. O *'Times'* what manners! If there were not a certain lack of proportion in the metaphor one might say that the *Encyclopaedia Britannica* were the thin end of the wedge, designed to expand the interval between the past and present of the *'Times'*. . . . It once set the world aflame by publishing, straight from the original text, the Berlin treaty. The full text of the treaty was printed with no particular head-line, with no other introduction than this: 'We are favoured with the following.' That was dignity. This . . ."

At *Punch,* the funsters took a lighter view:

> "You are old, Father Thunderer, old and austere,
>   Where learnt you such juvenile capers?"
> "It's part of the Yankee Invasion, my dear,
>   To galvanize threepenny papers."

Jauntiest of the critics were Edward Verrall Lucas, the poet and essayist, and Charles L. Graves. In later years of reflection, Lucas described his jibes as part of his "nonsense period." Their attacks first appeared in privately printed booklets, but in 1903 they were gathered into a red-covered volume titled *Wisdom While You Wait: Being a Foretaste of the Glories of the Insidecompletuar Britanniaware.* In front was reprinted the "Father Thunderer" verse and midway was another:

"You are old, Father William, yet nimble and fleet,
How kept you your sinews so supple?"
"By reading this Supplement, slick and complete:
You ought to subscribe for a couple."

This sly compendium of mockery listed among its "editors" Bell, William Hohenzollern, Sir George Newnes, and the brothers Harmsworth, and, as American editors, Mr. Dooley, Buffalo Bill, Mrs. Mary Baker Eddy, and John Wanamaker. In the mode of the *Encyclopaedia Britannica* advertisements, there were extracts supposedly from the *Insidecompletuar Britanniaware*. From the "article" on "America" the volume quoted:

. . . The Fauna of America is extensive and peculiar. Unlike other civilised countries, dangerous wild beasts and birds of prey are commonly encountered in the most populous districts. Nothing can exceed the ferocity of the Trust Fowl, while whole regions of New York are rendered unsafe by the ravages of the Tammany Bos and the Tammany Tiger. Yet alongside these examples of barbarous atavism, one encounters evidences of singular refinement and humanity. Mr. Roosevelt, though originally a cowboy, has set his face like a flint against the tyranny of the Beef Trust, and only a superficial observer would count Mr. Hay as a man of straw. Furthermore, the humanising influence of American culture is signally displayed by its principal exports, which include, amongst other products, J. Pierpont Morgan, canned peaches, Mr. Duke, duchesses, R. G. Knowles, coon songs, Quaker oats, Tabs, Christian Science, Virginia hams, cocktails, Sunny Jim, Honeysuckles, Bees, and Edna May. . . .

In the matter of liquid refreshment America has always set a high standard of excellence. As George Washington aptly observed, "I care not who makes the laws of this nation so long as their drinks are discreetly mixed.". . .

But the supreme boon conferred on the western world by this great Republic has yet to be revealed. All that is best in the present great Thesaurus of Universal Knowledge, the INSIDECOMPLETUAR BRITANNIAWARE; all the electrifying rag-time methods of our scheme of advertisement; all the "sideshows" in this superb and brainy bazaar are the products of the volcanic and voluptuous Transatlantic imagination.

Lucas and Graves laughed merrily at the lavish use of testimonials made by the original advertisements. They quoted the mythical indorsement of Ignace Paderewski, the famed pianist: "Ten volumes of your harmonious work make the most perfect pianoforte stool imaginable." And of Carrie Nation: "I don't know how my campaign against

the liquor saloons would ever have succeeded but for your timely publication. There is no plate glass that can stand against one of your
tomes. You should see Volume XXVII bringing down a row of whisky
bottles. It's great!" And of Eugene Sandow, the man of mighty
strength: "I now use your volumes exclusively in my schools of Physical Culture in place of the old-fashioned weights, bar-bells, &c." And
of H. G. Wells: "I have already given you an advertisement in *The Sea
Lady,* and can only repeat that for submarine reading your work has
no equal. The Atlantic is paved with it."

On the book's back cover, satirizing another kind of ad prepared by
Hooper and Haxton, were displays announcing that the *Insidecompletuar Britanniaware* covered sports since Ping-Pong, trade since J. P.
Morgan, medicine since pink pills, horticulture since Grape Nuts, and
politics since Winston Churchill.

Later that year, Lucas and Graves satirized the scholarship competition in another volume called *Wisdom on the Hire System.* It told of
the many prizes for those who replied most accurately to questions:
first was an eight-room, fourth-floor flat in Portland Place, to be named
Bellevue; the second a portrait model of the winner, "to be placed ad-
vantageously at Madame Tussaud's"; and the final eighty consisted
of "half an hour's stimulating converse with the gentleman who invents
the advertisements for the Ency. Brit." The volume contained "Scenes
in the Lives of Competitors," ranging from a sketch of Arthur Balfour
dancing a jig when informed he had been named a winner to one of a
gloomy casket labeled "He failed in Every Question." There were a
number of limericks titled "Rhymes for the Times." Inevitably, some
poked fun at the American invasion:

> There once was a clerk in a bank
> Whose prospects were perfectly rank;
> He developed such brain
> In competing for gain,
> That he's fit to shake hands with a Yank.

And others flicked humorously at all those who competed:

> There was once an ambitious K. C.
> Who said, "I'll a prize-winner be."
> He toiled every night
> Till his whiskers grew white
> But his answers were wrong—one in three.

There once was a slovenly Dean,
Whose hat wasn't fit to be seen.
With his prize-winning fruits
He purchased new boots,
But his gaiters were still rather green.

5

No more avid reader of these humorous booklets than Horace Hooper could be found in all London. Haxton raged and stormed up and down the High Holborn offices, vowing to sue for libel or thrash either Graves or Lucas, or both. Jackson frowned and worried about the harm such attacks might do to their attempts to sell the work. But Hooper chuckled.

"Greatest advertising in the world," he insisted. "They talk about us, that's fine. If they didn't talk, they wouldn't help us. It'll stir interest among people who might not even read the ads we've been running. Let's take it in good grace and you'll see how little effect they have on slowing down sales."

So the campaign, especially in the closing days of the year, continued. Hooper was in the midst of it all, checking copy for ads, rushing around the High Holborn offices, acquiring the admiring nickname from his closest subordinates of "Hell Every Hour" Hooper, although to his face they always called him "H. E." He rarely left the offices until late at night. Lunch was brought in from Claridge's or the Savoy or a nearby restaurant, and at the lunch hour he and the others spoke of nothing but the *Encyclopaedia Britannica* and how it could best be sold.

Orders streamed into these offices, although occasionally there was an angry reply, such as the prepaid telegram with the message, "From my bath, I curse you!" and the letter from a retired member of Parliament protesting, "You have made a damnable hubbub, sir, and an assault upon my privacy with your American tactics." To reasonable complaints Jackson was delegated to reply tactfully. Hooper busied himself with plans for carrying through collections. Fearful that many who made down payments might not follow regularly with the required additional ones, Hooper imported from New York a former policeman, William Miller, who stood six inches over six feet and weighed 310 pounds. He assigned to him a small van painted vermilion, with "Debt Collection Agency" in bright yellow on its sides, intending to send this garish vehicle into neighborhoods where defaulters lived, so that all could see, when the van stopped outside a door, who was slow in paying. But the truck was never used because of legal restrictions and, moreover, because only an insignificant percentage of purchasers defaulted.

There were reports of good sales in foreign lands—Australia, India, South Africa, and even Japan—where, increasingly since 1900, Hooper and Jackson had dispatched agents to set up offices. From Oswald Sickert, one of Haxton's aides, came a story of an experience in Australia, a tale that set the office staff laughing and, in various versions, entered the official lore of the encyclopaedia business. Sickert related that one sheep-farmer was so overwhelmed by the advertisements in his local newspaper about the tenth edition that he had sent in his guinea. When he was informed that his purchase had arrived at the local post office, he rode his foam-flecked horse fifteen miles into town to pick it up. As he arrived at the building, he yelled, "Where is it? Where is it?" Ushered inside, he was led to the large box. Feverishly he ripped off the top, quickly he tore aside the paper coverings, and then he stared in disbelief. "Books!" he bawled. "I ain't bought books, have I?"

6

The cost of the campaigns for the reprint of the ninth and the tenth edition had been considerable. Advertising in newspapers and periodicals totaled £203,000, and circulars, booklets, and letters to prospects another £90,000. But, as Hugh Chisholm soon made public in a long and lucid report, the campaign expenditures—and all the effort and even the gibes—had been worthwhile.

Using the occasion to strike back at the skeptics and critics of the Americans and their methods, Chisholm emphasized that previously the price of the *Encyclopaedia Britannica,* £37, had been prohibitive to many, that only rich men, libraries, schools, and well-to-do private institutions had been able to buy it.

"Apart from the existence of some exceptional obstacle," Chisholm wrote, "it seemed paradoxical that the British public should have been so much less appreciative than the American of a work which is a monument of British initiative and learning. . . . I have myself heard people in the United States attribute their success in life primarily to their having in early days bought the *Encyclopaedia Britannica,* and anyone who knows the American and realizes what has been done for their country by their general acuteness of mind, passion for applying knowledge, and quickness to appreciate the solid value of education agrees—no matter how patriotic a Briton he may be—that in our own country we have had some leeway to make up and that anyone who could give a proper stimulus in the right direction might justifiably consider the object a good one on its own account."

Those whom the various advertisements offended were guilty, in Chisholm's phrase, of "superficial and thoughtless criticism" and too much given to "glib and contemptuous talk about the ubiquity and excess of advertisement." "It is always possible to make fun of people who appear to have only one idea, and the devices adopted for interesting the public in the *Encyclopaedia Britannica*—novel, varied and picturesque as they were—have been the object of some clever skits, and a good deal of satirical parody. Nobody minds this poking of fun so long as it is not malicious. But while anybody with a sense of humour can appreciate the comical side of a persistent and vigorous attempt to arouse preoccupied and negligent humanity to a sense of its own interests by bombarding the portals of the mind from every conceivable vantage ground, this, after all, is the essence of clever advertising, and in the long run its only proper test is its success, provided always that the thing advertised really is what it is claimed to be."

Indulging his passion for statistics, Chisholm covered every aspect of the campaigns. One single full-page ad in the *Times* had resulted in orders worth £8,000. More than 200,000 persons had written to the newspaper since 1898 about the set. The number of volumes sold in the 300 weeks since the *Times* sanctioned the reprint of the ninth edition came to 1,500,000; their aggregate weight, 5,500 tons. The largest sale on any one day was more than 30,000 and in a single week more than 100,000. "The packing used for dispatching sets to subscribers would, if arranged in a solid block, have formed," exulted Chisholm, "an edifice as big as St. Paul's Cathedral and the Houses of Parliament combined." And an added fillip of information was that 500,000 goats had been requisitioned for the book bindings.

Of the reprint of the ninth, 30,000 had been sold, and so far, said Chisholm, 32,000 of the tenth edition had been disposed of—a figure, even with the price increase of December 19, that would eventually rise to 70,000. The total sales already amounted to £600,000, a bounty few had ever anticipated or even imagined possible. Few, perhaps, but Horace Hooper was among them; his fervor had never dimmed, and he quietly gloated when he learned that his predictions of the response to his selling techniques had turned out to be correct. At a dinner party a guest heard him citing Chisholm's statistics and remarked,

"Dear me, I wouldn't have thought as many people as that wanted the *Encyclopaedia Britannica.*"

"They didn't," replied Hooper. "I made them want it."

7

Because of the tangled and unorthodox nature of the Hooper-Jackson business operations—in the middle of 1903 they established a second American office in Chicago to provide a legal bridgehead for combating irksome copyright thieves in the Middle West—it was impossible to determine exactly the full profits of Hooper and Jackson, but from estimates and other recorded data it was evident each had made more than half a million dollars.

As for the *Times,* its salvation had come by means of its association with the Americans. Ever since the first contract in 1898, the newspaper had received ever increasing revenue each year, and with comparatively little effort. From 1898 to 1900, the annual profits from the *Times's* Publications Department, headed by those from the sales of the *Encyclopaedia Britannica* and followed by those from the sales, also arranged through Hooper and Jackson, of the *Century Dictionary, The Times Gazetteer,* and *Fifty Years of Punch,* had risen from £2,-000 to £22,000. The grumpiest of coproprietors could take comfort in this rise, and even more in the amount that had come to the paper from the sale of the *Encyclopaedia Britannica* alone since the cautious day in 1898 when Bell threw in his lot with the Americans. For that sum, robust and handsome, was £108,000.

9

Hooper's Revolution

Now, in the flush of this success, Horace Hooper was closer than ever to Bell and the *Times*. In spite of the glories of the sales campaigns, many executives and staff members of the *Times* scorned Hooper—and Jackson, though in lesser degree, since he was not so much in evidence as Hooper—for being too aggressive and too assertive. Some expressed fear that Hooper might wreck the paper. They disregarded or refused to have faith in his stated reluctance to become involved with its editorial side; Hooper would no more have proposed a topic for an editorial to Bell than he would have suggested altering details in the article on "Egyptology" in the *Encyclopaedia Britannica.*

Naturally enough, Bell was grateful to the Americans for helping to ease his economic burden. But his personal feeling, especially for Hooper, went deeper. He considered Hooper a shrewd, resourceful, and trustworthy man, in whom were combined idealism, generosity, and commercial acumen. Bell sometimes felt that Hooper was too impetuous, that Hooper's ideas were impractical, but he was never loath to listen to him.

A number of new contracts were signed with the two Americans. One, late in 1903, provided for the use of the *Times*'s name for a new edition of the *Encyclopaedia Britannica,* intended primarily as a reprint of material from the ninth and tenth, with such alterations and additions as might be necessary to update the work. Chisholm and W. Alison Phillips, his cousin and an able historian, spent months in an exhaustive examination of the earlier volumes, finally concluding that a mere reprint was hardly feasible because only 10 per cent of the material was fresh enough to be properly transferred to the contemplated edition. Their report spurred Hooper to a swift decision: "Now we can start from scratch and have a completely new edition! Completely rewritten! Knowledge has moved too fast and we must catch up with it." Ultimately, this proposal would create fatal dissension between Hooper and Jackson, but at this time it seemed logical and workable, and Chisholm was directed to proceed.

Another important agreement made Hooper and Jackson, respectively, advertisement director and circulation manager of the *Times.* The formal contract was signed in May, 1904. The two offered their services in an arrangement that involved no extra investment and little risk for the newspaper. By its terms, if the newspaper's annual revenue were less than £200,000, Hooper and Jackson were to make up half the loss. But if the newspaper made more than £200,000, the *Times* received half the excess. Hooper and Jackson were guaranteeing, in return for the right to associate themselves with the newspaper, that they could be so successful that no losses would occur.

Jackson, who was in the United States when this arrangement was made, cared little for it. Hooper sought to assure him. "We are undertaking a very much bigger thing than we undertook when we first started the E.B.," he wrote to Jackson, "and the profits to you and me individually will be greater, and very much greater. I believe I am honest when I say that we shall get half of the profits of the *Times* without the least particle of trouble. This is a strong statement to make, but I believe that is what we are getting, and what is more I believe they are perfectly willing for us to have it, and that we'll have to cast it up till you and I get into the place where we can't do anything more with the *Times* and then they'll have to give it to us for 10 years beyond that."

The extent to which Bell and evidently Arthur Walter were willing to permit Hooper to take control of the business end of the newspaper was jubilantly described. "It is understood that I am to take charge of the advertising department down there. I can reorganize the rates, I can sell quarter double columns or half double columns, I can put 3 or 4 canvassers on the streets of London canvassing for the advertising, I can write and circularize as many people as I want that we will do their advertising for them, charging them nothing or charging them something as we may see fit, in other words they'll let me do whatever I want in the advertising department down there."

When Jackson protested that he feared the *Times* might frown on the use of new advertising techniques in its columns, Hooper replied, "I want you to know that they are not weak-kneed in any way, shape or manner. . . . They are all delighted, all willing to do everything I ask them. . . . They are willing to let us say anything in our advertisements, do anything we want, and make everything we can suggest."

2

With customary zeal, Hooper undertook his new assignment. He placed Haxton in charge of recruiting salesmen and advertising copywriters, but he insisted, "I want to see every piece of advertising that we're going to put in the paper." Hooper directed that the half-dozen salesmen he would send, as he had put it to Jackson, "on the streets of London canvassing for the advertising," dress smartly, speak well, and be bold but not overbearing in their approach to prospective space-buyers. Hooper was an inspiring force, and in many of the advertisements that began to appear in the *Times*, his ideas and often his rhetoric could be detected.

Although little alteration was made on the traditional first page of personals and want ads, the appearance of the *Times* on other pages gradually began to change. Block ads, ads with illustrations, ads with heavy black type, and ads of two columns and three columns and of the full six columns appeared. While the new advertisements were not startling judged by later standards—or, for that matter, by the standards of less dignified newspapers of that day—readers of the *Times* were astounded that their solemn journal should have them. Even the personals seemed to assume a capricious mien: "Hubby still love little Muv. Come back to Father, who awaits his Hun. Baby brother and Hub both in despair." A new type of institutional advertisement was widely used. Written by Haxton, these ads appeared to the unpracticed eye to be feature stories, although, as in an effusive article about the Midland Hotel in Manchester, the italicized note atop the columns stated, "This announcement has been written by a member of *The Times* Advertising Staff after independent investigation, for which full facilities were afforded by the manager of the Midland Railway Hotels." Such article-advertisements dealt not only with pleasure places but with such establishments as the Keeley Institute, for which Haxton wrote "The Redemption of the Inebriate," after thorough investigation and assistance from a "medical practitioner of long experience."

There were large ads, with varied formats, from the makers of Hennessy's One Star Brandy, Martell's Cognac—hitherto content with old-style ads repeating the brand name in light type down half a single column—and Old Bushmill's. To the horror of old subscribers, Martell's Three Star Brandy was often featured on the same page with the parliamentary reports. And jammed together on pages that for years had never been violated were advertisements, large and small, for Cockle's Anti-bilious Pills for Brain Workers; Apollinaris ("The Queen of Table Waters"); Remington typewriters; the Lanchester motorcar, with photographs of that massive automobile, the "Ideal of Luxury, Silence and Ease"; and for furniture, teas, cocoa, watches, Allsopp's Lager, Eugene Sandow's Physical Culture School, magazines of the hour, and the National Movement against Consumption and Cancer. One full-page advertisement caused talk throughout London. In the center was a drawing purportedly of Plato "meditating on immortality before Socrates, the Butterfly, Skull and Poppy," and the page was spattered with quotations from poets and philosophers about life and the extent of man's existence and immortality. This high-flown prose and graphic art combined to assert that "the jeopardy of Life is immensely increased without such simple precautions as Eno's Fruit Salt—It rectifies the Stomach and makes the Liver laugh with Joy." And in the same classification was another that declared: "Only Live Fish swim up stream. Which Way are You Going? With a clear head to steer a strong body you can do things and win. Both can be built by proper food, brain food—Grape Nuts, the Most Scientific Food in the World."

As he had been obliged to do when the first advertisements for the ninth edition reprint appeared, Bell took to his letter-writing table to explain these innovations to subscribers. He, too, was annoyed by the character of the Hooper-inspired advertisements, but he could not overlook the revenue. "I can understand and sympathize," he wrote to one irate subscriber, "with anyone who dislikes advertisements. As a reader I dislike them myself. They increase the bulk of the paper, and, until one gets to ignore them, they are even irritating. I object equally strongly to paying rates and taxes, but I recognize that there are certain advantages, which I cannot have without paying for them, and that, on the whole, the advantages outweigh the inconveniences. . . . In the same way I think that if I subscribed to *The Times* and got a paper of 'immense influence and almost Imperial authority' for a sum that pays little more than the cost of the white paper on which it is printed and the delivery, a sum that certainly does not pay in addition the printers' bare wages, I should be inclined to look charitably upon the eccentricities, perhaps the vulgarities, of those advertisers who pay the whole cost of the staff, of the thousands of contributors, of the correspondents, of the telegrams sometimes costing 100 pounds a column, who, in fact, alone enable me to have on the white paper, for which I have paid, all that news and all that thought, care and intelligence which converts my white paper into an organ 'possessing immense influence and enjoying almost Imperial Authority.' "

3

To supplement income from these ads, Hooper arranged for Jackson to operate as circulation manager. He believed the lure to subscribe to the *Times* would be irresistible. "We are not going to make new newspaper readers," he explained. "We are going to take people who are now taking a newspaper over to our newspaper."

His idea was simple but, as it turned out, it had its several defects. Persons who had not heretofore held annual subscriptions to the *Times* could now obtain them at a rate reduced approximately 23 per cent. The new price was three pounds a year instead of three pounds, eighteen shillings. "A Novel Plan of Newspaper Distribution," read the explanatory pamphlets distributed throughout London. Hooper reasoned that as more subscribers were gathered and more newspapers sold, more advertisements would follow—and at justifiably higher rates. "Our purpose," read the booklet, "is to reorganize our budget, to reduce our revenue from one source and increase it from another." A strong appeal was directed to many who were not able to afford the *Times*, who borrowed copies, who bought secondhand copies, or who actually hired copies by the hour from news vendors. "The fact that *The Times* offers, at its present price, good values for the money," the booklet admitted, "does not alter the fact that there are many persons to whom threepence a day seems a great deal to pay for a newspaper."

Frankly experimental, this offer was good for a limited time, until June 25, 1904. To attract new readers, Bell rehired F. Harcourt Kitchin, a former editorial staff member, to edit a weekly financial supplement that would contain articles and reports on all staple industries of the country and occasionally a series of articles and reports from principal business centers of the world. When Kitchin drew up a prospectus and preliminary supplement, Hooper was elated. "This is the finest thing which has been produced by any newspaper since the world began," was his estimate, one that astounded the self-effacing Kitchin. Haxton yearned to create advertisements informing readers that Kitchin's supplement would impart to them secret information about the financial world. When Kitchin protested that this would be some miles removed from the truth, Haxton insisted that he could exaggerate and still not lie. The ads proves less sensational than Kitchin had anticipated, but still he was astonished to find himself referred to as "one of the most brilliant financial geniuses" of the day with "a network of great financial reporters all over the globe."

For all his efforts, Hooper's project was a failure. Although about thirty-two thousand new subscribers were gained, the additional expenses and costs were too high to make the venture even partly successful. News vendors were disgruntled with the plan and generally refused to co-operate, so that more men had to be hired to make deliveries to new subscribers. Neither did the circulation swell as much as Hooper had expected, a disappointment that bore the practical disadvantage of preventing him from raising advertising rates as he had hoped to do.

4

None of Hooper's ideas—neither the blaring advertisements nor the interesting supplements—provoked as much excitement and strife during his period of power at the newspaper as the formation of the *Times* Book Club.

Late in 1904, Hooper proposed to Bell that the newspaper open a lending library in one of London's busiest sectors and stock it with books that could be borrowed without fee only by *Times* subscribers, those already in the fold and newcomers who assuredly would be attracted by the service. Hooper confidently maintained that this device might well double the newspaper's circulation and increase the advertising rates, thereby more than offsetting any costs involved. Bell expressed great interest, and the two men went to various publishers to explain the new plan. Most of the bookmen were enthusiastic and agreed to supply the books at the usual rates allowed all booksellers and libraries.

With one of the mightiest of the publishers, Frederick Macmillan, Hooper was especially voluble. "This scheme," he said, "will not benefit the *Times* alone but all of you publishers. My experience with the *Encyclopaedia Britannica* has led me to think that a large number of books of all kinds can be sold if new methods, especially in advertising, are used. We will agree to supply on loan the books our subscribers want, and, of course, we will have to make large purchases from you publishers. We will want the best trade terms, and our contracts will be not for one year or two years but for at least four or five."

"What else is there to the plan?" Macmillan quietly asked.

Hooper waved his arm airily. "Of course," he said, "we shall be at liberty to do what we like with the books we have bought and paid for."

Sensing trouble, Macmillan declined to sign with Hooper, but most of his associates did, and so did Simpkin, Marshall and Company and smaller wholesalers.

Bell was soon infected with Hooper's excitement. "The scheme," he wrote to a friend in India in June, 1905, "is, briefly, to open a large West End office of *The Times* well stocked with books, some 25,000 volumes of that sort of quality likely to be asked for by readers of *The Times*." But he still had qualms, stimulated chiefly by his superior, Arthur Walter, who insisted that the contract establishing the Book Club repeat the guarantee that the receipts for the year would not go below £200,000.

When Bell conveyed Walter's reservation, Hooper pondered for several days, then finally agreed, but not before he had spoken his mind on how slowly the project was getting under way. "Look here," he told Bell, "I have to come down to this office and put my shoulder underneath you—and you are a good heavy man—and it takes me two or three weeks to push you round into a place. Then you and I have to push Mr. Walter into a place, and that takes a week or so. Then I have to go up to High Holborn and push my partner Mr. Jackson into a place and then I have to go out and enthuse the public. That didn't make much difference when I was a young man and had plenty of energy and to spare. But now it is too hard."

Thus prodded, Bell and Walter signed a contract establishing the

Book Club. It consisted of only twenty-one lines on two small sheets of paper and called for management of the Book Club by Hooper and Jackson, in exchange for a specific percentage of profits from subscribers gained through the club. It reaffirmed that the over-all revenue from this and other schemes would not go below £200,000 and that any gain from the selling of used books would go to Hooper and Jackson.

Premises for the Book Club were rented on Bond Street, off bustling Oxford Street, and books were purchased at net prices. Some publishers had signed contracts for a year; others, wary because of Macmillan's refusal to join them, agreed to supply books for only six months. All summer, excitement was kept high by advertisements in the *Times:* "All the newest books to read, and nothing to pay for the use of them. . . . You can buy them after you have read them." By subscribing for a year to the *Times,* the customer could take out three volumes at one time, more by special arrangement. "And he can buy the books he wants, after reading them, at—on the average—half the usual price." A chief librarian was hired, Janet Hogarth, formerly in charge of all women clerks at the Bank of England. Twenty thousand circulars were sent out, and ten thousand replies received.

"On the 15th of September, or thereabouts," wrote Bell to another friend, "we blow our trumpets, send out 700,000 more circulars, prospectuses, catalogues, etc., and shall see the result to a certain extent, for many have already their subscriptions with other libraries to the end of the year. . . . Before the end of the year we attack again those of the 700,000 that have not fallen victims, and shall, I hope, reap in a few more. Meanwhile"—and here he wrote with prophetic insight—"we shall have the booksellers in arms against us, and a battle royal between libraries, booksellers, publishers and *The Times.*"

5

From the moment the doors swung open on September 11, enthusiasm prevailed—and strife grew.

Vast crowds surging into the new library were photographed by men Hooper had hired. Miss Hogarth and her fifteen librarians bustled about, tending to the needs of long lines of subscribers. Hooper strode through the place, greeting all around him. And he adjudged the Book Club a vast success. Books were displayed on shelves and on tables. On the walls were posted lists of best sellers and books for good reading. "The book you want when you want it," read one poster, and another, "The book of the day."

But before the week was out, trouble developed. It stemmed from a more specific reference to the varied volumes that could be bought at the Book Club at reduced prices. Any member, if he desired, could purchase any book at prices ranging from 10 to 33 to 50 per cent below the original cost, depending on the age of the book. A number of publishers promptly protested, but Hooper waved them off. He recalled to the complainants their eagerness for the *Times* to start the club and reminded them that they had assured him they would spend in advertising a good percentage of every pound the paper spent in buying their books. "Almost without exception," he declared, "you told us you welcomed the *Times* into the book business because the book trade was in a bad condition and needed someone to stir it up. We are doing the stirring. In the end, we all shall profit."

But the protests continued. In October, the Publishers' Association, expressing fear that the *Times* Book Club would touch off a price-cutting war of the kind the publishers themselves had averted by an official pact in 1900, wrote to Bell, complaining about the "detrimental effect on retail trade." Bell replied that the secondhand books offered by the club would be those used by at least two subscribers and returned in such a condition that they could never again be sold as new. These books, he insisted, were not new books and could legitimately be sold at less than the "net prices" set by the publishers.

Temporarily, this appeared to mollify the publishers. Actually, the leaders of the industry were preparing a stronger attack at a more propitious moment. Meanwhile, the idea was catching on. Even Alfred Harmsworth, always watchful of the activities of his competitors or potential competitors, expressed qualified commendation. "It's quite a good notion," he said, "to sell off books at about one-half price directly they cease to be asked for by borrowers—if the publishers would allow it, which of course they won't." (Harmsworth had already been stimulated by the Hooper-Jackson example to enter the encyclopaedia business. A few months earlier, he had summoned an editorial aide, telling him, "Hooper and Jackson have spent a hundred thousand pounds making the British public conscious of one word, and that word is 'encyclopaedia.' I want you to cash in on that word." The first result was a prospectus for a *Monthly Encyclopaedia,* but this was abandoned in favor of a traditional kind, called the *Harmsworth Universal Encyclopaedia,* which was successfully sold on the Hooper-Jackson time-payment plan.)

While the publishers smoldered, the club continued to prosper and the lists of new subscribers to grow. On May 1, 1906, upon moving from Bond Street to larger quarters on Oxford Street, the Book Club announced in a six-column advertisement a huge sale. "The greatest sale of books that has ever been held," boasted the ad. No less than 600,000 books were offered, and though the total cost of these, based on established prices, would be £200,000, the *Times* Book Club was offering them at an aggregate price of £25,000. In this significant advertisement, the *Times* went so far as to call attention to a steadfast claim of Horace Hooper's:

It is the opinion of *The Times* that books have always been sold at too high a figure, that if their prices were reduced to a scale more in correspondence, for example, with the price of a newspaper, books would circulate in correspondingly larger numbers. In the course of two days, for instance, *The Times* itself prints in its columns and sells for sixpence as much news matter as is contained in an important biography published at 21 shillings net. The cost of the paper, printing and binding in the case of such a book may amount to one shilling and sixpence. The enormous balance of its price goes in profit to the publisher, author and booksellers, wholesale and retail. An enormous balance indeed, but by no means an enormous profit, because the quantity sold is small. *At our great sale such books will be sold for 23 and 30 pence.* Where do the books come from? *The Times* has purchased from the publishers direct, 500,000 books of different kinds; it has secured a further stock of 70,000 from dealers and other libraries, and has added to them books from the surplus stock of *The Times* Book Club. The books acquired direct from the publishers are, of course, entirely new. Of books from the other sources, any that have been used at all have been rebound in special bindings, and are therefore equal to new. The large discounts are possible because of the enormous scale on which our purchases were made.

Customers—subscribers and nonsubscribers alike—were invited to stock up their libraries with "the most important and valuable kinds of books." Special bargains were 250 assorted books of biography, travel, and fiction for only £23 and 1,000 in the same categories for £80.

By ten o'clock on the morning of the "jumble sale" Oxford Street was blocked with crowds. After the first buyers surged in, the doors were closed, and for the rest of the day, while the mob outside howled, the doors were opened at hour intervals for two or three minutes to permit more to enter. Again, photographers recorded the scene. Extra policemen were called to keep order, and much of their labor involved scurrying after persons who climbed barriers and attempted to get inside by other passages. Buyers bought by threes and sixes and dozens, and many had servants with them to carry their purchases to waiting carriages. Hooper, standing in the midst of the turmoil, exulted to a weary Miss Hogarth, "This is our biggest success of all!" And Bell, highly elated, hurried to his desk to write to a friend, "We have not only increased the number of our subscribers but we seem to have converted a large number into supporters, and if we are left alone there is, I hope, a dawn of a better day for *The Times*."

The publishers were furious. They asked Hooper and Bell to a conference on May 9. To Bell's office in Printing House Square came Edward Bell, president of the Publishers' Association, and C. J. Longman. Neither side seemed disposed to be friendly. Edward Bell later recalled testily that the managing director of the *Times* struck him as one with a decidedly oriental set of features, leading the irritated book publisher to believe rumors that Bell's real name was Moses Abel or Benjamin Moss, and assumed that Hooper, who stared across a table at him and said little, was obviously an American "of either Indian or Mexican extraction because of a certain duskiness of complexion."

The representatives of the Publishers' Association asked that their adversaries agree not to sell any surplus copies of new books at lowered prices for at least six months after publication. Although Bell replied, "We decline to do that," the book publishers, judging from a report filed later by Edward Bell, assumed that peace had been restored. "Hooper and Bell agree," Edward Bell told his colleagues, evidently without justification, "that the Book Club will offer any large amounts of unsold books to the publishers or the Booksellers Association before making them available at reduced prices to the public."

How grievously Edward Bell had erred or misinterpreted was apparent on May 17, when another sale was announced for the new headquarters of the Book Club. This one was heralded in a full-page advertisement: "The success of our Great Sale of Books has been astonishing—It has astonished even ourselves! It has surpassed all our expectations!"

Since that mammoth sale, two hundred thousand more books had been added. Those who did not wish to confront the expected crowd could fill out a form on the page by checking numbers corresponding to the one hundred books listed. Featured prominently on the list was a new two-volume biography of Randolph Churchill by his son, Winston, available to members of the Book Club at only thirty-two pennies a volume, about 40 per cent less than the established price. The list also featured the work of a brilliant new novelist, W. S. Maugham, titled *The Merry Go Round* ("The Story of a young barrister who marries a barmaid, because honour bids him") and reduced from six shillings to fourteen pence.

The publishers considered this a hostile act, and they retaliated. After many meetings, the Publishers' Association, on July 4, issued a resolution aimed directly at the Book Club. It stated that no new book could be considered secondhand until at least six months after publication. No book subject to discount through regular book-trade channels could be sold either new or secondhand at less than 75 per cent of the established price in the six-month period. Both of these terms were incorporated into a formal agreement signed by all major publishers, and, to strengthen their demands on Hooper and Bell, the publishers agreed, on the suggestion of one of the industry's leaders, John Murray, to cancel all advertisements in the *Literary Supplement* of the *Times* and for that matter, anywhere else in that newspaper until the *Times* signed the agreement.

To this, Bell, urged on by Hooper, responded with accusations of "Unreasonable threats!" and "Monopoly!" He now felt—and Hooper stood by to support him and prod him—that the fight with the publishers was over more than prices; it was one of principle. Hooper had impressed on him that there were more than profits to be made, more than prestige, more than subscribers. "The *Times*," insisted Hooper, "must serve a public that wants to be educated. We started serving them by letting them buy the *Encyclopaedia Britannica* at lower prices, and the booksellers didn't like that. But we won. Now the publishers and the booksellers are angry again. But it is our duty to spread books around to people."

Both Bell and Hooper felt the publishers had gone too far with this threat to cancel advertising because of the dispute. It showed, Bell cried, that the attitude of the publishers was that "of the rat to the ferret." He insisted that the Book Club was helping to create a bigger reading public and that all publishers of books would eventually benefit. Faced with the demand that he sign the new agreement or do battle, he chose to fight. Intoned Bell: "I must leave the public to judge between our conduct and that of the Publishers' Association, which condescends to retaliate in withdrawing its advertisements and boycotting one bookseller in order to enforce a regulation carried behind the back of that bookseller and avowedly directed against him alone."

The Book War was on in earnest.

Caricature by John Kay, the eighteenth-century Scottish painter and etcher, of two of the men responsible for the first edition of the Encyclopaedia Britannica: *Andrew Bell (left), its engraver and one of its publishers, and William Smellie, the Edinburgh scholar who was its editor.*

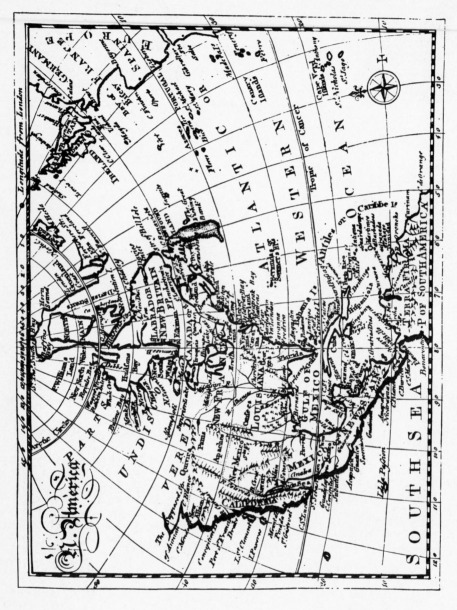

This map of North America as it was thought to be in 1771 appeared, with considerable details that were in many cases accurate and in others imaginative, in the first edition. It was one of 160 illustrations engraved by Bell on copperplate for the edition.

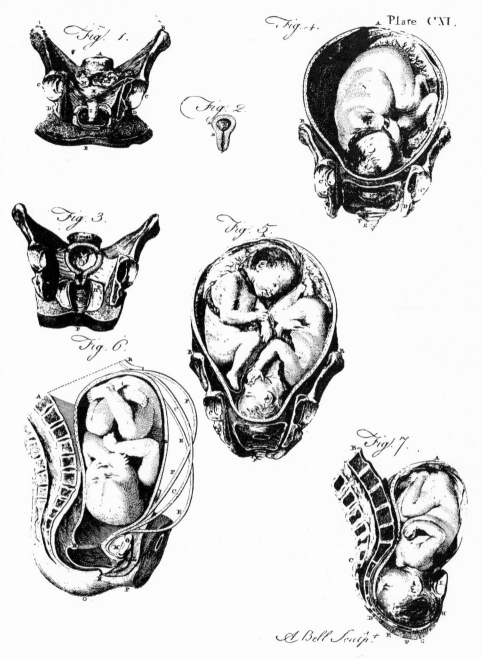

Bell's three full-page plates illustrating the article on "Midwifery"—of which one is shown here—so startled many purchasers of the first edition that they ripped the pages from the offending volume; others were so shocked that they threatened to take legal action against the publishers.

ANDREW BELL

In a formal, idealized pose

JAMES TYTLER

Eccentric but able, he was EB's *second editor*

In addition to the men shown here, another important figure in the encyclopaedia's early history was Colin Macfarquhar, Bell's copublisher who initiated the third edition. He died in 1793 at forty-eight, "worn out," wrote his biographer, "by fatigue and anxiety of mind."

GEORGE GLEIG

A clergyman who completed the third edition

38 Fowls of a Feather Flock together.

In addition to his editorial duties, James Tytler was fanatically interested in balloon ascensions. His several attempts to make successful flights were caricatured in 1784 by Benjamin West, who shows Tytler flanked by two sets of cronies. Tytler's various efforts all ended in failure.

Plate XXXVIII

Fig. 1. Noah's Ark
floating on the waters of the Deluge

Another plate from early editions showing Bell's conception of the size, shape, and occupants of Noah's Ark

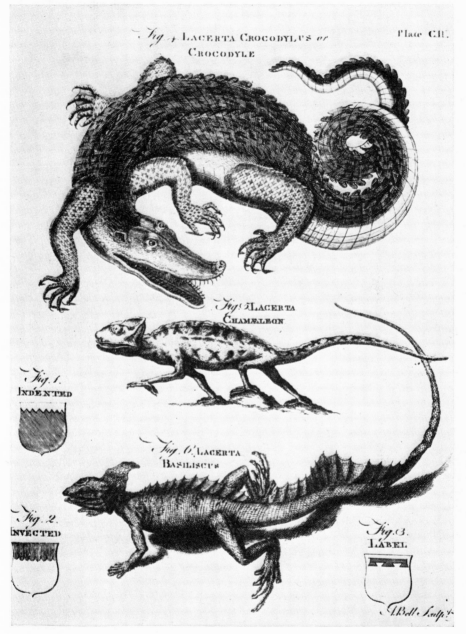

For "Zoology" Bell engraved a number of illustrations, of which these are striking examples. The crests at the left and at the lower right were inserted to fill space in the full-page drawings.

ARCHIBALD CONSTABLE

*The publisher who was called, among other things,
"The Crafty" and "The Napoleon of Publishing."*

MACVEY NAPIER

Editor of Constable's fifth edition supplement

JAMES MILL

SIR WALTER SCOTT

Contributors to the notable supplement

ADAM BLACK

Founder of the firm that published the distinguished ninth edition from 1875 to 1889.

WILLIAM ROBERTSON SMITH

His articles on religious subjects in the ninth edition aroused bitter controversy but helped dispel theological darkness,

THOMAS HENRY HUXLEY

In the ninth edition he was the foremost interpreter of the new trends in thought motivated by the writings of Charles Darwin on evolution.

HORACE EVERETT HOOPER

He revolutionized the operations—and the history—of the Encyclopaedia Britannica

WALTER MONTGOMERY JACKSON

Hooper's associate—later his adversary—at a high point in the encyclopaedia's career. Jackson also founded thriving publishing firms of his own.

CHARLES FREDERICK MOBERLY BELL

To help his London Times *he joined Hooper and Jackson in a daring—and successful—venture in 1898 to sell* Times *reprints of the* Encyclopaedia Britannica.

WILLIAM J. COX

His career with the Encyclopaedia Britannica *started in 1901 and was climaxed when he was the publisher of the "humanized" fourteenth edition in 1929.*

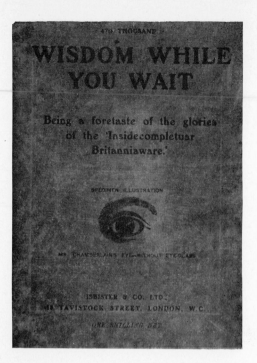

He failed in every Question.

London: Printed by Strangeways & Sons,
Tower Street, Cambridge Circus, W.C.

He omitted to send his Second Guinea.

Bringing Home the Winner.

British humorists delighted in parodying the Hooper-Jackson sales and promotional techniques of 1903–4. Shown here are the cover of one satirical book, Wisdom While You Wait, *and three typical illustrations from another,* Wisdom on the Hire System, *jibing a contest in which college scholarships were to be awarded to those readers who found the correct answers in the tenth edition of the* Encyclopaedia Britannica.

HUGH CHISHOLM

*A scholar-journalist who edited the eleventh edition,
1910-11, and wrote a number of articles for it.*

JAMES L. GARVIN

This erudite editor of the London Observer *was
editor-in-chief of the fourteenth edition in' 1929.*

FRANKLIN H. HOOPER

*Horace Hooper's brother, he served as Garvin's asso-
ciate before succeeding him in the early 1930's.*

WALTER YUST

*Formerly a literary critic, he has served as editor since
1938, a tenure longer than any predecessor's.*

Top of a full-page advertisement from the New York Times *of March 3, 1911, extolling the attributes of the eleventh edition, which was published under the imprimatur of Cambridge University.*

When Horace Hooper invaded South America two years before World War I, he dispatched this display wagon through the streets to compare the merits of the Encyclopaedia Britannica *with its competitors.*

THOMAS BABINGTON MACAULAY

His articles in the seventh edition on Samuel Johnson and on Oliver Goldsmith and his other contributions are considered small masterpieces of biography.

ALGERNON CHARLES SWINBURNE

To the eighth edition—which he called "that great repository of erudition"—this poet contributed brilliant articles on Mary, Queen of Scots, and John Keats.

EDWARD EVERETT

The famous orator was the first American ever to write for the Encyclopaedia Britannica. *His article, in the eighth edition, was on George Washington.*

MATTHEW ARNOLD

Distinguished poet and critic, he wrote on literary subjects for the ninth edition, acclaimed at the time of publication and later for its many scholarly qualities.

LEON TROTSKY

His vivid article on Lenin, his Russian Revolution associate, first appeared in the thirteenth edition.

H. L. MENCKEN

A steady and versatile writer on American literature and allied topics from 1922 until his death in 1956.

GEORGE BERNARD SHAW

His article, "Socialism: Principles and Outlook," written originally for the fourteenth edition, is a minor classic, still retained in the modern EB.

SIGMUND FREUD

The "father of psychoanalysis" wrote the first popularized description of his methods for the encyclopaedia in 1922 and again for the 1929 edition.

GENERAL JOHN J. PERSHING

This famous American military leader contributed articles in the 1920's on decisive battles of World War I.

IRENE CASTLE

In the 1929 edition she wrote about a subject in which she surpassed all of her competitors: ballroom dancing.

HARRY HOUDINI

Master magician and escape artist, he discussed "Conjuring" in the thirteenth edition.

MARIE CURIE

The thirteenth and subsequent editions carried her articles on "Radium" and other scientific subjects.

NIELS BOHR

He writes about the atom

RALPH BUNCHE

His topics deal with Africa

LINUS PAULING

His field is chemistry

GENERAL GEORGE C. MARSHALL

This distinguished soldier's subject is World War II

WILLIAM BENTON

A former advertising executive turned educator and public servant, he is publisher of the Encyclopaedia Britannica *and chairman of its Board of Directors.*

SIR GEOFFREY CROWTHER

Chairman of the board of the British company, he also is active as vice-chairman of the Board of Editors.

PRESIDENTS, PRESENT AND PAST

Robert Preble (left) has been president since 1951; his predecessor was Harry Houghton (right), now chairman of EB's executive committee.

Meetings of various boards are held four times a year. In this segment of one such recent session of the Board of Directors are (clockwise) Beardsley Ruml, social scientist and fiscal expert; William Benton; Adlai E. Stevenson, former Illinois governor and Democratic presidential candidate; Curtis Gager, industrialist; Robert Maynard Hutchins, head of the Fund for the Republic and chairman of Encyclopaedia Britannica's Board of Editors; and Sir Geoffrey Crowther.

IO

The Book War

For a full year the conflict continued. An angry Bell and a defiant Hooper assailed the publishers as the "Book Trust." The publishers called Bell a "captive of the American Syndicate."

The initial assault was made on September 25, when a half-page advertisement in the *Times* denounced the demands of the publishers as "an attempt at monopoly" and continued: "The attempted restriction is called for neither by the natural course of business nor by public convenience, indeed it runs counter to both, and *The Times* is desirous that all who care for books should know that it is determined at all costs to continue the system which the logic of business and the advantage of the reading public alike recommend."

For three consecutive days further denunciations flared under titles of "The Real Evil," charging publishers with purposely putting excessive prices on their wares; "A False Plea," upbraiding publishers for claiming they were acting in the interests of booksellers; and "A Glaring Injustice to the Bookseller," decrying as excessively restrictive the agreement the *Times* had refused to sign. The Publishers' Association countered by placing the *Times* on an official black list. Major publishers, responding to the suggestion of John Murray, started to withdraw their advertisements and, as each contract expired, declined to furnish the Book Club with new volumes.

More indignant than ever, Bell, as if to underscore his faith in Hooper, announced after the black-listing that the *Times* was extending Hooper's contract as advertising manager and giving the "alien American" further powers of hiring and firing in his department and complete sway over display ads. As for the cutoff of the supply of books, Bell and Hooper were momentarily hard pressed, but Hooper soon found ways by which he hoped to circumvent the publishers' boycott. The Book Club still had a contract with the big wholesale dealers, Simpkin, Marshall and Company, and books did come in from that source. Some publishers who were not members of the association were persuaded to continue their relations with the Book Club. Hooper also helped small shopkeepers in various localities build circulating libraries by giving them several dozen old and unwanted books. Thus established, these men were able to buy from all publishers at the usual discounts—after which they passed on the new volumes to the *Times* Book Club. These way stations were set up not only in London but as far away as northern Ireland and the Isle of Wight. They helped to ease the problem for several months until investigators for the Publishers' Association learned of the scheme and stopped sending supplies.

Despite the publishers' countermeasures and the withdrawal of their advertisements, Bell remained loyal to the traditions of the *Times*. In the same issues containing attacks on the "Book Trust" the *Literary Supplement* carried impartial, often highly laudatory, reviews of books published by the very objects of Bell's assault. All one might find in the supplement to indicate the hostilities was the announcement after each review, even the most favorable:

"The publishers of this book decline to supply *The Times* Book Club with copies on ordinary Trade terms, and subscribers who would co-operate with *The Times* to defeat the Publishers' Trust may do so by refraining from ordering the book so far as is possible until it is included in *The Times* monthly catalogue."

Its columns depleted of large-scale book advertising, the supplement emphasized the Book Club's own announcements in a column headed "Seen in the Book Shop." Among offerings in the midst of the battle were *The Life of Sir Richard Burton,* by Thomas Wright, published at twenty-four shillings but offered by the Book Club at seven shillings; "A Nice Edition of the Complete Works of Dickens," a twenty-one volume set reduced from 105 shillings to only 24; and a number of popular American books for which the *Times* had secured reprint rights. This latter group was headed by John Nicolay's *Life of Abraham Lincoln,* and the *Times* called snide attention to the difference between its price of four shillings, sixpence, and the twelve shillings, sixpence, charged by the "Book Trust" for Alonzo Rothchild's *Lincoln, Master of Men*—"and yet it is substantially the same as the four shilling, sixpence volume and shows no superiority in manufacture."

2

Everyone of importance, in and out of the British book world, seemed to join in the clamor.

The economist Dr. Arthur Shadwell was employed by the *Times* to write articles exploring the complex problems of book publishing, and in a series of seven dullish contributions he lengthily concluded that there was some right on both sides of the controversy. Henniker Heaton, a publicity-minded member of Parliament, drew up a petition signed by ten thousand "book buyers and book lovers of the United Kingdom" in support of the *Times,* the signers including the Lord Mayor of London, the Duke of Hamilton and other peers, representatives of church, medicine, and law, business magnates, and social leaders. This distinguished roster was printed by the *Times* over several full pages. George Bernard Shaw, as might be expected, sided with the *Times.* "How old is a book?" he asked, and replied, "A book is old sixty minutes after it is published." Shaw arranged for a special volume containing three of his plays, *John Bull's Other Island, Major Barbara,* and *How He Lied to Her Husband,* with this title-page imprint: "This edition is issued by the author for *The Times* Book Club." The historian George Trevelyan persuaded his publisher, Longmans, one of the few major firms still bound by contract to the club, to sell his *Garibaldi's Defence of the Roman Republic* at six shillings instead of twelve.

Other writers denounced the club. From the United States Gertrude

Atherton sent a bold message, "I want to be able to tell *The Times* to go to hell whenever I want to." Rudyard Kipling went on official record with his belief that the Book Club might eventually do away with all booksellers and that then all authors, cut off from booksellers, "would be absolutely at the mercy of *The Times*." And G. Herbert Thring, secretary of the Incorporated Society of Authors, drew up a long resolution condemning the Book Club in the name of the organization's membership comprising most of Great Britain's authors.

In response to the Athertons and Kiplings and Thrings and all others who opposed them, Hooper and Bell issued a pamphlet composed by Henry Haxton in characteristic prose. Titled *Fair Book Prices vs. Publishers' Trust Prices*, it explored the economics of book publishing and charged that the publishers had "maintained a truly Ephesian hubbub, in which the voice of reason was drowned in random damnation of an intruder daring enough not to fall down before their shrines." Did not these authors realize that the Book Club operations would bring wider distribution of books and greater royalties? Did they not see that the existing high prices and restricted circulation constituted the central citadel of the publishers' position? And who were these authors who were so blind to the advantages of the Book Club? "The curled darlings of the fiction market come forth from the lotosland where they dwell withdrawn from the vulgar bustle of commerce, or emerge from the vaporous private Utopias wherein they excogiate phosphorescent millenniums. In tones perhaps more shrill than the world expected to issue from these oracular retreats, they proclaimed at once their disinterested devotion to literature, their contempt for vulgar rewards, and their unbounded indignation at a reduction of their profits which, at the mere asseveration of the publishers, they believed to be imminent."

The booklet produced a prompt retort from the Publishers' Association in a pamphlet asserting that the Book Club was merely an "appendage to the *Encyclopaedia Britannica* promotional campaigns." "The American Syndicate," bristled the publishers, "has taken on the task of wrecking the time-honored arrangement of publisher and author and bookseller and public not with a view to enhancing the reputation of *The Times*, not to help authors and writers and readers, but for one reason and one reason alone: Revenue."

This was a rather incomplete view; as the battle intensified in these early months of 1907 it was evident that the Book Club was producing neither the revenue nor the increase in subscribers Hooper had anticipated. Yet he remained defiant. Met by reporters during a trip to the

United States, he sought to minimize the ferocity of the warfare by implying that most publishers were annoyed simply because the Book Club had been able to dispose of some books, notably the Churchill biography, which had not sold well at higher prices. "The Book Club is very popular with the people," Hooper was quoted in the *New York Times*. "It'll cost us some money, but we will win. It's important that we do, because books cost too much and ought to be brought down in price so more people could afford them." To this, *Publishers' Weekly*, spokesman for American book manufacturers, responded indignantly: "From every standpoint, practices such as those indulged in by *The Times* Book Club and other undersellers are not in the line of legitimate business enterprises, inasmuch as they do not 'make good' along the whole line." It predicted, quite prophetically, that the club would encounter more difficulty making headway because subscribers to the *Times* were not multiplying as rapidly as Hooper had expected; a typical refusal from one woman read, "I want to belong to a book club, not to a dispute." As much as £15,000 had already been lost to the *Times* in publishers' advertisements. *"The Times,"* was *Publishers' Weekly's* stern conclusion, "will have time to repent at leisure for its divagations in the book field."

The funsters and punsters again had their day with this latest of the Hooper adventures. E. V. Lucas and C. L. Graves once more were foremost among them, producing a small book on the book-club theme, this one titled *Signs of the Times, or The Hustler's Almanac for 1907* and dedicated "with the deepest sympathy" to the shade of John Delane, one of the greatest editors of the *Times* in earlier days. Mocking the *Times* as the London edition of the *New York Times* and as "The Only Paper Which Gives Itself Away Daily," it listed the editors in chief as Messrs. Hooper and Bell, the general manager as Mr. Hooperly Mober, the literary editor as Mr. Molby Belber, the city editor as Moberly Hooper, and the advertisement manager as Mr. Whooper.

In this jaunty almanac, Hooper and Bell were depicted as going far beyond the limits of a mere book club. On the first day of each month a striking new idea was proposed. For January there was a *Times* Meat Club, to which, of course, the Butchers' Association objected because of the offer of free hash. In subsequent months the mockery included such innovations as the *Times* Cooperative Clothing Club, with howls from the West End tailors and modistes; the *Times* Egg Club, with farmers and dairymen in high dudgeon; the *Times* Royal Academy, with Hooper offering to buy six Sargents at a 15 per cent discount and being attacked by art dealers; the *Times* Private Motoring Track from Croydon to Brighton "for *Times* subscribers only"; the *Times* Book Club Festival, with Bell and Hooper singing, "I love my love and my love loves me," and Jackson trilling, "How we brought the good news from New York to London"; the *Times* Cigar Club; and the *Times* Beer Club. All the silliness was climaxed by the establishment by the *Times* of a new religion for subscribers only—"The Community of Times Servers with the Right Rev. Moberly Bell as Chief Archimandrake, assisted by the Rev. The Judicious Hooper"—and an offer of £25,000 for the use of Westminster Abbey as a temple of worship.

Throughout were scattered drawings by a clever caricaturist, George Morrow, and mock advertisements. The one that best indicated the critical intent of this book showed Uncle Sam pointing a bony finger at the reader beneath a caption: "It's Your Money We Want."

3

The general furor over the Book Club roused some of the many coproprietors of the *Times* to action. For a decade or more several persons and groups had sought to inquire into the assets and losses and myriad details of the Walter heirs' majority control of the newspaper. The most persistent was Dr. Walter Knowsley Sibley, a descendant of the first John Walter and a holder of one-fortieth of a share in the *Times*. He had been an irritant to Arthur Walter and his brother Godfrey since 1900, when, acting in the name of his mother, Mrs. Clara Frances Sibley, he had raised questions about the way the Walters were managing the newspaper and receiving fixed fees for printing it. In 1905, Dr. Sibley had started suit against Walter, demanding to see the accounts of the business and suggesting incorporation of a company, an eventuality which would have compelled Walter to give up the printing division. Little developed on this matter until the end of 1906 when, at the height of the Book War, a compromise agreement was reached in which the Walters agreed to make a statement of the number of partners and their respective holdings and of the full assets of the partnership.

Dr. Sibley insisted that his action had no connection with the Book War, but his disclaimer lost validity as the strife grew. The Sibley group was especially indignant over the agreement with Hooper and Jackson extending their control of the advertising and circulation departments. There was continued muttering about the affiliation with "alien Americans" and "alien publications." To Dr. Sibley's insistent voice was added that of a Miss Brodie-Hall, also the holder of a small share, who called a meeting on June 19, 1907, to ask all coproprietors to join her in seeking legal action to set aside the agreements with Hooper and Jackson. The pacts had been made with the Americans, said she, so that Walter could insure his personal profits from the printing of the newspaper.

Arthur Walter countered with a meeting of his own, informing the coproprietors who attended that the agreements were in favor of the *Times.* It was already evident that because of the Book War, Hooper and Jackson had not yet gained a shilling of profit and, in point of fact, had spent nearly £125,000 of their own since opening the club, little of which had been retrieved and much of which would possibly never be regained. For a short time Walter staved off litigation.

4

It was at this point that Hooper stepped forward with a startling plan of his own—"Amalgamation!" All the holdings and extra ventures of Printing House Square—the *Times* itself, the *Encyclopaedia Britannica,* the Book Club, the printing business, even Hooper and Jackson, Limited—should be combined, insisted Hooper, into one gigantic firm. Such a corporation would be capitalized at £400,000, with securities offered for sale to the public; all other proprietors could be bought out or be offered new shares in exchange for their holdings.

There were discussions between Hooper, Jackson, and Bell in Hooper's Grosvenor Square town house. From them, Bell emerged a strident supporter of the proposal. He was now certain that the *Times* could never pay its own way under the existing organizational system, so unwieldly and so complicated, and that if the newspaper were to maintain its high standards, especially in its foreign service, it needed subsidies beyond any funds it derived from subscriptions, advertisements, or other traditional sources.

"We cannot do more for two years than balance receipts and expenditures," he wrote to Arthur Walter. Hooper's plan, therefore, seemed to Bell "our one chance of escape," and he laid before Walter charts and figures prepared by Hooper and Jackson. To the influential Lord Cromer, Bell wrote for aid and advice, emphasizing that under the proposed merger neither American would have—or desired, for that matter—editorial control of the *Times.* Hooper, by terms of the prospectus, would be manager of the Book Club; Jackson, manager of the Publications Department. "If the idea comes off," wrote Bell, "Hooper and Jackson will each of them be large shareholders—their interest will be mainly the financial one. They are, moreover, Americans, and not therefore imbued with British ideas about *The Times*." He was full of praise for both men. He had done business with them for nearly ten years, and, though their contracts had many loopholes, stated Bell, there had been no discord. "I have never known them to raise a quibble or a difficulty, and they have accepted all my figures without a query." The corporation, Bell explained to Lord Cromer, would be managed by two committees, one for the newspaper with headquarters at Printing House Square, the other for the subsidiary publishing and for the Book Club at Oxford Street. Bell was certain that within two years solvency and financial solidity would be established.

While Walter hesitated in coming to a decision, the Sibley and Brodie-Hall forces went into court with a demand that the complicated partnership be dissolved and the *Times* be placed on sale. On July 18, Justice Warrington ordered that this be done and appointed Walter receiver. Despite this development, Hooper pushed for a reply. He knew that a public sale, in spite of the legal ruling, was an eventuality none of the conflicting parties really desired, since it would be considered a heavy blow to the paper's prestige.

Still Walter hesitated. His major fear was that Bell and Hooper would continue a relentless fight with the book publishers, and this, for all of Hooper's apparent willingness to continue to absorb the costs of such a struggle, would have a damaging effect on the paper's reputation. He employed a firm of accountants and stock experts to examine minutely the Hooper proposal, and the reply was not enthusiastic. Hooper scorned this report, reminding Walter that had it not been for profits accruing to the paper from the *Encyclopaedia Britannica,* the *Times* might have been compelled to cease publication. Again he assured Walter, "I have no desire here except to straighten out a mess that will simply continue to get worse and worse. I have no wish to interfere editorially—although I do think the *Times* is sometimes too discreet." When Walter continued to vacillate, Hooper lost his temper. In October, he told the chief proprietor, "Look here, Mr. Walter, we have been talking with you almost three months now and have not, so far as we can see, advanced a step." Thus pressed, Walter decided against the Hooper proposition. His decision, leaving open the matter of the newspaper's sale, saddened Bell and angered Hooper.

5

Perhaps in irritation, perhaps reacting with hasty bitterness to Walter's rejection, Hooper now made a move that propelled him into a long stretch of bad fortune and new conflicts and brought him close to disaster.

Since 1903, John Murray, the London publisher who had proposed the cancellation of advertisements in the *Times* during the Book War, had held the contract for publishing the collected letters of the late Queen Victoria. For three years Viscount Esher and Arthur Christopher Benson had been intrusted with the task of gathering these letters, and now Murray announced that the first three volumes, covering the period from 1837 to 1861, would soon be issued by him. It was an event of considerable importance to all of Great Britain, and Bell, with a show of nerve that often served him well in crises, was determined to confer with Murray about the possibility that the *Times* Book Club might distribute the volumes.

Although considerable bad feeling existed between him and Murray—the book publisher had been among those who had accused the *Times* of foisting a long-published ninth edition of the *Encyclopaedia Britannica* on the public without stating it was a reprint—Bell strode into Murray's Albermarle Street office on October 15, two days before scheduled publication. Boldly, he stated his proposition.

"We are willing to lose a little money on it if you care to meet us halfway," he told Murray, "and we will take a very large number if you are disposed in this one case to deal with us directly. For the sake of the late Queen we should like to give the book as good a send-off as possible."

Murray saw his chance to end the Book War. "Nothing would give me greater pleasure than to do business with you again," he replied, "not only with regard to this book but all along the line. Can't you reconsider your decision as to the six-month limit for new books? If this were done, I think I could answer for it that not only mine but all other doors would be opened. I cannot, however, make an exception."

Solemnly, Bell shook his shaggy head and left Murray's office.

On October 18, the *Literary Supplement* carried a favorable front-page review of the volumes of letters, written by John Bailey, editor of the *Quarterly Review*. At the end was the usual plea to readers to desist from buying the book, and midway in the review was a paragraph written by Bell which he had handed a day earlier to the supplement's editor, Bruce Richmond, with the admonition, "Put it in!" It followed an especially laudatory paragraph of Bailey's and read, "But a grave mistake has been committed in the name of publication. This book is one that will create very wide interest—in one form or another it will appeal to every reader in the Empire, and it is difficult to overestimate its educational value if it were accessible to the classes who are apt to believe that wisdom lies only in a democracy. But the three volumes which might, one would imagine, have been produced at ten shillings, and which at a reasonable figure would have sold by hundreds of thousands, are offered to a privileged few at three pounds, three shillings."

Bell had written this at Hooper's instigation, for Hooper was now embarked on a daring drive to break the publishers' resistance. Hooper had already made arrangements with Edward Ross, one of his advertising aides, to write a long letter to the *Times* and, without Bell's knowledge, had given to Ross a mass of figures seeking to prove that publishers charged exorbitant prices for their books. Ross's first letter appeared the day after the review. It was long, angry, and full of denunciation and was signed "Artifex"—a rather unhappy choice, since the translation of the Latin word is "cunning inventor." It asserted that *The Letters of Queen Victoria* could easily have been put on the market for nine shillings. John Murray had paid nothing for the contents of the books, Artifex asserted, and stood no real risk in selling it. After citing the profit Murray could be expected to make from the sales, the letter grew bolder.

"Now, sir," it continued, "these figures in any case spell simple extortion. More than two thirds of the price charged for the book represents an arbitrary addition to the natural price of the book, which would be absolutely impossible if books were published under the ordinary competitive conditions applying to other productions. But this is no ordinary case at all. . . . I believe that I shall command the assent of the thinking portion of the public when I say that in accepting this task Mr. Murray has assumed a fiduciary position. Were he really imbued with the lofty and chivalrous sentiments which he has publicly professed, that aspect of the case would have presented itself to him very forcibly. He would have felt, too, that the credit and prestige of bringing out a book of this kind would be a reward which might well make him content with a relatively small pecuniary return. He would then have exerted himself to sell the book as cheaply as possible, and to make it accessible to the greatest possible number; and his reward would not have been wanting. Mr. Murray has seen things otherwise. He has exploited the great personality of Queen Victoria for his own ends, and carried the national interest in her doings for his own enrichment into 32 pieces of silver, to be precise."

The words were those of Ross, but the figures and sentiments were those of Horace Hooper. Warming up to his task, Artifex warned that the public would not be fooled by the high price of the book but would wait until it dropped, as had such others as *The Memoirs of Prince Hohenlohe,* twenty-six shillings in 1906 and only six in 1907; Captain Scott's *Voyage of the Discovery,* forty-two shillings in 1905 and ten shillings in 1906; and Sir Evelyn Wood's *From Midshipman to Field Marshal,* twenty-five shillings in 1906 and seven shillings, sixpence, in 1907. "So the hocus pocus goes on; there are more examples. . . . The public, at any rate, are no longer so easily deceived as they were, and the tables may be turned even upon Mr. John Murray."

Murray sped to his attorneys. They wrote to Bell, demanding an apology, insisting that all the statements in the letter were false. Bell's attorneys replied that an apology would soon be forthcoming and expressed their regrets that Artifex's letter might have been distressing to Murray. But no apology appeared. Instead, precisely one week after the first letter, another was printed, similarly inspired, similarly signed, similarly displayed. It repeated most of the data in the earlier letter but now added to its accusations the charge that Murray was guilty of "plunder" in charging what he did for the volumes of Queen Victoria's letters.

The time for demanding apologies was past, so far as John Murray was concerned. He instructed his attorneys to file a suit against the *Times* for libel. This done, a hearing was set for the following May. Before that contest, however, there was an upheaval in the fortunes of the *Times*—a development that would affect greatly the futures of Bell, Hooper, Jackson, and the *Encyclopaedia Britannica.*

II

A Man Called "X"

In spite of Arthur Walter's rejection of Hooper's plan of amalgamation, Bell continued to hope that Hooper and Jackson might be brought into active participation if a new company were formed. What Bell did not know was that Walter's brother, Godfrey, had quietly started plotting to organize such a company, one that would satisfy court and co-owners—and cast aside Hooper and Jackson and all their works.

Godfrey Walter had always confined his attention to the printing business. He was a shy, quiet man, ignorant of newspaper management, interested primarily in seeing that rental of the buildings and payments for printing were paid by the *Times*. But early in 1907, while Bell was in the United States receiving an honorary degree from the University of Pittsburgh, Godfrey Walter issued orders discharging a number of advertising salesmen. Although this clearly clashed with Hooper's command in this department, Hooper was too occupied with the Book War to make more than a token protest. Besides, some immediate savings were realized as a result of Walter's action, although when the busy season started the *Times* was caught short and losses ultimately outran whatever profits had been made.

Almost immediately after his brother turned down Hooper's proposal, Godfrey Walter had approached a number of wealthy, influential friends and public figures to discuss formation of a new company. From these talks emerged a tentative plan designed to quiet the protests of those coproprietors who had inveighed against the Walters and especially against the warfare that Hooper, Bell, and Jackson insisted on carrying on against the book publishers. The basis of the plan was to establish a company of which the *Times* would be a major part, and to appoint as the newspaper's managing director Cyril Arthur Pearson, owner of the garish *Standard* and lesser publications.

These discussions were secret, but details filtered out. And they traveled to the ears of the lieutenants of Alfred Harmsworth, now Lord Northcliffe, as mighty a press lord as Pearson and twice as ingenious and aggressive. On January 5, 1908, a tiny paragraph headed "The Future of *The Times*" appeared in Northcliffe's *Observer*. It read: "It is understood that negotiations are taking place which will place the direction of *The Times* newspaper in the hands of a very capable proprietor of several popular magazines and newspapers." Another newspaper, the *Daily Chronicle*, went further, naming Pearson as the *Times*'s potential purchaser.

Rumor bred rumor as these notices caught the eyes of the men certain to gain or lose by such a move. Many believed that Lord Northcliffe himself was the "very capable proprietor." George Edward Buckle, editor of the *Times*, thought it all a joke, intended to embarrass the Walters in their dealings with the coproprietors. Northcliffe was unavailable for comment. The Walters refused to talk. But Pearson declared, "There is nothing to it—but there may be some day."

Pearson was being discreetly technical. By the time he issued his partial denial he had already agreed, in a pact with the Walters, to become managing director of the *Times*. By terms of the pending agreement, which still needed approval by the courts, the new company would be capitalized at £850,000. It would merge the *Times* with the faltering *Standard* and also own the printing business. For his part, Pearson would sell his holdings in the *Standard* and the *Daily Express* to the new company for £150,000.

Spurred to action by the notices in the *Observer* and *Chronicle*,

Arthur Walter, who had complied completely with his brother in the plan favoring Pearson, gave Buckle, on the night of January 6, an item to be inserted into next day's *Times*. Buckle scanned it with unbelieving eyes.

"Negotiations are in progress," read the statement, "whereby it is contemplated that *The Times* newspaper shall be formed into a limited company under the proposed chairmanship of Mr. Walter. The newspaper, as heretofore, will be published at Printing House Square. The Business Management will be reorganized by Mr. C. Arthur Pearson, the proposed Managing Director." Then followed the disclaimer that any change would be made in the character of the newspaper or that it would be subject to party control.

Bell's first knowledge of these developments came when he returned that evening from Calais, where he had gone to greet his daughter on her return from a trip to India. When Buckle handed him Walter's statement, Bell's hulking shoulders drooped and his face grew suddenly white. Then he forced a weak smile and said, "Perhaps they will keep me as limerick editor." He walked slowly to his home to tell his wife and daughter the news. When they expressed indignation, he shrugged. "What's the use of being bitter?" he asked. "It only makes it worse for all of us."

But, as might be expected, Bell recovered rapidly. Within an hour he was at his desk scribbling a letter to Arthur Walter. "Forgive me if I say that I cannot help feeling deeply hurt," he wrote, "at the want of confidence you have shown in one who has tried to serve you faithfully, and who regarded you as a friend." He added crisply that he intended to work against the Pearson arrangement and offered to give up his salary as of January 1. "Your own interests," he assured Walter, "I regard as closely identified with those of *The Times,* and in no case will I work against *The Times.*"

Immediately, Bell set himself to determine means and measures by which he could raise money enough to thwart any plan to organize a new *Times* headed by Pearson, whom he considered one of the yellowest of yellow journalists and a man who would wreck everything he had tried to build since he had been summoned from the tranquillity of his post in Egypt.

2

From the beginning, Horace Hooper and Walter Jackson were deeply involved. They dreaded Pearson, for they were certain he would put a stop to the affiliation of the *Times* with their own enterprises. Already they had spent nearly half a million dollars on the forthcoming eleventh edition of the *Encyclopaedia Britannica*. They were planning, within a month, a new kind of work, *The Historians' History of the World*, with approval and sanction of the *Times*. They discussed briefly the possibility of making another effort to bid for the *Times*, but this time Jackson was even less agreeable to the venture than he had been a few months earlier, and all discussion on this matter was dropped.

On the morning the *Times* carried the announcement of the negotiations designed to make Pearson managing director, Horace Hooper sat glumly in the grillroom of the Savoy Hotel. As he dawdled over his breakfast, he was approached by Kennedy Jones, the shrewd and resourceful editor of the Northcliffe-owned *Daily Mail*.

"I see by the papers," said Jones, "that you are going to have a new proprietor at the *Times*."

"Well, maybe," snapped Hooper. "I guess that even in this country a man can't sell property which doesn't belong to him."

Eager to hear a fuller explanation of Hooper's remark, Jones seated himself and asked more questions. Soon Hooper was disclosing to Jones all he knew of the arrangements at the *Times*, of the conflicts of interest between the many coproprietors, of the fears the Walters held of any public sale of their newspaper, of facts and figures, of losses and profits. "Pearson won't have so easy a time," Hooper said. "There'll have to be approval from the court and the other proprietors before it goes through. It'll take time."

When Jones asked about the possibility of discussing with Bell his move against Pearson, Hooper nodded. "You ought to meet with Bell and get more details. And if you do, I want to be in on the deal. I don't want to make money. I'm interested only in one thing—to protect the interests of the *Encyclopaedia Britannica* and the rest. I'll be glad to help anyone who wants to fight on Moberly Bell's side against Pearson. But I can't be connected with this openly."

Eagerly, Jones asked, "How much would it take to buy out the proprietors so all will be content?"

"About 350,000 pounds should do it. The right kind of man backing Bell with the right kind of money could do it."

For Hooper his own meaning was clear: Lord Northcliffe was "the right kind of man." As for Jones, he thought immediately of Jones. "I held *The Times* in the hollow of my hand," he wrote later. For three frantic days he sought financial aid from Lord Curzon and others, but he was unsuccessful.

Then Jones apprized Northcliffe of what he had learned from Hooper. Northcliffe had long coveted the *Times*, but his immediate reaction was to shrug off Jones's suggestion that he enter the contest. "In her present frail state," he said, "an unseemly wrangle between two yellow journalists for the possession of the *Times* would be more than the old thing could stand." But when Jones told him that Hooper knew of considerable dissatisfaction among a segment of the coproprietors at the thought of Pearson's domination, Northcliffe informally authorized Jones to learn more and act as his representative in any eventuality.

For his part, Hooper gingerly approached Bell, who was still striving to secure enough money—or promise of money—to make a counterbid against Pearson. Bell had considered fleetingly alliances with a free-trade group and with another representing a German syndicate, but he had decided against both, saying, "I prefer the *Times* wrong and independent to the *Times* right and shackled." Nor would he consider an earlier offer from Hooper to abandon the *Times* and join him in his publishing ventures. "No, I'm going to smash the plan to wreck the *Times*. I'll fight to the end!"

But when Hooper now quietly proposed, "Why not work with Alfred Harmsworth?" Bell roared, "Never! Never!"

"But he's interested and he has the money."

"Never! The same objections I have to Pearson apply to the other one. Either of them would wreck the *Times*."

"If you won't work with him, he'll go over your head. Think it over. It may be your only chance."

Bell agreed to consider the new proposal. He prepared a list of prominent people who had enough money to buy the *Times* and submitted it to Lord Cromer, members of the Rothschild family, and other financial giants, asking each, "Please cross off the name of anyone to whose connection with *The Times* you would take serious exception." On every list the name of Northcliffe remained untouched.

Impressed by this response, Bell met with Jones, with Hooper close at hand. There were long and guarded discussions, at the end of which Jones sent a cable to Northcliffe, then at the Ritz Hotel in Paris. As always, it was sent in care of Northcliffe's valet, Brunnbauer. It read, in part: "Are you prepared to come into a deal which will upset negotiations eventually acquiring business ourselves?" and added that the man who could get the £350,000 necessary for the deal "would save organization for empire."

After a slight delay, Northcliffe indicated he was interested. More discussions followed between Bell, Jones, and Hooper. Bell insisted only that he wanted the integrity and character of the newspaper maintained. Hooper repeated his wish that his relationship with the *Times* be maintained. Jones listened quietly, assuring them both that Northcliffe would deal fairly with all involved.

On January 28, Northcliffe returned to London. Bell asked to see him but received no reply; he was eager to bring the negotiations to a decisive point because already rumors were circulating that an "unknown capitalist" was preparing to fight Pearson for control of the *Times*. One newspaper, the *Graphic*, actually went so far as to "reveal" that the men behind the plot to buy the newspaper were none other than Hooper and Jackson. Bell wrote to Arthur Walter denying this but explaining that there was one man, indeed, with whom he was dealing for purchase of the newspaper, a development not so displeasing to Walter now, for he and his brother were beginning to lose their zeal for the Pearson plan.

Finally Northcliffe made a definite move. Designating Hooper and Jackson to act as his intermediaries, with additional counsel from Kennedy Jones, he wrote, on February 3, "I am desirous of purchasing *The Times* on behalf of myself and others, and I authorize you up to June 30th, 1908, to negotiate for the purchase of the copyright thereof for any sum up to £350,000. I agree to be satisfied with the purchase at that price."

This led finally to a direct meeting between Bell and Northcliffe.

"Well, Mr. Bell," said the press magnate when they confronted each other a day later in the Sackville Street office of Northcliffe's accountant, "I am going to buy the *Times*. With your help, if you will give it. In spite of you, if you do not."

"I will help you," Bell replied.

3

Complex negotiations now developed which assumed elements of intrigue. Hooper and Jackson played helpful roles. Northcliffe frequently used the Americans as emissaries and often called on them for special information about the financial structure of the *Times*. Each of the principals assumed code names: Northcliffe was either "X" or "Atlantic"; Hooper, "Adelaide"; Jackson, "Demerara"; Bell, "Canton";

Kennedy Jones, "Alberta." In notes to his wife relating to any phase of the negotiations, Bell wrote only in Arabic, a language both had learned during their years in Egypt.

Northcliffe soon made it clear that if he put up the money he intended to achieve full control of the *Times*. Although he assured Bell that he meant to preserve the traditional character of the newspaper, he would countenance nothing less than complete command, even if his ownership must remain secret for a time. When Bell drew up a long list of requirements and guaranties he thought were essential, Northcliffe returned it unsigned, instructing his lawyer to inform Bell of his conditions. With a sigh, Bell sent back his acceptance of Northcliffe's terms: "It is understood that in the event of your acquiring *The Times* newspaper I shall act as your Managing Director for 5 years & carry out your absolute instructions. But you express your desire that the present policy of the paper in Home and Foreign Affairs should be continued under the editorship of Mr. Buckle and Mr. Valentine Chirol. In my former letter I desired to make no *conditions*. I merely wished to express what I believed to be your ideas."

Bell soon realized the first real triumph of his fight. On February 14, Pearson, informed by Arthur Walter that opposition to his participation in ownership of the *Times* had grown steadily since the first announcements, formally withdrew, and the way became clearer for Bell to drive toward the finish.

To throw the inquisitive ones off the trail and make others more receptive to his possible acquisition of the *Times*, Northcliffe himself wrote an article for the *Observer*, "The Truth about *The Times*." Appearing with no name attached, this two-column analysis hinted slyly of what might have happened had Pearson achieved control: Bell, "who rescued that journal from an apparently hopeless condition after the dark days of the Parnell Commission," would most assuredly, under Pearson, "receive his congé at very short notice. . . . In the interests of all concerned, the sooner the Court of Chancery takes the matter in hand and settles affairs, one way or the other, the more certain we are to have in the future, as in the past, a national uncommercial organ, admired, if not always liked, by all political parties, spacious enough to adequately report Parliamentary and legal proceedings, independent enough to be received everywhere as the representative of the Englishman."

This done, Northcliffe soon disappeared from London and headed for France, establishing headquarters at Boulogne to receive communiqués from Adelaide and Demerara, Canton and Alberta. Back in London, Bell, Hooper, and Jackson continued to consolidate gains already achieved. Pearson was out of the way, but a group led by Miss Brodie-Hall was still making fluttery motions to buy out the other co-proprietors. Bell already had £320,000 in the Bank of England, deposited there in his name by Northcliffe. And, as Northcliffe now informed Hooper and Jackson, he was prepared to raise that sum to £400,000 if necessary.

By the first days of March, the end was in sight. Arthur Walter, guessing at the identity of "X," assured his brother and his close associates that the move was all for the best. "It would be disastrous to the interest of all," he said, "if this contract is not confirmed." Bell made ready for the important appearance in court on March 16. On that day attorneys for Miss Brodie-Hall asked for a continuance. Justice Warrington shook his head and asked, "Are there any new offers?" Bell strode forward firmly with his offer to pay £320,000 for the *Times*, 10 per cent of it ready to be deposited at that instant. The judge approved and scanned the draft of a notice intended for next day's newspapers, and Bell hastily and happily sent to Northcliffe, now at Versailles, and to Arthur Walter the same message: "Gone through as we wanted." One additional message he wrote to his new master, "I hope it is unnecessary for me to say again how grateful I am to you."

4

For thirty days the name of the new head of the company now in possession of the *Times* remained an official secret, although one or two newspapers did hint at Northcliffe. Then William T. Stead, that ubiquitous journalist, made full disclosure in his *Review of Reviews*. The news spread, and Fleet Street and, indeed, all London braced for explosions at Printing House Square.

Hooper and Jackson anticipated little alteration of their own status. Having aided Northcliffe so intimately in acquiring the newspaper, they were confident he would show his gratitude in the proper manner. Warmly expressing his and Hooper's views, Jackson congratulated Northcliffe: "I must send you just a line to say how *very* glad I am that matters have come to such a satisfactory conclusion. . . . Not only the British Public but all friends of Great Britain will some day know what a great good you have done for the nation and it will be appreciated."

Northcliffe appreciated the message. Assuring the two Americans that no major changes were contemplated, he agreed to give them exclusive rights to publish and sell such subscription books as might later be mutually agreed on in the name of the *Times* and through its influence. Hooper and Jackson congratulated themselves on passing a crisis. The worst was now over, and, with Northcliffe in top command at the *Times*, with Bell presumably as strong, perhaps stronger, than before, they felt their position was solid.

5

Then, in May, the John Murray libel suit came to trial. It lasted four days, from May 5 through May 8, and was held before Justice Darling, a jurist who fancied himself a wit and who, judging from his brusque treatment of Hooper, disliked Americans, especially aggressive Americans.

At one point Justice Darling interrupted questioning of Hooper to ask, "How long, sir, have you been a publisher?" in a tone that implied, "How dare you be a publisher?" Hooper snapped back a ready reply, "All my life, since I was a boy." The jurist constantly interrupted attorneys for both sides, but the jury managed to learn from Bell that he believed the price for the Queen Victoria volumes could have been much less, from John Murray that sales had diminished after publication of the Artifex letters, and from Hooper that while he had indeed asked Edward Ross to write the allegedly libelous letters and had supplied him with thoughts and figures, such words as "extortion" and "plunder" were Ross's own. "I am against the excessive profits of publishers generally, not of Mr. Murray," said Hooper. Asked by Murray's lawyers what Ross meant by the references to thirty-two pieces of silver, Hooper grinned. "I think he thought it a bright way of putting it," he replied.

Justice Darling's summation took a full hour, but the jury needed only thirty-five minutes to return a verdict in Murray's favor, awarding him £7,500.

Even before this decision, however, Northcliffe had moved to end the Book War. On May 7 he went to see Frederick Macmillan at the book publisher's St. Martin's Street office. He was irritated, brusque, and direct.

"You must keep this very secret," he told Macmillan, "but I have purchased the controlling interest in the *Times*. Now the first thing I wish to do is to end this damned Book War on terms that will be satisfactory to all of us. We want to continue the Book Club. It has 27,000 members, most of whom subscribed to the *Times* to get the advantages of the club, and they all appear to be satisfied with the services they are getting. But it is all too expensive. Can we come to friendly terms?"

"I am certain that we can," replied Macmillan.

Soon talks progressed between leaders of the Publishers' Association and Kennedy Jones, whom Northcliffe deputized as his agent. Neither Bell nor Jackson nor Hooper knew of, or were invited to, these negotiations. In some phases disagreement developed, but eventually all major issues were resolved, and one decision, contrary to the assurances Northcliffe had given the two Americans who had aided him in acquiring the *Times*, was that after June 30 Hooper and Jackson would have no further affiliation with the Book Club.

Although the final settlement, hewing to the general lines of the net book agreement which Bell and Hooper had so steadfastly resisted, would not be drawn until September, Kennedy Jones took imperious command at the Book Club. He put all the librarians and attendants into blue uniforms and peppered them with daily complaints about why the blinds were still drawn at nine o'clock in the morning or why a certain assistant librarian turned her back on a certain subscriber. To mark the end of the Book War, Murray permitted the Book Club to distribute *The Letters of Queen Victoria* in a cheaper edition for only six shillings, and Jones, who fancied himself a master salesman of commodities both material and intellectual, undertook a campaign to dispose of thousands of the sets. All he actually did, however, when the books were available, was to pile them high in the Book Club's front windows, with dignified placards informing passers-by that to purchase the volumes of letters was a patriotic duty. Such appeals produced meager sales. Soon the books were removed from the windows and stacked in the basement. When Jones petulantly asked Janet Hogarth why the sale had been so disappointing, she replied like a true Hooper loyalist, "You want Mr. Hooper to sell this for you. He'd have had it in the Fiji Islands by this time!"

But Horace Hooper was in no mood to co-operate with Kennedy Jones. He felt he had been betrayed. Yet he was careful to keep his feelings to himself. Northcliffe was too powerful a personage, with or without the *Times* in his possession, for him to antagonize. He had already dictated Hooper's removal from the newspaper's advertising department; and an argument over the settlement of the Book War and what Hooper considered abject surrender to the book publishers would only jeopardize, Hooper well knew, the future of the *Encyclopaedia Britannica*'s eleventh edition, on which Hugh Chisholm and a large staff had been hard at work for nearly five years. Moreover, Hooper was soon involved in a new struggle, and his adversary was neither book publisher nor competitor but Walter Montgomery Jackson.

12

Hooper versus Jackson

During the hectic period of Hooper's control of the advertising department of the *Times*, the fury of the Book War, and the negotiations for Northcliffe's purchase of the newspaper, work had proceeded on the eleventh edition of the *Encyclopaedia Britannica*.

On the top floor of the building at Printing House Square, Hugh Chisholm presided over a staff of editors, subeditors, and departmental chiefs, with W. Alison Phillips as his chief assistant. In New York the editorial staff again was headed by Franklin Hooper, with all administrative details under the management of Charles Crawford Whinery, formerly an assistant editor of the *New International Encyclopaedia*.

The bulk of the editorial work was done in London. Although the majority of the contributors were acknowledged scholars, a new trend was discernible. Chisholm relied primarily on journalists for his working force and added many of his newspaper associates to the line-up of writers. Close to him was W. Garrett Fisher, who had worked with him on the *St. James's Gazette.* Chisholm himself was an unusually earnest worker, a kind of scholar-journalist. There were strange moments when he would drop his papers and sit moodily, making notes for an article in almost illegible script. Then, leaping to his feet, he would mumble, "My brain won't function," and hurry off to a large, soft chair at the Athenaeum Club or to a round of golf on the links. Despite such lapses, Chisholm read some 90 per cent of the papers that streamed into his office from the fifteen hundred contributors, and eventually he wrote half a dozen biographies, including one of Austen Chamberlain that filled twelve columns, and articles on "Parliament," "Representation," and the "Victorian Era in English History."

Chisholm was a man of strong prejudices. He held old-fashioned views on many subjects. Reading the article on "Obstetrics," he was shocked at some of the details and insisted that they be modified if not deleted, a request that led one subeditor, during a heated argument on the matter, to shout, "Well, we ought to have something on the subject newer than what Adam did for Eve when he was left alone with her in the Garden of Eden!" He was so ardent a backer of feminism that he seriously considered, at one time, excluding the article on "Woman," saying, "They are so much an integral part of the human race that it is unnecessary to write of them as though they are a race apart." He was dissuaded from this by his aides.

But in most ways Chisholm was an ideal editor for the kind of encyclopaedia the eleventh edition was to be. Well grounded in learning, he was, nevertheless, no pedant. He possessed wide knowledge, and he knew where to go to find information that he lacked. A man of imagination, humor, and balance, with a great ability to assess the value of subjects and their timeliness, he had the full respect not only of his subordinates but especially of Hooper.

As always, Hooper avoided any direct interference with Chisholm or the other editors. But even in the most heated periods of the Book War he took time to show his interest in what was happening at Printing House Square. At least twice a week he invited Chisholm and a few of the other editors to lunch with him at the business offices in High Holborn, where he listened to their problems and offered suggestions. At one luncheon, a subeditor, Malcolm Mitchell, responsible for sections on "Ancient History," "Archaeology," "European History," and "Biblical History," reported that no new accounts of the antiquities of Corsica or Sardinia had been prepared. Immediately, Hooper wrote out a check for £70 and handed it to Mitchell. "Send an expert to those places right away," he ordered, "and let's have a fresh story."

Hooper paid the closest attention to all business and production details. It was he who decided that the edition should be printed not on the customary coarse paper but on the thin, tough, opaque India paper, previously used chiefly for Bibles and prayer books. The suggestion for this precedent-breaking step had come from Phillips while the two were lunching one day at the Café Royal. At first Hooper replied that such a plan was too expensive, and the conversation turned to other matters. But after a few minutes, Hooper interrupted Phillips, crying, "Yes, by God! It can be done. I will have a specimen volume made up at once!"

Jackson made dutiful visits to High Holborn, but he was more occupied with his other publishing ventures than with the *Encyclopaedia Britannica,* his prime outside interests being a book-distributing firm in Boston and the Grolier Society in New York. Through the latter, he was mapping a campaign to sell a new children's work in the United States. For some years, a popular children's journal had been published under Northcliffe's auspices. Its founder and editor, Arthur Mee, had persuaded Northcliffe to bind copies of the newspaper into volumes and sell them in sets. In England its sale was large, but when Mee offered the American reprint rights to Major George Haven Putnam, that distinguished publisher rejected the idea. Jackson immediately snapped it up, and he was now putting the final touches on plans for selling the set all through the United States, calling it *The Book of Knowledge.*

2

At the height of their earlier successes, Hooper had voiced few complaints about Jackson's involvement in other publishing ventures. But now the stresses of the Book War, the Northcliffe betrayal, and the fears for the future of the eleventh edition all worried Hooper. More frequently he warned Jackson that many decisions had to be made about the forthcoming edition—if, indeed, there was to be any new edition; that close attention needed to be paid to it, personally and financially. When Jackson continued to disregard Hooper's insistent and single-minded plaints, Hooper exploded. In June, 1908, he made an angry threat to leave the business entirely. "For 10 straight years," he wrote to Jackson, "I have had to push you and Bell before I could get your help and co-operation to push the public, and I have no more intention of going on with it than I have of flying. I am perfectly satisfied to close up the business and let it go. I believe there would be no more trouble, that you and I each would not get more than a million dollars out of it, and I shall be quite happy to retire to the United States with that money and live quietly for the rest of my life. . . . I certainly think it is also fair to point out to you that for 10 years I have certainly done more than half of the work in the business and I think that you would also acknowledge that I have made more than half the money."

This heightened angry conflict between Hooper and Jackson. But there were even deeper causes of dissension. Hooper's enthusiasm for preparing an entirely new eleventh edition instead of reprinting what was salvageable from the ninth and tenth editions had never been fully shared by Jackson. However laudatory the idea was intellectually, it posed serious problems of financing. To meet these problems, Hooper proposed that either a public stock issue of $1,500,000 be floated in England and the United States to provide funds or that sufficient loans be made on the strength of the *Times*'s imprimatur to support such a venture. He envisioned publication of the complete set at one time and a simultaneous sale all over the world, with huge sums spent on advertising.

Jackson balked. A successful businessman, he could see scant reason to spend large sums to attain or attempt perfection when it might be perfectly possible to extract the best of the ninth and tenth editions and still have a successful sale. "I'm for bringing the new edition out as in the old days," he told Hooper. "Let's have one volume or a few at one time, sell them and get enough money for the next volumes, and so on. We can make the collections on them and use the proceeds to pay for the manufacture of the next lot. That way we won't have to borrow any money anywhere."

"Nothing doing!" replied Hooper. "I'm determined that the eleventh edition must be the greatest book ever published. I mean that from an editorial and scholarly point of view. And I'm willing to pour as much money into it as I can lay my hands on."

These basic differences in attitude—Jackson insisting on adherence to tried methods, Hooper on goals beyond immediate profit—drove the two apart. In September, 1908, Hooper went to Colorado for a month of the outdoor life he loved, living in tents in the mountains, eating elk and deer meat and bear steak. When the vacation was over, he met Jackson briefly in New York and renewed the talk—and the argument. At one point Hooper impetuously offered to sell out his interests in the British and American firms for $2 million, but Jackson refused to listen. Then Hooper offered to buy out Jackson for a similar amount, and Jackson declined to sell. The meeting broke up in anger, and Hooper sped to Chicago to plan new strategy.

In November, he wrote Jackson that the board of directors of the American company was to meet on the twenty-fourth of that month to discuss the status of the contemplated edition and steps that needed to be taken for its completion. "I am acting in the best interests of the company in calling this meeting," he informed Jackson.

Jackson refused to attend, implying that the meeting was not valid and that the directors—Franklin Hooper, Whinery, and Harris B. Burrows, now president of the American company at $25,000 a year —were merely "dummy directors" who would do Horace Hooper's bidding. As for Hooper's plans for issuing the eleventh edition, Jackson wrote, "I believe that if you were a well man your judgment would be quite the contrary." Hooper's idea was "a visionary and extravagant scheme" and could lead only to disaster. "I trust that reflection will bring you back to the exercise of your better judgment," concluded Jackson, adding the gratuitous suggestion that Hooper return to his camping outfit in the Colorado mountains because he evidently was in no mental or physical condition to contemplate the future of the business.

Hooper retorted that the meeting would definitely be held and that Jackson had better attend. It was important, he insisted, to determine whether they should continue in business and whether—and how— more money should be raised. "In regard to my mental and physical condition," he wrote, "I will say that I feel younger and better now than I have for ten years and I cannot but believe that you know this. . . . You yourself know that for the past eleven years I have had no illness, and I may add that I have not had one for almost thirty years." In another letter he again urged Jackson to come to the Chicago meeting. "Now why not behave sensibly and come in here and go out to Chicago and attend that meeting and put the information that you have right at your fingers' tips before the Board of Directors and let us make up our minds in a sensible, business-like fashion."

But Jackson, obviously advised by attorneys, continued to insist that if he attended such a meeting he might indirectly give sanction to any decisions made there and approved by a majority of the board. So the meeting was held without him—and action was carried out weakening his role in the business. Hooper, his brother Franklin, Burrows, and Whinery voted changes in the bylaws of the corporation that gave Horace Hooper sole rights to conduct the business as he saw fit. They also granted him full authority to borrow enough money to see the eleventh edition through to completion. At the same time, Burrows resigned as president and Horace Hooper assumed the post, while Jackson, nominally listed as the firm's treasurer, was stripped of all but clerical duties.

Evidently Hooper intended this as a strong warning to Jackson that he meant to push forward with the eleventh edition. He sent a letter to Jackson hinting that the door was not closed to him and stressing that matters were in a serious state. "To bring out the new book, it seems very plain that some financing would be necessary to bring us to this point even. Even when it comes to buying paper, ads, etc., we need at least 200,000 pounds more. . . . The whole question as to whether or not we should liquidate and close up the business entirely or whether we should raise the money and complete the new book is something so very important that I have as yet been unable to understand your refusal to seriously consider the question."

Instead of replying, Jackson sailed for England. Hooper pursued him on a later ship, but when he landed he found that Jackson had sailed back to the United States. "This action on your part, taken in conjunction with various similar actions on your part in the past," Hooper admonished Jackson in a new letter, "makes it necessary for us to go ahead without further consultation with you. The interests of the business demand it, and while I regret that you did not stay here and conclude matters, it seems to me that there is only one course of action left open to us. . . . Your entire policy has been to make agreements to do things and then not live up to your agreements."

The momentum of their quarrel increased. Soon Jackson was writing to Hooper accusing him of being "insincere and dishonest," of plotting to deprive him of all control by installing his "dummy directors." "Do you soberly and seriously think that your conduct is fair, even if you believe you are within your legal rights? Do you not realize in your own heart that you are merely betraying the confidence I have rested in you and showing yourself unworthy of my trust? No wonder that constantly in speech and letter you protest your honesty of purpose! Do you not protest a bit too much?" This, Jackson admitted, was strong language, but he used it, he added, "to stimulate your conscience, to arouse your sense of shame or honor, or to contrast before your own eyes your honest self with your recent conduct. . . . Why not be honest with yourself and with me, and have done with this petty chicanery?"

Hooper, coached by his attorney, Jacob Newman, one of Chicago's shrewdest, replied calmly. "I have your letter of January 4th," he wrote. "As the letter is quite evidently not written by you, though of course you sign it, and as the man who wrote it evidently does not know very much about the facts in connection with this business, I do not attempt to answer it. There is hardly a correct statement made in the letter. The only part that needs any answer at all is in regard to going into Court. . . . I shall be only too pleased to have you test the matter of partnership in Court."

3

Thus challenged, Jackson conferred more frequently with his lawyers. By May, 1909, the headlines read: "Hooper and Jackson at War."

The fight was now in the open for all the public to see. On May 27, Jackson filed a suit in the Superior Court of New Jersey at Trenton. He named as defendants both Hoopers as well as Burrows and Whinery, charging them with plotting to exclude him from real participation in the management of the business. He denounced as illegal the board action of November 24 amending the bylaws. Again, as in his letters, he called Hooper's associates "dummy directors," selected to do as Hooper commanded. He complained that he had been deprived of the right to sign checks on company funds, as he and Hooper had done ever since they became associates. He charged Hooper with seeking to harm the business through unnecessary waste and disposition of assets. And he named inoffensive, scholarly Franklin Hooper, interested only in his editorial duties, as his brother's aide and accomplice.

The suit centered on a vital point. Jackson insisted that he and Hooper had a formal legal partnership and that Hooper had violated that partnership. He asked that the courts now disband the partnership and appoint a receiver to make an accounting of all finances, and he demanded an injunction to restrain Hooper and the others from withdrawing money from company accounts or disposing or transferring their shares.

In the bill of particulars, Jackson disclosed some of the details of his disagreement with Hooper over how the eleventh edition was to be issued and also revealed their roles in the sale of the *Times* to Northcliffe. When this disclosure was made known to the new owner of the *Times,* he refused immediate comment, but he sent word to Bell that he wished to see him about a decision he had long contemplated.

Hooper's reply to Jackson's suit denied all the charges, admitting only that there had been a difference of opinion about the publication of the eleventh edition. Still he sought to make peace. Less than a week after Jackson's legal assault, Hooper encountered Jackson in the lobby of the Belmont Hotel in New York and told him that one of his lawyers had relayed the report that Jackson was willing to buy his interest in the *Encyclopaedia Britannica* for $750,000 and a royalty of $10 a set. Jackson admitted this was true.

"Well," said Hooper, "I'm willing to accept it, but there are several conditions."

"What are they?"

"The first one is that you will agree to complete and issue complete the *Encyclopaedia Britannica,* eleventh edition, within the year."

"That is impossible," replied Jackson.

"Very good," snapped Hooper. "Then that ends it. Now do you want me to make an offer?"

Jackson chewed on an unlit cigar and nodded.

"My offer," said Hooper, "is this. I'll give you $450,000, pay it in two years, with a $5 royalty on each set sold. The royalties will come to at least $300,000."

Jackson shook his head and walked away.

Thwarted, Hooper filed a long affidavit on June 15. He traced their joint careers, denying vigorously that they had ever been legally partners. "It is not possible that any of the employees of Hooper and Jackson or of the Encyclopaedia Britannica Company . . . considered that Jackson and I were partners. All the business that was transacted in the offices of these companies was transacted in the name of one corporation or the other, depending upon the kind of business. The only sign on the door of the London office is 'Hooper and Jackson, Ltd.' The only sign on the door of the New York office is 'The Encyclopaedia Britannica Company.' Neither the name of Jackson nor myself nor our names together, except with the word, 'Limited,' have ever appeared on any door. The letter-heads used and the bills used were all those of the corporations. . . . Of course, everybody understood that the stock of the two corporations was principally owned by Mr. Jackson and myself, and I may have spoken of Mr. Jackson as my partner in the sense that we were associated together in these corporations, and I may have written some letters in which I used that expression, but nobody ever entered into a contract with Jackson and myself as partners."

4

These documents, disclosing intimate details about the sale of the *Times*, produced prompt and near-catastrophic reactions in London. Two days after Hooper's affidavit was made public, he received a curt letter from Bell, written at Northcliffe's behest. The *Times*, Bell's letter stated, was giving Hooper notice that it was canceling its contract made in 1903 for the eleventh edition. A clause in that contract provided for a ninety-day period before the agreement became invalid; so Hooper now had ninety days in which to scrap plans for the edition or secure new support for it.

All that summer, Hooper fought to prevent disaster. He cut Burrows' salary by $10,000 and his brother's from $10,000 to $7,000. He sought new loans from banks, but without the name and reputation of the *Times* behind him he found only dribbles instead of the greatly needed flood of funds.

In the midst of these unhappy circumstances, Judge James E. Howell in the New Jersey court handed down a ruling granting Jackson a limited injunction. While Judge Howell found that no strictly legal partnership existed between Hooper and Jackson, he held that they were "joint adventurers" and therefore were bound by precisely the same rules as partners. In his summation, Judge Howell expressed judicial surprise at the haphazard way in which the men ran their business, at their "indiscriminate commingling of accounts." He noted that none of the companies in which the pair was involved had paid them salaries and that instead of declaring dividends on their corporate stock they drew profits from the business' bank accounts as they saw fit. The affairs of the firms, at least until that memorable and controversial November board meeting in Chicago, were carried on merely by consultation and agreement between Hooper and Jackson, "and they appear to have made and unmade these corporations, in which they were equally interested, at their will." Judge Howell set a later date for further hearings, proposing that meanwhile attorneys for both men seek to come to a workable solution.

Jacob Newman immediately filed an appeal from this decision and prepared legal action on the British front by claiming, in a suit in the Chancery division of the High Court of Justice, that Hooper was entitled to carry on the business as he wished in spite of Judge Howell's ruling. And Hooper paused and took account of the status of the eleventh edition. He found that $696,618 had been expended on editors' salaries and contributions since 1903. Cash on hand was only $44,-506. Money still technically due from the prior sale of the tenth edition was $1,600,000, most of it uncollectable. What payments were being made were coming in at the rate of $3,000 to $4,000 a month, quite useless for large needs. Between this time, early in September, and the date on which he hoped to publish the full eleventh edition—the schedule had been moved forward six months from January, 1910—he needed at least $700,000 more. Originally the cost of the edition had been estimated at $750,000, but it now appeared that the actual amount would be twice as much.

Consequently, Hooper directed Chisholm to give notice of a suspension of work to those employed on the eleventh-edition preparation. Because of dwindling funds, the active editorial staff had already been cut to about thirty-five, and these persons now were told that within a month operations would cease. All reading of copy was halted, as well as all setting of type by R. and R. Clark in Edinburgh, and day after day Chisholm and his editors idled in the offices or went out to play golf.

5

In this dismal period, lawyers for both sides continued to seek an equitable peace. Robert McCarter, former attorney-general of New Jersey, represented Hooper in the New Jersey litigation, and Jackson's attorney was Sherrerd DePue, a boyhood friend of McCarter's with an office adjoining his in Newark's Prudential Building. Heeding Judge Howell's admonition, the two worked out a plan to bring an end to the conflict. They proposed that Hooper make a buy-or-sell proposition to Jackson, with a deadline of forty-eight hours. If Jackson were to refuse Hooper's offer, he was to make one of his own. McCarter conveyed this idea to Hooper and he agreed to draw up such an offer.

On September 27, 1909, Hooper's proposal, lengthy and detailed, arrived at the offices of Henry Wollman, another of his lawyers, with instructions to convey it to McCarter and DePue. This plan provided that Jackson have a three-month option to buy out Hooper for $750,-

000, with $100,000 in cash when the option was taken up and $50,000 every third month till the full amount was paid. Fifty-one per cent of the stock of both the British and American companies was to be placed in the hands of trustees until all the $750,000 was paid, and provision was to be made for the eleventh edition of the *Encyclopaedia Britannica* to be printed within two years. No salaries to any executives were to be more than $10,000 a year, but the existing staff of the *Encyclopaedia Britannica* was to be retained and the rest of the set issued "on the same scale, and with the same care, expense and scholarship already completed."

Within the week, Hooper, now in England, followed this letter with a cablegram: "It is understood that offer is only rough draft and if accepted either way formal contract with full details will be drawn at once." Then came still another cablegram directing that when the plan was shown to Jackson, it must be accompanied by a letter emphasizing that the offer was not binding until followed by a formal contract with complete details.

The tangled and tragicomic events that ensued were to form the basis of new litigation later, but it is clear that massive misunderstandings, consciously or unconsciously motivated, bred massive complications.

McCarter was shown both cablegrams but shied away from revealing their contents to Jackson. "I'm afraid," he told DePue, "that if we put the idea of a formal contract covering full details in bold type before Jackson's eyes, it will break off negotiations."

DePue agreed, but he promised to inform Jackson that the plan was only tentative and that no final settlement could be agreed upon without the detailed contract.

When Jackson, unaware of these specified restrictions, read Hooper's long memorandum in DePue's office, he immediately accepted the terms. On October 7, he sent Hooper a cold note: "I beg to say that I accept your offer to sell me your interests and that I assent to the terms therein stated by you." Then he went with his lawyer to McCarter's office and formally handed McCarter his acceptance, saying that he had the money for the deal. McCarter, as he later testified, believed Jackson had implied that he had the full $750,000, but Jackson actually meant that he could, at a moment's notice, get the $100,-000 for a down payment from a friend, John M. Graham of Boston's International Trust Company, using his stock in the Grolier Society as collateral.

Whatever the understanding—or, more precisely, the misunderstanding—Jackson considered himself legally the owner of Hooper's interests in the business. Puffing grandly on a cigar, he strode into the *Encyclopaedia Britannica's* New York offices and informed Whinery he had bought out Hooper. "I do not want you to attend any more directors' meetings," he told Whinery, "because I have now purchased Mr. Hooper's interest, and I do not want anything done that will be in any way inimicable to my interests, or resolutions passed, or anything of that sort." To James Clarke, his and Hooper's old associate, he wired: "Have closed deal and bought Hooper's interest."

When Hooper learned of what Jackson had done, he instantly cabled Wollman: "When delivering option did you as instructed by cable deliver also letter regarding agreement to be drawn up? . . . Do absolutely nothing meanwhile." He became more apprehensive when a wire arrived from Burrows: "Jackson buys astounded. Congratulate you. Commiserate Frank and myself advise concerning future plans." Again a cable flew from Hooper to his lawyers: "Cables worry me. . . . Did you follow my instructions?"

On October 11 news of the negotiations leaked to the newspapers. Stories on this day, headed "Settling Encyclopaedia Suit," stated erroneously that the suit brought in New Jersey was soon to be withdrawn because "negotiations have been in progress by which Mr. Jackson will receive a huge sum—said to be several hundred thousand dollars—in return for relinquishing his claim." The next morning the more nearly accurate reports were that the dispute between Hooper and Jackson was on the verge of settlement, that Jackson had decided to buy out Hooper.

Actually the battle, far from being settled, was renewed by Hooper. On the very next day he heard from Chisholm about a terse cable the editor had received from Jackson: "Have bought out Hooper. Writing." At once, Hooper shot off to Jackson a cable notifying him that all remained as before. Yet Jackson would not be moved. Stubbornly, he now considered himself the virtual owner, although not a penny had exchanged hands, and when he received a letter from Hooper's London lawyers, Burns, Berridge and Company, directing him to attend a meeting of the directors of the British firm, he cabled: "Am equitable owner all shares company having purchased Hooper's interest. No directors' meetings should be held."

But a directors' meeting was, indeed, held, with Hooper presiding and with new members of the board in attendance: his brother,

Burrows, and W. Garrett Fisher. Again, as in Chicago, the balance of power was shifted to Horace Hooper by a majority vote. The new board, Hooper piously avowed later, was named so that the business could be carried on if he suddenly dropped dead. And when Jackson finally arrived, there was little he could do for the time being but storm and stomp and threaten new legal action.

6

In the midst of this exchange, Hooper received a number of letters commiserating with him about the suspension of work on the eleventh edition. One of these came from Professor Phillips, who had grown to admire the brash American much as Bell, in an earlier and happier day, had.

In reply to Phillips' expression of sympathy, Hooper enunciated his deep feelings about the *Encyclopaedia Britannica* and hinted that this latest maneuver was only an expedient. He wrote:

I cannot express to you my feelings on reading your letter. For the last four or five years it has been my one great ambition to bring out the 11th edition of the Britannica, and make it, from an editorial and scholarly point of view, the greatest book that has ever been published. It is needless for me to add that I wanted to make money, and more, that I expected to do so; but if it had been for money alone I should have made that book very different from what it has been made. We could easily have produced a book at half the cost by doing hack work and taking a large share of it from the 10th edition; but I felt that I should like to know that I had been instrumental in producing a greater book, and in better form, than any other man. This may seem to you like vanity, but it was really a desire to do something that might leave the world a little bit better for my so doing.

The goodness of the book I don't think I deserve great credit for. The conception of the idea was mine, but the carrying out has been due to Chisholm, yourself and your editorial force, and I don't mind telling you that I really believe that it is too great to be crushed by any such methods or suits as Mr. Jackson has started so far, and I still hope that the book comes out, if not under my management, at least under somebody's who is competent, and will get a good sale of the book. You may rest assured that it took me a long time to make up my mind to give notice to the men who had worked so faithfully on the staff down there.

From this correspondence there evolved a course of action designed to rescue Hooper and his *Encyclopaedia Britannica,* a move based on audacity and a supersalesman's skill.

13

The Contract with Cambridge

Long before he was harassed by litigation and financial difficulties, Horace Hooper had talked with Phillips about the eventual establishment of the *Encyclopaedia Britannica* as a public institution, guided editorially, and eventually financially, by a great university. For Phillips, the main advantage to such an arrangement was that it would insure the maintenance of editorial excellence and high standards of scholarship and would provide the public with a warrant of topmost quality. Hooper agreed, but he now saw more than intellectual advantages. On the strength of the backing of a university, and without any financial risk to that university, he surely could secure the loans he needed. And, properly exploited, such an affiliation would certainly result in large sales and payment of royalties to the university.

So when Phillips again proposed that he seek out such a sponsor for the *Encyclopaedia Britannica,* now that the connection with the *Times* was severed, Hopper replied, "Go to it. Do what you can." Formal arrangements could be made later. "As for now," he told Phillips, "offer a royalty of 10 per cent on our sales. Tell them I'm sure it will bring them a good deal of money."

Phillips registered at the Mitre Hotel in Oxford and made his first overtures to the managers of the Oxford University Press. Impressed with Hooper's offer, they went so far as to request Phillips not to approach any other university until they could come to a decision. Phillips considered this an extremely hopeful sign. But in the end the university rejected the proposal, yielding to the objections of those who were chary of any affiliation with the Americans who had sold their volumes—however successfully—so flamboyantly.

Hooper accepted the rejection with philosophic calm. "Phillips," he said, "they think I was trying to bribe them. I offered them too much. You go to Cambridge now—and offer them just half."

And to Cambridge the obedient Phillips went. Here he encountered a preliminary reception that was unusually warm, and he was soon able to bring together Hooper and Richard T. Wright, aging secretary of the Cambridge University Press Syndicate, the members of which were popularly called "the Syndics." Wright had been responsible for publication of the distinguished *Cambridge Modern History,* and in his closing years in his post he hoped to bring off another publishing coup, preferably a profitable one. To the other Syndics he emphasized the great advantages of an alliance with Hooper and the *Encyclopaedia Britannica*—how such an association would involve no risk and much profit to the university.

Hooper himself appeared several times before the Syndics to enumerate the benefits that would accrue to Cambridge. He impressed them all with his earnestness and his zeal for producing an edition that might well become the best of all editions, an instrument of adult education with which one of the world's distinguished universities might with pride and propriety be affiliated. One of Hooper's strongest adherents, won over by his persuasive arguments, was the head of the Syndics, Montague Rhodes James, noted scholar, medievalist, writer of ghost stories, and provost of King's College, a shy, unworldly man. He and Hooper took long walks together on the college grounds, James nodding his head steadily as Hooper, arms waving, peppered him with arguments.

"To me," Hooper would say, "the *Encyclopaedia Britannica* is like the Bible. It's something holy! And who else but Cambridge should have it? It's got a great reputation, like Cambridge. It's reputable, like Cambridge. And we're revising it completely. New articles! New plates! There's no financial risk, and I'll give the university a handsome commission on sales!"

Hooper invited James and other scholars among the Syndics to examine the work already completed, and they did so assiduously. Beyond some slight errors, they pronounced it all excellent. Before agreeing to a formal contract, Wright and James asked if Cambridge might examine all other articles, present and future. To this Hooper eagerly assented and promptly issued instructions to Chisholm to send all material to James for examination. "It looks good," he chortled happily, "I think we've got them."

2

This tentative approval by Cambridge University seemed a propitious omen.

Confident that the Syndics would sign a contract with him, Hooper again moved forward with his plans for publication of the eleventh edition. The Edinburgh firm of R. and R. Clark resumed setting type, and final arrangements were made, too, for the printing of sets to be sold in the United States. Hooper had begun negotiating for American publication late in 1908. He was in New York trying to decide between several Boston firms when he met George R. Carpenter, one of the younger executives of the thriving Chicago printing house of R. R. Donnelley and Sons. Carpenter persuaded Hooper to take a one-day trip to Chicago to visit the Donnelley plant. Hooper, after inspecting the extensive facilities of the firm's Lakeside Press, forgot Boston and invited Carpenter to come to England for further consultations. Carpenter and his young bride found, on their arrival at Southampton, that Hooper, in a typical burst of grandeur, had chartered the royal railroad coach to transport them to London. Eventually a satisfactory schedule of costs and printing processes was worked out, and now Donnelley had the order for the composition, presswork, and binding of the encyclopaedia in the United States. Among those in the complicated negotiations for this contract who were as impressed with Hooper's devotion to, and passionate interest in, the *Encyclopaedia Britannica* as Bell had once been and as Montague Rhodes James now showed himself to be was the printing firm's head, Thomas E. Donnelley, who accompanied Carpenter to

London for the final signing. Donnelley saw in Hooper a man who combined the sometimes conflicting traits of idealism and hard business sense, a man of whose drive and energy and brain power there could be little doubt. Although Hooper was still engaged in legal controversy with Jackson and had only indefinite hopes of securing the kind of money necessary to complete the eleventh edition, Donnelley satisfied himself that the contract should be signed, and soon a persistent flow of copy came to the Chicago plant.

Almost simultaneously, Hooper won an important legal battle. Just as he and Jackson were squaring off again in the courts, this time in Chicago—Jackson filing a new suit to restrain the transfer of shares to anyone, Hooper demanding $300,000 "for damages suffered by us through the pestiferous litigations directed against the company"—the Appellate Court of New Jersey reversed the lower tribunal's decision that had declared the two men "joint adventurers." "We hold," read the high court's decision, "that the parties are not partners as to the corporate property, but merely stockholders in two foreign corporations, distinct legal entities." Any effort to restrain transfer of shares was illegal, read the new decision, and the New Jersey court had no jurisdiction in the matter.

This dissolved the earlier injunction against Hooper and stamped approval on his actions ousting Jackson from any role in running the business. And it prompted some peace overtures from Jackson.

Before long, Jackson was in Hooper's office at High Holborn. "Horace," he told Hooper, "I've had all the litigation I want. I've had a lot of advice and I'm through now."

Hooper motioned to an adjoining desk. "Take your place over there and sit down and attend to business."

When Jackson protested that he would take orders from neither Harris Burrows nor Garrett Fisher, Hooper replied, "They have given you no orders. There is no desire on anybody's part to give you orders. I don't care to give you orders. Why work your imagination as to whether there are orders or not orders to be given to you? Go attend to business!"

Jackson sat in angry silence for a few minutes, then strode out of the office.

Later, Hooper's attorney, Jacob Newman, met Jackson in London and proposed that he rejoin Hooper and work with him in producing the eleventh edition. Jackson wanted to know if Hooper had made any progress in getting Oxford or Cambridge to back it.

"I don't know," said Newman, "but I know this. The sensible thing for you to do is to go right back to the business. Take up your work where you left it off, and I give you the assurance that everything will be just as it was before the trouble arose. You'll draw the same amount of money Horace draws, both of you shall have a salary to be agreed upon, and all the old feeling will be annihilated."

Jackson's answer, according to Newman's later testimony, was, "I do not believe I can do that. My lawyers will not permit me to give up my lawsuit."

3

By this time Hooper was no longer concerned with pending or future suits by Jackson. For on July 31, 1910, Montague Rhodes James, having pored over many articles with his associates, informed Hooper that a contract could be drawn. On August 8, the pact was prepared, agreed upon, and signed by Hooper and A. W. Mason, vice-chancellor of Cambridge University.

Hooper's triumph was great, although by the contract's terms restrictions and burdens were placed on him. Complete inspection by the university of all plates for the eleventh edition was mandatory. The first fourteen volumes were to be ready for final examination by October 1, with publication on December 1. The last half and the index were to be inspected within four months and published by April 1, 1911. Penalty payments were to be made if the company failed to deliver the plates for inspection promptly. All costs were to be borne by the company, including expenses of preparation, editing, contributors, artists, office maintenance, typesetting, paper, binding, and warehousing, "and it is expressly agreed that the University Press shall in no way be responsible for any of such costs or expenses." In addition, Hooper agreed to set up offices in London's Fetter Lane, where sets of the *Encyclopaedia Britannica* would be displayed and orders taken, and to pay for the rental of these offices, plus all costs of advertising, salaries of order clerks, and traveling expenses of the Syndics on matters relating to the eleventh edition.

All advertisements were to be submitted to the University Press for approval or disapproval within three days. All University Press decisions on advertising matter were to be final. No false statements of any kind were permissible, and all ads were to be specific on the point that subscribers would not be obliged to pay a single instalment until the complete set was delivered. Orders for the work would be taken either through selected booksellers, from the outlying offices of the University Press especially set up for this purpose, or directly from the company. Prices, subject to change, also were specified in this strict contract; they ranged from fifteen to eighteen shillings a volume in cloth binding before publication to twenty to thirty shillings after publication, with higher charges for better bindings. Owners of old ninth editions could trade in their sets for an allowance of four to five pounds. Tenth edition owners could do likewise for an allowance of four to six pounds. The contract even provided for the return of bookcases at one pound each.

Royalties were pegged surprisingly low. On each January 1, April 1, July 1, and October 1, Hooper was to forward a statement to the University Press of all orders received at the London and branch offices. Every January 25, April 25, July 25, and October 25, Cambridge University would receive six shillings for every set ordered in the preceding three months—a far lower amount than had been rejected by Oxford. Within six months, however, an amendment to the contract raised the royalties to six shillings for each of the first twenty-five thousand sets sold, seven shillings, sixpence, for each of the next twenty-five thousand and ten shillings for all remaining.

The University Press was protected against subscribers' claims of non-delivery, damages, expenses, or violation of copyright. It reserved the right to appoint a chartered accountant at any time to inspect company books relating to orders. The contract was only for the eleventh edition, but a measure of how successful Hooper had been in persuading James and the other Syndics was evident in the proviso that a twelfth edition, if any, would be prepared under the editorial supervision of the university.

Despite the many restrictions and hampering clauses, Hooper felt triumphant, especially when he reflected on the meager royalty rate the Syndics had been willing to accept. There was more cause for rejoicing. In signing the contract, the university had implicitly approved the prospective edition as a commendable publication and had added greatly to Hooper's prestige. Even more significantly, at this important time, a signed copy of the contract waved in front of stern bank officials worked miracles. Within a week, banks which had been willing to lend Hooper no more than £40,000 gladly increased the amount nearly fivefold. Again, Hooper had won, and he now set his mind to the task ahead of completing the edition and making the public aware of its value—and availability.

4

On October 21, two months before the first half of the work was due, the advertising campaign was officially started with a dinner at Claridge's, London's most expensive hotel. An impressive assemblage presided over by the university's chancellor, Lord Rayleigh, gathered to cheer the union of Cambridge with the *Encyclopaedia Britannica*. Hooper himself paid meticulous attention to every detail of the dinner, from the hiring of the musicians to the devising of menus bound in the eleventh edition's own green sheepskin and the selection of cigars offered in boxes that were replicas of individual volumes of the *Encyclopaedia Britannica*.

There were huzzas when Lord Rayleigh announced that the heads of both the great English-speaking nations, President William Howard Taft and King George V, had agreed to accept a joint dedication. There were enthusiastic cries of "Hear! Hear!" when speakers praised Cambridge University, when other speakers commended the men who had made the old *Encyclopaedia Britannica* and were now completing the new. "The University," declared S. H. Butcher, president of the British Academy, "has acted on the principle laid down . . . in 1693 that the Cambridge Press must make the advancement of learning its object. . . . The University is a living organism, its roots are in the past, and it is a thing of gradual growth; it looks to today and to tomorrow and its hopes stretch out into the future." Hugh Chisholm, recounting the steps by which the new edition had come into being, had laudatory words for Cambridge: "By disseminating through all its educational channels the contents of this book, it will really be doing a great work to advance popular culture and give a real impetus to the desire for accurate knowledge."

Soon the first advertisements, considerably less florid than their predecessors, began to appear in British newspapers and magazines. The preparation for these had been long, careful, and sometimes irksome to Hooper, who occasionally found himself regretting the provision that gave the university the right to censor ads. At one point he showed Phillips the copy for an ad that described the *Encyclopaedia Britannica* as "THE SOURCE OF ALL KNOWLEDGE." Gently, Phillips remonstrated that this claim was a bit absurd, but that it might be fitting to announce that the set contained the "KEY TO ALL KNOWL-EDGE," since one of the publishers' professed objects was to stimulate purchasers to use the encyclopaedia as a guide to further study. After staring at the draft for half a minute, Hooper sighed. "O.K., you're right."

On another occasion, after a series of one-column announcements bearing a list of outstanding contributors and a specimen illustration or two, Hooper decreed a change. "We've got to set a time limit on our offer," he told Phillips and Oswald Sickert, now advertising manager in place of an ailing Haxton.

Phillips objected to any change, maintaining that Cambridge University would consider time-limit ads undignified. He prepared several dignified ads and offered them to Hooper.

"Yes, Phillips," said Hooper, after he had examined them. "That's a very good idea." And turning to Sickert, he asked, "Didn't we try that form of advertisement a long time ago with the tenth?"

"Yes, we did."

"And how long did we try it?"

"For a week."

"And what happened to the sales?"

"They went down like that," replied Sickert, lowering one hand so that it grazed the floor.

"And when we went back to that old system of 'If you don't buy it today it will be sixpence dearer tomorrow,' what happened?"

Raising his hand above his head, Sickert replied, "Why, the sales went up like that!"

Hooper grinned at Phillips, winked at Sickert, and soon there were time-limit ads for the *Encyclopaedia Britannica*—all approved by the Syndics. Not only did these urge customers to place their orders as speedily as possible, but they noted that even a twenty-one-shilling volume, word by word, would be the "cheapest bargain imaginable." "It gives the purchaser 1,800,000 words for 21 shillings, whereas the ordinary book contains only about 200,000 words." They told of that major innovation in publishing—the "wonders of India paper"— which shrank the six feet taken up by the old-style sets to less than three feet. They enumerated the 400 compositors required to set up the edition, the 250 tons of metal, the 1,500 tons of paper, the 150 tons of millboard, the 1,500 miles of thread, the 5 tons of ink, and the 10 tons of glue. And, in Hooper tradition, they advised: "Don't hesitate! Send in your order now!"

5

From the start of the sale there arose the inevitable chorus of complaints, with an already antagonistic group, the British booksellers, leading the pack.

Through their organ, *Publishers' Circular*, they complained that their percentage of profit for handling orders was too low. Hooper offered 5 per cent of the purchase price, but the booksellers insisted on more and suggested that the price be raised. Letters to *Publishers' Circular* inveighed against the instalment plan of buying popularized in the book field by the Americans—"Customers will not buy other books until they finish paying for their sets of the *Encyclopaedia Britannica*." Many upbraided Cambridge for joining an alleged plot against booksellers, and even when Hooper raised the profit percentage to 7½ the outcry continued. Cambridge responded by withdrawing its advertisements from *Publishers' Circular*, and the publication, in an editorial titled "The First Duty," asserted that the university had an obligation to the booksellers of England and not to Hooper and his "American system" of direct selling to customers which either by-passed booksellers or allowed them infinitesimal profits.

The hubbub that always attended the publication of a new edition of the *Encyclopaedia Britannica*—certainly since the advent of Hooper and Jackson—continued. Bell loyally directed an article to be written in the *Times* commenting favorably and hopefully on the union of Cambridge and the *Encyclopaedia Britannica*. The newspaper had dropped its affiliation with "the knowledge that other no less responsible hands will continue a work which, by its efforts, has now been established on new and secure foundations. . . . The University Presses of Oxford and Cambridge are not on the same footing as ordinary publishing concerns. They have a trust to discharge to the nation in the promotion of higher educational interests. The Cambridge Press has given many proofs that it recognizes this responsibility, but has never undertaken a work more consonant with its character than the present."[1] The dignified *Athenaeum* noted that many considered the affiliation even more startling than that with the *Times*, because Cambridge "with a special regard for its own products has

---

[1] Bell's final years with the *Times* were less than happy, although he worked as diligently as ever. He died at his desk on April 5, 1916, while writing a letter on a copyright controversy.

rather held aloof from the world outside its borders that courted its recognition and approval."

Forced to defend itself, Cambridge, with James its principal spokesman, replied to its decriers and critics. A pamphlet was issued with a full explanation—but with few details of the contract—of the arrangement with the *Encyclopaedia Britannica*. "The association of the University with the publication amounts to a guarantee that it is a trustworthy guide to sound learning, being not only up-to-date, but also the work of experts who are entitled to speak on their several subjects. The new volumes represent the elaborate organization and arduous labour of eight years, and the editor, while retaining certain articles of permanent value, has been getting new ones in many countries." The university, admitted the pamphlet, had nothing to do with organizing the encyclopaedia's staff, planning its production, or selecting writers. "What the Press has done," wrote James, "is to satisfy itself that the new edition of the *Encyclopaedia Britannica* is a work which will do credit to Cambridge."

When, in November, Hooper and Sickert started a campaign to distribute thousands of booklets all over England with extracts from articles, the highbrow *Cambridge Review* snidely commented: "The pamphlet opens with a popular lecture on astronomy by Sir Robert Ball, by shewing what the distance from star to star means in figures. The words contained in the Encyclopaedia are almost equal to the amount of sovereigns Mr. Lloyd George hopes to wring from the wealthy taxpayer; the cost of production would almost keep Mr. Rockefeller or Mr. Carnegie for a calendar month; the amount of India paper used would make a bag large enough to contain this earth and leave enough to spare an envelope for the moon. . . . A charming lady whose face we may not behold is reading it with its cover bent backwards like a sixpenny novelette, to show that unlike some of our own books occasionally borrowed by our friends, you may bend but cannot break the back of the *Encyclopaedia Britannica*. Finally, a strong man is shown with a look of stern determination on his face carrying the set of volumes in its case, to shew that those who refuse to buy will be debarred from performing feats of strength from which Sandow might shrink. All this proves how wide awake the place is."

More critical letters and articles appeared during the remainder of the year and in the first months of 1911, and James continued to respond with spirit. He defended the action of the Syndics in putting the university's imprimatur on the new edition and found little justification for criticisms of advertising methods. Other professors and influential men at Cambridge upbraided him for joining Hooper and reminded him that Cambridge University Press had been among the strong anti-Hooper forces in the Book War. But this gentle scholar, now whipped about in an academic tempest, stood firm by his promise and asked that judgment on Cambridge's action be withheld until the full edition could be impartially and judiciously examined. "The essential question," he wrote, "is whether or not the Syndics were right in the high estimate they formed of the merits of the new edition. Time will show that, and they await the verdict with complete confidence."

14

"High Tide Mark of Human Knowledge"

Neither academic criticism nor embittered carping nor waspish disagreements could slow down Hooper's promotional campaign for the eleventh edition. Instead of slackening in the face of the uproar, he increased his pace on every possible front. "I'm living up to the contract one hundred per cent," he declared. "I'm doing it my way, and the university is going to get clean, honest royalties."

More dinners for selected groups of contributors were held, all at the Savoy Hotel. At one, attended by 150 writers on historical and religious subjects, Chisholm humorously disclosed that technically King Edward VII could be considered a contributor. Early in the work on the new edition, Chisholm had decided to include illustrated plates with the proper colors of the insignia of the principal British and foreign orders of knighthood. Upon inquiry, he found that most books on the subject had incorrect colors. Since King Edward held most of the orders, it was suggested that he be asked to assist. Permission was given, and an artist spent time at Buckingham Palace conferring with the monarch, who displayed an interest not only in the preparation of the plates but in all the processes involved in the publication of the work. At another dinner, this one for scientific experts, Chisholm tolled the count of the 1,507 contributors, noting that in this impressive total there were 168 fellows of the Royal Society, 53 presidents or secretaries of learned societies, 47 members of the British Museum staff, 53 members of staffs of similar institutions, 47 staff members of various laboratories and observatories. A special dinner was held also for women employed by the *Encyclopaedia Britannica*, with Janet Hogarth, who had been shifted from the Book Club in 1909 to head the indexers for the eleventh edition, keynoting the evening: "The *Encyclopaedia Britannica* has given women the chance to demonstrate their rightful place in the learned world."

Even more than in England, the sales campaign was intensified in the United States, a logical step since sales there still outnumbered those in the British Isles. The American drive was touched off by a sumptuous dinner in January, 1911, at the Hotel Plaza, where the guests included Alexander Graham Bell, Woodrow Wilson, James Bryce, Joseph Cannon, Joseph Choate, Admiral Dewey, and J. Pierpont Morgan. As if to answer the critics of Cambridge University's connection with the edition, Chisholm emphasized that the Cambridge University Press "has the greatest faith in the book and the most confident belief that it . . . will do uncommonly well." He noted, too, that the new edition was designed not merely for British readers but for "English-speaking peoples" and paid warm tribute to his American aides.

The ad campaign, which was to cost $1 million for the year, also stressed the Cambridge University affiliation and the breadth of the encyclopaedia's subject matter. The international character of the many contributors was always cited: "Men of Action, Men of Learning, and Practical Experts from Twenty-One Countries *Have Cooperated* with Sixty-Four English and American Editors *to Produce* the NEW EDITION OF THE ENCYCLOPAEDIA BRITANNICA." A breakdown by professions and occupations was featured to show that the contributors included 327 historians or archeologists, 161 theologians, 126 ministers, diplomats, and government officials, 107 biologists and agriculturists, with the remainder comprising dozens in each category of sociologists, economists, geographers, explorers, mathematicians, physicists, meteorologists, lawyers, physicians, surgeons, engineers, architects, businessmen, manufacturers, and naval and military officers. While the greatest number of contributors still came from England and Scotland, the total of American contributors was now well ahead of those from Germany, France, Canada, Italy, Austria-Hungary, the Netherlands, Japan, India, Belgium, Australia, Switzerland, Serbia, Norway, Turkey, Sweden, or Denmark.

A typical ad was the one appearing in the March 3, 1911, issue of the *New York Times,* spread over a full page and headed: "THE SUM OF HUMAN KNOWLEDGE." The attributes of the edition were enumerated vividly, from its "complete and modern exposition of thought, learning and achievements to 1910" to the savings possible if orders were placed before May 31; "only $4 a volume for ordinary paper bound in Cloth, or $4.25 a volume for India paper bound in Cloth (the Ninth Edition having been sold when first issued at $7.50 a volume, Cloth, which will be the ultimate price for the Eleventh Edition)."

Besides the daily newspaper ads, four-color displays in twenty leading magazines also invited readers to write for sample booklets and pamphlets. Every inquiry, of course, was scrupulously followed by a swift procession of booklets, pamphlets, testimonials ("Who would have thought it possible that an encyclopaedia could ever compete with the latest novel?"), statistics, and the inevitable "Hurry Up!" telegraph blanks.

By the middle of May, the intense campaign had already made itself felt. A total of twenty thousand sets had been signed for in the United States alone. But Hooper considered this too few for all the money spent. He ordered a daily assault, and a fresh torrent of ads was produced, with results that were happily appropriate to the purpose. By May 18, the total stood at twenty-three thousand, and six days later this was increased by four thousand. Each figure was duly reported in the press. Every one of the ads warned, in sixty-point type, how many days remained to take advantage of the lower prices. Finally, when the deadline was reached, the number of sets ordered at prepublication prices in America was thirty-three thousand—nearly as many as had been sold of the ninth edition in Great Britain over the fourteen-year period from 1875 to 1889.

No sooner had this time limit passed than a new campaign started, emphasizing, as autumn approached, the suitability of the *Encyclo-*

paedia Britannica as a Christmas gift. As much attention was paid in these ads to physical qualities as to intellectual values—especially the India paper, "which can be crumpled into a ball and ironed out smooth again," and the reduced weight and size ("In this format the volumes, though containing from 960 to 1,100 pages, are only 1 inch thick").

In England, during the pre-Christmas months, the sales promotion was persistent if less extensive. As in America, photographs were used more frequently than in previous campaigns. One was of a dignified young lady bending over a bookcase containing the new edition. Another, showing a young man carrying an entire set in his arms, had as its muscular model Arthur Croxton, whom Hooper had hired in 1909 as business manager in the British office. Croxton, a man with a bent for the theater, was hard at work planning some promotional literature when Hooper told him, "Say, you look intellectual and handsome enough for a photograph. I should like to see the effect of an average man carrying a set of our new India edition. If the twenty-nine volumes can be held with comfort by one man, it will be an impressive advertisement." Croxton posed willingly, but he came to regret it, for he was plagued for months afterward by friends who twitted him about his great strength.

Croxton traveled extensively in these busy months throughout the British Isles, placing ads, drumming up business among booksellers, trying various promotional devices. At the Caledonian Hotel in Edinburgh, he met the actor H. B. Irving, son of Henry Irving. Croxton showed Irving, whom he knew from his days as a writer for the *Tatler*, a specimen copy of an India-paper volume. "Listen," he said, "you're playing *Hamlet* tonight. Why not give me a lift here by bringing on this volume instead of the usual script when you're instructing the actors in the play scene?"

Irving agreed. But Croxton's idea turned out to have little advertising value, for the audience could hardly notice what book Irving carried with him as he strode about the stage declaiming. Only one person did detect the difference, and he was a stagehand who whispered hoarsely, "Hoot mon, ye've got the wrong prop in your hand."

2

The high intellectual standards that had characterized its predecessors still dominated much of the new edition. And there were so-called modern tendencies. Its forty million words totaled only 3 per cent more than in the ninth edition, but they were broken up into many more articles under new headings, intended for easier reading. The long omnibus treatises of earlier editions appeared now as three or four articles, so that where the ninth edition had seventeen thousand treatises and monographs, the new edition contained forty thousand. This arrangement of articles tended to make the eleventh edition a practical reference work for laymen rather than an erudite work largely for scholars and educators. In his Preface, Chisholm called careful attention to this quality: "The object of the present work is to furnish accounts of all subjects, which shall really explain their meaning, to those who desire accurate information. Amid the variety of beliefs which are held with sincere conviction by one set of people or another, impartiality does not consist in concealing criticism or withholding knowledge of divergent opinion, but in an attitude of scientific respect which is precise in studying a belief in the terms, and according to the interpretation accepted by those who hold it."

Among the other signs of a strong drift toward popularization was the use of more current material, notably in an increased number of biographies of contemporaries. Many of these were no more than a paragraph or two in length, but their inclusion added to the character of the work as a reference aid; after all, the subtitle of the edition as carried on the front page now read, "A Dictionary of Arts, Sciences, Literature, and General Information."

Another change was in the improved readability. Commenting on some of the sections on religion, the observant *Athenaeum* stated, "The world of intelligent readers and busy literary workers should be thankful to find that there are learned theologians and critical investigators who can, when the occasion demands it, lay aside stiff and technical phraseology, and say their say in simple, direct and perspicuous English." And, at the end of its analysis of the complete edition, the *American Historical Review* concluded that the work had "literary charm and readableness."

The index, praised by the *Athenaeum* as "a model of well-ordered compactness," was designed primarily to aid the general reader. The extensive bibliographies, which some experts considered too long and sometimes out of date, were also meant to help the intelligent layman who considered his *Encyclopaedia Britannica* not as the final compendium of knowledge but as a stimulant to further study.

Yet, though the encyclopaedia had been seemingly transformed from one chiefly for specialists to a more popular work for laymen, the bulk of the material still bore the marks and quality of authoritative scholarship. Indeed, one American critic, Louis Heilperin, after full examination of the complete set, reflected the opinion of those who believed the edition was still top-heavy with technical articles. In the first of a series of articles for the *Nation*, he hailed the edition for its diffusion of general information, calling it "a monument to the learning of the Anglo-Saxon race such as no other people has ever reared to itself." Later, after studying the volumes more carefully, Heilperin took note of the technical sections, characterizing the set now as "a storehouse of information for people of all cultures, upon which is reared an imposing super-structure, accessible only to a few, comprising the weightiest elements in the whole edifice—the lengthy scientific treatises designed for the specialist."

Some critics maintained that neither specialists nor laymen would profit from the edition. A typical complaint was that there was too much for the general reader, too little for the scholar. Others used the publication of the eleventh edition as an occasion for the general comment that the purpose of such works was to spread knowledge, not to create a nation of smatterers, those who read encyclopaedias only to learn something about everything but nothing very profoundly. Inevitably, there were critics who frowned at what they considered an imbalance. London's *Nation* wondered why "Charity" received twenty-six full pages and "Crime and Criminology" only seven columns and criticized some of the articles on music, edited by the musicologist Donald Francis Tovey, because Debussy received only half the space devoted to the technical discussion of the bugle; Handel, Bach, and Beethoven little more than the flute, clarinet, and bassoon; and Berlioz less than the harmonium.

But for all the criticism, deserved and undeserved, the general reaction was highly favorable. Even London's *Nation*, most severe of the observers, considered the edition vastly superior to its predecessors and contemporaries: "We conclude by wishing for the Encyclopaedia Britannica the great success which it deserves. It is a wonderful treasure house of human knowledge, and a great glory to our nation." Another British publication, *Connoisseur*, lauded the work and metaphorically declared, "Like a reservoir in which water from all streams of knowledge has been collected, it offers an unfailing supply to those who want information on practically every subject. If this one work constituted a man's soul library, he would, if he mastered it, be learned above most of his compeers." Especially pleasing to most of the commentators was the nearly simultaneous publication of all twenty-nine volumes, an innovation that, as the *Independent* remarked, "made it possible to keep the articles open to the last moment, so that the new Britannica has the charm of freshness, the enviable privilege of speaking the last word." This publication also called attention to the fact that, although some had expressed indignation at American ownership and supervision of what had been a Scottish publishing venture for the preceding 142 years, the quality of the set had not been injured nor had it decreased.

The *American Historical Review*, whose critic, George Burr, deplored the popularization of some sections, nevertheless declared that to compare the new edition with any other encyclopaedia in the English language was clearly idle. "Its advent," he wrote, "is a noble step toward the good day when the learning and art of all the world shall be enlisted for the creation of that international work which alone can be a really faithful mirror of advancing knowledge." Other American critics agreed that there was no longer cause for complaint that the work was too insular in its views. Referring to it as "A Reference Library for the English-Speaking World," the *Review of Reviews* declared, "In turning its pages one is almost startled to find a column of information about his native town in the Middle West—a place that had never been thought worthy of so much as a stickful of type in any American reference book. In other and more important fields of knowledge the same catholicity of selection and treatment has been observed. Perhaps it is an indication of the relatively more important place that America holds today in the world's civilization as well as a tribute to the editorial genius that conceived and brought to fruition this monumental work, that every one of the volumes is alive with the intellectual and material progress of the new world."

3

From the religious quarters where such an uproar had been raised over certain articles in the ninth edition there was silence now. "We have gone far from the fury raised over W. Robertson Smith," commented London's *Nation*. "No longer is there any attempt to conceal the most radical hypotheses which criticism may have ventured or reject their hypotheses." And the *Spectator*, closely examining all the religious and scriptural articles, found them to be as "severely scientific as the articles on Physics or Secular History. They claim attention and

convince the mind and they are all written with reverent good taste—
reverence has become good taste since honest scholarship has been
freed from obloquy."

But from certain Catholic critics there issued a harsh attack, not on
one man, as in Smith's case, but on all who had been involved in
publishing and editing the new edition. Leading the assault in England was the *Month,* a Catholic publication in London which had, as
far back as 1886, termed an article on the Jesuits in the ninth edition
"an invective, not a history, a repository of accusations." When the
new edition appeared, the magazine again denounced the article on
the Jesuits. This one was written by the Rev. Ethelred Taunton, described as a Jesuit, whereas the earlier article had been the work of
F. W. Littledale, a theologian at Dublin's Trinity College. Asserting
that few changes had been made, the magazine added, "To keep
seventy per cent of Littledale's article while dropping thirty is to rob
the result of all reliability." Although Littledale's accusation against
the Jesuits in connection with the instigation of the Thirty Years' War
had been considerably softened, the *Month* asserted, "It is not based
upon a study of the original, is full of partiality and overstatement of
fact, as well as allegations of bad motives and of pernicious doctrine."
Throughout 1911 the *Month* continued its acrid campaign. It charged
that the *Encyclopaedia Britannica* was guilty of "unscholarly bigotry";
that the "anti-Catholic animus" of several writers on subjects involving
Catholicism was well known; that all articles on the Catholic church
were "thoroughly Protestant and necessarily incorrect"; that the "acme
of contemptuous indifference to Catholic feeling" was reached in an
account by Viscount St. Cyres, a non-Catholic, of the "Church in
Europe since the Reformation." This latter article was, according to
the *Month,* "full of bitter animus against orthodox Catholicism, bris-
tling with misrepresentations, conveyed by phrase and epithet, by
assertion and innuendo. . . . If they let Kropotkin write on Anarchism, why not Catholics on Catholicism?" And finally, bitterly: "The
Encyclopaedia Britannica is a non-Catholic production, which means
practically that it is anti-Catholic, for the claims of the Church
Catholic are so unique, so far-reaching and fundamental, that they
cannot be ignored or misrepresented without distortion of the truth.
He that is not with her is against her."

Less violent, but no less critical, were the views of another British
Catholic magazine, the *Tablet.* Its first reactions to the eleventh edition were roseate—"a revelation and a delight. . . . what used to be

a work for laborious reference has suddenly become a library to read"
—but soon the tone changed. More temperate than the *Month,* this
publication was careful in its charges, making no broad accusations but
calling to the attention of readers certain errors of interpretation and
information in articles dealing with Catholicism. At one time, for instance, it complained of insufficient discussion of the Augustinian
canons, citing errors in the treatment of the administrative relationship
of the canons to the central church.

In contrast to attacks by United States publications, the *Tablet*
seemed a fervent defender of the *Encyclopaedia Britannica.* First
there appeared a pamphlet titled *Poisoning the Wells,* issued under
auspices of the American Federation of Catholic Societies and generally believed to have been written by the Rev. John S. Wynne, S.J.,
one of the editors of the *Catholic Encyclopaedia.* The booklet approached the vilification of Chisholm, Phillips, and their editorial staff.
It labeled the new edition "unscholarly, sectarian, and offensive" and
cited dozens of examples to prove its point. It denounced what it
called a "rationalistic and anti-Catholic spirit" and called on all good
Catholics to refrain from buying the set. The Jesuit monthly *America*
mirrored these charges; its editor, the Rev. T. J. Campbell, S.J., wrote:
"The frequently unveiled contempt of the usages, rituals and sacra-
mental agencies not only of Catholicism but of Christianity, combined
with the absence in many of its writers of any knowledge above material things and a deplorable dullness of vision in what pertains to the
spiritual world, will always make of the Encyclopaedia Britannica a
most exasperating book for Catholics of every degree."

In replying, Chisholm and Phillips made use of the columns of the
friendliest of their Catholic critics. Soon there appeared in the *Tablet*
a list of Catholics who had written for the *Encyclopaedia Britannica*
some two hundred articles on churches and church history, including
the Abbé Boudinhon, professor of canon law at Catholic University in
Paris; His Eminence Cardinal Gibbons of Baltimore; and Father
Joseph Braun, a German scholar. Their works, together with scores
of other articles from Catholic pens, seemed, stated the *Tablet,* "sufficient proof of the good intentions of the editors—intentions which
many difficulties conspire to leave in some cases unfulfilled, difficulties, some of them, which even the editors of the Catholic dictionaries
and cyclopaedias have not wholly escaped." Phillips' letters noted that
virtually all the articles dealing with Catholic subjects had been
examined by Abbé Boudinhon or some other distinguished Catholic.

When Father Wynne, in a letter to the *Tablet*, claimed that the editors had promised that only Catholic writers would write on Catholic subjects, Chisholm sent a reasoned rejoinder. Denying any such promise had been made, he wrote, "Such a course in the *Encyclopaedia Britannica* would be impracticable with any attempt to write history from an impartial but critical standpoint. We did not ask a Buddhist to write on Buddhism, a Mohammedan on Mohammedanism, or a Mormon on the Mormons. We did, however, I believe, take every reasonable precaution by the cooperation of men of all sorts of religious belief, against the misrepresentation of the nature of the doctrines held by different churches and different religions."

Others soon joined in the controversy in the columns of the *Tablet*. Father Aidan Gasquet, O.S.B., abbot president at Sant' Anselmo in Rome, denied the charges in *Poisoning the Wells*, especially those accusing Chisholm of assigning articles on Catholicism to "bigots and anti-Catholics." "The charge is undeserved and consequently unjust," he wrote, disclosing that he had been asked by Chisholm to examine many articles and that his suggestions for their improvement had been scrupulously followed. Father Wynne promptly responded with an itemization of "new errors" in, among others, the articles "Divorce" and "Attrition." E. Cuthbert Butler, another Catholic contributor, sided with Father Gasquet, asserting that any purported promise by the editors to secure writers "friendly to Catholicism" surely could not be understood "as a promise to secure such a treatment of the great questions of religious controversy as should be theologically satisfying all round to all the people who hold all the divergent beliefs concerning them, for this is plainly impossible." The *Tablet's* editorials grew calmer and more friendly, now criticizing the "controversial rhetoric and the exuberance of transatlantic hyperbole" in *America* and in *Poisoning the Wells* and declaring that the pamphlet writer had not proved his charge that the *Encyclopaedia Britannica* had made "a shameful attempt to perpetuate ignorance, bigotry, and fanaticism in matters of religion." Many of the purported errors, stated the magazine, were not so much factual as interpretative. One example cited was the pamphlet's expressed horror at this sentence in the article "Attrition": "It is held among the Roman Catholics that in the sacrament of penance attrition becomes contrition." Many savants held to this view, although others, notably St. Thomas Aquinas, had presented opposite opinions. The encyclopaedia's error, stated the *Tablet*, was neither malicious nor rooted in bigotry, but merely one of citing the belief as universally Catholic.

One firm Catholic supporter of the *Encyclopaedia Britannica* in America was Carlton J. H. Hayes, historian at Columbia University. Asked by the *Independent* to make a close examination of the charges and countercharges and the original material on which they were based, Hayes, after a six months' study, absolved the editors of practically all the accusations made in *Poisoning the Wells*. He noted some errors of fact and deplored the assignment of Catholic subjects to Viscount St. Cyres. But he added: "Now it is one thing to accuse the editors of mistakes of judgment in selecting contributors, or even of lack of proper attention to the detailed revising of the wide range of religious subjects, but it is another thing to denounce their work everywhere, in season and out of season as 'a shameful attempt to perpetuate ignorance, bigotry and fanaticism in matters of religion.' That is impugning their motives; that is reading them out of the society of scholars. And before subscribing to that conclusion, we should naturally await the presentation in a passionless, critical manner of weighty and convincing proofs. . . . But when the candid student, be he Catholic, Protestant or agnostic, reads the pamphlet that contains the crushing charge and painstakingly sifts its eighteen pages of evidence, he may almost be entitled to wonder if some one besides the editors of the *Britannica* has not been perpetuating ignorance, bigotry and fanaticism in matters of religion."

Hayes made an important point in his analysis that applied not only to the case at hand but to all charges of prejudice against specialized or general encyclopaedias. "Suppose," he wrote, "that a zealous Protestant, or better still, a brilliant parodist, would criticize the *Catholic Encyclopaedia* in this pamphlet form, ascribing the merest slips to bigotry and Popish prejudices. He might enjoy himself and be amusing to others. He might conceivably, with the ill-informed, injure the sales of the publication; but no trained person would suspect him of scholarship. The type of scholarship which defaces this pamphlet against the *Britannica* must in future be avoided if Catholics are to convince the editors of the twelfth Edition of the great encyclopaedia, and the intellectual generally, that Catholic learning has truthfullness, authority and strength."

An unofficial end to the whole disturbing affair was announced by the *Tablet* at the end of 1911, with an editorial, "A Pax Britannica."

Father Gasquet and Professor Hayes had gone to the root of the matter, it declared. "The point of controversy of real importance is, not whether there are misstatements and mistakes in articles which deal with Catholic matters, historical and dogmatic, but whether the managers and editors made deliberate choice of writers who might be expected to set forth false views about the Catholic Church and its beliefs. . . . The right way to regard the Encyclopaedia Britannica is to think of it as, what in effect it is, a great library. We do not think it necessary to boycott the library at the British Museum because there are some anti-Catholic and offensive volumes on its shelves. We use it for what is good in it. Why should we mete out any different measure to the Britannica? For our part, we think it wiser to weigh the grain than to count the chaff, to make the willing acknowledgement of what has already been done to free the Britannica from an old reproach, and to look forward with confidence to the Twelfth Edition for the continuance and completion of what has been so well begun in the Eleventh."

Its final statement was especially incisive on the nature of encyclopaedias. Recalling that even the *Catholic Dictionary*, with its official imprimatur, received harsh censure from Catholic critics when it appeared, the editorialist advised, "The ways of Encyclopaedists, in the best of circumstances, are hard. Let us not make them harder by hurling unjust accusations of want of good faith against those who have for the first time in this country tried to do justice, and with a large measure of success. Their failures, where such there are, will be more fully remedied by an exhibition on our side of some of that spirit of fair play which we bespeak of them."

Thus, on a note of philosophical realism, the *Tablet* cooled the controversy and ended its editorial, "This correspondence may now cease."

4

An echo of the earlier fuss raised by academicians at Cambridge University sounded just as the Catholic issue began to fade. A fly-sheet addressed to the Syndics was circulated demanding that none among them who had been party to the contract with the *Encyclopaedia Britannica* be reappointed to duty. Its signers were Archdeacon William Cunningham, one of the earliest of the critics, and a number of other faculty members and alumni. "No information has been given as to the rights which the University has acquired and the obligations which the University has incurred, but the publication of this work, although it has been undertaken by the Syndics on their own authority, has not been treated as a transaction in the ordinary course of their business." From advertising and from a prefatory note in the first volume dated from Cambridge, the impression had developed in some quarters that the university was responsible for the preparation and production of the work. "We believe," concluded the statement, "that the reputation of the University has been injured by the representations which have been made; that this reputation has suffered and is suffering, by the methods taken to advertise the work, and on these grounds we enter our protest."

In this dispute, as in the days when Hooper and Jackson had issued their *Times* reprint of the ninth edition, the fact seemed to be that those who opposed the venture simply refused to read or, having read, to understand plain statements. Over and over again announcements issued jointly and separately by Hooper and the Syndics emphasized that the work of preparing the edition had started—indeed, was more than three-fourths completed—when Hooper first approached the Syndics. It is true that in his advertisements, especially in America, Hooper strongly suggested that Cambridge University had had charge of the entire project—even to listing the ads under the sponsorship of "Cambridge University Press (Encyclopaedia Britannica Department)"—but these ads were approved by the Syndics and actually conveyed no false information.

Stressing that the contract with Hooper was secret, as were all their agreements for the publishing of books, the Syndics made another reply to their critics. "The Encyclopaedia differs from other books only in its magnitude. We are satisfied that it was a work which deserved the imprimatur of the University, and that by its publication we were contributing to the spread of knowledge. We recognized that a work so costly in production could not meet with an adequate sale unless widely advertised; we accept full responsibility for our policy; and, without contending that we have never at any point made a mistake, we believe that that policy promotes the interests entrusted to us by the Senate."

For the time being, this exchange closed the case. When several of the professors were not reappointed Syndics, the opposition acclaimed this a minor victory. Gradually controversy and discussion subsided, with final adjudication to come later.

5

Hooper paid no great heed to all the criticism. He was certain Chisholm could reply adequately, and he could always turn for any needed solace to the laudatory estimates, such as the statement of William A. E. Axon, a critic for the *Library*, a respected quarterly review of bibliographical and library lore. Axon spent a solid year in studying the edition. "What is the average student's verdict after a year's use of the EB?" he asked. "Most readers will, I believe, say it is one of satisfaction. It reaches a high standard of accurate and full statement on important matters, and rarely fails to give some information even on an obscure or little-known subject." Despite some defects —omissions, slight discrepancies, disproportionate amounts of space —his final conclusion was gratifying. "It is, when all deductions have been made, the most useful of all books of reference, and represents the combination of learning, research, co-operation and organization in a higher degree than perhaps any other of the monumental works of literature and science. It is the high-tide mark of human knowledge. And it is knowledge brought to the service of all."

As seriously as Hooper respected the *Encyclopaedia Britannica* and the knowledge and learning it symbolized, enthusiastic critical ovations would have been far less sweet had not sales figures turned out to be what he had anticipated. Now the year of 1911 was over, and his triumph over innumerable difficulties and obstacles was complete. The year-end report showed his company's net assets to be $4,100,000, certainly an agreeable complement of the praiseworthy words in the newspapers and magazines. Everywhere that his encyclopaedia was being offered for sale, the response was gratifying. Refreshed and exuberant, Hooper felt ready for what lay before him.

15

Triumph—and Gloom

Walter Jackson had taken no part in the sale of the eleventh edition, but he was far from idle. He was promoting his own enterprises and preparing new legal assaults against Hooper. His *Book of Knowledge,* with all copyright difficulties resolved, was catching the fancy of the American public, as parents discovered that their children enjoyed reading its brief, illustrated articles on a variety of common subjects. Jackson was equally successful with publishing enterprises in South America, which he had invaded in 1908, shortly after his first quarrels with Hooper. Sensing an opportunity for profits through furnishing the Spanish-speaking peoples there with books comparable to the favorites of the English-speaking world, he was busily selling, through local agents, the *Biblioteca internacional de obras famosas,* a twenty-four volume compendium of the best-known works of prominent European authors.

Jackson had plans for still another publishing venture, but before he could get it under way he filed a new suit against Hooper, this one destined to be the last. On August 30, 1911, in New York's supreme court, he demanded $5,200,000 from his former associate, basing the claim on the muddled negotiations of 1909 when he had accepted the "offer" made by Hooper from England. By failing to live up to that agreement, Jackson now charged, Hooper had caused him to suffer financial damage in that sum. Jackson also accused Hooper of illegally excluding him from the business and of appropriating for himself and his close collaborators "excessive salaries and compensation."

The case was set for trial early the next year. Meanwhile, Jackson pushed forward with his South American project. To help, he called on one of Lord Northcliffe's most prized editorial lieutenants, John A. Hammerton, a keen journalist, editor, and encyclopaedist. The two had worked together amicably when the various intricacies of transferring copyrights to the *Book of Knowledge* from Northcliffe's *Children's Encyclopaedia* were being untangled, and although Hammerton was snobbishly disdainful of most Americans, he regarded Jackson as a sound businessman.

"I'm contemplating an ambitious publishing scheme in South America," Jackson told Hammerton, "and I'd like you in with me. How much are you making with Northcliffe?"

"One thousand pounds a year."

Jackson waved his arm, a trail of smoke coming from his ever-present cigar. "Not enough! I'll give you five thousand a year for five years, plus royalties."

Hammerton wavered a bit, but in the end he agreed to join in Jackson's enterprise for at least two years. Soon he was at work on his assignment—editorial supervision and production of a Spanish encyclopaedia whose plates and rights for distribution in South America Jackson had acquired from its owner, Montaner y Simon of Barcelona, Spain's leading publisher. Not only was Hammerton to handle editorial revision, insertion of articles of interest to South Americans, and modernization of illustrations, he was also to originate all newspaper publicity and advertising in the South American press. The work was to be titled *El diccionario enciclopédico hispano-americano,* and R. and R. Clark, printers of the *Encyclopaedia Britannica* before the gradual transfer after 1909 of the full printing to Chicago's R. R. Donnelley and Sons, were to handle production in Edinburgh.

Hammerton was barely aware of Jackson's fight with Hooper, but he was intrigued with Jackson's instructions to him as he began adapting the original edition for South American readers. "Whatever notes, clippings, and correspondence you are throwing away, I want you to burn," Jackson warned him. "In fact, you had best burn all that's in your wastepaper basket."

"Why on earth should that be necessary?" asked Hammerton.

"Well, I can only tell you that in America we stop at nothing to get to know what our competitors are doing, and a good tip to the dustman used to be a favorite way of finding out. You'd be surprised at what can be learned about the activities of anyone when you can examine his wastebasket at your leisure."

Despite the warnings, advance information of Hammerton's work did reach Hooper. Immediately, Hooper hired a staff of Spanish-language experts to plow through Jackson's Spanish encyclopaedia to discover possible breaches of copyright. The researchers soon found that two articles—one on "Encyclopaedia" and the second on "Dictionary"—had been lifted entirely from the *Encyclopaedia Britannica's* tenth edition.

But Jackson, too, had spies in the enemy camp. When Hooper demanded that his attorneys get an injunction to restrain Jackson from selling his encyclopaedia, Hammerton soon learned of it. He acted swiftly. Thousands of the books destined for South America had already been printed and bound in Edinburgh and packed for shipment, but Hammerton wired to R. and R. Clark: "Hold everything." Then, working feverishly with two Spanish assistants, he rewrote the offending articles and quickly dispatched them to Edinburgh, where they were substituted for the originals and the volumes involved were rebound.

Meanwhile Hooper had filed for his injunction, but process-servers sought Hammerton and Jackson in vain. Hammerton and his wife, already on their way to Buenos Aires, sped to Lisbon. Jackson secreted himself in London hotels under assumed names until the new volumes were ready to be produced in court with the purloined articles gone and new ones substituted.

Thwarted, Hooper vowed to follow the flight into South America. But first there was to be a final legal battle with Jackson in New York.

2

For this clash, each man came arrayed with formidable legal talent. Hooper's chief attorney was Samuel Untermyer, a man of sharp wit and sharper tactics, a master of cross-examination and incisive questioning who rarely raised his voice but who could easily upset a balky witness. Jackson's chief counsel was Sherman L. Whipple, one of Boston's best courtroom strategists, aided by the estimable lawyer-diplomat Joseph H. Choate.

All through January and February, 1912, the hearing proceeded before Justice Martin Bischoff. Most of the testimony revolved around the misunderstandings aroused by the Hooper cablegrams of October, 1909. Over and over again, Jackson, a stern and assured figure in the witness chair whenever he was questioned by Whipple, insisted that his acceptance of Hooper's "offer" made him technically the owner and that he had a right to all subsequent profits. When Hooper's New Jersey lawyers had informed him of the offer, he declared, he was not only prepared to pay $100,000 down for the business, but could just as easily have put up the rest of the $750,000.

Slowly and with excruciating patience, Untermyer sought to show that Jackson's suit had been instituted only because Hooper had been unusually successful in marketing the eleventh edition—in his own way and by methods formerly frowned on by Jackson. Skilfully the canny lawyer brought out Jackson's real feelings about the affiliation with Cambridge and his stubborn insistence that, despite the happy outcome of Hooper's plan, his own system would have been better.

"Now the interposition of the Cambridge University, or the publication of this book under its auspices, made a tremendous change in the situation, did it not?" asked Untermyer.

"Made a tremendous change in what situation?"

"In the prestige under which the book would be issued."

"I do not think so, especially."

"You do not think," asked Untermyer, raising his voice slightly, "that it made any difference whether Jackson and Hooper issued the *Encyclopaedia Britannica* or whether it was issued in the name of the Cambridge University Press?"

"I do not say that."

"I understand you to say that—did you mean it?"

"You were not comparing Hooper and Jackson. . . . I doubt that it made much if any difference, as between the name of Cambridge University and the name of a reputable London publishing house, but that is simply a matter of opinion."

As the colloquy continued, Untermyer placed Jackson in the guise of a rather naïve man in his views about publishing promotion.

"The prestige of the Cambridge University Press as publisher of great books is very great, is it not?"

"I do not know anything about the prestige," replied Jackson.

"It exercises great care in publication work, does it not?"

"I am not familiar with its publications, except in one instance."

"You considered, when you made that contract with the *Times,* that its assuming the publication of the work would be of great value, did you not?"

"At that time, but not later."

Then:

"And yet the name of the Cambridge University Press as publisher you do not think was of any great value, do you?"

"Did think or do think? I do not exactly follow your question."

"At the time you heard of it you did not think it was of any value, did you?"

"I did not think it was of any especial value."

"And you don't think so yet?"

"As compared with some other first-class publishing house?"

"As compared, for instance, with whom?"

"Adam and Charles Black, or Charles Scribner's Sons."

"You think that the name of Charles Scribner's Sons would have as great an effect in the publication of a book of that kind as the Cambridge University Press?"

"Perhaps not over the world."

But later:

"I understood you to say that Scribner's or Black's name on a publication that goes all over the world would be just as good as the Cambridge University Press?"

"I am inclined to think so."

Jackson also insisted he could have produced the eleventh edition more efficiently and without great indebtedness to banks by issuing single volumes periodically. This was how the Blacks had done it, how the *Century Dictionary* had been brought out. But Hooper had insisted that it be issued his way—as a single unit. "Hooper said this method of production and sale would be very much more successful than any other way," testified Jackson. "I disagreed with him, and said that I thought that not only would that not be the case but I thought, that I was sure, that it would be a very much more costly way, involving the risk of money and taking a hazard that perhaps we were not putting out just the most effective kind of advertisements, and that sort of thing." By the method of publishing one volume at a time, estimated Jackson, the edition could have been issued within a two-year period.

Untermyer was quick to pounce on this theory.

Did not Jackson know, he asked, that when the Blacks so issued the ninth edition, only about forty thousand sets were sold?

"I know that this is not so," snapped Jackson.

"Do you? Well, what is the fact of the ninth edition, when issued by the Blacks, according to their method of doing this business?"

"The fact is they sold in England and the Colonies between nine and ten thousand sets. Scribner's sold in round figures fifty thousand sets of their edition, and the pirates, who pirated here in America, sold three or four hundred thousand sets."

"We are not speaking of pirating of the edition! That was stopped."

"It is the same edition."

"We are talking of sales of the authorized edition."

"You said ninth edition."

Later, Untermyer pressed Jackson on this point. "At any rate, I am asking you how many sets the Blacks sold or how many were sold of the authorized edition by the method you have described of selling books, if you know."

"About sixty thousand."

"Are you sure about that?"

"I am not absolutely certain, but I have had access to their books."

"Wasn't it under forty?"

"I think not."

"Do you know that there have been thirty-three thousand sets sold within one year of this eleventh edition?"

"I believe that to be so."

"Do you know whether any such feat could have been accomplished by the method you have in mind?"

"I think so."

"When it took the Blacks fourteen years to sell forty thousand or thereabouts?"

"They did not use the same methods of sale."

"And I understand you to say that the Blacks were quite as good for all purposes of publication all over the world as the Cambridge University?"

"I am inclined to think they were considerably better."

"You think they would be better."

"I do."

"You think that to the ordinary purchaser of a book of that character, the name of Blacks all over the world would mean as much as the name of the Cambridge University?"

"No, but with that particular book, because their name had always been associated with it."

"Now you know that the Cambridge University exercises an active supervision over this work, don't you?"

"I have been told so, yes."

"Didn't you know that the articles were read by the professors, members of the faculty, there, before they were permitted to be printed, every one examined?"

"I have heard so."

"And don't you know that there were many of the members of the faculty who wrote the articles themselves?"

"I assume that is so."

"And yet I understand you to say that the bringing of the Cambridge University into this transaction in August, 1910, did not in any way change the situation."

Haughtily, Jackson answered, "I have already replied very fully to that."

Naturally enough, Hooper took advantage of his session in the witness chair to deny all of Jackson's charges. An interesting admission by him was that one of the purposes of shutting down production and editorial work on the eleventh edition shortly after the *Times* served notice of cancellation of its contract was—besides the obvious one that sufficient money for the edition was lacking—to "bring Mr. Jackson to his senses."

"What do you mean," asked Untermyer, "by bringing Mr. Jackson to his senses?"

"I meant that he would realize that it was to his interest to stop litigating and come and attend to his business."

"You never had any desire to acquire that interest, had you?"

"At no time at all," replied Hooper, fixing his flashing eyes on Jackson.

"And when you were negotiating for acquiring it, was it for yourself or for other people who worked with you in the business?"

"At no time that I have ever made an offer did I wish to buy it for myself."

"You were satisfied with what you had?"

"Absolutely."

Candidly and not without some smugness, Hooper revealed all the details attendant on securing the imprimatur of Cambridge University. He enumerated the difficulties he had encountered in attempting to obtain loans before signing the contract with the university—"A bank that had previously loaned us money refused to loan us more than £40,000." He gave a picture of the post-contract situation—"After Cambridge took it, we were able to borrow from one bank in London £185,000, which we could not have borrowed if it had not been for the fact of the Cambridge agreement." And then he disclosed how the financial situation had improved since the more dismal days when the *Times*'s contract ended.

The net assets in October, 1911, were a little more than $4,100,000, compared with assets of $2,383,877 shown in the balance sheets of October, 1909. "And is the situation improving every day?" asked Untermyer.

"It is."

The success or failure of the undertaking, explained Hooper, depended "on a great many things. . . . It depended first on being able to get money enough to advertise it widely. It depended on the name that guaranteed the book. It depended on being able to get that book out and delivered to the people. It depended on what we call in the trade the scheme, that is, the plan, under which we advertised it."

"Now you say that advertising had a good deal to do with it?" asked Untermyer.

"Everything."

"What did you spend in the first advertisement of that book?"

"During last year we spent over $1,000,000 in advertising."

"In advertising. And what was the result in the way of sales?"

"Thirty-three thousand sets."

"As the result of one campaign of advertising?"

"Yes, roughly speaking, about seven or eight months."

"Had any such thing ever been known in the history of bookselling?"

"Never!"

"Or anything approaching it?"

"Not within a great distance."

The New Jersey lawyers—except for Sherrerd DePue, who had died —were all summoned and questioned closely by both sides. Each contradicted most of the testimony of his opposite number, although it was clear that the bungling and, in the last analysis, the litigation had resulted from withholding Hooper's all-important proviso that no sale agreement was final without a written contract.

By March 26, 1912, Justice Bischoff was ready with his decision—and it was entirely in Hooper's favor. The jurist held that the contract offer was not binding because Hooper clearly contemplated that it was to be followed by a more formal agreement containing details that were not in the preliminary offer. Hooper's original terms were too indefinite to be legally sound, especially in their reference to the fact that 51 per cent of the stock of the companies was to be held by a trustee for the benefit of the seller until the entire purchase price of $750,000 was received.

After Justice Bischoff had dismissed his suit, Jackson trudged wearily from the courtroom to the offices of the company from which he issued his South American sets. He sat on the edge of the desk of his secretary, Margaret Schneider, and stared out the window. Then he lit a cigar, puffed for a few seconds, and sighed. "I'll never have a partner again, Miss Schneider, not even if I have to sell shoestrings like that little fellow down on the corner," he said.

3

Jackson's lawsuits against his former associate were over, but his clashes with Hooper were not.

Now Hooper took out after Jackson in South America. On stationery of the Grolier Society, Jackson wrote to Hooper denying that he was selling any Spanish translation of the *Encyclopaedia Britannica;* a rumor to this effect had disturbed several meetings of Hooper's board of directors. Jackson's protestations notwithstanding, Hooper dispatched Henry Haxton, long since recovered from the illness which had prevented his participation in the eleventh edition sales campaign, to Buenos Aires to check on Hammerton's progress.

Hammerton had performed a remarkable job. Although he had previously frowned on American methods, he had yielded to Jackson's advice to employ American-style selling. The time-payment plan was used everywhere; at the opening of one campaign seven men were stationed at a counter, where books were displayed, to take downpayments, and these came so rapidly that the gold pieces were swept into wastebaskets behind the counter.

After a preliminary survey, Haxton organized a counterattack against Hammerton and the *El diccionario enciclopédico hispano-americano.* He organized a procession through Buenos Aires streets of horse-drawn carriages with large posters attacking Jackson's publication as obsolete and unworthy. Behind the carriages came men with sandwich boards inscribed with abusive criticism of *El diccionario enciclopédico hispano-americano* and extolling the merits of the *Encyclopaedia Britannica*.

"Which book is right?" Haxton's sandwich signs and newspaper advertisements demanded. *"El diccionario enciclopédico hispano-americano* says that Queen Victoria is still Queen of Great Britain, but the *Encyclopaedia Britannica* says the present sovereign of Great Britain is George V. WHICH BOOK IS RIGHT?"

Haxton had slipped since the days of the early campaigns. This kind of appeal misfired badly. Not only was it patently unfair—the Spanish encyclopaedia, despite the error, carried a full and accurate biography of King George—but it aroused little interest among the residents of Buenos Aires, who were more concerned with biographical information about their own rulers and their own land. Moreover, Jackson's publication had an obviously wider appeal siince it was in the language of the country, whereas the *Encyclopaedia Britannica* was in English. As a matter of fact, Hooper had, in earlier years, considered publishing a Spanish translation and had sent a representative to Spain to make preliminary arrangements for securing sales representatives in Spanish-speaking countries, but this plan had been abandoned.

4

When Haxton's campaign proved ineffective, Hooper realized the futility of making new efforts to best Jackson in South America. Already his rival was invading other sections of that continent with more literary products. The prolonged litigation had cost Hooper close to $500,000 in lawyer's fees and court expenses, and the threat of new suits had not entirely passed. So Hooper called his cohorts back from South America and, thereafter, through the outbreak of World War I, concentrated on other projects closer to home.

Always concerned with the problem of keeping the *Encyclopaedia Britannica* as up to date as possible, Hooper had proposed in 1911 that a biennial reference book be issued, recording events of importance and historical developments and trends in each two-year period preceding publication. For the first such book, which he hoped to publish in 1913, he sought Chisholm as editor. As it turned out, Chisholm was available. After he had completed his labors on the eleventh edition, Chisholm had been asked by Lord Northcliffe if he were interested in the post of editor-in-chief of the *Times*. Chisholm was completely amenable and agreed to notify Northcliffe when he returned from a visit to the United States on a promotional campaign for the eleventh edition. But when he did so, Chisholm found that the position had been given to another. He readily accepted Hooper's offer, and, with Janet Hogarth—now wed to W. L. Courtney, editor of the *Fortnightly Review*—as his first assistant, he set out to do the job. Most of the articles in the single volume, published in 1913 as the *Britannica Year Book*, were the handiwork of contributors to the eleventh edition; Chisholm himself was responsible for half a dozen, including a sixty-seven-page review of English history for 1911 and 1912. The book's subtitle was formidable: "A Survey of the World's Progress since the Completion in 1910 of the *Encyclopaedia Britannica*, Eleventh Edition, Comprising a Register of Current Events and Additions to Knowledge in Politics, Economics, Engineering, Industry, Sport, Law, Science, Art, Literature, and other forms of Human Activity, National and International, up to the end of 1912." Of its 1,126 pages, nearly a quarter were devoted exclusively to information about the United States, including a diary of events of importance in 1911 and 1912, various statistical tables, a list of the members of the Sixty-third Congress, and tabulations by states of votes cast in the presidential elections of 1908 and 1912. Its reception was moderately favorable, although some quipsters, remarking upon the speed with which it had been prepared and issued, labeled it "Wisdom without Waiting."

Another of Hooper's ideas to stimulate wider use of the *Encyclopaedia Britannica* was the issuance of reading guides. The first of what was intended as a series came out in 1913, a handbook containing sixty-six courses of "systematic study or occasional reading." By use of the guide and a set of the *Encyclopaedia Britannica*, readers could obtain, according to the advertisements, a wide educational background. The guide also stressed the utilitarian aspects of the *Encyclopaedia Britannica* as firmly as its educational and philosophical values. The six parts into which the guide divided the "wealth of material" to be found in the *Encyclopaedia Britannica* included itemized suggestions for "those engaged in certain occupations, or preparing for them"— farmers, dairymen, merchants, manufacturers of textiles, chemists, insurance men, architects, printers, binders, papermakers, and "all who love books"—some thirty occupations in all; for those desiring reading to supplement or take the place of school studies in music, ethnology, philosophy, science, and the arts; for those interested in such "questions of the day" as education, training of defectives, alcoholism, trusts, finance, suffrage, or international relations; and for those seeking information about recreation and vacations (motoring, a specimen trip from New York to the White Mountains of Vermont, mountaineering, dancing, acting, and the like). The *Encyclopaedia Britannica*, the guide emphasized, had much in it to bring light and knowledge to children. There were scores of sample questions whose answers were to be found in the volumes: "What makes people snore?" and "Why do stars twinkle?" and "Why is winter colder than summer?" and many more.

Hooper's third project, broached early in 1914, was to publish a *Junior Britannica*. Mrs. Courtney and a staff were assigned to make up a sample volume of articles taken from the senior edition and shortened, rewritten in plainer language, and well illustrated with photographs and drawings. Work was started, too, on a Japanese history. Published the following year, it was an especially beautiful volume on India paper, with fifteen hundred illustrations by Japanese artists and many halftone plates and maps. Captain Francis Brinkley, editor of the *Japan Mail*, edited it with the co-operation of Baron Dairoku Kikuchi, former president of the Imperial University at Kyoto. And an arrangement was put into effect in this same year to use the plates of the ten-volume *Century Dictionary* for a single-volume edition on India paper, to be sold by Hooper's firm on a royalty basis.

If this period was a busy one for Hooper, it was also a fateful one. Early in 1914, he and his associates pondered the best way of settling all difficulties with Jackson. Business was thriving, profits were mounting. As long as this continued, Hooper feared new legal onslaughts from Jackson, despite Jackson's ever-growing concentration on publishing interests in South America. After many consultations, Hooper decided to make one further effort to settle with Jackson. Working through an intermediary, Frank Eagan, a friend of Jackson's and a financier of considerable repute respected by both men, Hooper made an offer in May, 1914. He would buy out Jackson's interests with the implicit understanding that such a move would bar further lawsuits. This time Jackson agreed. A settlement was effected by which Hooper acquired his holdings in the American and British firms for a sum that, with later adjustments and additions, eventually amounted to $900,-000. (After his final break with Hooper, Jackson continued to prosper in South America. When he died in 1923, two sons, H. Chapin Jackson and W. Montgomery Jackson, disposed of their father's Grolier Society and other publishing interests and concentrated on expanding the South American business. In the ensuing years their company, W. M. Jackson, Inc., grew to a two-thousand-employee, $10 million firm, with retail stores and publishing plants in eleven countries, mainly throughout South America, with products ranging from encyclopaedias to children's books in Spanish and Portuguese.)

5

Hooper made this important move with confidence that his future was bright, that profits from his many enterprises would more than make up the payments to his former associate. "I have a dozen other ideas brewing," he told Chisholm, "and they'll all make money for us." Hooper, enjoying the life of an affluent British squire, lived in Dunstable with his wife and four sons on a vast country estate which he called Cheverels. The home was staffed by many servants, and there were two Mercedes automobiles and two chauffeurs. On the grounds of the property were five gardens, with a gardener for each. Hooper frequently took time off from work and legal troubles to go hunting in Alpine forests, to charter a vessel on which to take his family for a trip in the Norwegian fiords, or to motor through France and Italy in the newest model automobile. He was no longer the lithe fellow who had so startled England with his campaign for the *Times* reprint of the ninth edition. In a little more than a decade, he had grown heavy and paunchy. His once slick mustache drooped carelessly, his hair was patched with gray, and pince-nez spectacles covered his bright eyes. But he was happy that his troubles with Jackson seemed over. Sales of the eleventh edition not only in England and the United States but in Australia, Japan, India, and other countries were high; the prospects for paying off debts, even with the costs of legal fees and the settlement with Jackson, seemed favorable; the chances for expansion of new ideas seemed good.

But this optimistic outlook suddenly dimmed with the outbreak of war in Europe in July, 1914. Sales began to drop sharply. The system of collections from purchasers shuddered, shook, and virtually collapsed. The idea of a children's encyclopaedia was abandoned; plans for further biennial supplements were forgotten. The staff at the London office was reduced to a few loyal but dejected workers. By the time the "Lusitania" was sunk, Hooper was ready to shut down the London office and return to the United States with his family. Characteristically, after closing his country and town houses, he cabled to Germany's ambassador in the United States, Count Johann Heinrich von Bernstorff, whom he had grown to know in connection with acquiring certain German copyrights for the *Encyclopaedia Britannica*. Informing Bernstorff that he and his family were sailing on a Dutch ship, Hooper demanded that all German submarines be advised of this and accordingly desist from making any torpedo attack. As he said his farewells to Chisholm and Mrs. Courtney, he promised to work diligently in behalf of influencing American opinion in favor of the Allies. As for his own future, he grinned and told Mrs. Courtney, "Don't worry. I can't be downhearted for long, even if you turn all the lights down on me.

16

Hooper's Last Efforts

Horace Hooper's return to the United States—he and his family settled in a large house in Morristown, New Jersey—coincided with a decisive phase of a project he had started when sales of the Cambridge edition of the *Encyclopaedia Britannica* slipped at the outbreak of the war.

To an editorial conference one day in 1914 Franklin Hooper had brought a photograph of a page from the encyclopaedia. Horace scanned it, exclaiming over the clarity of reproduction in the photograph half the size of the original page. "It's beautiful!" he cried. "Why can't we bring out an edition that's smaller in size page by page and sell it cheaper—sell it to people who can't afford our big one?"

On investigation, Hooper learned that such an edition could be produced at less than half the cost of the larger one. Moreover, he grew enthusiastic about the possibility of spreading the name and fame of the *Encyclopaedia Britannica* into sectors of population presumably unaware of it. He found a sales and distribution medium in the company owned by his friend and frequent golfing partner, Julius H. Rosenwald, the Chicago millionaire and philanthropist. Rosenwald's firm was the huge mail-order house of Sears, Roebuck and Company, with no less than five million customers.

Hooper proposed to Rosenwald and his vice-president, Albert Loeb, that, for a percentage of profits, the big firm should sell the photographed set through its catalogues and handle billing, credit, and collections. "This will give Sears a chance to be associated with one of the greatest trade names in history, the *Encyclopaedia Britannica*," said Hooper, "and we'll put it out at a cost that will appeal to your customers." So persuasive was Hooper that he convinced both Rosenwald and Loeb that instalment sales of the work, which Hooper proposed to call the *Handy Volume Encyclopaedia Britannica*, could be made profitable for them.

One of Hooper's aides, James F. Patton, a Canadian, was installed in the Sears, Roebuck and Company offices in Chicago to work out the sales plan, and R. R. Donnelley and Sons was commissioned to produce the cheaper set. The project was well under way by the time Hooper returned to the United States. The Donnelley firm was busy with a first printing of 50,000 copies, with twenty-two presses needed to handle the text alone. Hooper promptly made himself available for interviews, informing reporters, "I honestly believe that any young man who takes this set of books and studies it regularly and conscientiously will get from it a better education than he can obtain at the average university. And now it has been put—or will soon be put—at the disposal of any young man who is willing to make a slight effort to obtain it." He affirmed and reaffirmed that any medium that spread knowledge was important above all necessities of life. "I am of the belief," he told reporters, "that it is immoral for valuable information to be shut off away from people. Throughout the years this great storehouse of information, this *Encyclopaedia Britannica*, has existed, but the people who needed it most could not partake of its benefits. I believe that knowledge should be diffused. And this is the idea back of the 'Handy Volume' edition of the *Encyclopaedia Britannica*—the idea that we have no right to keep, by means of high prices, this great university away from the ambitious young men and women who should be its students." Sales of the *Handy Volume* would easily reach a million, Hooper estimated.

But before the sets were completed and advertising for them initiated, financial reorganization was imperative. There had been many drains on the company's working capital since publication of the eleventh edition a few years earlier: payments to Jackson in settlement of the vexing legal conflict, extensive costs of the litigation itself, the sudden halt in instalment payments by many thousands of purchasers in Great Britain with the onset of the war, and continued expenses. Hooper was, moreover, beset by debts to British and American banks which had made loans to him earlier, and he was heavily committed to printers and paper-suppliers for the *Handy Volume*. In need of more funds, he turned to his attorney, Samuel Untermyer, and Untermyer, aware of profits to be made not only from the sale of the *Handy Volume* but of other possible editions to come, drew up a plan of adjustment. In September, 1915, the Illinois firm was disbanded and a new one organized under the laws of New York as the Encyclopaedia Britannica Corporation, with 7,000 shares of preferred stock at $100 with an 8 per cent interest rate, and 25,000 shares, at $100 each, of common stock. Untermyer and several associates, including his son, Irwin, bought the 7,000 shares at $90 each, thereby yielding $630,000 in fresh capital for Hooper's new enterprise. Hooper and various of his associates held most of the common stock.

Thus bolstered, Hooper proceeded with the *Handy Volume* sale. Each book was an exact reproduction of its Cambridge edition counterpart, except for narrower margins and smaller type. Whereas the original books measured 8¾ by 11¾ inches, the present ones were 6½ by 8½ inches. The most attractive feature, well stressed in the advertisements prepared by N. W. Ayer, was the price of only fifty-five dollars, with low monthly instalments after an initial payment of only one dollar.

2

Actually, Hooper seemed to be in direct competition with himself, for sales crews under the direction of his brother-in-law, William J. Cox, were also at work selling the more expensive edition. All this appeared to be a replica of the "cheap book" technique developed years before by Hooper's Chicago mentor, James Clarke, but Hooper insisted that only through such methods could the whole company be made solvent. This scheme illustrated how reluctant Hooper was to stay within the framework of a sound business, to devote himself to making it strong and financially stable, and how eager he was for new promotions and new devices. Such thinking reflected the quirk in Hooper's character as a businessman. It had provoked the expensive clashes with his more conservative associate, Jackson. It had propelled him toward catastrophe several times. It might, even now, cause new calamities.

Yet the Hooper luck held—for a time. From October, 1915, until mid-1916, 55,000 sets of the *Handy Volume* were ordered, many of them in rural districts where no salesman or book advertisement ever had penetrated. And the sales of the major set suffered no harm. Cox's crew in New York offered a good example of the kind of ingenuity employed by encyclopaedia salesmen of that era, for this group, under the direction of Cox's young son, Warren, was unusually successful in producing orders.

Before his affiliation with the *Encyclopaedia Britannica*, Warren Cox, who had theatrical yearnings, had worked with the Washington Square players. Put in charge by his father of seventy-five salesmen throughout New York, Pennsylvania, and New Jersey—the first time salesmen were extensively used—Cox prepared a sales talk that actually was a sales act, with lines to be memorized and rarely altered. Each prospective salesman was put through a three-week training course. Besides the usual elements of salesmanship, Cox taught a few extra pointers. One device was for the salesman to ask, very casually, if the customer were interested in sheep or ships or any other subject and, often before the prospect could even reply, quickly to look up one of these subjects in the index volume. "Why, what d'you know?" the salesman would blurt out. "Why, there are pages and pages on this!" Then a quick shift to the specific volume and the precise pages and an invitation to the customer to survey the great mass of material.

An especially successful salesman was Charles Wollken, a former newspaper reporter who specialized in selling to office managers. An imposing, articulate man, Wollken strode past astonished secretaries into inner offices, confronting amazed executives with, "Sir, I am making a survey for a fact-gathering organization. Can you tell me who Heraclitus was?" Rarely was the answer anything but, "I don't know." Thereupon Wollken produced charts, pictures, and, of course, copies of *Encyclopaedia Britannica* volumes, informed the prospect where he could learn all about Heraclitus, then proceeded with a sales talk. Brash as this method may have seemed, Wollken's record showed sales

—or, at least, down payments—in two out of every three attempts. He prided himself on the speed of his sales approach; he rarely spent more than half an hour on a single prospect.

There were salesmen like Edward Noonan, who operated only in towns near colleges. He always made arrangements with the local druggist to work behind his soda fountain where, at opportune moments, he inveigled students and professors alike into discussions of the *Encyclopaedia Britannica*. Before long, as records of the period vividly show, Noonan managed to get a down payment; each druggist for whom he worked shared in Noonan's commissions.

Another star salesman was Elias Manchester Boddy, who presented himself to Cox one cold morning after arriving in a freight car from the West Coast. Hungry and in need of a shave, Boddy asked for a job. Cox told him, "I'll give you money for a shave and something to eat, and I'll hire you if you can make a sale within the hour." In far less than the specified time, Boddy was back with a down payment from the owner of the cigar and newspaper stand in the building at 342 Madison Avenue that housed the offices of the *Encyclopaedia Britannica*.

Boddy was assigned to a district where sales were rare—the Bowery. Years later, after a career as a newspaper publisher in California, Boddy recalled his experiences there: "I found that even the stinkiest old flat in the heart of the Bowery often housed fine families of immigrants. I would work each day until I found a family with teen-age youngsters who could speak English. I would make a date to come back when Papa and the working brothers and sisters were home after supper, and then I made a large chart showing how the whole family could get a college education from a set of the *Encyclopaedia Britannica*. I even held classes for those who bought." Boddy established a vastly satisfactory record by this technique, often earning as much as $250 a week in commissions.

Boddy achieved another sales coup by convincing the top officials in the New York police and fire departments that the *Encyclopaedia Britannica* was indispensable to the efficiency of their uniformed men. With permission of the authorities, Boddy visited one fire station and one police station after another, striking up conversations with the men on controversial subjects, then springing on them the information that the final answers were all to be found in the latest edition of the *Encyclopaedia Britannica*. Ultimately, about 90 per cent of the firehouses and police stations visited by Boddy were equipped with sets, for which the men paid by dropping a dime or a quarter at least once each week into a cigar box alongside the *Encyclopaedia Britannica* bookcase.

3

Critical reaction to the *Handy Volume* was skimpy but quite harsh in at least one quarter. Although in the *Outlook* Henry Hoyt Moore hailed it as "a handsome, impressive and remarkably compact set of books," another critic in the outspoken *Reedy's Mirror* in St. Louis hammered away heavily. The magazine itself had already called stern attention to the sale of the *Handy Volume* as "something of a swindle," because its price was 46 per cent below that of the original edition, and had accused Hooper of perpetrating "the same old slippery trick." Then, in a series of articles in the same magazine, Willard Huntington Wright, a journalistic dilettante, a writer on art, philosophy, and aesthetics, and a confirmed iconoclast, made a vigorous attack upon the eleventh edition of the *Encyclopaedia Britannica* for being "bourgeois, evangelical, chauvinistic, distorted and unfair." He was infuriated because some British writers, artists, and musicians received more space than some Americans, Germans, and Russians. He listed two hundred names he considered worthy of inclusion that were omitted. The edition, he wrote, was "a narrow, parochial, opinionated work of dubious scholarship and striking unreliability," characterized by "misstatements, inexcusable omissions, rabid and patriotic prejudices, personal animosities, blatant errors of fact, scholastic ignorance, gross neglect of non-British culture, an astounding egotism, and an undisguised contempt for American progress." Behind all this Wright spied a plot to mislead the English-speaking public as to the achievements of Americans.

When these accusations were collected and printed under the title of *Misinforming a Nation* early in 1917, Wright himself was severely attacked for misleading statements, half-truths, and untruths. "The confusion of thought, the mixed metaphor, the affectation of needless and banal French words, and the spiteful and shallow temper . . . pervade the book," stated the *New York Times*. In the *New Republic*, Francis Hackett remarked that in a work of 30,000 pages it was inevitable that some defects and deficiencies would appear, then added, "It is unfortunate for Mr. Wright's remorseless purpose that he has proceeded in an unscientific spirit and given so little objective justification of his criticism. What he has to say is said in a nasty spirit." In the very intellectual *Dial*, Henry Blake Fuller conceded to Wright the privilege of using a critical pickax on "this extensive, big-bulking edifice" but suggested he would find it more entertaining and enlightening to examine virtually any other major encyclopaedia. Wright, complained Fuller, "gets to be rather wearying and irritating. One is irked by his disproportionate preoccupation with the arts. . . . He clangs; he clanks."

4

Despite adverse comment and the seeming competition between the original edition and the *Handy Volume,* sales of the less expensive set continued to thrive. Wages in the United States were high, unemployment low. Hooper's second campaign for the *Handy Volume,* now selling for sixty-five dollars, started strongly in the autumn of 1916 and improved month by month.

But with America's entry into the world conflict in 1917, President Wilson asked that instalment buying be curtailed so as to maintain the nation's economic stability. Among the first to be affected by this presidential directive were those who sold subscription books and sets on time payments. Orders for the *Handy Volume* dropped drastically. Worse yet, so did the payments. The terms for the full-sized edition went as low as five dollars down with the balance in fifty-four payments, plus a free copy of the one-volume *Century Dictionary* as an added inducement. But all was to no avail. Unsold sets remained in storage, and collections on sets sold trickled in very slowly or not at all.

The banks which formerly had come to Hooper's aid in times of distress now refused to renew their loans because of uncertain, warborn financial conditions. Soon a creditors' committee was organized under the direction of Percy Johnston of the Chemical National Bank, and a program was mapped in which all new business was halted and all efforts were concentrated on collecting payments due the company and on paying debts. In June, 1918, all officers of the company except Horace Hooper resigned, and his salary was cut from $3,500 to $1,800 a month. The creditors' committee named Charles F. Ross, nominated by the Chemical National Bank, president; he retained Charles Whinery as the man best qualified to help untangle the firm's affairs. Together, they began calling back all sets on which customers had defaulted, and these now descended on the Sears, Roebuck plant in Chicago by the thousands. In addition, scores of other customers discontinued payments and shipped their sets back to the company.

To raise needed cash, Hooper organized a sale of many of the antiques he and his wife had purchased during their years abroad. Mrs. Hooper was an especially astute collector, and the auction, open only to major antique dealers from all sections of the country, netted $200,-000. To effect savings, the family moved to a smaller house in Bedford Hills, Massachusetts. Although Hooper had little to do with the operations of the *Encyclopaedia Britannica* all through 1918 while the Whinery-Ross team ran the firm, he kept a watchful eye on its affairs and knew of the progress being made in paying the greater part of his companies' debts. Anticipating the time when the affairs of the *Encyclopaedia Britannica* might be turned back to him, he contemplated, as often before in dire situations, a plan to eliminate future crises—this time, however, a plan that would yield him no profit but would insure the existence and integrity of his beloved *Encyclopaedia Britannica.*

5

In March, 1919, Hooper sailed for England to seek help in carrying out his new idea. At the Savile Club in London he outlined the details to W. Alison Phillips, Chisholm's assistant in preparing the eleventh edition and, since its publication, professor of modern history at the University of Dublin.

"I think a fund should be raised to buy the *Britannica* and establish it as a public institution under joint control of, say, the Royal Society and the British Academy," suggested Hooper. "In that way the prestige of the book will be enormously increased for all time. And the sale all over the world will bring big profits, as much maybe as a million pounds. And that money could be used for endowing scientific or some other kind of research. What do you think—and will you help me?"

As he had done nearly a decade earlier, when Hooper, confronted with another financial crisis, had proposed an alignment with a major university and had sought his aid in securing the imprimatur of Cambridge, Phillips agreed to serve as an emissary. Like Hooper, Phillips believed that if the *Encyclopaedia Britannica* were firmly endowed, thereby avoiding periodic financial distress, it could be a forceful medium for bringing together learned men of many countries and for creating greater intellectual co-operation and better understanding among nations.

From Sir Frederic Kenyon, president of the British Academy, he elicited approval of the general program and a promise to present it favorably to his group. The head of the Royal Society, Sir Joseph Thompson, was less enthusiastic, but he made it clear to Phillips that his objections were inspired not by the nature of the plan but by the unsuitability of the mathematical and physical articles in the volumes for educational purposes. Yet he, too, agreed to consider the idea in greater detail.

While these negotiations progressed, the faintly smoldering issue that had developed over Hooper's contract with Cambridge University for publication of the eleventh edition was publicly revived. Although for all practical purposes the contract and the actual affiliation had ended four years earlier—with payment, incidentally, to the university of some £16,000 as its share of royalties—the university's senate, on May 7, issued a resolution condemning the advertising still being used in various parts of the world as "unworthy of the dignity of the University."

This development hampered Phillips, although he was able to bring together Hooper, Sir Frederic, and others of the British Academy amenable to his plan. In a meeting a month after the public announcement from Cambridge, Hooper received assurances from this group that his idea would win favor in a final consideration. Hooper also met with the leaders of the Royal Society and was asked to draw up a specifically detailed memorandum for their consideration. When this was done by Phillips early the following October, the result was as had been anticipated: the members of the British Academy voted for it, the Royal Society voted against it. This, of course, was fatal to the grand scheme. Although the Royal Society declined to make public its reasons for the rejection, it was generally known that its members still were haunted by the memory of the waspish criticism a minority of academicians had leveled against the Cambridge Syndics when they affiliated with Hooper. The tone and scope of advertising of all products all over England had broadened since the first of the eleventh edition campaigns, so that the public now was inured to methods far more lurid and blatant than Hooper's. "But the Royal Society, an ancient and dignified body," wrote Phillips later, "may perhaps be forgiven if it shrank from the prospect of being exposed to the fire of contumelious criticism which had been so recently directed against the University of Cambridge. It was, however, a pity."

6

Hooper wasted little time lamenting the adverse decision emanating from the community of scholars and educators. He turned once more to the community of businessmen, specifically to Julius Rosenwald.

Partly because he was a good friend to Hooper and partly because he was convinced that profits could be derived from the sale of the *Encyclopaedia Britannica,* Rosenwald came to Hooper's aid. On February 24, 1920, Sears, Roebuck and Company purchased the *Encyclopaedia Britannica's* copyrights, plates, unsold volumes, and assorted merchandise for $1,330,000, retaining Hooper as publisher. Heartened, Hooper proposed that a three-volume supplement to the eleventh edition be prepared, and to this Rosenwald assented. A month after the purchase he signed a contract with Hooper by which the enterprising bookman was advanced $325,000 to prepare the supplement not later than December, 1922.

With the enthusiasm that had characterized all his previous efforts, Hooper swept into the new job. Once more he recruited Hugh Chisholm as editor. Since publication of the 1913 yearbook, Chisholm had been on the staff of the *Times,* not as editor-in-chief as he had once anticipated, but in various subsidiary editorial posts, in each of which he had served with distinction. But when Hooper, in a chance meeting with Chisholm at New York's Lotus Club, offered him the editorship of the supplement, Chisholm accepted and sailed for England to assemble a staff. Once again, he hired Mrs. Courtney as his first assistant, and the High Holborn offices were reopened, cleaned, dusted, and made ready.

The theme of the volumes, Hooper wrote Mrs. Courtney, must be "The Wonderful Decade." "These volumes ought to be made up so that the history of the War dominates the whole book. I am hoping that it will be made so that people will want to buy it just for its history of the War, whether they own the Britannica or not. . . . We cannot afford, of course, to ignore men like Lloyd George, President Wilson and many others, but men who are on the border line, and really ought to have an article and are not very important, we can well afford to miss without it bothering us! The same remarks apply to a great many other subjects, but we cannot get the military side or the historical side too well done. Literature, for instance, is one of the subjects that can be passed over with great ease and not do much harm, and it is quite within a possibility that this is true of art. Of course, you understand, that I do not mean that these articles should be ignored, but I mean that a great deal of space should not be given to them."

Hooper obviously intended to take a more active editorial interest in the supplement than he had in any of its predecessors. He insisted that Chisholm make an earnest effort to recruit as contributors men who had played vital roles in the recent war, both in friendly and in enemy nations. George Saunders, formerly correspondent for the *Times* in Berlin, aided in enlisting German contributors and supervised translation of their writings. Contributors of repute included the president of the new republic of Czechoslovakia, Thomas Masaryk; Professor Henri Pirenne, rector of the University of Ghent in Belgium; Professor L. V. Birck of Copenhagen; H. N. Bronmer of the Netherlands legation in London; Baron Alstromer, the Swedish chargé d'affaires in London; and Erik Colbran, an official of the League of Nations.

Hooper left the United States for London in April, 1921, to be closer to the editorial operation; the final volumes were still to be printed by the Donnelley firm in Chicago. He worked long hours in the High Holborn office he now shared with Chisholm; the summer was a dry, hot one, and he sat at his roll-top desk in his shirtsleeves, poring over piles of proofs, occasionally consulting with Chisholm, often calling out in his high-pitched voice for a messenger or an editorial assistant.

In that year he brought over his eldest son, Horace, Jr., and put him to work around the office. Young Hooper, a freshman at Williams College, had been summoned by his father two days before his final examinations. He was given a small salary and an allowance of two pounds a week for clipping coupons in the circulation department and writing preliminary advertisements under the direction of the re-enlisted Henry Haxton. Later young Hooper went out on the road with sales crews, invading such cities as Manchester, Leeds, Birmingham, and Edinburgh. In each he paid for advertisements in the largest newspapers and in exchange was permitted to set up a display and desk in the lobby of the newspaper office. There he sat, ready to answer difficult questions asked him by merely flipping the index of the eleventh edition and finding the proper section in the proper volume. Everywhere but in Edinburgh the instalment plan was considered a boon; in that city the thrifty customers generally scorned the "easy payments" and offered full cash.

Another member of Horace Hooper's family also joined him—his brother-in-law, William J. Cox, who, since suspension of business in the dreary months of 1918, had prospered as the vice-president of a plumbing supply firm. Cox was reluctant to leave the certainties of pipes and faucets for the uncertainties of the unpredictable encyclopaedia business, but Hooper made him an offer of $10,000 a year to become American sales manager, with a commission practically guaranteed to yield another $10,000 or $15,000. Besides, he was assured that he need stay with the *Encyclopaedia Britannica* only six months. "I just want you to help get things going," Hooper told him, "and then you can go back."

But Cox was never to return to the plumbing supply company. Working long hours, eating irregularly, Hooper suffered a mild heart attack late in 1921. Harassed by myriad details, he had grown increasingly fretful with his subordinates, even snapping at his son. Although he tried to relax from the strain of preparing the supplement by playing bridge almost every night in his suite at Claridge's, he grew tense and harried. When the attack came, he was advised by his physicians to shift some of his responsibilities and duties; so Cox was named president of the company. But Hooper, as might be expected, retained active direction even when he was compelled to rest a few hours each day in his rooms.

Orders for the supplement came in rapidly. Sixty-five thousand copies of this so-called twelfth edition, comprising the three new volumes plus the eleventh edition, were to be sold in the next four years. But even his curtailed activities proved too arduous for Hooper. In March, 1922, after the first two volumes had been issued and commendably received, he was stricken again and ordered back to New York. From his hospital bed, especially when he appeared to be improving, he retained his interest in the project, cabling his congratulations when the third and final volume was issued on May 6, then writing to Chisholm and Mrs. Courtney about the possibility of publishing reading guides for use with the edition. Released from the hospital with a warning from his doctors to rest for a good part of each day, he still mapped out other projects. He grew steadily worse, and on June 13 came another seizure, this one fatal.

7

There were tributes and estimates. Some called him a genius, others marveled at the combination in him of hard businessman and idealist.

In retrospect, Hooper's flair for sales showmanship and promotional devices was his strongest point. As his career proved, he shied away, as Walter Jackson rarely did, from carrying on the day-to-day duties essential to the operation of a business enterprise. His interest in the diffusion of education verged on the fanatic. To some of his critics, he appeared as "a ranker who loved to be accepted as a gentleman." But this, even if true, was a small part of his total personality. Essentially Horace Hooper was a master salesman and a dazzling innovator, passionately devoted to the important product he had to sell, always certain that he could create in a vast public the desire for that product, convinced to the end that as a medium of popular education his *Encyclopaedia Britannica* was without a peer. He recognized, in his time, the popular thirst for knowledge, and he devised a means of satisfying that thirst—and of stimulating it further.

In its editorial on his death, the *New York Times* offered an apt evaluation: "In the view of the public, his success lay in the originality, boldness and brilliance of his operations. But that was merely the surface. The deeper source was his faith in the intelligence and the ambition of a great mass of citizens. Many professional educators of note have done less than he toward popular enlightenment."

Part Three

Part Three

17

Prelude to 1929

For most of the decade after Horace Hooper's death, the affairs of the *Encyclopaedia Britannica* were directed by William J. Cox, whose on-and-off service had been of considerable value ever since 1901 when Hooper had first summoned him to London. Unlike Hooper in personality or temperament, Cox, a lean and lithe man, was taciturn and reserved. He never smoked, and no underling ever dared approach him with cigarette or cigar in hand. Like Hooper, Cox had little formal education, but as a young salesman in his pre-encyclopaedia days he had obtained this high-school diploma by attending special classes at Columbia University and had gone on to take college courses in law, civics, and economics. An avid reader, he, too, had great respect for writers and scholars. That he was an able sales executive had been shown by his direction of the campaign for the

Handy Volume. Whether his ideas and methods could sustain and nourish the company and the encyclopaedia itself now remained to be seen.

One of Cox's first acts was to exhort Rosenwald to sell back the *Encyclopaedia Britannica* to him and Mrs. Hooper, to whom Horace Hooper had left his shares of stock in the encyclopaedia company besides $250,000 in life insurance. Rosenwald was easily persuaded; in the wake of the postwar depression, he had already taken severe action in slashing expenses and in cutting down on ownership of factories and other subsidiaries. In August, 1923, for the comparatively small sum of $265,000, ownership of the encyclopaedia reverted to Cox and Mrs. Hooper. The ledgers of Sears, Roebuck showed that in the venture since 1920 the mail-order concern had sustained losses of $1,800,000.

Now Cox—president of the newly formed company at $25,000 a year—withdrew the *Handy Volume* from the market and issued a "New Form Edition." It combined two volumes of the Cambridge edition into one, with narrower page margins, and, priced at only $100, amassed a respectable sale of some twenty-five thousand in the United States and Great Britain in the next two years. In 1924, under Cox's stimulus, there was published a two-volume collection of articles by eighty journalists, statesmen, military leaders, and various world figures, all reputed authorities in their respective fields. *These Eventful Years,* Cox called it, and its subtitle read "The Twentieth Century in the Making as Told by Many of Its Makers." Although there actually was little new or vital in this compendium, its interest historically —and for future generations of encyclopaedists—lay in the attempts to secure contributions from those importuned to write for it and, frequently, in what they had to say for themselves.

2

George Bernard Shaw was one such prospect. He was asked by Franklin Hooper, whom Cox appointed to edit the volumes, to write on "Communism in Russia" at what Hooper described as "the maximum *Britannica* rate." Shaw replied with mock modesty that such an assignment was quite beyond his abilities. "I do not know what has happened in Russia," he wrote, "and cannot find out. Even if I were to visit Russia, as I have been invited to do, I should come back not much wiser than I went as to the economic moral of the experiment. Besides, the experiment is not yet consummated. I have not the least notion of what 'the maximum Britannica rate' comes to in figures; but situated as I am at present, with a heavy budget of permanently remunerative work waiting to be completed, I do not believe that anything I could do for you would be worth what it would cost you to induce me to do it. None the less, I am much obliged to you for the invitation to contribute, and I should do the particular job you propose for its own sake if I were qualified to do it justice."

Also unable to accept Hooper's invitation, but for different reasons, was the great Hindu nationalist leader, Mohandas K. Gandhi. In reply to a letter requesting an article on his passive resistance movement came an official note from the Home Department, Bombay Castle, India, informing Hooper that prisoners were permitted to write and receive only one letter each month, limited strictly to private matters, and that it was "not possible, therefore, to pass on your letter to prisoner M. K. Gandhi." The gentle militant was then serving a term for "conspiring to overthrow the government," a sentence soon to be commuted after an emergency operation for appendicitis.

Several experts agreed to contribute but later declined because of their enmity toward other contributors. Émile Bourgeois, the French historian, was on a lecture tour in America when Hooper asked him to write the chapter on modern French history. He was on the point of assenting when, almost as an afterthought, he asked, "Who are some of the others who will contribute?" Hooper told him, "Well, Signor Nitti, the former premier of Italy, is one, and . . ." Bourgeois yelled, "Nitti!?! Pah!" Then Hooper mentioned the name of James Louis Garvin, the editor of the *London Observer*. Bourgeois shouted, "Garvin! Garvin!! I will not contribute! I cannot be in the same book with Monsieur Garvin. He said that France was imperialistic!" Despite his refusal, Bourgeois calmed down long enough to recommend as his replacement Albert Thomas, who had held half a dozen jobs in the French government.

Several contributors expressed surprise when they learned they would be paid. "I am keeping the check," wrote Dr. James Brown Scott, the expert on international law, "although I must say that I did not expect anything except a copy of the volume in which the article appeared. . . . You are setting a very pleasant but dangerous precedent. However, do not let it worry you, as it will not be held against you." Two other contributors returned their checks: Ambassador M. Hanihara for his article on "Japan" and Dr. Wellington Koo for his on "China." "I do not wish it to appear," explained Hanihara, "that I have written for a pecuniary consideration, but I am quite satisfied with your assurance that it has, in some measure, helped to complete the proposed publication."

A number of contributors—notably the Germans—made various stipulations before assenting. Admiral Alfred von Tirpitz, the "German sea dog," agreed to write on the German navy only on condition that *These Eventful Years* contain no vilification of his country; in his reply, Hooper indicated his willingness to comply, but added, "I must be the judge of what constitutes vilification of Germany." General Erich von Ludendorff, the erratic chief-of-staff of the wartime German army, insisted that all letters be written to him in German, although he was capable of reading and corresponding in half a dozen languages, including English. Assigned to furnish a general article on the German army, Von Ludendorff wrote instead on "Germany Never Defeated," in which he expounded the thesis that his country's loss was due, not to America's entry into the war, but to "the damnable precept of German social democracy." Another kind of German was the antimilitaristic Maximilian Harden, twice imprisoned under the German imperial regime. Hooper sent half a dozen letters before he finally tracked down Harden and secured his agreement to write on "Germany's Place in the Sun." Evidently fearful of assassination, Harden asked that no extracts from his chapter be published separately. "I am obliged to add to this remark because a misrepresentation could result by this," he explained, "and in the strange conditions of our life, an earnest danger would result! My bitter experience in these affairs teaches me to be careful."

From Sigmund Freud, Hooper obtained an article on his methods of psychoanalysis. From Bertrand Russell came an incisive discussion of government by propaganda. The central figures in the Battle of Jutland, Admiral John Jellicoe and Admiral Reinhard Scheer, described that decisive naval encounter. John Foster Dulles, then counsel to the American Peace Commission, wrote on reparations; Bernard Baruch, on the Allied debts; H. G. Wells made "A Forecast of the World's Affairs." Half a dozen women were among the contributors, most notably Mme Marie Curie, who wrote about radium, and Lady Rhondda, an active British feminist. Not only did Lady Rhondda engage in frequent transatlantic arguments with Hooper about changes in her article on the subject she knew best, but she held back the proofs when they appeared with the working title of "The Triumph of Women." Her sex, she insisted, had not yet obtained a complete triumph and any article bearing her name and that title would mislead scores of ladies who should be busy at the feminist ramparts. Not until Hooper agreed to permit her to alter the title did she return the corrected proofs; the heading then read, "The Political Awakening of Women."

3

This firm reliance on internationally recognized specialists in contemporary matters as well as timeless subjects prevailed through the thirteenth edition, which consisted of the basic eleventh edition plus three volumes to replace those issued in the last months of Horace Hooper's life. In addition to the continued concentration on such contributors, this edition included more articles relating to the United States and the Western Hemisphere.

Cox began preparations for the thirteenth edition in 1925, selecting as editor James Louis Garvin, the Irish-born journalist whose writings in the *London Observer* intrigued him. Garvin, then fifty-seven, had been a leading editorialist for the *Newcastle Chronicle* at twenty-three, and then for over a decade had written brilliantly on literature, politics, and foreign affairs for the *Fortnightly Review*. Since 1907 he had been editor of Lord Northcliffe's *Observer*, and that publisher considered him one of the world's greatest living journalists. Garvin had worked miracles with Northcliffe's newspaper, a moribund weekly journal when he assumed editorship. By making it a blend of newspaper and magazine, devoting as much space to literature, music, art and drama as to news and opinion, he managed, in a few years, to increase its circulation tenfold to a quarter of a million copies. Few British journalists wrote about America with such comprehensive and sympathetic understanding, and during the war Garvin had been one of the ablest interpreters of the American point of view to Great Britain.

It was Garvin's pro-American attitude that persuaded Cox to offer him the editorship at $10,000 a year. In a letter praising his *Observer* articles and asking him to lunch at the Reform Club in London, Cox wrote, "You are the one friend of America I have met in high British circles." As editor, Garvin was assured absolute authority. "Nothing will go in that you say won't go in," promised Cox.

So important was the appointment of Garvin considered in the United States that the *New York Times* devoted a full column to the announcement under the by-line of its London correspondent, T. R.

Ybarra. An editorial followed in which Americans were advised that they had "the best of reasons" for taking an interest in Garvin's selection. "Naturally," stated the editorial, "the exuberance of his pen and the confidence of his prophecies will have to be somewhat restrained when he passes from current journalism to the sober and enduring record of science and history. But there can be no question of his competence for the work he is now to undertake, whether on the score of intellectual ability, knowledge of who the experts are whom he must call upon, or executive aptitudes. Those who know him best are most sure that he will both command success and deserve it."

Garvin made his intentions explicit in a number of interviews. Not only would the encyclopaedia continue to be based on scholarship and learning, he said, but "the deliberate design is to restore international unity in these matters of intellectual co-operation, which was broken by war and has remained too long and too widely interrupted in peace." He hoped, too, that the new edition would be more cosmopolitan "to help to accumulate what may be called the common stock of civilization."

Because of his journalistic background, Garvin was expected by many observers to change the writing style of his contributors for easier reading. But when a reporter asked him, "Do you intend to jazz up the set?" Garvin grinned and replied, "Well, I've asked Albert Einstein to do the section on space and time." The *Brooklyn Eagle* commented, "Anyone who has tried to read Einstein will sigh with relief. There can be no danger that the new editor plans to make the EB light reading for light heads." With a newspaperman's eye for contemporary events, Garvin asked Leon Trotsky, then carrying on bitter ideological battles with his archfoe, Joseph Stalin, to write the biography of Lenin, the father of the Russian Revolution. Trotsky turned in the article, a reasonably accurate and unimpassioned one, and received $106 for it a few months before he was banished to Turkistan.

In the United States, where Franklin Hooper still served as American editor, a striking array of experts in varied fields was recruited. H. L. Mencken, Henry Seidel Canby, Robert Morss Lovett, Carl Van Doren, Louis Untermeyer, and W. E. B. DuBois divided among them the subject of "American Literature." The point of view in their articles, from Mencken's on the American language to Untermeyer's on the new poetry of Edgar Lee Masters, Vachel Lindsay, Edna St. Vincent Millay, and Edwin Arlington Robinson, was clearly liberal, stressing the spirited life of American literature and reflecting the modern flow of ideas. In other fields, there were articles by other well-known Americans: Henry Ford's on mass production, actually ghost-written for the auto magnate by Samuel Crowther; Harry Houdini's on conjuring; Andrew Mellon's on finance; Amos Alonzo Stagg's on football; Colonel E. M. House's on the Paris Peace Conference; Bernard Baruch's on war debts; and General Lincoln Andrews' on bootlegging and liquor smuggling. Contemplating all this, Bartlett Cormack, in the *Bookman,* wrote, "Hail, Columbia! The Great Authority has gone modern, and, significantly, American, with an enthusiasm and to an extent that must shiver the timbers of the Old Subscribers of both England and the United States who have used that encyclopaedia to assure themselves that whatever is true is dead, and sung, 'Rule, Britannica!' when any question of authority lurched up to disturb the Conservative Peace."

What that bitter critic Willard Huntington Wright now had to say, in view of his earlier charges of the encyclopaedia's anti-Americanism, was undetermined. Wright was busy in other fields. Under the pseudonym of S. S. Van Dine, he had become the author of a series of best-selling murder mysteries, occasionally contributing articles to magazines on the theme, "I Used to Be a Highbrow."

4

Like Cormack, C. K. Ogden, an especially astute critic, in a lengthy review in the *Saturday Review of Literature* expressed satisfaction with "a notable advance . . . in all that pertains to the American scene. . . . The gradual widening of the Britannica horizon is also evident in the effort to meet the needs of the average family as well as of the librarian and the specialist. Never, we feel, has such a comprehensive record of human endeavor been offered in so small a compass. . . . For, when all is said, these 5,000,000 words are a more worthy record of our time than anything that has hitherto been published." The liberal *Nation,* commending the edition, sarcastically commented on the joint dedication of the edition to President Calvin Coolidge and King George V: "This majestic panorama of the world's knowledge, this grand survey of the terrestrial globe from the Aaland Islands to the Zuyder Zee, this great cooperative effort of the patience and learning of our civilization is dedicated, humbly and 'by permission,' to a pair of amiable gentlemen neither majestic nor learned —George of England and Calvin of America. Not since the present

Prince of Wales assumed his presidency of the Royal Society has any such cosmic joke been solemnly perpetrated."

In a long and thoughtfully detailed analysis, an anonymous critic in the *New York Times* maintained that for all the trumpeting about a more readable style, a certain abstruse quality was still evident in many of the articles that made up the three new volumes. This was especially true of the scientific articles, the reviewer wrote, thereby emphasizing a perennial hazard of encyclopaedists. "And the trouble . . . has always been that on the one hand they tell the expert nothing except what he already ought to know, while on the other hand their terms are so technical that to one who is not an expert they tell little or nothing." Unlike previous critics, this one had a suggestion on how to overcome this defect. "Of this perplexity it is perhaps presumptuous to suggest a solution. But we are impressed by the success with which the similar situation is mastered by the authorities who deal with literature. They make no attempt to summarize the poems, the novels, the dramas and the other books which have been produced within the period under consideration, but are content to offer signposts for the guidance of the student who must himself consult the masterpieces, so indicated. We have thus not a photograph of the country to be traversed, but a map with the roads clearly marked. We cannot but think that the same method of reference applied to science might save a good deal of valuable space and yield what is really needed in an encyclopaedia. To summarize in a page or two the most recent developments of mathematics is, after all, a hopeless task. But it is not hopeless within a page or two for a great mathematician to give invaluable guidance, at once to authorities like himself and to students, as to where the latest developments are most responsibly stated."

Despite defects he deplored, the reviewer made certain in his full evaluation to note the encyclopaedia's good attributes. "These criticisms," he concluded, "are doubtless outspoken. It must be remembered always that the production of the Britannica is largely a labor of love and that it represents an immense sacrifice of time and energy on the part of world-wide comradeship of erudition. Criticism is intended, then, to be constructive. It is animated only by the belief that the Britannica, as it stands, represents a service to society the importance of which it is not easy to estimate. The book is one which should be available for every boy and girl of ability. It should be placed in the home, and, when placed, it should be used. The automobile, after all, carries you only a part of the way. Here is a vehicle which travels over all time and all space, an observation car whence you can survey the universe."

18

"A Monument of Learning"

Diligently, Cox read every word in the reviews of the thirteenth edition and sensed, quite accurately, that the times demanded strong editorial action. So he embarked on a major undertaking: preparation of a fourteenth edition. Its production ultimately would involve thirty-five hundred contributors, hundreds of office and editorial workers in New York, and scores of typographers, engravers, and printers in Chicago; its cost finally would amount to $2,500,000; it would contain great masses of new material, and its publication would, for that era, climax the growing trend in what would be described, approvingly or regretfully, as the "humanization" of the *Encyclopaedia Britannica.*

For this complex undertaking, Garvin was selected as editor-in-chief, Franklin Hooper as American editor. Besides close editorial associates in their respective offices, each had twenty-seven departmental advisers. Garvin's included Julian Huxley for biology and zoology, Dr. Abraham Wolf, professor of logic and scientific method at the University of London, for philosophy and psychology, and Captain B. H. Liddell Hart, military historian, for military affairs and aviation. Hooper's advisory board included John Dewey for philosophy, Roscoe Pound, dean of Harvard Law School, for law, and Dr. Isaiah Bowman, director of the American Geographical Society, for geography.

While these men and their associates drew up lists of potential contributors, Garvin and Hooper, by letter and by personal conference, discussed methods and format. "Constructing an encyclopaedia," Garvin noted, "is like building a battleship. One wants to have the heaviest armor in existence to keep out all torpedoes and shells. One wants to have the biggest guns in existence to sink all other ships, and one wants to have enough coal space to sail all around the world very fast. All of these wants cannot be fulfilled. Something has to be sacrificed." Such dedication to sacrifice had to prevail, especially when contributors who were requested to scale down their articles harangued and even threatened Garvin or Hooper. Both agreed that the distinctive style of the *Encyclopaedia Britannica* must be maintained, with a large number of headings and with articles of reasonable length. "*EB* must not become merely a dictionary," warned Garvin. He objected occasionally to the cutting up of long articles into too many divisions, although Cox, who took an active part in the preliminary preparation, insisted that such a practice would make it easier for readers who neglected the index. It was Cox's steadfast idea that the volumes be made usable for the greatest possible number. "Personally I can't understand," he wrote to Garvin, "why anyone should object to making a book for the *many* instead of a book for the *few*."

Financing such a project seemed a monumental task. Certainly not enough revenue could be derived from sales of previous editions or special publications, and Cox balked at negotiating bank loans. While the contributors were being selected and preliminary editorial preparations made, Cox sought to persuade the University of Chicago to take over the company and publish the forthcoming edition in conjunction with Cambridge University, if the British institution could be induced to renew its connections with the *Encyclopaedia Britannica*. Supported by a promise from Julius Rosenwald of a gift of $1,000,000 to the University of Chicago, Cox opened informal discussions with Max Mason, the university's president, and some of the trustees. But the plan fell through, primarily because a majority of the trustees, despite Rosenwald's proposals, expressed doubts that the amount was adequate for a new edition or that the university would be able to manage such a business competently. So, as he had done with Hooper, Rosenwald continued to help Cox. At Rosenwald's behest, Charles Kittle, then president of Sears, Roebuck and Company, agreed to purchase ten-year, 7 per cent, sinking fund gold debentures for $1,064,000, a sum Cox insisted would be more than enough to see the proposed new edition to completion. He was heartened, too, by Rosenwald's assurance, "Don't worry about money. Don't put a limit on cash. Get out the best encyclopaedia you can."

In April, 1927, Cox set September, 1929, as a final publication deadline, slyly—although inaccurately—warning his editors and staff members that, unless the work were ready by that time, R. R. Donnelley and Sons, the printers in Chicago, would fine the firm $1,000 a day for every day's delay. Once again he assured Garvin that he intended to keep away from the editorial phases of production and concentrate primarily on drawing up an extensive sales campaign. "I do hope," he wrote to Garvin, "that we will have an encyclopaedia that will be more popular in its appeal than the eleventh edition. You are free, of course, to do as you wish. But I think that all definitions should be in the simplest possible language and all processes described in a clear way and illustrated as far as possible—and in general more things should be expressed with pictures."

2

In London, editorial offices were established on Regent Street in the Imperial House—nicknamed the "Monkey House" as pressures mounted each month. Garvin was a talented journalist but not efficient as an editorial organizer, especially for so complex an undertaking. In all the time it took to prepare the edition, he appeared at the editorial headquarters on no more than a dozen occasions. He preferred to work at his home, Gregories—once occupied by Edmund Burke—in Beaconsfield, some twenty-five miles from London. To this house he summoned his editorial aides. The most prominent among them were two bright young newspaper writers, E. Ibbetson James, the managing editor, and Raymond W. Postgate, a departmental editor who, besides newspaper work, had written books on a variety of subjects, his most recent being *Murder, Piracy and Treason*. In the office as a managerial aide was Mrs. Margaret Dorothy Law, whose earlier experience working with high-powered personalities had been gained as an advertisement writer for Harry Gordon Selfridge, the Chicago merchant who had come to London with revolutionary ideas about retail salesmanship and, after a cool reception, had finally been brilliantly successful with his American-style department store on Oxford Street.

From Gregories, Garvin issued a multitude of instructions, messages, advice, warnings, and admonitions to his editors and subeditors. To Gregories were transmitted perplexing problems, controversies over space allotments, and requests for permission to reject articles. These missives were pasted into large ledger books, later comprising what came to be known in *Encyclopaedia Britannica* archives as "Garvin's Bible," a full record of methods and problems involved in creating an encyclopaedia and an instructive guide for future editors.

In "Garvin's Bible" was his admonition that in articles about companies no mention be made of profits or dividends; and since many such editorial contributions came from presidents of the firms themselves, this seemed a wise precaution for the sake of objective information. In an article about Swinburne, Garvin noted that the word "magnificent" ought to be omitted from what was otherwise an excellent analysis: "It is almost a supreme word—deserved by few, not by him, he is resplendent, a different thing." In larger matters he was equally careful, as in the article on H. G. Wells by Ellis Roberts; he ordered it scrapped because he thought it might offend Wells by its rather snobbish tone. (If he was aware of this order, Wells scarcely reciprocated, for when the edition was published, he was among its most ungenial critics, an attitude ascribed by mutual acquaintances to his animosity in political matters toward Garvin, whom Wells characterized as "a volcano erupting gruel.") Garvin was watchful, among other things, of the wording and tone of captions to appear beneath the work's many photographs. At one time he dispatched Postgate to New York to scrutinize all captions lest they smack of journalistic sensationalism. "To an educated mind," he wrote Postgate, "they often seem crude, sometimes not quite so literate as to English, and conveying notions like those of an old-fashioned elementary school. . . . These texts are singled out of the pictures and upon their prominence the eye falls. People might easily get the idea from this (before they had the time to go through the EB pages) that the whole work was on a low standard of writing and thinking, whereas it is on a *very high one."* From his store of varied facts about widely assorted subjects, Garvin was able to discourse as authoritatively with a subeditor about whether Burmese woodcarving was superior to Japanese woodcarving as about the precise personality quirks of a historical figure. Asked whether he approved a biography of William Congreve, the Restoration playwright, he replied, "Yes I do, very much, but knock out that utterly false touch about 'carpet slippers'—no mind was less soft, he was marble in style, love and money." When Franklin Hooper sent on a long article on "Etiquette," Garvin replied tartly, "In no case, unfortunately, can I accept any responsibility for the article. It would be parodied in *Punch*, caricatured right and left, make us all superbly ridiculous and knock down the reputation of the EB. It might well appear in a quite different kind of publication, for in itself it is not ill done; but it is quite impossible for it to appear in any kind of publication associated with my name. It must be omitted. I deeply regret to say this."

The inevitable and vexing problems of allotment of space were usually settled amicably, if after many exchanges of letters and cables. Nearly all contributors wrote more than their assigned number of words. Most accepted the order to do their own editing calmly enough, but occasionally a rebel protested. When Dr. Cloudesley Brereton, the British educator, was asked by Hooper to cut his article on "Schools and Curriculum," he stormed into the "Monkey House" and announced to all around him, "I shall fight to the last ditch any suggestion that the article be killed or a single word deleted from it! If Mr. Hooper is not willing to take my declaration to this effect, I shall appeal to Mr. Garvin. If Mr. Garvin supports Mr. Hooper, I shall then air the whole matter in the public press, and if this fails, I shall print, at my own cost, a pamphlet stating the whole case and distribute it gratis!" Because there was nothing essentially erroneous in the article and the reduction in length had been suggested only to save space, a solution was achieved by cutting elsewhere in the edition, thereby avoiding the trouble threatened by the blustery pedagogue.

Another who caused difficulties was Lord Dunsany, the Irish poet and novelist. An expert chess-player, he had agreed to write on "Chess Problems." When his article arrived, it was in his highly individualistic style, but it had virtually none of the technical details about the subject itself; its opening line read, "The chess problem— which may be described as the critical position in a supposititious game of chess when one's antagonist announces, 'Mate!' in a given number of moves, no matter what defence you adopt—is to the game of chess what poetry is to conversation." Lord Dunsany not only refused to alter a single word, but he maintained a rigid attitude about his stylistic innovations. A subeditor appealed to Garvin for advice. "Tell Lord Dunsany," counseled Garvin, "that to our great regret our printers inform us that they are far past the word 'Chess' and have been compelled to leave a blank space and that completion is urgent. The only thing left for us is to arrange for a new and shorter article, though Lord Dunsany's honorarium will of course be remitted to him." He then advised the subeditor to call a local chess club and ask the secretary to write "a compact and unvarnished article of not more than 500 words."

Cox's son, Warren, who had turned to painting and lampshade manufacturing after his service in World War I, had been named art editor of the edition, and he proposed to Garvin that at least a third of all the space be devoted to art—including lampshade-making. But Garvin allotted a total of only 250 pages, adamantly insisting that within these prescribed limits the subject could be adequately treated. Yet when Hooper proposed that the general article on painting be eliminated in favor of concentration only on specific artists, Garvin cabled him: "Astounded procedure disastrously foolish destroying editorial responsibility and Britannica character. Even Chambers Encyclopaedia has good general article on painting as on music. Absolutely indispensable otherwise we would be hooted by every European country." On another artistic matter, Garvin was curtly stubborn. The Westminster Catholic Federation wrote demanding that Paul Gauguin's painting of the Madonna be omitted from the edition. Replied Garvin: "We wish to thank you very courteously for your letter. Our arrangements do not permit of change."

Beyond anticipated difficulties and normal complications, certain scandals threatened for a time to hold up production. In the spring of 1928 it appeared that some 100,000 words on economic matters might be delayed when Sir Leo Chiozza Money, the dapper and brilliant economist and member of Parliament serving as departmental editor for economics, was arrested with a Miss Irene Savidge on a charge of engaging in improper conduct in Hyde Park. Both were freed in court, but a parliamentary inquiry stirred the land when the police were accused of having used third-degree methods in forcing Miss Savidge to testify against Sir Leo. What concerned Garvin and his editors, however, was the delay this unsavory event caused in the production of the articles Sir Leo was scheduled to procure. Despite their qualms, the economist managed to turn in all his assigned material just as the other articles for the volume were being put on a steamer to the United States en route to the Donnelley plant in Chicago. Another unexpected mishap delayed the articles on the geography of art. The French expert to whom they had been assigned was surprised in his mistress' flat by her husband and was shot and seriously wounded; the police padlocked his apartment for several weeks during the course of the investigation.

3

In the United States, Franklin Hooper, a modest and somewhat prudish man, was shocked by these scandals; he was the kind of editor who frowned even on such a phrase as "pregnant with possibilities." But he was too occupied with his phase of the imposing task to spend much time bemoaning the morals of contributors. He and his closest aides, notably Walter Pitkin of Columbia University, kept to the job of obtaining needed articles, reading and inevitably scaling them down to required size, and sending them on to the printers.

In the months before publication, considerable interest was centered on celebrities who had been recruited to write for the edition, although such contributors constituted an infinitesimal percentage of the total list. Among the newcomers famed more for their exploits than for scholarship were Gene Tunney, the heavyweight champion, assigned to write on "Boxing"; Irene Castle, the ballroom dancer, on "Dancing"; Alfred E. Smith, on "New York"; Helen Wills, on "Tennis"; S. L. "Roxy" Rothafel, the theater magnate, on "Stage Lighting"; and Alfred Dunhill, on "Tobacco Pipes." Lon Chaney, the movies' "man of a thousand faces," and Otis Skinner, the American actor, collaborated on "Make-up," and Lillian Gish and other motion-picture players wrote on their profession. A *New York Times* editorial reacted to this "knock-out idea" with considerable skepticism. "The man who has made the most money in Wall Street," it stated, "would probably not be the best encyclopaedia authority on the stock market. The richest man in the world would perhaps not be the wisest choice for an article on finance. With all deference to the cleverness of the idea, the humble suggestion may be made that possibly there are better ways to collate an encyclopaedia."

Advance publicity—and there was much of it—about these personalities unfortunately obscured the importance of scores of authoritative contributors from the United States and elsewhere. Collaborators on the long article about the London Naval Conference, for example, were Henry L. Stimson, who had headed the American delegation, and J. Ramsay MacDonald, the British premier, who also contributed a special piece about the development of the Labour party. Elihu Root, former Secretary of State, wrote about the Permanent Court of International Justice; Roscoe Pound, about legal education in America; and Justice Charles Evans Hughes, about the Monroe Doctrine. In the ranks of contributors, too, were eighteen recipients of the Nobel Prize, including a trio of American scientists: Robert A. Millikan, A. A. Michelson, and Arthur Holly Compton. James T. Shotwell, one of Columbia University's leading professors and once an editorial aide on the eleventh edition, wrote on historical subjects; General John J. Pershing, on the late war; Frank B. Kellogg, a former Secretary of State, on "Outlawry of War"; Charles F. Kettering, the wizard inventor and president of the research division of General Motors, on "Motor Car"; and the psychologist Dr. John B. Watson, on "Behaviorism." Senators William E. Borah and Arthur Capper, college presidents, industrialists, novelists, lawyers, doctors, statesmen, military leaders, and scores of other authorities made up an impressive roster of American contributors.

From Pershing's article Hooper felt compelled to delete a sentence reading, "Lack of definite preparedness cost America immensely in human life and treasure and might have been disastrous if the Allies had not gained time for the American effort to materialize." Albert Einstein's article on "Space-Time" was written in flawless English and remained one of the few untouched by an editorial pencil. James Truslow Adams, the historian, had to be watched carefully for misspelled words. Julius Rosenwald's "Philanthropy" was patently sound, although events shortly to develop in the American economy were to make a mockery of a section that read, "Philanthropic endeavor in America differs from that of other countries in its greater variety and in the larger proportion undertaken through private initiative as compared with that carried on by the state. . . . Moreover, as little poverty exists and there is no pauper class, welfare work is carried on in a more confident spirit, with the expectation of making social relief ultimately needless."

Of the thirty-five hundred contributors, nearly half were Americans, a proportion greater by some 40 per cent than the number in the eleventh edition or the intervening supplements. And these men and women wrote not only on subjects connected with their own country but on many with no national limits. There were several collaborations that produced unsatisfactory results. Sometimes, when parts of an article were by an Englishman and the other parts by an American in order to present an international viewpoint, the transition in tone and language and, indeed, in attitude, was accomplished with a dislocating jerk or with needless repetition. Because readers throughout the world studied the English language largely from British texts, the encyclopaedia generally used British spelling and British terms. Yet one assiduous scholar found almost as many American terms replacing the British equivalents—"progressive education" instead of the European "new education" and "motion pictures" instead of "cinema"—and another noted that in the article "National Parks and Monuments" only American parks and monuments were described.

4

Before the volumes were ready for reviewers and purchasers, there was an important shift in ownership. By the middle of 1928, it was apparent that considerably more than the original $1,064,000 Cox had thought sufficient would be required to complete the project, and already some new articles had to be cancelled and older ones from the preceding edition retained. Again and again Cox came to Rosenwald, recalling the promise that whatever additional funds were necessary would be furnished. Finally, after close to $2 million had been allotted, it was proposed by Rosenwald's top executives, primarily Albert W. Loeb, that, instead of handing out more money, Sears, Roebuck and Company once more assume ownership of the encyclopaedia. By mutual agreement, this was done, mainly by exchanging Mrs. Hooper's holdings for Sears, Roebuck stock and by buying up all remaining shares, including those held by Samuel Untermyer and associates; the money paid for these shares totaled some $500,000. Cox remained publisher, calmed by assurances from Rosenwald that he would not be interfered with by any Sears, Roebuck officials.

In another sector of the enterprise, there were preliminary rumblings about the proposed contents of the edition, principally from British critics reacting to the increased amount of space allotted to American subjects and the greater dependence on American scholars. In September, 1928, fully a year before the edition became available, the debut issue of *Britannia,* a weekly edited by the British novelist

Gilbert Frankau, charged that the American publisher of the *Encyclopaedia Britannica* had demanded of Garvin that all articles on eastern political questions be written by Americans. To this Garvin replied characteristically, "In the whole farrago there is not one grain, not one atom, not one little jot nor tincture of truth. The American gentleman concerned is incapable of suggesting anything like that. The King's subject concerned is known to be among the last men alive to whom such a stipulation could be safely breathed."

When the volumes did come out, the cries were renewed in other British quarters. At Oxford University, the college newspaper, the *Isis,* accused the *Encyclopaedia Britannica* of "being run by a nest of Americans at a huge profit." And the *New Statesman* asked, "Why *Britannica?* Anglo-Saxon perhaps or Nordic or Anglo-American, but certainly not British. A British encyclopaedia, for example, would not inform us that members of the House of Commons enjoy the privilege of free travel on British railways; nor in a record of great trans-oceanic flights would it put Col. Lindbergh at the top of a list and make no reference whatever to the two Englishmen who crossed the Atlantic successfully eight years before him." A sour view of the "humanization" of the encyclopaedia was expressed by London's *Saturday Review:* "With many merits, perhaps particularly in the treatment of science and of recent political history, the Fourteenth Edition of the *Encyclopaedia Britannica* has been vitiated by an attempt to anticipate the demands of the plain man which is here out of place. It will meet most of the requirements of most people most of the time but it is not the final resort of the student. Should it come to be regarded as that, the public will have a poorer idea of what in certain departments constitutes knowledge." Mildly deploring this same trend, the *London Mercury* offered a tongue-in-cheek explanation: "In no other country in the world except America will you find that happy combination of intellectual curiosity and surplus cash. No encyclopaedia, conceived on such a scale as this one, can live without America. America pays the piper, and not unreasonably demands the right to call every alternate tune."

When a letter from Dr. W. D. Simpson, librarian of Aberdeen University, in the *Times Literary Supplement* expressed disagreement with certain statements in the article on "Fathers of the Church," other letters were received defending the article. But for some undisclosed reason the *Times* refused to print these, prompting Dr. Simpson, a conscientious polemicist, to comment, "That's too bad of the supplement.

That's not fair." Letters criticizing the edition, however, continued to appear in the *Supplement*. Garvin personally sought a reason for the sustained attacks and decided to his satisfaction, if not to his pleasure, that they were being made in retaliation for Sir Robert Donald's article on "Newspapers," in which no mention was made of the *Supplement* and a reference noted that Geoffrey Dawson, editor of the *Times*, was "a man who in fact had always taken great steps to safeguard his personal authority." Capitalizing on the anti-American feeling, the Educational Book Company, controlled by Lord Camrose, issued new prospectuses stressing—in red letters—that its *Harmsworth Universal Encyclopaedia* was a British production. Its salesmen also struck hard at the "American influences" in the new *Encyclopaedia Britannica*. Both practices were eliminated after Mrs. Law held a number of conferences with Lord Camrose, during which she convinced him of the unfairness and even the immorality of such methods.

5

In the United States, the new *Encyclopaedia Britannica* was generally received enthusiastically—in most instances for the very reasons that some British critics were so cool. Although he decried the prepublication publicity that stressed the contributions of the Tunneys, the Fords, and the Irene Castles, the historian Allan Nevins extolled the new concepts exemplified in the edition. "There is popularization," he wrote in an extensive article in the *Saturday Review of Literature*, "but not at the expense of accuracy or erudition." As for "Americanization"—"The English editor notes in his introduction that there are 130 million Americans and Canadians against 50 million people in the British Isles, and the United States has become the richest, strongest, and most vibrantly active nation in history. . . . The center of gravity of the English-speaking world has decisively changed, and the editors make the proper deduction."

Yale University's president, James R. Angell, added his praise in the same publication, asserting that in his special fields of philosophy and education he had sought in vain to discover material errors. And he made a strong point for the emphasis on modernity in the edition: "To give Bishop Berkeley a little over a page and to comparative psychology fifteen pages, probably reflects correctly current interest in these two subjects, even among intelligent folk."

With this, Henry Noble MacCracken, president of Vassar College, agreed strongly in the *Bookman*. "It is, above all, an encyclopaedia of the Twentieth Century; an encyclopaedia of the time; almost of the day. . . . Yet, though this edition is a mirror of our age, the great past has not been slighted. . . . In short, the *Encyclopaedia Britannica* puts a girdle around the world, not in forty minutes, as Puck promised to do, or in twenty days as the Zeppelin did, but in twenty-odd volumes. . . . On top of the little stand, the household telephone will give access to the speech of men; while on the shelves below, the *Encyclopaedia Britannica* will wait to serve our need for the written word, as a great clearing house of civilized intercourse."

The edition's modernity was applauded in the American *Nation* by Louis Heilperin, an expert on encyclopaedias. "No encyclopaedia, however lavishly equipped with editors and paraphernalia, can ever hope to be quite up to the minute, for men will die, or resign, or be promoted or demoted, and things are not always today quite what they seemed to be yesterday; but the *Britannica* comes as near to being up to date as any reasonable standard can demand. . . . The new *Britannica* is a monument of learning and editorial competence. If something of the finer flavor of culture which characterized the earlier editions is lacking in this one, and what is offered bears often, in unaccustomed clearness, the stamp of practicality, it is because a new age is upon us and efficiency has taken culture in hand."

Various experts acclaimed the sections dealing with art and especially the scores of illustrations, some two hundred of which were in full-page, dazzling color. Although Clennell Wilkinson in the *London Mercury* decried Warren Cox's "personal weakness—a passion for lampshades," exemplified by a lengthy article by Cox on lamps and shades, he admitted, in discussing the work's illustrations: "Nothing as good could have been produced in England. . . . They tempt you to begin to read here and there, and once you do that with this new encyclopaedia, it is not easy to stop. That, to put it shortly, is the great distinction of the 14th edition, that it will be read by all sorts of people, both in England and America, and will undoubtedly do more for the cause of education and culture than all the previous editions put together, which is no small achievement, when all is said and done."

The art critic of the *New York Times*, Edwin Alden Jewell, writing about the work involved in producing the many halftones, the color illustrations, and the engravings, told of the seventy-five draftsmen who created new drawings, of the four photographers who prepared the multicolor pages, and of the more than a hundred men and women whose duty it was to secure from everywhere in the universe the needed photographic material. As for the many articles under the general heading of "Art," there obviously were statements and opinions, remarked Jewell, with which not all would agree. "But is not controversy, when based upon sober and dignified appraisal, also a fact? And by way of bolstering this semi-innovation, the editors have made an effort to secure as many justifiably divergent points of view as possible, so that within the volumes themselves a reader will unearth plenty of controversy. This makes the work sparkle; gives it a living quality undreamed of by those who in the past set out to prepare an encyclopaedia."

In the heartland of the United States, Howard Vincent O'Brien, the popular columnist for the *Chicago Daily News,* wrote: "In the new edition . . . the editors have recognized that life has been getting along and have tried to catch up. The older editions were content to give the scholarly data for the literate. Users were supposed to be interested only in such things as the genealogy of Publius Crassus and the municipal government of Peshawar. Now, account has been taken of the vastly increased complexity of life and there is pictured 'how to' information in commendable variety. The unlettered citizen is told, in simple language, how to do all sorts of useful things, from carving a duck to the best way of cleaning a panama hat." This "how-to" characteristic, frowned on by the scholarly who would forever recall reverently the ninth and the eleventh editions—although they also contained such articles—was, indeed, a highly praised attribute of the new edition, for besides those mentioned by O'Brien, this *Encyclopaedia Britannica* could furnish for its readers knowledge of how to sew, box, swim, dance, fence, and skate; play golf, tennis, or auction bridge; operate a radio, movie camera, or automobile; manage a home; cook; plan and plant a garden; make lace; tie knots; or weave baskets.

6

William Cox was greatly pleased with the estimates from approving critics, especially so since few commented on the inclusion of a number of outdated articles. He himself had no doubts about the work's excellence. "It is a magnificent encyclopaedia," he wrote to Garvin when one of the first copies was placed before him, "the best ever, the nearest thing to everybody's guide, philosopher and friend, the most universally helpful and enlightening book since books were, an original service to the world today and a credit to us all."

Whatever arguments might be presented against this evaluation, it was true that the fourteenth edition, though some scholars might deplore its "practical" aspects, its "humanization," and its intensified effort at popularization, marked one of the most significant changes in the *Encyclopaedia Britannica* since its origin. In each major edition there had been reflections of the times and the intellectual climate. Each was larger in size than the last, with the editors, as the perceptive critic, Glennell Wilkinson, wrote in the *London Mercury*, "all the time taking a most unnatural, uneditorial kind of pride in the mere size of the monster they had created." This drift toward increased growth in both size and scholarship had reached its apex in the famous ninth edition, a compendium of scholarship in the most literal sense. From the point of view of scholars the ninth was easily the finest, but from other points of view it was not. "Why not admit frankly," asked Wilkinson, "that the old Encyclopaedia, as regards all its more important and learned contributions, was becoming intolerably long-winded and dull? No one but experts could understand its expert lenguage. The 14th edition, on the other hand, because it had to be Americanized had also to be humanized, to quote from its advertisements, in order to meet the requirement of a new kind of reader. And humanized in a very large proportion of the work, and that not the least scholarly, has simply meant plain English, and a merciful brevity, and a few explanatory words now and then to help the ordinary reader over some style."

Henceforth there would be two principal schools of thought about the *Encyclopaedia Britannica,* and, indeed, about the general nature of all encyclopaedias. One would insist on the scholastic superiority of previous editions, holding that the shift in emphasis, despite the host of Nobel Prize winners and other men of extensive learning represented in the fourteenth edition, was detrimental to the established reputation and scholarly character of the work. The other would continue to espouse the idea of making the encyclopaedia more understandable and thus more appealing and desirable to a far greater mass of persons, while at the same time retaining its scholarly authority. This latter group thought of the *Encyclopaedia Britannica* not only as an authoritative source of knowledge, but as a publication, within reasonable physical limits, designed to stimulate, inform, and instruct. It contended that the work should be edited not merely for a learned minority but for all who seek self-improvement.

7

Throughout a steady advertising campaign that ran for a full year before the edition's publication in 1929, Cox, quite naturally, stressed its "humanization." But almost as much attention was drawn to the scholarly reputations of the contributors as to the articles on such new subjects as television, shop-front design, family budgets, and the medical and legal aspects of aviation. With some pride, it was noted that famous articles from older editions—Macaulay's on Dr. Johnson, Bunyan, and Oliver Goldsmith; John Addington Symonds' on the Renaissance, Italy, and Machiavelli; and others by Swinburne, Tovey, and Bryce—were reprinted with only slight revision.

Cox's idea of selling the set was not to send out hordes of salesmen but to carry on a campaign through letters and magazine and newspaper advertisements designed to produce orders by mail. In this period and through the rest of his tenure with the *Encyclopaedia Britannica,* he employed no more than a dozen salespeople. These few worked in "mop-up" operations after specific areas had been suffused with sales letters, circulars, booklets, pamphlets, and brochures, the latter expensively produced and sent to community leaders who might be expected to purchase a set and comment to friends and neighbors on its many virtues. One of the handful of salespeople was Mrs. Alice P. Ballard, who covered all Los Angeles and the surrounding area. In 1955, still employed by the *Encyclopaedia Britannica* in a selling capacity in that territory, she recalled her early experiences: "I started with a bundle of papers and a couple of little booklets under my arm walking from door to door, telling them of the great 14th edition that was coming off the press, stirring up the whole neighborhood with the wonderful news that Nobel Prize men were writing for it. It sold for $118, $10 down and $10 a month, and was to go to $129 in September, 1929, the publication date. I did house-to-house and office buildings and schools and librarians."

For all their industry, such workers as Mrs. Ballard accounted for a mere 10 per cent of the total sales during Cox's term with the company. Another 10 per cent was derived through a bookshop maintained on the ground floor of the tall building at 342 Madison Avenue that housed the *Encyclopaedia Britannica* offices in New York. There, Mrs. Lavinia Dudley, who divided her time between selling and editorial duties in the office, marked as a high point of her experience the day she sold not one but five full sets to Charles Evans Hughes, later chief justice of the United States Supreme Court.

The rest of the twenty thousand sets sold in the first year of the fourteenth edition—despite the depression—resulted from mail and newspaper campaigns. Many hundreds of thousands of pieces of advertising literature were dispatched in the prepublication months, and as many or more afterward. There were routine, direct, sales letters and also letters with "snob appeal." This was an expensive method, and some of the minor executives in the organization—and a number of the executives at Sears, Roebuck and Company—sought to persuade Cox to employ more salesmen or to seek to use the channels of the vast mail-order company, but he remained steadfast.

In 1930, the year after the edition had been published, Cox continued his mailings and magazine and newspaper advertisements. To help in the ad writing, he hired a young literary columnist whose articles in the *Philadelphia Public Ledger* had attracted and held his attention. He was Walter Yust, who had been a newspaper man since the days when he worked for the old *Philadelphia Telegraph* while a student at the University of Pennsylvania. After several years of service with the YMCA during World War I and as a reporter on other Philadelphia papers and a writer of short stories and literary criticism in Chicago, Memphis, and New York, Yust had eventually become literary editor of the *Public Ledger,* writing a pert, witty column, "Of Making Many Books." In one of three about the *Encyclopaedia Britannica,* he had stated, "It [the *Encyclopaedia Britannica*] comes in twenty-four comfortably printed volumes, bearing enough words to fill literally 500 ordinary sized books. And the book reviewer sits down to it, certainly, very like a chap who has been ordered to eat and digest a battleship."

The columns so interested Cox that he asked Yust to come up to New York. During Yust's visit, Cox offered him a job as assistant to Franklin Hooper, with a promise that on Hooper's retirement he would be named editor. But after Yust accepted and signed a two-year contract as an assistant editor, he found himself writing advertisements. Although Cox had hired a large advertising firm to prepare copy for magazines and newspapers, he invariably found fault with its creations and passed them on to Yust for rewriting and revision. One of Cox's favorite words was "monumental," and he impressed on Yust the importance of working it into as many ads as possible.

Even as the economic depression grew worse, Cox stubbornly continued his expensive system of promotion. In 1931 a series of monographs was issued, each a collection of material from the *Encyclopaedia Britannica* on subjects from gardening to Chinese art, from theaters and motion pictures to mammals and birds. Each contained the most striking color and halftone illustrations from the original volumes, reproduced on the slickest paper. These monographs were available in the bookshop for two dollars each, but many were sent without cost to selected prospective customers in high-income brackets.

8

The persistent depression, the drop in sales and prices (at one period the price for the least expensively bound set slipped to $67.50), and the death of Julius Rosenwald early in 1932 led to a rupture of Cox's relations with the *Encyclopaedia Britannica* and Sears, Roebuck. While Rosenwald lived, Cox was assured—although the philanthropist took no direct part in the detailed affairs of the encyclopaedia—of strong moral backing in any disagreements with top executives of the mail-order firm. But with this support gone and in the face of rising promotion costs and drops in sales, Cox soon was under pressure from the executives, principally Robert E. Wood, the former army general who was now its president.

Wood, who had come to Sears, Roebuck in 1924 after pioneering in the opening of retail stores for its major rival, Montgomery, Ward and Company, had always considered Rosenwald's acquisition of the *Encyclopaedia Britannica* a business error. The encyclopaedia was not the appropriate kind of enterprise for the giant mail-order firm. He argued that the business was far too risky and erratic, and the records of the years immediately following 1929 supported this view. Wood had a high personal regard for the fourteenth edition as a sound educational work, but he looked with the eye of a dour realist upon balance sheets that showed annual decreases in sales of the set. So he made several proposals to Cox. One was that less money be spent for advertising; it seemed unlikely that encyclopaedias, however worthy, could be sold to hard-pressed Americans while the nation continued to be economically ill. Another was that instead of continuing to concentrate on mail-order selling, a system be established to sell the set through the hundreds of retail branch stores which Wood had opened for Sears, Roebuck throughout the country.

To such suggestions, Cox replied firmly and negatively. All through

1932 he was summoned to Chicago periodically to discuss his differences with Wood and executives of Wood's persuasion. At the end of that unhappy year, Cox offered to resign; he had become tubercular and physicians advised him to quit. His resignation was accepted, with customary official regrets and a settlement of $60,000. He spent a period of convalescence in the Berkshires and later wrote a column of general comment—titled, in tribute to J. L. Garvin, "The Observer"— for the *Register* in Torrington, Connecticut. The man named to replace him—and to assume responsibility for changes considered vital to the existence and character of the *Encyclopaedia Britannica*—was a Sears, Roebuck veteran, Elkan Harrison Powell, whom his friends and associates called "Buck."

Innovations and Increases

In Powell, the *Encyclopaedia Britannica* had for the first time a chief operating executive with no previous experience in the making or selling of encyclopaedias. His background was diversified: he was educated at the University of Chicago, spent some years as a professional football player and as an appraiser of property in litigation, and was, for a decade, advertising manager and secretary-treasurer of Sears, Roebuck and Company. A hobbyist fond of painting and photography, he was a man who shunned arguments and quarrels, especially political debates, which he considered time-consuming.

At first, he had no real enthusiasm for his assignment; he even neglected to tell his wife of his appointment as president, and she learned of it through a family friend. But he had been directed by General Wood to examine and reassess the *Encyclopaedia Britannica* with a view toward placing it, depression or no, on a paying basis.

When his appointment was made known to the older hands at the *Encyclopaedia Britannica* offices, they expected to be swept into the street. But within weeks after Powell assumed his job, he had won their support, especially by his frank admission, "I don't know anything about books or bookselling." He instilled a new importance into Franklin Hooper's position as editor, and the elderly man was soon hard at work on suggestions not only for editorial improvements but for promotional booklets to spur sales. When Powell learned that Walter Yust, despite his excellent editorial experience, was writing advertisements, he called him off such duties and officially named him Hooper's associate.

Powell's first accomplishment was to establish spirit and order in the New York offices; he commuted regularly from Sears, Roebuck's Chicago headquarters in the initial year of his presidency. And then he turned his attention to selling methods.

At first Powell sought to dispose of volumes by advertising them in the mail-order firm's catalogues and by displaying them in selected company stores. When this proved futile, he gradually abandoned Cox's expensive mail-order system and proceeded to organize a direct-sales organization. This was no easy task. Many of the men hired as salesmen were honest and efficient, but others were old-style sharpers who devised their own sales talks and promised their prospects more than could be delivered. Sharp practices by some of these veterans produced letters of complaint from customers who felt they had, in one way or another, been bilked. Scores of salesmen were hired and discharged, and in the first years of his tenure Powell had three sales managers before he found, in lean-faced, intense Louis G. Schoene-wald, the man to head the new sales system.

Schoenewald had come to the *Encyclopaedia Britannica* as a salesman in the last months of Cox's presidency. Like Powell, Schoenewald knew little of bookselling before this affiliation, having previously been in charge of sales for the Aeolian piano company in New York. When the depression caused a slump in the piano business, Schoenewald spent four months looking for new connections. Before selecting the *Encyclopaedia Britannica*, he made his own survey of the reference-book field, then offered his services just as the switch from Cox to Powell was being arranged. In charge of the five-man New York crew when Powell assumed office, Schoenewald had been helpful and instrumental in the switch to direct selling.

Shortly after Schoenewald was appointed national sales manager, he instituted in the twenty-four sales offices then operating a system similar to that in the New York headquarters. Its basis was simple enough and not unlike the theory underlying all types of so-called specialty selling: "The *Britannica* is sold with shoe leather. It doesn't matter in what section of the country you are selling. People in any part of the country buy a product for the same reasons, whether it is a vacuum cleaner or a *Britannica*. The technique of selling is basically the same everywhere. In the South we talk a little slower and we visit a little longer. But we say the same things."

Under Schoenewald a method was devised of training salesmen to memorize their talks and never to attempt impromptu deviations. The earlier way of haphazard house-to-house canvassing—the so-called "cold turkey"—was discarded almost entirely. Instead, salesmen made appointments by telephoning a prospect's office or home. Wherever possible, each sales talk took place with both husband and wife present. Slowly, sometimes through trial and error, sometimes through wholesale dismissals of incompetents or shyster salesmen, the transition to direct selling proceeded. Before long it became the established method, to be sharpened and improved with time.

2

In the decade from 1933 to 1943, while sales crept slowly upward from a low of 4,559 a year, other alterations were made in both the editorial and business divisions of the *Encyclopaedia Britannica*. One of these was a system of continuous revision of the editorial material. This resulted not only from a reluctance on the part of Sears, Roebuck officials to expend any great sums for completely new editions and from demands by salesmen that the set be kept as current as possible, but also from an examination by Franklin Hooper and Walter Yust of the editions from Smellie's first to Garvin's fourteenth. They had been directed to make this investigation by Powell, who had asked these questions: Was it possible to abandon the system of numbered editions? Could revisions in the editorial matter be made so that all information might be brought as up to date as possible in annual printings? How much of the material was more or less stable and not subject to alteration from year to year and even from decade to decade? What was the minimum size of printing orders? How often could the set be printed with revision of a specific percentage of the material at each printing?

For a year Hooper and Yust carried on their study. Then they were ready to report that a system of continuous revision would be not only possible but beneficial. The traditional method of producing new editions or supplemental volumes to existing editions had involved needless waste of funds and always bore the disadvantage of having earlier volumes out of date when the final volumes were issued. The manpower problem had been persistently vexing. Once the first flush of an edition's appearance had paled, only a small editorial department and fewer salesmen were needed. But with each new edition, editorial staffs had to be greatly enlarged, usually with difficulty and often at added expense, and sales and promotion personnel had to be recruited anew.

Yust and Hooper consulted with experts in the many fields covered by the *Encyclopaedia Britannica*. Then they advised Powell that the scholarly consensus—though subject to amendment—was that 75 per cent of the work's material was reasonably "fixed" and might, for a decade or more, remain unchanged but subject to periodical editorial review. The remaining 25 per cent demanded constant watchfulness and regular revision, some sections more than others. With these considerations in mind—and doubtless influenced by the fact that a number of competitors had already instituted their own continuous revision systems—the annual revision plan was adopted. The forty-one thousand articles then in the work were divided into thirty classifications. Each classification was to be scrutinized by authorities and those in the categories that required more or less constant surveillance were to be revised throughout at least twice in the next decade. Since this plan was then frankly experimental, it was deemed subject to alteration, and, indeed, it has been changed to some degree in ensuing years. But the basic idea still prevails: continuous revision to keep the set as up to date as is humanly possible without printing, at regular intervals, completely new editions.

Within a year after this important decision, the company offices were centralized in Chicago, first in the Sears, Roebuck plant, later in the Civic Opera Building on Wacker Drive. Chicago was considered an excellent site from which to direct the expanded sales organization. And with this move other innovations developed, some designed specifically to spur sales, some to improve the editorial product and services.

One of Yust's assignments—he was soon to succeed Franklin Hooper as editor-in-chief—was to undertake a long-range textual restyling of the work. Toward that end, the skilled designer, Rudolph Ruzicka, was hired, and he modernized display pages and end pieces and end sheets, besides devising a sleeker, more attractive binding. Yust also instituted new editorial controls, principally an adjustment of the index. In the earlier editions, references to information in the maps were contained in the regular index. Revisions, when they were made, were haphazard and inaccurate. To separate the index to maps from the text index and to set it up as an index by itself, seventeen indexers worked for two years, checking and correcting each reference against the editorial material in the volumes themselves and amplifying inadequate entries. This indexing has been carefully maintained ever since, though the lore of the company of that period is dotted with entries about inexperienced workers who classified "Virginia Reel" under Biography, "Defense Mechanism" under Military, "Gallstones" under Geology, "Incest" under Business, and "Pope Innocent" under Law.

Shortly after the move to Chicago, an edition for children under twelve was published by the company. This sprightly work, titled *Britannica Junior,* derived from the purchase early in 1934 through R. R. Donnelley and Sons of a twelve-volume children's set called *Weedon's Modern Encyclopaedia,* whose owners had fallen into debt to the printing firm. Immediately after its acquisition, 60 per cent of its text was revised, and eventually it was rewritten and restyled entirely to become one of the company's strongest assets.

Another product ultimately became successful as a stimulant to sales of the full set, as a revenue producer, and as a historical record. Schoenewald's salesmen persisted in asking for an annual supplementary publication as an adjunct to the system of continuous revision. So Powell, taking his cue from Horace Hooper, revived the idea of an annual volume and called it the *Britannica Book of the Year.* The first, issued in 1938, covered the principal happenings of the preceding year in interesting text and with some 200 pictures furnished by *Life* magazine from the thousands it had printed in 1937. The loan of the photographs, certainly one of the most salable features of the book, was facilitated by R. R. Donnelley and Sons, printers of both the magazine and the encyclopaedia. The attractive book was available to all, but at a substantial discount to *EB* owners. In a joint preface, Franklin Hooper, performing his final editorial duty before retirement, and Yust emphasized this quality. "It answers demands on the part of the public," they wrote, "for an authoritative handbook recording what has happened in a single year. It consolidates the significant facts, whether statistical or historical, of the year."

To signalize publication of the *Book of the Year*, a dinner attended by many of the scholars, journalists, public figures, and officials who contributed to the book was held at New York's University Club. It served a double purpose because it also marked the retirement of Franklin Hooper from active work as editor. Then seventy-six and still spry, Hooper had served in various editorial capacities for forty years—four decades in which his staunch faith in the *Encyclopaedia Britannica* as the greatest of all reference works had not swerved for an instant. Although in his last years with the company he had attempted to draw up ideas to stimulate sales, he had rarely been able to understand the need, even in the hectic heyday of his peripatetic brother, for promotional campaigns and sales drives. He had always felt that people should buy the *Encyclopaedia Britannica* without urging, for he believed that, next to the Bible, the *Encyclopaedia Britannica* was the greatest and most important book in existence.

Before the dinner, Hooper became ill and went to a room in the club to rest for a few hours. The dinner, meanwhile, progressed. At its end, P. W. Wilson, a former member of the British Parliament, arose to eulogize Hooper and the *Encyclopaedia Britannica*. Wilson was halfway through with his speech when Hooper, shaky and pale, appeared in the dining room. He insisted on walking to his place at the speakers' table; then in a weak and frail voice he began his farewell speech. As he continued he seemed to grow stronger, and soon he was standing stiffly erect and speaking clearly, while the entire assemblage listened in respectful silence.

3

An editorial division that grew rapidly during this period was the Library Research Service. In 1936, it was officially established under the direction of Mrs. Aimee Buchanan, William Cox's former secretary, who, with two assistants, undertook to reply to those set owners seeking additional information on a wide range of subjects. Purchasers were then entitled to ask as many questions as they wished for ten years after buying the set. Within four years the service—which salesmen found to have strong customer appeal—had broadened considerably. The variety and number of queries had also multiplied, and Mrs. Buchanan's staff increased.

Mrs. Buchanan early received unusual queries. "Please tell me about the care and feeding of worms in captivity," pleaded one seeker for knowledge, and he was satisfied with a reply covering seven single-spaced pages. And there were other unique questions: "Please send me information on a rock in a Southeast Asian country which is kept suspended in the air by the humming of the natives." "What is the cause and cure of child psychology?" "How many dog and cat cemeteries are there in the Union of South Africa?"

Mrs. Buchanan's researchers scoured Chicago libraries for answers to even the most unlikely questions. They failed to find sufficient replies to only 1 per cent of them, even when the number of questions greatly increased. By 1940, as the service grew more and more popular, each purchaser of the *Britannica* was given a sheet of fifty gummed coupons limiting him to that many questions for the next ten years, and Walter Yust, having been named editor on Franklin Hooper's retirement, stipulated that only questions to which answers were available in library sources would be handled.

Another popular technique in a completely different field spread the name of *Encyclopaedia Britannica* in these years. In 1939 one of the nation's favorite radio programs was "Information Please," devised by Dan Golenpaul and featuring a panel made up of Clifton Fadiman, the literary critic and editor; John Kieran, nationally known sports writer; Franklin P. Adams, columnist and professional wit; and Oscar Levant, the concert pianist. Powell suggested to Golenpaul that the *Encyclopaedia Britannica* be given to listeners who stumped the panel. This was a good promotional stroke, but some salesmen reported that many prospective customers were delaying their purchases because they hoped to win a set from "Information Please." To combat this, Powell and Schoenewald assured full cash refunds if within three months any purchaser won an "Information Please" prize, and this promise was maintained through the three years' affiliation with the show. In this period, only one hundred sets were given away annually, a pittance when assessed against the national publicity and promotional value derived from the association with the highly original panel quiz show. (A similar type of promotion was effective in later years, when the *Encyclopaedia Britannica* was the indisputable authority for various television quiz shows, especially "The $64,000 Question" and "Twenty-one.")

4

The result of all this was a gradual gain in sales and revenue. Yet General Wood continued to insist that the mail-order company was far out of its intellectual and business depths in continuing to maintain and sell the *Encyclopaedia Britannica*. Futhermore, the firm had been embarrassed by complaints about some of the more aggressive salesmen. Wood, therefore, was prepared and eager to dispose of the encyclopaedia to a logical recipient.

To sell it to a commercial institution seemed unwise and, indeed, was hardly discussed. Such an act would not only detract from the work's prestige but might be deemed incompatible with the responsibilities Wood and the company had inherited from the original interest of Julius Rosenwald. A sounder move would be to turn over the *Encyclopaedia Britannica*, at advantageous terms, to an educational institution that could be relied upon to maintain the reference work's standards and reputation. And at this time, the University of Chicago —certainly a logical recipient—was indirectly being prepared for such a role by one of its most energetic officials, William Benton, an advertising wizard turned educator.

Part Four

20

Benton's Gamble

William Benton's shift from New York's Madison Avenue to the campus of the University of Chicago in 1936 had, in a sense, fulfilled a family tradition. His forebears included teachers, professors, ministers, and missionaries. His father, Charles William Benton, was a Yale man and a Congregational minister who left Connecticut in 1880 for a teaching post in the state university at Minneapolis, Minnesota, where he remained for thirty-three years, many of them as chairman of the department of romance languages. His mother, Elma Hixson Benton, taught country school in her native Iowa at thirteen, at twenty-five was Minnesota's first woman county superintendent of schools in Ottertail County, the state's largest, and she continued to study and teach all her life.

Benton was born in Minneapolis on April 1, 1900, and spent his boyhood there and later, after his father died, on a bleak homestead in Montana. He helped work his way through Shattuck military school in Faribault, Minnesota, by selling scrapbooks for student memorabilia, special binders he designed for the school paper, and class emblems, pins, and embossed stationery. After a year at Minnesota's Carleton College, he went to Yale on a scholarship, became a contributor to the *Yale Record*, and eventually its chairman and editor. On the debating team, an associate and friend was Robert Maynard Hutchins, like Benton the son of a minister-educator; his father was William James Hutchins, president of Kentucky's Berea College.

After he received his degree in 1921, Benton joined the famous sales organization of the National Cash Register Company, whose founder, John H. Patterson, then known as "the father of scientific salesmanship" and "the Napoleon of sales promotion," had beaten financial panics and had built a $50 million business, of which the key sales slogan was "Analyze! Visualize! Dramatize!" From this milieu to the then youthful field of national advertising was a short step, although Benton's mother had hoped he would become a lawyer or "do something respectable like teaching or the ministry." He went to work in August, 1922, as a twenty-five-dollar-a-week copywriter for Albert D. Lasker's Lord and Thomas, then the largest advertising firm in the country. After service with another agency, which grew to become Batten, Barton, Durstine and Osborn, he and Chester Bowles, a former assistant whom Benton had hired and helped to train, opened their own advertising office on July 15, 1929, with a staff of three employees. Even after the onset of the depression, the firm of Benton and Bowles survived—and prospered. In the next six years, annual billings rose from $40,000 to $18,000,000, and by 1935, although the company had only five clients and all its accounts were concentrated in a single office, Benton and Bowles stood sixth among the advertising agencies of the world. In that year, too, Benton decided to retire from the advertising business. When the firm had been set up in 1929, Bowles had promised to buy him out whenever Benton wanted to get out, and at a good price. So, in December of 1935, Benton contracted all his stock in the agency to Bowles and their partner and associate, Atherton Hobler, and planned a round-the-world trip and a search for new ventures and vistas.

2

One morning in the spring of 1936, three weeks after his official retirement, Benton had a visitor. He was Robert Maynard Hutchins, now president of the University of Chicago. Hutchins came with a problem and a proposal. Early in 1935, Charles Walgreen, head of the multimillion-dollar retail drugstore chain, had alleged that his niece, Lucille Norton, was being subjected to "Communist influences" in her social science survey courses at the university. After a cursory inquiry in which Walgreen was disturbed to find that among dozens of books listed as required reading were the *Communist Manifesto* and *New Russia's Primer,* Walgreen had withdrawn Miss Norton from the university. The action had led to a hearing by a state senate committee. Although the committee cleared the university of all the charges made by Walgreen, the university was left with a touchy public relations problem; of the city's four daily newspapers, only one, the tabloid *Times,* was then friendly to the university. Hutchins asked Benton to come to Chicago to study the problem of modern university public relations in general and the Walgreen case in particular.

Benton went, and soon he was immersed in the intellectual tempest on the university campus. He interviewed trustees, professors who revered Hutchins and those who opposed him, newspaper publishers, public officials, and business and professional men. Then he collected the notes and documents gathered in four weeks of day-and-night interviewing and wrote a privately printed and distributed book titled *The University of Chicago's Public Relations.* This contained suggestions for improving the university's status in the public eye, for attracting desirable students, and for prompting the wealthy to give money to the school, which, as Benton saw it, were the inherent aims of good public relations. Benton even went so far as to ask whether the name of the University of Chicago should be changed to dissipate the taint of local gangsterism and the scandal of payless paydays for the city's school teachers and, further, to make clear that the university was a great private institution like Yale and Harvard and in no way supported by public funds. Hutchins' observation at the time—which was used as the book's opening sentence—spoke for many who read it: "No book like this has ever been written before; surely not about a university." (Each trustee was asked to return his copy after reading it, because of the confidential nature of the proposals, but one evidently never did. In 1954 Edward G. Bernays, the public relations expert, told Benton he had purchased an annotated copy for fifty dollars from a rare-book dealer and considered it the most astute treatise of its kind he had ever seen.) Through personal discussions with Walgreen, Benton helped solve the Walgreen problem so well that by early 1937 the drug magnate, after conferences with Hutchins, had given the university $550,000, which, with another $250,000 secured elsewhere, went to establish the Charles R. Walgreen Foundation for the Study of American Institutions, with lectures and research designed to "forward the development of good citizenship and the improvement of public service."

Benton now considered his affiliation with the university at an end. But he was persuaded to remain on half-time duty—spending six months each year away from his Connecticut home—as an academic vice-president of the university. His acceptance was partially prompted by an interest in opportunities afforded by such methods of communication in education as motion pictures and radio; in the latter field, his advertising firm had achieved prominence as the major customer first of the National Broadcasting Company and then of the Columbia Broadcasting System. He was to continue this half-time academic work for six years and then spend another two years on one-quarter time.

One of his first assignments from Hutchins after Benton became vice-president in October, 1937, was the writing of a recommendation for the Rockefeller Foundation regarding ERPI (Electrical Research Products, Inc.) Classroom Films, Inc., which had been organized as a subsidiary of the American Telephone and Telegraph Company in 1929 to develop the classroom-film field as a market for sixteen-millimeter sound projectors, on which AT&T owned patents. The first talking films designed wholly for classrooms had been made by AT&T on the campus of the University of Chicago. Benton's proposal for establishing a philanthropic corporation, with a foundation grant of $4 million, that would take over ERPI and develop classroom films on a major scale, was rejected by the foundation, but he continued to be fascinated by the potentialities of films as a medium of education and he often sat in on many university classes to study their use.

In addition to his academic duties, Benton helped to provide backing for the radio broadcasts of the University of Chicago Round Table, the highly popular program that brought together distinguished faculty members and outside authorities in weekly discussions on timely and timeless subjects. Another Benton-inspired radio series was "The Human Adventure," which dramatized projects and research being carried on at the university and was then adjudged by critics to be the most highly advanced of public service programs. Benton wrote articles for the mass magazines, made broadcasts frequently over national radio networks, visited newspaper publishers and their editorial staffs, and spoke widely on behalf of the university. (In addition to his work at the university during this period, Benton became a founder and vice-chairman of the Committee for Economic Development; was an original and key consultant to Nelson Rockefeller when he was appointed co-ordinator of Inter-American Affairs; and acquired ownership of the Muzak Corporation, a firm that piped background music into manifold institutions.)

3

Late in 1941, a memorandum atop the inevitable pile of papers and letters on his desk attracted Benton's attention. Written by W. K. Jordan, general editor of the University of Chicago Press, it reported on a meeting of various scholars at which agreement was general on the "desirability and practicality of preparing a new edition of the *Encyclopaedia Britannica*." The group maintained that a new edition, completely rewritten, seemed in order, although all agreed that considerable preliminary discussion with other savants was essential before any full decision could be reached. The discussion had been stimulated by a similar meeting held earlier in New York and called by David Stevens, vice-president of the Rockefeller Foundation.

Benton's curiosity was swiftly aroused by the problems cited in Jordan's report: Should the *Encyclopaedia Britannica* be made "more scholarly?" Should it be completely rewritten in the mold of the ninth edition? Would a super-scholarly encyclopaedia stimulate research in important fields? Musing over Jordan's memorandum and noting that "the discussion strayed on several occasions to the difficult problems of costs and distribution," Benton wondered what kind of people bought the set, how it was marketed, and how many were sold each year. Eager to learn more, Benton arranged a meeting with Hutchins and General Wood, chairman of the Sears, Roebuck board. There was informal discussion of whether the firm would sell the property, the purchase possibly financed by the Rockefeller Foundation. There was talk of the encyclopaedia's business history since the days of Horace Hooper, and Wood told of the unsuccessful effort in 1928 to interest the University of Chicago in taking over the company and of subsequent discussions—just as futile—involving Harvard and the Massachusetts Institute of Technology.

Soon Benton dispatched a memo to Hutchins: "Might not there be some possibility that Sears, Roebuck might give the *Encyclopaedia*

Britannica outright to the University (there might be important tax savings)? Or might there be the possibility that Sears, Roebuck would maintain ownership and would make a major investment in bringing out a new edition, provided funds could be secured to insure a break-even basis at least for the project?" For a week or more, Benton and Hutchins discussed possibilities and probabilities, viewing the financing of the *Encyclopaedia Britannica* by the Rockefeller Foundation or some other agency as potentially important in prestige for the university and in scholarship for the encyclopaedia.

But the Rockefeller Foundation appeared not to be interested in financial involvement. Nor did some individuals whom Benton sounded out. When Benton turned to his friend, Henry R. Luce, the *Time-Life-Fortune* magazine publisher, urging him to buy the rights to the set and turn them over to the university as a gift, Luce showed no enthusiasm and questioned, among other matters, the merit of retaining the name *Encyclopaedia Britannica*. "Neither Bob nor I share your fears," replied Benton. "We feel this name is generic—we doubt that one American in a thousand associates the name with England." In a note to Hutchins reporting on his exchange of letters with Luce, Benton wrote, "I told him that the name had had 150 years of promotion."

Then, in the midst of the early talks and the memos, came a decisive luncheon with Wood on December 9, when Benton and Wood met at the Chicago Club to discuss the attack on Pearl Harbor two days earlier and related matters. As the waiter served coffee, Benton suddenly asked, "General, don't you think it's rather unwise for a mail-order house to own the *Encyclopaedia Britannica*—and isn't it even more unwise in wartime?"

"Yes," replied Wood. "Sears should never have acquired it in the first place."

The discussion continued. As they rose from the table, Benton suggested making a gift of the encyclopaedia to the University of Chicago. Without replying, Wood walked silently downstairs for his hat and coat. As his car drove up to the club door, he turned to Benton and said, "All right, Bill, I'll give you the *Britannica*."

Benton sped to the university, bursting in on Hutchins to tell him, "Call the general! Tell him Bill Benton just arrived in your office and says that he has given the *Encyclopaedia Britannica* to the University of Chicago! See what he says!"

With Hutchins, Wood verified the offer by telephone. "Of course," he added, "I didn't mean that we would give you the cash and receivables we have in the corporation. I'm sure Bill understands that. We can't give you our inventory either, that is, our present stock of books and the books being printed. You'll have to come up with about $300,000 for the inventory. But all the rest of it, the plates and the copyright and the good will, everything else is yours as a gift to the university."

4

Benton now assumed the role, as he was later to describe it, of "professional beggar." Where was he to get the $300,000 and the money for working capital?

He turned first to one of the university's good friends, Lessing Rosenwald, a trustee and the son of the man who had helped save the *Encyclopaedia Britannica* in its dire days during and after World War I. Rosenwald listened patiently, but opposed any plan to have the university take over the publication. Benton then sent letters to friends everywhere. He lunched with magazine publishers, newspaper owners, and philanthropists. But he could stir no interest in raising the necessary money. When one reply gratuitously offered the advice that the name of the work be changed to simply "The Encyclopaedia," Benton retorted, "It's one of the best known trade names in the world. Compared to the name *Encyclopaedia Britannica,* Coca Cola and Chevrolet and Kodak are mere passing fancies."

As Benton continued his search, Wood offered a liberal plan of paying for the inventory: a $100,000 down payment, the remaining $200,-000 to be taken out of profits. Later the general secured his directors' approval of a plan to lower the price for the inventory to $200,000, with half to be paid on delivery of the gift and the rest to be transmitted over five years at only a 2 per cent interest rate. Still later he proposed a ten-year plan. He furnished Benton with earnings reports, sales records and other essential data. In a very important concession, Wood worked out an arrangement by which his company's bank would, for the next five years, lend the encyclopaedia company 90 per cent on the face value of all instalment accounts as soon as sales were made. Perhaps more important, Wood agreed that during this period all collections for sets sold on the instalment plan would continue to be the responsibility of his firm's experienced and efficient credit-and-collection network.

In the ensuing months of 1942, Wood continued to come forward with additional favorable terms. If the university, after accepting the gift, failed to make a success of the venture after a year's operation, Sears, Roebuck and Company would take it back and assume all liabilities. If the university accepted the ten-year payment plan for the inventory, Sears, Roebuck and Company would make a gift of $50,000 in cash to the university to be used as working capital. Wood estimated that this sum was enough for the purpose; Benton's own estimate, after many conversations with *Encyclopaedia Britannica* officials and his own financial friends and attorneys, was between $100,-000 and $150,000. This was not because Benton questioned Wood's judgment; rather, he thought it wise to provide extra assurance to the university trustees, most of whom were frankly incredulous at the $50,000 estimate, inasmuch as their own advisers had informed them that at least $750,000 was required.

To Wood's new offers Benton replied with gratitude. He sent to Harold H. Swift, the meat-packing firm executive who headed the university Board of Trustees, a letter detailing the generous proposals and urging that the university provide any additional working capital needed. And to Hutchins Benton wrote that although he realized the business risks involved in the venture, he believed that the university might gain $300,000 a year in profits that could be used to increase salaries and services.

But despite the offers by Wood and the persuasive memos from Benton, the university trustees were divided. The proposed gift, Wood's liberal terms, and the question of putting up working capital constituted the sole topics of discussion at many special trustees' meetings in the closing months of 1942. Several trustees were downright suspicious of the bounty. Some considered it "a dead horse" and remembered the times when the company had approached utter ruin; the university, they warned, would be put in a precarious financial position if, after accepting, it were faced with a wartime governmental decree stopping the time payments for encyclopaedias and other reference works. Others argued that the university could not successfully run a business of this kind, that it was too volatile and too speculative an enterprise, that university ownership would be "the dead hand of disaster at its neck." The salesmen of the *Encyclopaedia Britannica,* some feared, would prove embarrassing when they invoked the university's name in the presentations to prospects. William Scott Bond, the board's vice-chairman, issued a circular letter to all the trustees expressing doubts about whether the trustees of the university

—indeed, of any private university—had the legal right to put up working capital and to underwrite the responsibility of a business involving such financial risks. Benton argued that if it was legal for the university to buy common stocks, it was legal to put money into *Encyclopaedia Britannica* stock. He recalled that Wood had told him, "Bill, don't pay too much attention to the financial record of the business under Sears. If you will interest yourself in it and go to work on it, you can build it. Tell your trustees this is a five-million-dollar gift."

As the year drew to a close and Wood's deadline neared, Hutchins lost heart. Riding home with Benton one night after an especially prolonged discussion with a special board committee at the Chicago Club, he sighed and told Benton, "Bill, they're going to turn it down."

5

In the face of this and in view of Wood's ultimatum that the offer would be withdrawn on the approaching January 31, Benton made a gambler's decision. He had just received $100,000 in payment for his preferred stock in Benton and Bowles. He offered to put up this $100,000 as working capital. Besides, he agreed to become chairman of the board of Encyclopaedia Britannica, Inc., and to take personal responsibility for its management and development.

A special committee of trustees set out to study this proposal. Hutchins urged acceptance, suggesting that because Benton was furnishing the $100,000 and was to assume all the risks and the responsibilities of the new company, he should have common stock in the company. In this, Hutchins had the support of board chairman Swift. Hutchins stressed that the University of Chicago was the "logical repository" for the *Encyclopaedia Britannica.* He was interested, he told the trustees, not merely in having the university make money but in bringing the institution and the publication together for education's sake. There was no assurance, Hutchins cautioned, that the Sears, Roebuck offer, once rejected, would ever be repeated. "There is every chance that it will not. This is another and major reason for acting now."

At this critical point—one year to the day of that December 9 Chicago Club luncheon—Wood increased his offer once more. He informed Benton that because his firm stood high in the excess-profits tax brackets, his treasurer had advised him to make the $300,000 in inventory an outright gift. "He'll give us the whole thing, lock, stock, and barrel," exulted Benton in a memo to Hutchins. "No notes and no payment for inventory." This left only the issue of working capital.

Now there were new meetings and new discussions as Wood's deadline neared. More trustees were won over to Benton's proposal, now that working capital was assured by him and the university could avoid responsibility for management. On January 14, 1943, only two weeks before the deadline, the special committee recommended to the full board acceptance of the gift and of Benton's proposal "because of a) the educational merit of *Britannica*, b) the possibility that the property may continue to earn substantial profits, and c) the prestige value of *Britannica*."

In the official contracts signed that February 1, royalty and stock-division schedules were established. In return for advice and counsel from its faculty, the university would receive, for each of the first 10,000 sets sold, $1, with $5 for each of the next 5,000, $7 for each of the next 5,000, and $10 for each of those over 20,000. Thus, on 10,000 sets the royalty would come to $10,000, on 15,000 to $35,000, on 20,000 to $70,000, and on 25,000 to $120,000. The scale of royalties on *Britannica Junior* was half this, and each atlas sold was to yield fifty cents to the university. The royalties to be paid, Benton hoped, would ultimately come to hundreds of thousands of dollars annually.

The stock distribution was patterned after that of *Parents' Magazine*, as worked out by the General Education Board of the Rockefeller Foundation, which originally financed it. The common stock was divided into thirds. Because Benton was providing the working capital, he was given two-thirds and the University of Chicago one-third. But the University of Chicago was given the option of buying half of Benton's stock after eighteen months of operation for $50,000, just what Benton had paid, thereby giving to it two-thirds of the stock. The university, for its further protection, was given preferred stock equal to $850,000 in prior claims against assets in event of liquidation. This was approximately the asset value of the company when Benton began to operate.

It was agreed that three of the nine directors of Encyclopaedia Britannica, Inc., should be university trustees and that the company would not enter into new ventures without the consent of at least two such members. Benton was not to dispose of his own stock without first offering it to the university. Later he proposed and signed a contract stating that, in the event of his death, the university would have the option for one year thereafter of buying enough stock from his family to give it control, the price to be "the fair value thereof."

6

In a long letter to Swift, Benton assured him that he would strive to make Encyclopaedia Britannica, Inc., a thriving company. He promised that changes considered essential for retaining and improving editorial excellence would be instituted, reminding Swift that the university had the right to withdraw its imprimatur from the work if editorial standards declined. "If the *Britannica* venture does not work out successfully for the University," wrote Benton, "I shall carry the responsibility and may lose $100,000. If it does work out successfully, the University can acquire two-thirds of the stock ownership, leaving me with a minority interest which, as business experience indicates, is often of little value in a corporation run for the benefit of the majority owners." For their part, the university trustees advised Benton to run the corporation on sound business lines and to be guided by the market and by competitive standards and conditions rather than by the customs or pay scales of the university.

Soon the myriad technicalities were smoothed out, and Hutchins made formal acknowledgment: "It is a development closely related to the University's interest in extending educational facilities to the widest possible number." To explain the contract between the university and Benton, he summoned the faculty to a meeting in Mandel Hall. There Hutchins enumerated the efforts made by Benton to acquire working capital and cited financial gains that he hoped would accrue to the university. And in his witty way, after noting that Benton had finally put up the working capital himself, he remarked, "Vice-President Benton has been the victim of his own propaganda."

21

Of Books, Films and Great Books

The general public reaction to the transfer was favorable, best typified by a *Chicago Daily News* editorial which agreed with a statement by Hutchins that the University of Chicago's connection with the 175-year-old publication was closely related to its interest in extending educational facilities to the greatest number of persons. Virtually the only derogatory statement came from a Spanish radio commentator in Madrid: "The encyclopaedia forms the mind of a people and the British mind will henceforth be molded by Chicago University. It must be said that Chicago has been better known for its slaughterhouses than for its contributions to science."

At first some of the executives of Encyclopaedia Britannica, Inc., were skeptical about the merits of the affiliation. Except for Powell and Schoenewald, few had been aware of the lengthy negotiations. Some declared privately that if the university were to dominate the organization they would resign; others were eager to co-operate completely. It soon became evident that there was scant cause for apprehension. Meeting Walter Yust, Benton expressed admiration for him and for the *Encyclopaedia Britannica*. "I want you to call me Bill," he said. "I'll come up with lots of ideas. I always do. I get about five hundred ideas a week and if one or two of them turn out all right I feel I've had a successful week."

Benton was named chairman of a revised board of directors that included, in addition to Hutchins, M. Lincoln Schuster, the book publisher; Paul G. Hoffman, head of the Studebaker Company; John Stuart, board chairman of the Quaker Oats Company; Beardsley Ruml, the social scientist and fiscal expert; Henry R. Luce; and Chester Bowles. (Fifteen years later, Hoffman, Stuart, Hutchins and Ruml were still serving. Among their associates were Adlai E. Stevenson, industrialists Walter Paepcke and Curtis Gager, and advertising executive Albert W. Sherer.) A board of editors was established; it was to meet four times annually with Yust and his managing editor, John V. Dodge, to discuss policies and procedures ranging from the feasibility of publishing reading guides for encyclopaedia owners to specific improvements in the methods of continuous revision. At its head was Hutchins, and foremost among its members were the University of Chicago professors Robert Redfield, Richard McKeon, and Ralph Tyler, respectively authorities in anthropology, philosophy, and education.

2

After the transfer, the primary objectives continued to be the maintenance and betterment of the *Encyclopaedia Britannica* itself, but a number of subsidiary ventures were undertaken and completed. In the first months after assuming the board chairmanship, Benton renewed his interest in classroom movies. The ERPI company was still available for the right buyer, and he began to plan for Encyclopaedia Britannica, Inc., to acquire the firm which, though quite small, with only a $300,000 annual sales volume, had built up the country's largest and most important classroom film library. Intensive talks began with Kennedy Stevenson, financial vice-president of Western Electric, the AT&T subsidiary that owned ERPI, and continued through most of 1943. Because Encyclopaedia Britannica, Inc., had no money to pay for ERPI and consequently had to pledge its assets and credit to consummate the deal, purchase arrangements were complex. But by November 25 the encyclopaedia company was the new owner of ERPI at a cost of $1,000,000 payable over the next decade, during which time another $1,500,000 was spent in building and developing the films firm. The purchase included hundreds of films which remained persistently popular; as recently as the late 1950's surveys showed that the three films still used most frequently in the country's classrooms, *Colonial Children, Adventures of Bunny Rabbit,* and *Gray Squirrel,* were part of this group. Four months after this purchase, the Eastman Kodak Company turned over to the company about three hundred of its famous Eastman Teaching Films on subjects ranging from agriculture to science. This group, even then suffering from the competition of sound movies, is now rarely used, but its acquisition late in 1943 made Encyclopaedia Britannica Films, Inc. by far the leading company of its kind.

Profits from the purchase of the films company, Benton told the university trustees, would be desirable, but he cautioned that no gains could be expected for at least ten years. He stressed a more important motive: "This new relationship will enable the university to use its resources and knowledge to develop an educational tool which expands the range of material available to the teacher as no other device can do."

In recent years, under its president, Maurice B. Mitchell, formerly an executive of the Muzak Corporation, Encyclopaedia Britannica Films, Inc., has moved forward as acknowledged world leader in audio-visual education. As the use of classroom movies spread, the company grew in size and scope. Many new films, made at its studios in the Chicago suburb of Wilmette and on location in forests, factories and foreign lands, were added to its original library. Many of the films have been translated into thirteen foreign languages, virtually the only ones of their kind with world-wide distribution. Each film is designed for use in teaching and is so made that students can learn faster and better with it than without it. Consequently, great care in production and preparation is taken. Before a film is begun, researchers go over the full field of texts and courses on the specified subject. Curriculum specialists are consulted for advice, and every movie is made under the supervision of an associate in research and production and with the guidance of an expert or a scholar. New techniques have been extensively used, and as the films company has progressed technically and intellectually, its creativity has increased. A massive project in scientific education, the filming of an entire high-school course in introductory physics, totals 162 half-hour movies in color. It was produced in 1956 in Pittsburgh in co-operation with local school officials and the Fund for the Advancement of Education and, in Mitchell's view, "may well revolutionize the teaching of the sciences in United States schools." Special efforts in cultural fields have resulted in films like *William Shakespeare*, produced in Great Britain for literature and theater-arts classes in high schools and colleges, a movie "so extraordinary," according to Cecile Starr, educational films expert for the *Saturday Review*, "that one must think twice before beginning its praises, for fear of overpraising it." During 1957, sixty-two new films were added to the company's library.

Profits from these and hundreds of others have been modest at best. Financially, there have been no significant returns and no dividends on the several millions of dollars invested since 1943. But the company is considered increasingly important because of its contributions to education, and profits are anticipated in the years ahead, for the future for teaching and learning through audio-visual means is limitless.

In October, 1943, it was announced that Hutchins would edit a collection of the great writings of Western civilization. Earlier that year Benton had proposed such a collection when he and his wife were students in a Great Books group, jocularly known as the "fat men's class" and comprising many Chicago business leaders and their wives. The class was conducted by Hutchins and Mortimer Adler, then professor of philosophy of law at the University of Chicago. An intense intellectual with a peppery manner of conveying learning and information, Adler, called by Hutchins "The Great Bookie," had originated and developed discussion groups at which persons of much or little learning talked about the ideas of those whom Adler considered the most original thinkers of the Western world.

Adler joined Hutchins in the task of preparing the collection. To aid in choosing the volumes a distinguished editorial board was named, including Stringfellow Barr, president of St. John's College; John Erskine, one of the pioneers in the study of notable writings of the ages; and Mark Van Doren, the poet and teacher. The initial budget was estimated at $500,000, with a separate allotment for an "index of ideas." Original estimates were that such an index, the entries of which would be correlated with the selected writings, would require a small staff, an appropriation of only $60,000, and about two years' steady work. Adler began with a handful of helpers in two cellar offices near the university. They drew up a list of four thousand basic ideas. For months Adler whittled away at this list, decreeing which topics should be discarded, which might be incorporated with others. More than a year after the time that had been deemed sufficient, he finally pared it to manageable size—102 major ideas from "Angel" to "World," subdivided into three thousand subtopics. Then started the task of reading through the 443 works of seventy-four men, from Aristotle to Tolstoy and from Homer to Marx, and finding all appropriate references to each of the ideas and subideas. At the peak of this job Adler's staff, by now occupying a rambling graystone building provided by the university and promptly dubbed "Index House," numbered fifty, plus a clerical force of seventy-five. The scholars went through all the books four times at a rate of six ideas a week, ultimately making some 900,000 decisions about dropping or changing references.

Finally, in 1952, nearly nine years after its inception and at a cost of some $2 million, the project was ready for printing: a fifty-four volume set of the *Great Books of the Western World*, comprising thirty-two thousand pages filled with twenty-five million words. Two of the volumes, representing well over half the money spent, constituted the *Syntopicon*, Adler's "survey of ideas" with essays on each of the 102 ideas. A third was Hutchins' *The Great Conversation*, in which he emphasized that great books constitute a most effective means of understanding not only an existing society but the people within it, that they contain the notable ideas which, recognized or not, dominate any particular society, and that there is no comparable repository of Western tradition and thought.[1]

There were critics—the most irascible was Dwight Macdonald in the *New Yorker*—who found reason for disparagement. Some believed that Hutchins was too dogmatic and doctrinaire. Some debated the choice of books and of ideas. But most agreed that the project was unusually impressive, to be compared favorably with the appearance of the first dictionary and the first encyclopaedia. Though critical of some of the set's aspects, in his review in the *New York Times* Gilbert Highet called it "a majestic set" and "a noble monument to the power of the human mind," and added: "They [the books] are a new and valuable proof of the high level of contemporary culture, worthy to be

[1] Hutchins had left the University of Chicago in 1950 to become associate director of the Ford Foundation.

set beside our thronged symphony concerts, our uncomfortably but encouragingly crowded art exhibitions, and other activities which are the reverse of 'U.S. materialism.'"

Besides helping to edit the work, Hutchins was instrumental in distributing the largest single lot through Paul Mellon's Old Dominion Foundation, which made a grant to buy 1,600 sets for libraries throughout the country. Subsequent sales went slowly, largely because of the need for building a special staff, but by 1956 a concentrated campaign was started, with the books priced at $298 and made available on the established *Encyclopaedia Britannica* twenty-four-month time-payment plan.

Another ancillary venture was the formation of the Collection of Contemporary American Painting sponsored by Encyclopaedia Britannica, Inc. Originally developed from an idea to commission painters to produce special illustrations for *Britannica Junior*, the collection of 121 paintings first went on view at the Art Institute of Chicago in April, 1945; in the group were works representing all contemporary styles and schools, from the academic to the abstract, from realism to impressionism, from Frederic Waugh to Stuart Davis, and from Grant Wood to Salvador Dali. And in the next five years the paintings were exhibited in forty major American cities, with attendance gratifyingly running into the millions.

Editorialists and art critics praised the company for stimulating the interest of the public in its national art, and various commentators declared that other business institutions had been given a cultural objective at which to aim. The show brought prestige to American art, aided the reputations of individual artists, and, as had been hoped, helped to spread the name of its sponsor. Noting that the show's catalogue displayed prominently the title of *Encyclopaedia Britannica*, Harry Salpeter, the respected critic, commented wryly: "If you reserve a small margin of your mind for the credit line, you will be doing no more for one of the leading cultural institutions of the English-speaking world than you do for the manufacturer of a dental cream through whose enterprise the humor of Bob Hope is made available to you."[2]

3

In mid-1944, the University of Chicago trustees were obliged to decide whether to take advantage of the institution's option to buy for

---

[2] At the end of the tour, Benton bought the collection, retained some of the works, sold some, and gave many to schools and other institutions.

$50,000 half of Benton's stock, thereby getting two-thirds ownership of the company. A negative decision was quickly reached.

Benton had assumed that if the company thrived the university would exercise its option, and he would then become the minority stockholder. The company had prospered in sales and profits beyond all anticipations, and already the university had received over $300,000 in royalties, but the option was now rejected. A new argument had implemented the old fear of having the university become responsible for the *Encyclopaedia Britannica:* The university was doing so well through its affiliation and benefiting so handsomely from the company's prosperity that any change in the relationship was thought unwise.

There were some easy explanations for this prosperity. Since the start of World War II, in contrast to the problems that had brought Horace Hooper close to ruin in the First World War, sales had risen, as they had, in fact, for most encyclopaedias. And they continued to rise for the duration of the war. Only paper shortages and insufficient printing and binding facilities prevented a more rapid increase. This boom resulted from war-swollen incomes and a lack of durable consumer goods; thousands of persons who had always wanted a top-quality reference work now found themselves able to afford and acquire one. Exempt from governmental credit restrictions, encyclopaedia makers tightened their monthly terms and still secured more customers.

As gross sales mounted, so did net profits. And this prosperity, in the opinion of some of the *Encyclopaedia Britannica's* top executives, seemed destined to continue indefinitely. They held to this view even after the war ended, when a slow shift should have been anticipated in consumer buying toward the kind of goods hard to get or unavailable during the war—automobiles, refrigerators, radios, vacuum cleaners.

Spending on current and fresh ventures remained high. One new one, based on Horace Hooper's venture after World War I, was *Ten Eventful Years,* a four-volume history of the decade preceding 1947. Elaborate plans were made for it. Contributors were selected from among the personages involved in the events of that period—generals, rulers of nations, diplomats, scholars. They included such women as Eleanor Roosevelt and Mme Chiang Kai-shek. But not much forethought was given to the means of selling the set. Published in September, 1947, it recorded the major happenings of 1936–46, disclosed many details—from the number of Nazi submarines lost to the sources for such war-inspired words as "scuttlebutt," "quisling," "commando," "gutbucket," and "bazooka"—and afforded what friendly critics characterized as a fascinating and instructive glimpse backward into a significant decade. But the set had no sustained sales appeal and had to be adjudged a failure.

Another enterprise was the invasion of the competitive retail book market by the establishment of a department called the Encyclopaedia Britannica Press. Some 2,400,000 paper-backed books for children were produced inexpensively, their illustrations taken from Encyclopaedia Britannica Films stills. But they languished in warehouses, for few of the top men in the company had knowledge or experience in this area and no skilled sales promotion department had been organized to sell the books. The venture was eventually discontinued, although the books later were successfully used as promotional premiums for *Britannica Junior*.

Persistently expensive was the continuing preparation of the *Great Books of the Western World,* with monthly costs often soaring to $80,000. In addition, two floors were rented for the firm in Chicago's stately Civic Opera Building, where formerly less than half a floor had been sufficient; this increase was in part necessary because the working force had doubled by the end of 1946 and in part due to the requirements of the films company, whose headquarters had been shifted from New York. Later the films company was moved to the Chicago suburb of Wilmette and entailed additional costs by helping to finance the purchase of homes for some fifty employees and their families and by leasing a large bank building, which was remodeled into offices, with a movie studio across the street.

Such adjustments and expansions were hardly unusual; companies of all kinds which had charted large earnings in the war years anticipated greater ones in the postwar period. The executives at Encyclopaedia Britannica, Inc., were following this trend. In addition to projects in progress, there were others discussed: an encyclopaedia of music, supplemented by long-playing records; an edition of the Bible based on the King James version but with new and special interpretative material; an almanac; and pocket-sized books with extracts from the *Encyclopaedia Britannica*.

But by the middle of 1947 such ideas, though interesting and worthwhile, were discarded, for expenditures had grown increasingly vexatious and, worse yet, the company, suddenly and critically, swirled into a crisis.

22

A Crisis Met and Solved

In 1946 estimates based on accelerated sales in the war years were that annual gross sales of the *Encyclopaedia Britannica* for the following year would amount to close to $32 million. Consequently, orders were placed for paper and for the printing of enough sets to cover this anticipated demand. But as the year drew to a close it became evident that the estimates had been unrealistically high. Sales had begun to fall off, and large numbers of uncollectible instalment accounts were accumulating fast. The prospects for 1947 looked far less attractive than they had a few months earlier, and it was too late for cutbacks and reductions in orders given to R. R. Donnelley and Sons. Yet, even this overestimate in printing requirements would have been of small import—in the reference-book field, swollen inventories can be worked off with a little time—had it not been for another larger, and far more critical, problem.

Ever since the days in Great Britain when Horace Hooper had instituted time-payment plans with his sale of the *Times* reprint of the ninth edition, most purchasers had paid by monthly instalments. By 1946, more than 80 per cent of *Encyclopaedia Britannica* owners were in this category, and their payments constituted the principal source of incoming cash for the company. Before turning over the *Encyclopaedia Britannica* to Benton and the University of Chicago, Sears, Roebuck and Company had provided various important services: financing, supervision of production, management of accounting and credit passing and of collections. The credit-and-collection services, it was agreed at the time of the 1943 transfer, would be maintained for at least five more years through the six hundred Sears, Roebuck retail stores, each staffed with people trained and experienced in this work. This was a considerable asset, for the retail stores were able to investigate prospective purchasers promptly, rejecting those who were not desirable credit risks. From 1943 through 1946, the Sears, Roebuck credit staff saw to it that bills were sent promptly, that monthly payments were made on time, and that when accounts fell behind, appropriate steps were taken to collect on them.

At World War II's end, General Wood was eager to expand his merchandising operations not only in the United States but in South America. Because he would require his capital and his credit people for this expansion, he asked Powell if Encyclopaedia Britannica, Inc., could assume its own credit-and-collections operations as soon as possible, instead of waiting for the five-year deadline specified in the 1943 contract. Aware that no preparations had been made by the encyclopaedia company to train or acquire sufficient personnel to assume this important phase of the business, Wood told Powell, "I'll send our people over to train your people." Powell agreed to the plan. He assured Benton—who was meanwhile absorbed in his postwar duties as Assistant Secretary of State in Washington—that the company would actually save money by centralizing collections in Chicago under its own direction.

In December, 1946, more than a full year before termination of the 1943 agreement, the shift started. Ninety skilled credit-and-collection employees were transferred from Sears, Roebuck to the *Encyclopaedia Britannica* offices to train workers assigned to or hired especially for the new undertaking. They stayed for about three months, then returned to their own jobs. The force that remained was supposed to be sufficiently trained.

But it was soon alarmingly apparent that the training period had been far too brief. Moreover, no such group, however well trained, could be expected to duplicate the credit-and-collection of some six hundred on-the-spot credit managers in Sears, Roebuck's far-flung stores. Within two months after April, 1947, the new system broke down so badly that the customary envelopes for forwarding payments were not even being sent out. Collections dropped off by hundreds of thousands of dollars monthly. Scores of customers made their payments voluntarily, but often, when their money reached the main office, no one knew where to put it or to which accounts to credit it. In addition, with local credit controls relaxed, many salesmen took orders from customers who were poor or, at best, marginal credit risks.

By the early fall of 1947 it was evident that not only was the collection system in a state of disintegration but sales were far below estimates. And R. R. Donnelley and Sons, in the midst of its own expansion program, was asking for payment of a printing bill of $400,-000. The encyclopaedia company, in its dealings with the huge printing firm, had, since the transfer of 1943, adhered to the early-payment schedules worked out by Sears, Roebuck; under these, payments were to be made as soon as paper was purchased and printing proceeded.

Contrary to the optimistic predictions of the previous year, it now appeared that the company might end the year 1947 with a substantial deficit.

3

That September, when Benton resigned as Assistant Secretary of State with commendations from President Truman and Secretary of State Marshall, he left Washington accompanied by Harry Houghton, president of Muzak Corporation and a member of Encyclopaedia Britannica, Inc.'s Board of Directors since 1945. On the trip to Chicago he told Houghton the essential facts of the crisis and asked him to undertake a swift survey. Canadian-born, in his mid-forties, Houghton had a reputation for salvaging ailing companies.

Once in Chicago, Benton made clear Houghton's status in a letter to Herbert P. Zimmerman, then president of R. R. Donnelley and Sons. "I have told Buck Powell," he wrote, "that Harry Houghton is to act as my full representative, with full authority. I know you will give Harry your own views, with complete frankness, and I would be grateful to you if you can find time to pass them along to me." He was disturbed, added Benton, about erroneous estimates of sales, the soaring of operating expenses, and commitments on such new ventures as *Ten Eventful Years*, the *Great Books of the Western World*, and Encyclopaedia Britannica Films.

Houghton examined ledgers and account books. He talked to Powell and Schoenewald and with lesser executives whose warnings had not always been heeded. Unable to borrow on inventory, Houghton managed to get the company out of some of its commitments for printing and paper. After stern discussions, the tempo of development on the *Great Books* project was slackened; its current operating appropriation was reduced by more than two-thirds, and the staff for the *Syntopicon* was skeletonized. Officials at the University of Chicago listened patiently and sympathetically to the details of the company's plight and agreed to forego immediate payment of royalties, accepting long-term debentures for the $468,000 due that year. (Since 1943 the university had already received $1,408,944 in royalties, which had been assigned to its general education fund.) From the sale of surplus stocks of paper, $92,000 was procured.

At a board meeting the following January, Powell reported the dire news: total sales for 1947 would be $16,428,000, about half the amount that had been predicted earlier. Benton loaned the company $351,000 of his own money and this, together with other assets that could be gathered immediately, enabled payment of the Donnelley bill, the only one overdue. One reason for Benton's action was that the banks with which the company dealt refused to extend more generous terms although—as they were under contract to do—they did increase the loans against the instalment accounts receivable to the agreed limit of $7,800,000.

4

Yet all this was not enough. Significant changes had to be made in the tottering credit-and-collection system. Against the objections of Schoenewald and other executives who insisted that this specific problem would somehow solve itself, Houghton set out to revamp the operation. To supervise the reorganization, he installed Robert Conger, the firm's operating manager in charge of manufacturing, processing, and warehousing since 1945. Before joining the company Conger had directed a widespread door-to-door collection organization for the mail-order firm of Spiegel, Inc., and had helped to build that company's chain of retail stores and order offices.

One of the first of the Houghton-Conger proposals was to require that all monthly payments for sets be collected through the local division sales offices scattered over the United States instead of by the Chicago headquarters. "It won't work," argued the skeptics. "You're never going to get division managers to concern themselves with that kind of detail."

There were other differences of opinion. Basic disagreements grew in virulence. Early in 1948 Powell resigned. Named to succeed him, Houghton sent letters of instruction to each of the company's sixteen division managers, and he also made personal visits to key division offices. "You've been salesmen up to now and only salesmen," was Houghton's message. "Now you must be salesmen and executives. From now on you're responsible for collections as well as for sales in your areas. The better the collections on the sales that your men make, the better the credit risks and the higher your commissions and your net earnings."

Schoenewald had predicted that if such a demand were made, the division chiefs would assuredly resign. Yet not a single man left after Houghton's new system went into operation, with Conger in charge of credit and collections. In the spring of 1949 Schoenewald's resignation was accepted; Paul E. Seaman, the company's division manager in New York, was transferred to Chicago to replace him as vice-president in charge of sales.

5

Houghton had carried out his assigned task well. Within six months the company, aided further by stringent economies, cautious budgeting, and a reduction in the working staff, was steady once more. But despite the progress, Houghton told Benton, what was really needed now to head the company was a top-flight operating executive with years of experience in the encyclopaedia business. After a survey of candidates during 1949, the choice narrowed to three and finally to one, Robert C. Preble, a veteran in the specialized world of subscription book publishing.

A sales-minded individual since his boyhood in the Chicago suburb of Oak Park, Preble had sold calculating machines and books during his summers at the University of Illinois, where he also worked on the staff of the *Daily Illini*. Six months after graduation in 1921, Preble had become office manager for Midland Press, a Chicago publisher of reference books; when he resigned in 1925 over disagreement with the firm's editorial and sales policies, he was a vice-president. He joined the W. F. Quarrie Company, then publishers of the *World Book Encyclopaedia,* and remained with that firm and its corporate successors for more than two decades, filling the positions of advertising manager, editorial director, national sales manager, treasurer, and executive vice-president. At the time he was approached, Preble was contemplating resigning to establish a business of his own. But Houghton and Benton were persuasive. That November Preble was installed as executive vice-president and, after he had surveyed all phases of the company from its home offices to its sales methods, he was named president at the beginning of 1951.[1]

As the new president, Preble reversed or abandoned various administrative and personnel procedures, reassigned responsibilities in accordance with his own estimate of an individual's talents and experience, and established, unlike most of his predecessors, a practice of discussing general policies fully with department heads and subordinates. He kept the prices of both the *Encyclopaedia Britannica* and *Britannica Junior* from advancing in the next half dozen years— despite increases in the costs of paper, printing, and binding—by insisting that the various firms involved in their manufacture perfect more efficient production techniques. As a result of economies, funds became available for a stronger editorial-revision program. Salaries of clerical workers were adjusted upward, and departments with outmoded methods were streamlined. In July, 1951, new offices were established on an upper floor of a building off Michigan Boulevard, at half the annual rental of the Opera House quarters. The cumbersome structure of the company's national sales organization was revamped. Certain divisional sales territories were realigned, with each division subdivided into local districts. The long-time compensation program of salaries plus bonuses for achieving sales quotas was discarded. Instead, division and district managers were virtually established in business for themselves on a profit-sharing basis, their earnings dependent on the cash collected in their respective territories and on their own efficiency in controlling the costs of producing sales.

A mail-order division became popular and profitable. Its key attrac-

[1] Benton was now in the United States Senate, having been appointed in 1949 by his ex-partner, Chester Bowles, then governor of Connecticut, after the retirement of Senator Raymond Baldwin. Elected in 1950 to fill out Baldwin's term, Benton remained in the Senate until 1953. His term was characterized by his support of the Hoover Commission's reorganization proposals, by his fight for appropriations for the "Voice of America," and by his constant attack on Wisconsin's Senator Joseph McCarthy, whose eventual censure stemmed from Benton's demand for McCarthy's expulsion from the Senate.

tion was the *Britannica Book of the Year,* notably improved in editorial content and in illustrations. A later editorial innovation in the *Book of the Year* was the inclusion of "broad subject surveys." In the 1955 volume, one was "Atomic Energy: Today and Tomorrow" with articles by Lewis L. Strauss, chairman of the Atomic Energy Commission, and by scientists engaged in atomic research. The other, "Latin America," stressed the developing awareness throughout the world of the importance of Central and South America to the United States and other free countries. Benton himself contributed a significant 27,000-word report in the 1956 edition. It dealt with the techniques of propaganda, indoctrination, and education in the Soviet Union and was based on his intensive and spirited discussions with U.S.S.R. government officials, artists, educators, civil servants, writers, and administrators during a visit there in 1955. In the article and in other writings and speeches Benton stressed the evidence he found of the tremendous advances in scientific development and education in the Soviet Union and of the vast training programs there of specialists in every phase of the expanding Russian economy and in scientific ventures.

Another project that proved successful in this post-crisis period was publication of the interesting two-volume *World Language Dictionary* developed by Preble from plans he brought with him when he joined the company. Published in 1954, the first volume is the Funk and Wagnall's *New Practical Standard Dictionary,* but much of the second, running to 540 pages, provides a basic list of the 6,400 most-used English words with their equivalents, in parallel columns, in six other languages—French, German, Italian, Spanish, Swedish, and Yiddish. An additional section realphabetizes the words of each language and contains phonetic pronunciations and explanations of grammatical rules.

6

Other publications, begun in earlier years, continued to thrive. The fifteen-volume *Britannica Junior* is the only encyclopaedia in existence designed solely for school children through the ninth grade. Its closest rivals contain material for students in the upper elementary grades and high school and even for adults.

Since its acquisition in 1934, *Britannica Junior,* whose editor, Don E. Walter, is a former teacher, has been revised in varying degrees no less than twenty-three times. Youngsters themselves selected the type in which the set is printed. A vote that was taken favored large ten-point type, and the work has used this size ever since. Other similar experiments with illustrations, length of sentences and paragraphs, and maps were conducted. Material in *Britannica Junior* is selected with the counsel of a special University of Chicago advisory committee of educational experts together with editorial consultants and librarians from other major American universities. And the principles guiding the selection of contributors to the junior edition are akin to those for the parent—but with one major difference. Each original manuscript for *Britannica Junior*—whether by Roscoe Pound, former dean of the Harvard Law School, on "Law," by Emily Post on "Etiquette," or by Vilhjalmur Stefansson, the Arctic explorer, on "Eskimo"—is turned over to a staff of eight "text simplifiers" for examination in accord with established principles of vocabulary for the grade-school child. The simplified copy is returned to the contributor for rereading to make certain that no changes have been made in meaning or implication. New contributors are often selected from among writers of best-selling books for children; always the stress is on obtaining authorities in their fields.

Each revision, too, has brought a greater number of illustrations, especially of those in color. The number of diagrammatic drawings also has increased from edition to edition; all help to reduce to simple terms either various mechanical operations, such as the working of a gasoline engine, or physiological functions, such as human breathing. Through diagrams and specific and unencumbered instructions, young readers can learn, among many things, how to lay out a baseball diamond or make objects out of soap, wood, or paper, how to sew, cook, identify birds, animals, and flowers, or build a campfire. Maps of varying sizes constitute an important section. Again, as in the text, both index and maps, even with the mass of detailed information, are highly legible.

The work's first volume is the *Ready Reference Index*. This is no mere listing or sublisting of articles in the other fourteen volumes but, as a writer in *Grade Teacher Magazine* once described it, "the key which unlocks the vast store of information in the complete set." The procedure is handy: The child first looks up the major topic in which he is interested. Next to the word is its pronunciation with standard dictionary diacritical markings, and next to this is a full but simple definition of the word. Then, in heavy type, the volume and page of the complete article on the word are given. And finally are listings of subtopics, charts, pictures, and maps.

Another subsidiary publication is the *Encyclopaedia Britannica World Atlas*. The first edition, issued in 1942, was the product of a meeting of world geographers sponsored by the company to discuss the composition of an "ideal" world atlas. Since that time the atlas has gone through twelve editions, each an improvement over the last. It includes not only the general and detailed maps one would expect to find in any reputable atlas but also special data and information intended, in the words of G. Donald Hudson, *Encyclopaedia Britannica*'s geographical editor, to "contribute to the progress of avoiding periods of stress among the peoples of the world and to the need for understanding each other's lives and living."

The latest edition of the atlas shows vividly this orientation of subject matter to a world perspective. It contains geopolitical maps and summaries of each of the world's political units set up in statistical tables listing areas, populations, transportation facilities, communications, major crops, number of livestock, minerals, forest products, chief items of manufacture, value of foreign trade, and major export and import commodities. A section on geographical comparisons contains data on famous waterfalls, oceans and seas, islands, lakes, rivers, peaks, canals, dams, and bridges. The glossary of geographical terms and the index are thorough and detailed. As in the senior and junior encyclopaedias, there is continuous revision, employing the experience and knowledge of British, Canadian, and American geographers and the research efforts of scholars and scientists in geology, climatology, history, political science, economics, and anthropology.

7

Since 1954, much time and effort have been expended in reshaping the company's policies and methods in Great Britain.

During the years after Horace Hooper's death, there was no official British division of the company, since all sales and business were handled through the overseas branches of Sears, Roebuck and Company. By 1945, London headquarters were on Dean Street in the Soho district, occupying two picturesque but inadequate buildings, one of which, rumor had it, was once the home of Lord Nelson's paramour, Lady Hamilton. The editorial director then was William D. Clark, a journalist who had served with the British Information Service in New York and as a press attaché in Washington during the Second World War. Later Clark resigned to join the staff of the London *Observer,* and John Armitage, editor of the *Fortnightly* and a specialist in educational matters, was named London editor. A. E. Dolphin, who had started with the company as an accountant in the last days of Horace Hooper, was appointed managing director and served until his resignation in 1953.

One of Preble's objectives after assuming the presidency was to modernize the British subsidiary. The editorial and business offices, by 1956, had been moved from the Dean Street buildings and were consolidated on the top floor of a modern office building on Belgrave Street. Bookkeeping methods dating from the age of Charles Dickens were replaced by new accounting machines. Printing and binding of volumes in England was simplified and increased. Production methods and policies in the fully owned subsidiary now more closely follow the American example. Armitage's primary duties involve liaison with committees of scholar-advisers from the universities of Oxford, Cambridge, and London, as well as responsibility for all articles written by authorities in Great Britain and the Commonwealth and, indeed, all over Europe. He also edits the British *Book of the Year,* which is wholly different from the American edition. Salesmen are hired, trained, and directed as are their American counterparts. Sales director is S. D. Keetch, who has absorbed American-style selling techniques, with some modifications. Avoiding flamboyancy or "gimmicks," Keetch's force of over two hundred has steadily brought yearly revenues to a point where *Encyclopaedia Britannica* is the leader in the subscription book field in Europe. Until his sudden death in 1955 while sailing to the United States, Hector McNeil, former Secretary of State for Scotland in the Labour government, was in over-all charge as chairman and managing director of the British subsidiary. He was succeeded as chairman by Sir Geoffrey Crowther, who, in his nearly two decades as editor of the *Economist,* was among the firmest exponents of staunch Anglo-American alliances; he was added to the boards of the encyclopaedia company and to the films firm as well as to the Board of Editors. The post of managing director went to Graham Martin, a businessman who for a previous decade had filled the same position with the British Relay Wireless and Associated Companies.

The company's health has improved year by year since the crisis of 1947–48. Stock earnings are plowed back to be used for sales expansion and improvement of the encyclopaedia itself and affiliated ventures, and for such new projects as, in 1957, the *Enciclopedia barsa,* a fifteen-volume work with a consultants' board made up of the heads of leading universities of Latin America, Spain, and Portugal.

A striking indication of its condition has been the amount of royalty payments and other cash benefits given to the University of Chicago under the contract of 1943. Toward the end of 1955, Benton, in a letter to General Wood reporting on the company's financial standing and the piling up annual royalties for the university, commented: "Larry Kimpton [Lawrence A. Kimpton, Chancellor of the University of Chicago] not long ago told me that the *Britannica* is going to rank in university annals as the university's second largest donor, second only to John D. Rockefeller."

Early in 1957 the encyclopaedia company paid more than $2 million to retire the university's preferred shares and remaining debentures; also, the university canceled its option to buy the block of stock which would give it, upon Benton's death, control of the firm. In a personal report to the trustees, Benton noted that for that very year the university's cash income from the affiliation would amount to $700,000, bringing to $4 million its total share from the fifteen-year association. He also predicted that if sales volume remained at existing high levels the university would derive another $4 million over the next five years. Whereupon the trustees responded with a resolution of appreciation, describing the history of the affiliation since 1943 as "a brilliant and inspiring story of achievement" and citing Benton and his associates for "their capable operation of this fine business enterprise and for the remarkable contribution that their efforts have made to the growth and development of the University of Chicago and to education in general."

Avowed realists in an enterprise that must compete on commercial levels without debilitating its standards and reputation, the executives of Encyclopaedia Britannica, Inc., are aware of the basic causes— beyond the financial and managerial skills of its operating officials— for the status that has been maintained and, in recent years, strengthened.

The first is the quality of the *Encyclopaedia Britannica* itself, the responsibility of many editorial executives and their aides, advisers —scholars, educators, and scientists—and assorted authorities from the greatest universities of the English-speaking nations, and thousands of contributors from all over the world.

And the second is the special abilities of the people who sell the *Encyclopaedia Britannica.*

Part Five

Part Five

23

The Modern EB: *How It Is Edited*

In editorial methods and procedures, the modern *Encyclopaedia Britannica,* unlike its predecessors, represents a kind of complex journalism. Its system of continuous revision, in effect since publication of the fourteenth edition, sets up rigid deadlines and strict schedules, requires constant scrutiny of its contents and a steady watchfulness on world events necessitating textual alterations, and makes imperative keeping its information as up to date as is possible in a set of books whose forty-one thousand articles comprise more than forty million words.

Vital to this system is a corps of permanent advisers, some seventy-five scholars on the faculties of the University of Chicago and other major American universities and from Great Britain's London, Cambridge, and Oxford universities. Each of these advisers has a definitely assigned function: to watch articles within his field of specialization. Each counsels the encyclopaedia's editors on the necessity for current revision of an article, the need for additions, deletions, or entirely new articles, and the contributors most competent to make such changes or to write fresh material.

By methods devised by two veteran editorial workers, Mrs. Mae McKay and Mrs. Harriet Milburn, a large editing staff checks articles, works on the important index volume, and handles and controls the flow of copy from contributors. The task is a constant one, for to supplant the numbered editions there have been, since the fourteenth edition in 1929, new printings at least once each year and sometimes more frequently. Some changes have been minor—a shift in a statistic, a change of personnel, a correction of a spelling error. But some of the larger revisions have involved changing or rewriting as many as four million words and recruiting over four hundred new contributors.

Inevitably, new information seldom fits neatly into established revision schedules. With the explosion of the atom bomb at Hiroshima and subsequent fast-moving developments, a full article on the subject was required swiftly, and to make room for it four full pages of new material were inserted in the proper volume. Made suspect, too, by the explosion, were some five hundred other articles, from "Alchemy" to "Uranium," which had to be checked—and, in many cases, altered —by editorial workers before the onrushing deadline for a scheduled new printing. When Elizabeth II became the British queen in 1952, more than a few royal biographies and articles on English history were affected. Her accession added a Roman numeral to the first Elizabeth. Further, because of the British custom of referring to virtually all government offices, official celebrations, and prizes in the name of the sovereign, all through the work were scattered references to the high court of justice known as "King's Bench Division," "His Majesty's Stationer," and "King's Scouts." These had to be changed. Yet there were exceptions to the rule, such as the "King's Cup Race," which retained its old designation. The "King's Prize" for shooting, on the other hand, had to be altered, as did the British anthem, now "God Save the Queen."

Most frequently in need of periodic revision are the scientific sections. In some scientific fields, changes can be anticipated; all articles in these classifications are scheduled for review by specified monitors at short intervals. But sometimes unexpected developments occur. In 1953, when anthropologists declared that the Piltdown man's jaw was a hoax, and thereby revised many suggested theories of modern man's origins, editor Walter Yust and his aides immediately consulted the index for references. They were relieved to find that the article on the subject did note that many experts had always expressed doubts about the find. But it also stated that the jaw represented an individual of early Pleistocene times. The article was not scheduled for full review until 1956. But to report the hoax as soon as possible, without waiting for that printing or for a special discussion of the subject in the *Book of the Year,* the editors quickly consulted one of the advisers on anthropology. And he specified how, with a minimum of patching on the actual plates from which the article was printed, interim alterations could be made immediately.

Wars have always caused drastic changes—and editorial headaches. Destroyed monuments and buildings, migrations and increases or decreases in population, new boundaries, new alliances, political shifts, the establishment of new independent states—all must be recorded in the reference work as soon as possible, for readers are quick to note such omissions. An example of how political changes can be vexatious is the checkered history of Vilnyus, the European city also known as Wilno and Vilna. Before 1938 it was in dispute between Poland and Lithuania; then it was seized on March 17 of that year by Poland, captured by the Soviet Union in September, 1939, ceded to Lithuania a month later, taken again by the Soviet Union on June 15, 1940, lost to Germany on June 22, returned in the summer of 1944 to Soviet control, and ultimately established as the capital of the Lithuanian Soviet Socialist Republic. Doggedly, the *Encyclopaedia Britannica* editors followed and recorded the shifting fortunes of this city and of others similarly affected.

Physical catastrophes send the editors scurrying to the latest printing of their work. In 1950, researchers had just completed some three hundred editorial changes to incorporate the latest findings concerning heights of peaks, lengths of rivers, and populations of cities in the vast Himalayan mountain range. Almost simultaneously with the completion of this detailed job, heavy earthquakes were reported in that area. The mountains were said to be "crawling southward" under the influence of violent earth shocks; some peaks were abruptly rising and others were falling, rivers were changing their courses, whole villages were disappearing. All the toil that had preceded the news of these disasters had to be repeated for the next printing.

As with a newspaper, certain kinds of material can be prepared before a specific event. As soon as the Presidential candidates of all parties are nominated, for instance, assignments are instantly made for full biographies of each nominee, and appropriate photographs are assembled. At the same time, shorter biographies are also prepared. When the results of the national election are known, the full biography of the winner and the pictures are sped to the printers, as is the shorter biography of the loser. Similarly, if and when Alaska and Hawaii are admitted to statehood, the *Encyclopaedia Britannica* will be ready; changes will be necessary in at least 514 articles and in the big full-color plate now showing the forty-eight-starred American flag. Occasionally, a new edition has been held up just beyond a set deadline to record a late development. When Franklin D. Roosevelt died suddenly, the editors were able to insert this event into the work along with information about his successor, Harry S. Truman. When Pope Pius XII was critically ill, the printers were asked to hold pertinent sections of Volume XVII ("P" to "Planti") as long as possible; this was done, although the crisis was passed when the pontiff took a turn for the better and survived his illness.

2

At the heart of the complex system designed to maintain the flow of fresh material into those areas where alterations are most frequently required is the copy-control section built over the years since adoption of continuous revision. But there are essential preliminaries to the work of copy control. Two years before each new printing, Yust carefully studies the schedule of some thirty subject classifications into which the millions of words are divided. After conferences with his immediate aides and after studying recommendations from scores of editorial advisers, he selects the articles deemed in need of revision. When the lists of articles to be revised are drawn, they are dispatched to the specific advisers at American and English universities for the names of likely contributors. Generally the suggestions of these scholars on the need for change and the best possible contributors are followed, since they are all prime authorities in their respective fields. But occasionally an adviser is challenged, as when one proposed that the biographies of Octavia and Miranda Hill, nineteenth-century pioneers in British housing, be deleted for "more important matter," inasmuch as neither was especially well known outside of England. This suggestion evoked from John Armitage, the set's London editor, the protest: "I feel faint at the suggestion. Miranda may . . . depart from the title but Octavia stands second in our line of 19th century heroines to Florence Nightingale. Her name is honourably mentioned in any review of housing, and housing managers cannot pass their examinations without a knowledge of her life and work. . . . If Octavia does not rate as a great woman, there is none." The adviser was overruled and neither of the Hill sisters was eliminated.

Dates, names, and essential details about the articles to be revised are recorded by the copy-control section on large cards in a mechanical device variously known among the hundred editorial workers as "the Robot" or "the Monster." With the flick of a switch, it can disclose the precise status of every article. Indeed, every bit of data about a specific article, from the moment a prospective contributor is asked to handle it to the date on which the corrected proof is sent to the printer, is known to the Robot and remains known not only for the current edition but for those of the future. The Robot has rarely lost a challenge. A group of advisers clustered around it once defied a young lady in charge to inform them what had happened to the article on "Goldfish." She flipped a knob, looked at a card, then turned to one of the professors, saying, "Why, you've been holding it for two months and we've been trying to get it from you." Another inquired about an article in his specialty and was quickly informed, "The contributor has died and we are expecting a suggestion from you for a successor." When the adviser expressed surprise, explaining that he had only just heard of the contributor's death, he was told of another editorial worker whose task it is to examine each day's obituary notices in the *New York Times* and apprise the Robot of the demise of any contributor.

On receipt of the names of proposed contributors, letters of solicitation, specific in content and intent, are dispatched to them. They state briefly what is wanted and by what date, and that the rate of compensation is five dollars for reading each page of printed text and two cents a word for writing the revision, a rate established at the time of the publication of the fourteenth edition. The invitation is sometimes rejected, but rarely because of low payment. Most experts and scholars realize the prestige attached to being asked to contribute to the *Encyclopaedia Britannica*, and less than 2 per cent of those invited have ever declined.

An avid statistician once reckoned the number of processes from the time the copy is solicited until it appears in its proper place in the proper volume some nine months later to be 569. When the contributor accepts his assignment, a copy of the article in the latest printing is sent to him, and the date is entered on the proper card in the Robot. A favorite story in the editorial lore of the company involves the head of a history department in a western university to whom a historical article, many years unchanged, was sent. In agreeing to revise it, the professor was aroused enough to write, "I'll be glad to do this for you. The article is badly organized, inaccurate and full of errors of both omission and commission." An investigation revealed that the critic was the man who had written the earlier article years before—a discovery that remained undisclosed until the new treatise had been received at the editor's desk.

Most writers of major articles are given at least a year to prepare their manuscripts; not until a month before the scheduled delivery of the article is the author prodded to produce it. Immediately upon receipt, the words are counted and payment is promptly made. This policy was instituted because of Yust's own experiences as a free-lance writer, when quick compensation, however small, often elated him more than a delayed check, however large.

The next step for the manuscript is the Robot, where receipt is recorded and a note made of illustrations furnished or needed. Along the route, the copy is read by the specialist advisers for authenticity, then checked several times by editorial workers. After Yust and his assistant editors read it, either the manuscript is approved or a rewrite is decreed. Never is any material rewritten by anyone save the contributor himself. Any article that is difficult to read or obtuse is sent back to the writer with a request that he clarify the bothersome sections. Although few specific instructions are sent to contributors, it has been deemed wise to ask physical scientists, who often write on technical matters which cannot be explained simply, to adhere to a few general rules. The opening paragraph of these instructions reads: "Each article under each heading should begin with a clear statement in one sentence of the meaning and scope of that heading, comparable to an extended dictionary definition. The first paragraph following that heading should be an amplification of the first sentence, possibly with a discussion of subheadings and the like if the article is to be a long one. If it is to be very long with a number of sections, there should be a short list of contents by section-titles and division-titles."

An article that does not require rewriting by the author and is finally approved is turned over to typists who retype it on copy-fitting paper. Subeditors then reread and check the article. They prepare layouts of the actual page where the article will be placed. By this time it is known whether the revised article will be longer or shorter than the original. For either eventuality, a solution is ready. In a Killer-Filler file are lists of short articles that advisers have suggested can be eliminated from the page or adjoining pages without arousing protests from readers or impairing the basic purposes of the encyclopaedia, and collections of likely entries, mainly brief biographies or extended definitions, that can be inserted if a new article runs short. If the Killer-Filler file cannot produce reasonable balm for the situation, part of the new entry, if too long, is set in smaller type or, often, an additional page is inserted.

Back to the copy-control section goes the article, once it has been tailored to fit. Initials of the contributor are affixed to the manuscript, and it is then transferred to indexers who arrange their cards on a circular device they call their Lazy Susan. They not only make direct changes but also note all cross-references, "see also's," and related data that may be affected by additions, deletions, and other changes.

A few more technical steps, and the copy is ready for the linotype operators at R. R. Donnelley and Sons's Lakeside Press. This occurs after proper notations have been transmitted to the Robot about the myriad details of specific articles. Proofs are sent to the writers for final checking and last-minute changes; all proofs are read, too, by editorial experts. In previous years proofs were rarely sent to contributors, but Yust put this into effect shortly after he became editor, for he realized the importance both professionally and psychologically of such a method. He also recalled with what indignation George Bernard Shaw replied when offered not proofs but a typed copy of his fourteenth-edition article on socialism. "Do not bother about sending me a typescript," Shaw scrawled on one of his postcards. "I have the carbon duplicate of the one I sent you, besides an earlier-corrected draft from which it was fair-copied. But if I cannot have a proof (which is really shocking) at least let the printer set up from my copy and not from a copy of it; for if the printer's errors are reinforced by the typist's errors, and both edited by an American proofreader who will conclude that I must mean exactly the opposite of what I had written (accidentally omitting the nots) the result will be disastrous."

3

Shaw is one of forty-three Nobel Prize winners among the four thousand contributors to the *Encyclopaedia Britannica*. Most of them, like Shaw and Einstein and Sir Norman Angell ("Outlawry of War"), Hans Adolph Krebs ("Citric Acid"), General George C. Marshall (a section of "World War II"), and J. J. R. Macleod ("Insulin"), were asked to contribute after they had won this honor. But some were contributors even before their selection: Ralph Bunche ("Beira," "Belgian Congo," and "Nairobi"), who wrote for the set four years before he won the Nobel Prize in 1950, and Professors Linus C. Pauling ("Theory of Resonance," "Valence," and "Ice") and Glenn T. Seaborg, author of six articles from "Actinium" to "Transuranium Elements."

Shaw's article, interestingly enough, has been little altered since its publication in 1929, although some additions have been made to it. This is true of other major and minor classics written for earlier editions that remain useful to students and scholars and casual readers alike. There are among them Thomas Babington Macaulay's biographical essays on Samuel Johnson, Oliver Goldsmith, and John Bunyan; Sir Donald Francis Tovey's writings on music, more than three dozen articles from "Aria" to "Wagner, Wilhelm Richard"; G. K. Chesterton's vivid, contentious treatise on Charles Dickens; Sigmund Freud's essay on "Psychoanalysis," with additions enumerating advances in the important field in which he pioneered; and Julian Huxley's authoritative "Courtship of Animals."

4

The exigencies of time and expense often make it impossible for the continuous revision method to include as many changes as editors and readers would like. To help fill the gaps are the *Book of the Year* and the Library Research Service, both of which have developed here and in Great Britain since their beginnings in the 1930's.

The first of these, in addition to its subject surveys, contains more than a million words in its annual one thousand articles, reporting on developments and news during the previous year in activities varying from "Accident Prevention" and "Infantile Paralysis" to "Tariffs" and "Zoology." Each issue is new in content, but the list of subjects remains essentially stable. Editorial procedures resemble those of the parent set, but the time between receipt of manuscripts and finished volume is only five months. Deadlines for contributors are spread from mid-September to mid-December, with most articles due by the end of October. As with the encyclopaedia, a multitude of details including a great deal of reading and checking of data is involved before final copies are sent to the printer.

Since its origin, the function of the Library Research Service has been to reply to readers' questions on subjects not covered either in the set or in the yearbook. Each purchaser has the right to ask a maximum of fifty questions over a period of ten years, but no replies are given to seekers of medical or legal advice or specific professional or commercial information. In its first years, the service received questions that could often be answered by reference to only one or two books. But as readers became more conversant with the privileges of the valuable department and the amount of information that it could supply, the questions grew more involved and more difficult.

The service sends its researchers for information to many institutions, from the Chicago Public Library to New York's Library of Engineering Societies to the San Francisco Public Library and, of course, to the Library of Congress. Owners of the *Encyclopaedia Britannica* receive, in answer to their inquiries, individual, single-spaced reports, from four to as many as thirty pages long, made up of extracts from the highest authorities and supplemented by a bibliography to spur further individual study.

The department has always been stubborn in its refusal to be stumped. Actually, its rate of defeat has been about 1 per cent. On the other hand, the following is a representative list of reports sent out in a single day after researchers had collected their material:

Admission of China to the United Nations: Pro and Con
Security Measures and the Threat to Civil Liberties
Communism in the Schools
The Future of the Coal Industry
Statistics on the Sale of Soft Drinks in Bottles and Cans
The Guaranteed Annual Wage
Designing Skiving Tools
Statistical Quality Control for the Electronics Industry
Marketing Dehydrated Alfalfa
Organization and Operation of a Fabric Mart
Making Decorative Tiles for Table Tops
Construction of a Buffet Sideboard With Hutch China Cupboard
Interplanetary Navigation
Tibetan Concept of Morality
Maya Indian Baptismal Rites for Children Aged 3–12
Psychoanalytical Interpretation of the Works of Dostoevsky and Shakespeare
Current Soviet Theories on the Origin of the Solar System
Lanchester's Equations on the Phugoid Theory of the Flight Path
Nature Study for Children
Children's Fears
Federal Aid to Education

For owners of *Britannica Junior* an adjunct to the Library Research Service is designed to aid parents and children. Pamphlets, booklets, and bibliographies are available for set owners on an extensive range of problems, from "Babies: Their Care and Training" to "Cultural Activities for Children," in addition to specific reports on questions involving quarrels among siblings, activities for rainy days, eating habits, home duties for children, vocational opportunities, and sex instruction.

5

Despite all precautions, checking and rechecking, and expert proof-reading, letters complaining of errors, omissions, defects, misstatements, or misinterpretations in E B are inevitable. Keen attention— even when the writer's return address is a state mental hospital and his missive an eight-page farrago of nonsense about how to achieve perpetual motion or square the circle—is paid to all letters. Sometimes these communications provide useful clues to new information and do catch mistakes which slipped past everyone on the 569-step route from contributor's desk to printed page. Every form of criticism, whether in letters or publications, is diligently investigated; many are referred to the contributor and to the relevant adviser. In an average year the most prevalent plaints, constituting some 70 per cent of the total number received, charge errors of fact or omission, yet careful editorial checks show that less than 6 per cent of such grievances have any validity.

Charges of non-inclusion are sometimes as difficult to down as the belief that rewards are offered for finding errors; that myth has persisted since the days when the company offered a prize of a dollar to any boy or girl who found a mistake in the early editions of *Britannica Junior*. Such awards were given only for a year or two, but letter writers still cagily ask about the "big prize" before disclosing the nature of the purported error. One correspondent in Ohio, when informed that the company would be happy to learn what mistakes he claimed to have found but had to decline to pay any premium, replied, "I, as a lawyer, sell my professional services. If you do not deign my information worth at least $50, let us drop the correspondence forthwith." At that, the Ohio lawyer was comparatively mild in his request. Demands others have made include (1) a new set of the *Encyclopaedia Britannica* plus the *World Atlas* and *World Language Dictionary*, (2) $5,000, and (3) a position as an assistant editor.

6

For many years, no critic or scholar has had cause to write about the set with such vehemence as those who attacked William Robertson Smith's treatises on religious subjects in the 1880's or as Willard Huntington Wright did in his peevish *Misinforming a Nation* in 1917. Some of the bitterest attacks in recent years have come from the Soviet Union. In 1952, when the Soviet Union was claiming Russian origin of most of the great inventions, they assailed the editors of the *Encyclopaedia Britannica* as "modern savages" because Guglielmo Marconi instead of A. S. Popov was named the inventor of the wireless telegraph and James Watt instead of I. I. Polzunov was called "father of the steam engine." This, however, was not the first assault by the Soviets. Four years earlier, William Benton received a translation of an article in Moscow's *New Times* titled, "How the *Encyclopaedia Britannica* Distorts History." It was filled with allegations that "lies and fabrications" made up the work's articles on the Union of Soviet Socialist Republics. Benton forwarded copies to Hutchins and Yust for comment. Hutchins' reply was characteristically brief and pungent: "Nuts!" But Yust made a point-by-point rejoinder, carefully refuting the charges that the work had neglected the role of the Communist party in the Russian Revolution, that there was no mention of the Stakhanov movement to reward laborers for increased production, that the heroic defense of Stalingrad received not a word of attention, and that the official *History of the Communist Party of the Soviet Union* was unlisted. Besides citing page and line in his rejoinder, Yust suggested a more careful use of the index. By 1955, relations were more tranquil. Benton, visiting the Soviet Union, interviewed the editors of the Soviet encyclopaedia and asked if they were satisfied that the *Encyclopaedia Britannica* devoted a fair amount of space to their vast country. They replied affirmatively but insisted that their encyclopaedia was superior because of its "complete objectivity," although admitting that all articles were written, as B. A. Vvedensky, editor-in-chief, asserted, "from the position of our world outlook—Marxism-Leninism." After he returned to the United States, Benton dispatched copies of the latest printing of the *Encyclopaedia Britannica* to a number of Soviet officials whom he had met, including Premier Nicolai Bulganin and Klementi Voroshilov.

Despite the fact that *Encyclopaedia Britannica* has been American-owned since 1901, charges are still made that it is "pro-British"—a charge counterbalanced by critics who deplore its "Americanization." Many such letters begin, "Of course, I would not expect to find this in a British publication, but . . ." and then proceed to ask answers to questions as farfetched as "What was the name of the Dobermann Pinscher that won the best-of-breed in New York in 1921?" or "Why can't I find the maiden name of Molly Pitcher's mother in your set?" In one instance, Yust had special satisfaction in replying to an Anglophobe who demanded to know why Washington's Farewell Address was not included. "You point out," wrote Yust, "that *Britannica* does not reprint in its entirety Washington's Farewell Address, and you ascribe this to 'British bias.' You may have noted that the Declaration of Independence and the Constitution are printed in full. If you wish a copy of Washington's Farewell Address, let me refer you to the publication, 'Speeches and Documents in U.S. History.' It was published this year by Oxford University Press, whose main address is London, England."

Although articles on religion are rarely subjected to the type of criticism encountered by similar writings in earlier editions, occasional complaints are received about bias against specific creeds. Sometimes, in interesting contrast to the outcry of certain Catholic critics against articles in the eleventh edition, objections are heard that the articles on Catholic subjects have been subjected to "clerical shearing" by high-ranking members of that faith. One hasty critic insisted that all religious articles marked "X" at the end indicated such "censorship." What he did not know—but was quickly made aware of by the editors—was that the "X" signified that a subeditor had inserted current information or had made minor revisions. Actually, the current practice is to ask leaders of religious faiths to advise and verify factual points and, in the case of controversial issues, to ask the writer to compare opposing viewpoints. Since the 1957 printing and subsequent ones, certain articles pertaining to the New Testament, which had drawn frowns from Roman Catholic and Protestant clergy, were rewritten to the satisfaction of both groups by Professor Jaroslav Jan Pelikan, a young Lutheran minister and member of the University of Chicago's Federated Theological Faculty.

7

Other sample queries and complaints: A man in Atlantic, Iowa, demanded to know if Jesse James was still alive and added, "I'll take your word for it." The reply was soon dispatched: "We too have heard rumors that Jesse James is still alive or that he did not die in 1882 but lived to be over 100 years old. However, it seems that all of the authoritative sources agree that he was killed in 1882." A woman from El Paso, Texas, wrote to acclaim her father the inventor of slot machines, and would the *Encyclopaedia Britannica* like to acquire the patent? Back went the reply that the *Encyclopaedia Britannica* never engages in such transactions, plus a bibliography to give the woman clues as to whether anyone preceded her father in devising this boon to mankind. A man from Mylo, North Dakota, complained that, although the work he had purchased was handsome and fascinating, he was appalled to find no Mylo, North Dakota, on any of the maps. To him was sent the answer that lack of space prevents the inclusion of towns with only 110 inhabitants. Another woman insisted on a definitive answer to her query about whether a sexually inactive man is more prolific intellectually. The careful reply, based on material gleaned from the Library Research Service, was that some men can be both romantic and intellectual and some cannot—with examples from history of each. A high school sophomore wrote, "You state that all arachnida possess an endoskeleton, but my biology teacher says they possess only an exoskeleton." The question was referred to Alexander Petrunkevitch, Yale professor emeritus of biology, who replied to the student that arachnida possess both an exoskeleton and an endoskeleton.

When one of his staff members informed Bruce Gould, editor of the *Ladies' Home Journal*, that in 1768 the *Encyclopaedia Britannica* had four sentences on the atom and five pages on love but that in the current edition there were nine pages on the atom and nothing on love, Gould queried Benton, an old friend of his: "Is it true that the *Britannica* ignores love? And, if so, why?" In reply, Gould received not only a list of index references to "love" in articles ranging from "Libido" to "Ethics, History Of," but also an interesting extract from the second edition's article on the subject:

The symptoms produced by this passion are as follows: The eye-lids often twinkle; the eyes are hollow, and yet appear as if full with pleasure; the pulse is not peculiar to the passion, but the same with that which attends solicitude and care. When the object of this affection is thought of, particularly if the idea is sudden, the spirits are confused, the pulse changes, and its force and time are very variable; in some instances, the person is sad and watchful; in others, the person, not being conscious of his state, pines away, is slothful, and regardless of food; tho' the wiser, when they find themselves in love, seek pleasant company and active entertainments. As the force of love prevails, sighs grow deeper; a tremor affects the heart and pulse; the countenance is alternately pale and red; the voice is suppressed in the sauces; the eyes grow dim; cold sweats break out; sleep absents itself, at least until the morning; the secretions become disturbed; and a loss of appetite, a hectic fever, melancholy, or perhaps madness, if not death, constitutes the sad catastrophe.

To this Yust, commenting on the fact that the original article on "Love" was dropped after the eighth edition, added, "Perhaps previous editors agreed in a sense with the young lady on our staff who suggested the following reply to a similar criticism—'Love is better experienced than read about: the opposite is true of the atomic bomb.'"

Polite replies have been sent to less reasonable correspondents, including the man who maintained angrily that the principle of the rotary engine is spurious and offered the *Encyclopaedia Britannica* all rights to his treatise, "Fallacies in Rotary Design"; the befuddled student who wrote, "I want to ask you the Constitutional Convention of what year was composed of how many men appointed by the legislatures of what several states"; and the woman who insisted that only the editor could give her the formula for inhibiting growth of mold on her set of *Encyclopaedia Britannica*. (The answer was: "Wipe them with a rag which has been wrung out in a solution of half vinegar and half water, then rub the covers with a good paste wax.")

8

Yust's momentary irritation at discovering that a letter writer is correct and the *Encyclopaedia Britannica* is wrong has invariably been replaced instantly by a feeling of gratitude toward the correspondent. Mary Beard, wife of the historian Charles A. Beard and herself a scholar, once protested that too much space was given to biographies of men and not enough to those of women. Yust made a count and found that Mrs. Beard was justified. Of some thirteen thousand biographies, less than eight hundred were those of women. He wrote to thank Mrs. Beard for the information—then put her to work preparing the biographies of women she thought should have a place. Another correspondent, politely, but with a slight indication of petulance that such a stupid error could be made, wrote to inquire whether a formula printed in the encyclopaedia as "Cp equals $8.81 + 0.019T + 0.00000zzzT^2$" should not really read "Cp equals $8.81 - 0.019T -$

0.00000zzzT²?" Yust checked with the adviser and contributor and replied, "You are correct, sir, and we are grateful to you." Yust has sent similar expressions of gratitude—after appropriate checking— to writers who reported that Russia's coldest temperature was not 94° below zero at Verkhoyansk but 103° below zero at Oimyakonsk; that in Volume IV, page 22, a certain "not" should be "now" and on page 628 of Volume XVIII, "external" should read "eternal"; that in Volume XIII the latitude of Yakutsk is given as 62° 5′ and in Volume XXIII as 62° 1′; that Martha Washington was listed as "the first Lady of the Land" instead of "the first First Lady of the Land"; that Wisconsin is called the "Badger State" not because, as explained in the work, it has many badgers, but from the way—as Yust was informed in an indignant letter from a sixth-grade class in a Milwaukee school— in which miners of southwestern Wisconsin burrowed into sides of hills for metal.

Whenever Yust has found his attention called to genuine or alleged errors by the same correspondent over a period of months or years, he knows that he will soon receive from that writer a letter starting, "Dear Sir, You will be interested to know that I have just finished reading every word in all the 24 volumes of the *Britannica.* I believe I am the first person who has ever done this." Yust acknowledges the accomplishment with admiration (he, himself, has never read the set through) but advises the proud writer that others have laid similar claims. Their places in life are as varied as their names, ages, and the time it took each to do it. A. Urban Shirk, a Little Neck, Long Island, sales manager, went through the twenty-four volumes in four and a half years. A youngster named Robin Weir, of Galloping Tiger Ranch, Delray Beach, Florida, began to read the set when he was fourteen and finished when he was nearly eighteen. An architect, J. Lloyd Conrich, of San Francisco, read his set at a leisurely pace over seventeen years. "I enjoyed it all," he wrote to Yust, "even to discovering such extremely interesting things as the number of muscles in an elephant's trunk, and that people used to wean babies on warm beer." A retired minister, George Roberts, took only three years to finish his set, finding only the articles on physics and chemistry " 'hard reading,' these being uncongenial to one who never studied them and who invariably flunked mathematics in school." George F. Goodyear, a Buffalo, New York, chemist, started to read in the second volume when he was a student in Harvard Law School and wanted to learn about astronomy. He continued to read at the rate of about a thousand pages a year and finished in twenty-two years. George Bernard Shaw always claimed that in his youth he had read the complete ninth edition at the British Museum—except for the scientific articles. But to C. S. Forester, the famous British novelist and creator of Horatio Hornblower, belongs an interesting distinction: he read through two separate editions.

9

Yust delights in hearing from all such claimants, as he does from the critics, both serious and petty. A sensible man, he recognizes that "facts" are not always incontrovertible, and he expects that there will always be questions and inquiries and complaints both from the well-meaning and the carpers. Some expect him to be an authority on everything in his encyclopaedia, but Yust can reply, as Diderot once did, "I know indeed a great enough number of things, but there is hardly anyone who does not know his subject better than I." Strong in his belief that his is the greatest of all modern encyclopaedias of a general nature, Yust is zealous in his efforts to keep that standard high. But, being a man of easy wit, he can smile with pride, knowing that a jest often expresses an evaluation as effectively as a critical essay, when he reads in a newspaper this advertisement:

FOR SALE!
COMPLETE SET OF ENCYCLOPAEDIA BRITANNICA!
NEVER USED—MY WIFE KNOWS EVERYTHING!

24

The Modern E B: *How It Is Sold*

On any day or night of any week there is an *Encyclopaedia Britannica* salesman sitting or standing in a living room, a kitchen, a study, a den, an office, or in some less conventional place, with material from his sales kit spread before him as he "tells the story" to a potential customer.

He—or she, for there are women so employed, too—has reached the particular site through one of several circumstances. Perhaps the prospect was referred to him by a satisfied user of the encyclopaedia. Perhaps the name was secured through a systematic telephone canvass of residents in a particular neighborhood. This prospect sent in a coupon that appeared in a magazine advertisement; that one signed his name to an inquiry card he came upon in a wire rack at the corner drugstore; a third knew of a friend who had recently bought the fifteen-volume *Britannica Junior* and has written for information; another responded to a knock on the door by a salesman using the "cold-turkey" method of canvassing from house to house.

However the salesman has reached this point, he is engaging the prospect in a project of which the ultimate aim is to sell the *Encyclopaedia Britannica*'s ten-year educational program—involving the acquisition of the latest printing of the twenty-four-volume set, the *Book of the Year* for a decade, the *World Language Dictionary*, the *Britannica World Atlas*, the privilege of employing the Britannica Library Research Service for a decade, and home-study guides. The prospective customer may be a "hard sell" or an "easy sell." Even before the sales talk begins, he may say, "Mister, I'm the toughest nut to crack and I have no use for an encyclopaedia," or insist, "This isn't for me, I don't read anything but pocketbooks and comic magazines," or inform the salesman, "I know all the answers and there's nothing the *Encyclopaedia Britannica* can teach me," or, somewhere in the conversation, say, "I can't afford a set of books, even anything as worthwhile as the *Encyclopaedia Britannica*." These and other responses seldom balk the salesman. He may be a hard pusher and whisk through his presentation. He may, if he is skilled and experienced enough, decide within five minutes that there is no point in continuing his sales talk. He will rarely argue; no salesman likes to win an argument and lose a sale. If he belongs to the expanding class of *Encyclopaedia Britannica* salesmen who maintain that qualitative selling eventually leads to quantitative selling, he will be politely persistent and agreeably aggressive. If he succeeds in convincing his prospect of his need for the *Encyclopaedia Britannica* and closes the sale, he is less likely to say a conventional "Thank you" than "I wish to congratulate you." If he fails to make a sale he is less likely to pout or glare and stride out than he is to say, "Thank you for your courtesy."

Obviously, such salesmen have come a long way from the kind of booksellers once described by R. L. Duffus as men of "glittering eye and well-oiled tongue," each with "a large and heavy foot which he was ready to wedge into a doorway." Those old-time agents of an earlier era, bold and truculent, often carried samples slung from a harness under their coats. They were primarily wanderers who swept into a city or a neighborhood, turned a quick profit, and moved away swiftly and silently. They preyed on ignorance and often charged prices three to four times the physical or intellectual value of the books. They sold *Life among the Mormons*, tomes advising women how to acquire and keep a husband, collections of "art treasures," one-volume cyclopaedias "encompassing all knowledge," thick biographies, and dullish histories. Even after the ranks of such book agents, particularly numerous in the last decade of the nineteenth century, had thinned, there were shady practices in the business of selling so-called subscription books. With reason, prospects were wary of anyone who announced that he had come to bring enlightenment and culture to their households. But as time passed the people grew wiser and less susceptible to chicanery, and where the people were not alert, various governmental agencies and Better Business Bureaus were.

With the *Encyclopaedia Britannica,* the goal remains the same as it was in the days of Andrew Bell or those of Horace Hooper—to sell the set to people who ought to have it. And though techniques have changed and types of salesmen have changed with them, that goal always is kept in sight, and the essentials of achieving it—locating a potential prospect, getting an interview, and making a presentation that should produce an order if one is obtainable—are basic and firm.

2

The backgrounds of the men and women who sell *Encyclopaedia Britannica* are as varied as the reference work's subject matter. Many have been involved in saleswork since their early adulthood. The vice-president in charge of sales, Paul E. Seaman, was, at nineteen, a member of a horse-and-buggy crew peddling clocks, linens, silverware, tablecloths, and Smyrna rugs in country towns in Pennsylvania. Seaman started with the *Encyclopaedia Britannica* company in 1942 in Connecticut, and proved adept enough to sell two sets a day for eight consecutive weeks. Sent later to Philadelphia as a district manager, he brought that city up from the bottom in sales to a place among the leaders, then effected a similar improvement as division manager in New York. An advocate of selling on weekends—"You can get them right after payday and when they're more reflective"— he and his New York salesmen tallied more than a million dollars a year in weekend business alone. In 1949 he was transferred to Chicago to become vice-president in charge of sales.

Into the ranks of his salesmen have come persons who formerly were reporters, counselors, free-lance writers, artists, engineers, lawyers, cab drivers, sales clerks, professors, used-car dealers, doctors, high-school principals and teachers, military men, musicians, and ministers. Some gravitated to the firm because their parents had owned older editions of the *Encyclopaedia Britannica* and they themselves had developed respect for it. Many are former salesmen of other encyclopaedias and other subscription books who explain, "I was tired of fighting *Britannica* so I joined it." James C. Bradley—"Doc" Bradley—served for a decade as an ordained Presbyterian minister, as executive secretary of the New York Federation of Churches, and then as one of the top executives of the American Bible Society; he invented display plates for automobiles and once headed a company that made and sold the plates; and he edited church literature. With EB since 1946, first as a salesman in the Bronx, then as district manager there, he eventually became division manager in Chicago. Hubert Graeme Cook, a Toronto district manager, was formerly a professor of English, a lecturer on oriental affairs, a world traveler. As a salesman of other books, C. T. Jorgensen worked in Mexico, Canada, and South Africa. C. A. Flanders, a Houston, Texas, salesman, was a second mate on a tramp steamer when he first heard of the possibilities of selling *Encyclopaedia Britannica*. Len Meyer never progressed in formal schooling beyond eighth grade but educated himself to a college level by avid reading and study; he served as an ace salesman for the United States Rubber Company for eight years before taking up his *Encyclopaedia Britannica* sales kit. There are several former actors, but most people from the theater are not successful in this kind of activity; EB sales experts have found that, although selling is itself a form of dramatic acting, ex-performers tend to improvise too freely and too frequently on the sales talk that has been found to be most successful through test and trial and use.

Most new salesmen are hired through advertisements in the newspapers; many are recommended by other salesmen. All hiring is done by district managers, who insist they can tell after half an hour's conversation whether the prospective salesman will be an asset to the company. Each applicant is given a standard personality and intelligence test, but there are qualities sometimes undetected in such examinations that district managers look for in those they interview. Does the man speak easily and convincingly? Is it obvious that he likes people and would like to serve them? Does he seem pleasant and courteous? Is he physically healthy? District managers are advised against "desperation hiring"—the kind that finds a manager, perhaps fearful that without enough salesmen his sales will drop, saying, "I hire anyone because you never can tell by looking at a man whether he will sell books."

Once hired, the salesman begins his training period. He knows that no quotas are set, that his earnings depend entirely on sales; his commissions range from 15 per cent upward, depending on the volume of sets sold over a specific period of time. There are, consequently, no theoretical limits to what an *Encyclopaedia Britannica* salesman can earn. A few newcomers have been known to hit selling streaks that netted them weekly earnings as high as $1,000. Many experienced salesmen earn more than either their district or division managers, whose compensation is computed on a percentage of total sales in their respective sectors. A bonus system for salesmen augments earnings derived from commissions.

In training, the salesman learns something of the general history of the *Encyclopaedia Britannica* and how to line up prospects—by making telephone calls, by using references furnished by satisfied customers, by checking newspaper stories for the names of recent graduates, even by the seldom-used "cold-turkey" method. Each is assigned to a field trainer, a man of considerable experience, whom he watches as a sale is attempted. When he is deemed ready, the trainee himself initiates sales calls and makes his presentation while the trainer sits by observing, mentally noting errors and faulty technique. Later, trainer and trainee discuss every phase of the presentation, from the "opener" (the exact words used to present the sales talk) through the "spread" (the laying out of various pamphlets and display material about the set and subsidiary publications) to the "close" (the step before actual consummation of a sale, with collection of the initial instalment, or the folding up of all material used in the presentation preparatory to leaving).

By the time the man is adjudged ready to proceed by himself, he knows the basic sales talk and has already had considerable experience in meeting those many situations that not even the most foolproof sales talk can anticipate. Before he sets out, he is warned against getting "gravy orders"—orders from friends and relatives who may be eager to start him off well in his new endeavor. For at least six months, Seaman's directive advises, a new salesman must sell to strangers, and then if he is proceeding successfully he is permitted to approach those he knows well.

3

To secure his prospects, an *Encyclopaedia Britannica* salesman uses the telephone a great deal. He may spend as many as three hours each morning calling people whose names have been referred to him or picked from selected lists or have turned up on "wire-rack cards." The latter developed from experiments devised by Seaman and his national sales manager, Clay Cole, in Indianapolis and Kansas City. Arrangements were made in those cities to place small wire baskets full of cards in drugstores, gift shops, and other places where books or magazines were sold. Store owners were promised a dollar for every card mailed in. The tests brought thousands of replies but hardly any sales. Many store owners had told their customers, relatives, and friends, "I'm in a contest and I win if I get the most signatures," and the loyal patrons had signed their names to requests for information about the latest printing of the *Encyclopaedia Britannica*. When the salesmen went to follow up these leads, they encountered scant success. After some $7,500 had been spent, the experiment was dropped and its defects studied. When it was resumed in Chicago, all concerned, including the customers, were advised that no contest was involved.

However the salesman makes his appointment, his next step is important. If his telephone call to a prospect results in a favorable response he sets up a specific time for a presentation. Most of these appointments, especially if the presentation is to be made to a married couple or a family with children, are set for between six and nine o'clock at night. This is an interesting change from the selling techniques of the 1930's. Then, from 90 to 95 per cent of the sales were consummated during the day in offices and factories or in homes. When Seaman was district manager in Philadelphia, he noticed that a prospect approached at work would frequently advise the salesman, "Come back tomorrow, I'll have to ask my wife tonight." He set his men to work evenings and on weekends and broadened this system throughout the sales organization when he took over all sales for the company.

The actual sales presentation is simple on its surface, yet, as all salesmen know, psychologically complex, strewn with intangibles that may suddenly thwart or suddenly produce an order. Each salesman eventually learns the individual techniques that will make him successful, but the best of them are wary of applying to one prospect the same technique that may have won him an easy sale with another. Improvisation is often necessary, but free-wheeling improvisation can prove a losing gamble. The *Encyclopaedia Britannica* salesman invariably begins by disclosing how he happened to get the prospect's name (although the prospect has already been duly informed on the telephone, in most cases). Then he proceeds to explain the "ten-year educational program." This involves an elucidation of the virtues of the latest printing, the exhibition of a sample volume of the set with its specially inserted colored plates and interesting articles, and the display of a folder about such subsidiary publications that can be part of the over-all purchase plan as the *Book of the Year*, the *World Language Dictionary*, the *Britannica World Atlas*, and other accessories. Price is not mentioned until toward the close of the talk, when the terms of payment are explained in detail.

4

Often a salesman is interrupted before he reaches the vital point of price in his talk. For every objection the salesman needs an answer. In the lore of *Encyclopaedia Britannica* salesmen are many anecdotes telling how a certain phrase or a sentence in the midst or near the close of a presentation helped to effect a sale.

Randolph Jones of Boston was experiencing considerable difficulty with a young married couple whose main objection was that they had recently bought a lot on which they hoped to build a house. "Maybe when the house is built and we're settled in it, we can afford to think about getting a set of the *Britannica*," the husband said. Jones replied, "You know, the *Britannica* is something you can put in the middle of the lot and build your house around." The man and woman stared at each other, nodded simultaneously, and wrote out a check.

A husband and wife in Seattle were approached by J. S. Dalton in their new home. Dalton sat on a nail keg and they sat stiffly on orange crates as he spread out the material from his sales kit and made his presentation. The husband decided to buy the set, but each time he prepared to sign the order card, the wife snatched the pen from his hand. After the third time, Dalton, who had noticed on the walls framed mottoes advocating temperance, remarked to the wife, "Isn't it too bad that there are so many thriving saloons in this city? And isn't it better to have a husband who wants to spend money for the culture and education of his family instead of for liquor?" The woman's features softened, she said firmly, "Yes, it is," and then she signed the order. Dalton is renowned in salesmanship annals for a feat he accomplished after his car slipped off a wet Oregon road and hung perilously over a cliff. Two passing motorists dragged him to safety. Remarking on his narrow escape, one of the rescuers noticed Dalton's sales kit and asked several questions. Dalton replied. Within half an hour, his rescuer was signed up to buy a set of the *Encyclopaedia Britannica*.

The key words that spark a sale may fill more than a sentence or two. In Ironwood, Michigan, Earl E. Theiss had finished presenting his program to the president of a Parent-Teachers Association group. Both the prospect and his wife wanted to buy the set for their two teen-age sons, but added, "We will eventually, but not now." Theiss replied casually but earnestly, "Suppose ten years from now you may be sitting here the same as now. Then the thought may go through your minds, 'Did we do all for those two boys of ours while they were still with us and not away?' It will be too late then. Procrastination is the thief of time. Putting off until tomorrow what we should have done today is bad." Then he thanked the couple and started down the street. One of the boys quickly overtook him. "Did I do something wrong?" asked Theiss. "No, my folks want to buy the books," was the reply.

5

The presence of children or conversation about children are potent aids to salesmen. Zachary Caully, a former singer and Broadway stage manager, encountered considerable opposition from the head of a Manhattan household who scoffed at every laudable sentiment Caully expressed about the encyclopaedia. Had the wife not objected, the man, who weighed 250 pounds, would have thrown Caully out of the apartment. Caully asked if there were children and the man replied, "Yah, the older one is smart but the young one don't wanna learn nothin'. Now get outta here." Caully persisted in discussing the children and held the man's attention. But otherwise he made no progress. Just as Caully was preparing to leave, the older boy ran into the house, his face scratched and blood running from his mouth. "My teacher gave me a composition to write," he explained tearfully, "and I went to the library to look it up in the *Encyclopaedia Britannica*, and there were two other boys ahead of me and later we got into a fight and they beat me up." The father stared hard at Caully, then roared, "Gimme that order blank! I'll buy that set!"

Len Meyer had spent a frustrating hour with a merchant who repeated, "I don't need any set of books," and his wife who kept admonishing him, "Don't listen to that salesman, he'll hypnotize you." As Meyer began to fold up his materials, he said, "Of course, this set does have great advantages for anyone with intelligent children in the family." "Smart children!" snapped the merchant. "My eleven-year-old boy is the smartest kid in his class." Meyer resumed his talk. Within ten minutes the man called to his wife, "Bring a check, I'm buying the set!" After the set was delivered, Meyer called on the family with a special gift for the youngster, a two-volume *Popular History of the World*. When he left, he had been supplied with three names of "sure prospects" given to him by the wife.

Selling *Britannica Junior*, C. A. Flanders paid a call on a dairy farmer near Modesto, California. While the farmer milked his cows, Flanders told him of the benefits of the fifteen-volume set for children. The farmer was losing interest, complaining that his children's schooling was expensive enough. At that moment one of the children, who had been playing in the barnyard, threw a rock through the living-room window. "I give up!" the farmer yelled. "It costs me money just to talk about their schooling!" Taking a calculated risk of irritating the farmer, Flanders said, "If the schools aren't teaching your children to behave, and you are having difficulties with the problem, too, something has to be done. We consider our articles on 'Child Psychology' and 'Child Behavior' one of the greatest accomplishments of the new *Britannica Junior*." Replied the farmer: "How much for cash?"

An unusual case in which an infant aided in producing sales involved Fred Huserik, a veteran salesman in Seattle. He and an associate were in charge of an *Encyclopaedia Britannica* booth at a country fair near the Yakima, Washington, Indian reservation, when a young Indian woman asked if she could leave her tiny baby, carried by her papoose-style, with them for a short while. When they assented, the woman hung the cradle board from a nail protruding from the wall and strolled away. Attracted by a pair of big round eyes staring out from atop the blanket, a crowd gathered. Huserik took quick advantage of this and promptly secured three orders. As the morning wore on, the baby made no whimper, no sound, but stared impassively at Huserik. More spectators stopped to look at the child —and another set was sold. By early evening, after Huserik had ministered twice to the baby's various needs and the young mother had returned, Huserik had sold five sets and secured a dozen leads for further sales.

6

In EB annals are numerous accounts of how a kind of diplomacy—spoken or silent—proved effective despite strongly expressed feelings of hostility, interference from outsiders, or a prospect's desire for a cheaper encyclopaedia.

On a cold-turkey canvass, Donald Fleetwood encountered a glowering man who immediately declared, "Friend, you'll just waste your time with me. Nobody can sell me anything! I've got no use for salesmen of any kind." Fleetwood asked the man what he did for a living and was told he was an assembly worker at the local Ford Motor Company plant. "Did you ever stop to realize," asked Fleetwood, "that if there were no salesmen to sell the product you help assemble that you would not have a job?" For a second or two the man mused, then asked Fleetwood to step into his apartment; half an hour later he was enrolled as an owner of the *Encyclopaedia Britannica*.

"Doc" Bradley was making a presentation to a lawyer in Hastings-on-Hudson one summer afternoon when a neighbor strolled over, took one look at the spread before the prospect, and scoffed, "Buying a set of books, eh?" Bradley quickly countered this disruptive comment by telling the neighbor, "Just a minute, sir, I'll be over to see you after I finish here." He had resumed his talk when the prospect's mother-in-law came toward them and, seeing the sample volume and various booklets and placards, cried, "Books! What do you want with more books? You've got the place full of books now!" The prospect glared, reddened as Bradley discreetly remained quiet. Then he asked, "How much did you say this was?" Bradley told him the price and the man, staring hard at his mother-in-law, wrote out a down-payment check.

To a prospect who hesitated about buying the *Encyclopaedia Britannica* and hinted he would be interested in a cheaper set, Gregory Grover, a veteran Chicago representative, once responded: "If you could choose between two kinds of college education for your son, the usual education or the superior one for a comparatively slight additional amount, wouldn't you want your son to have a better education? Well, the full set of *Encyclopaedia Britannica*, together with the valuable research service, can mean the difference between an average education and the superior education which *Britannica* will assure."

Grover's rejoinder won for him the company's 1953 contest for "tested sentences" and was duly recorded, for the benefit of fellow salesmen, in the firm's monthly publication, *EB News*. The prime object of this magazine—beyond informing all salesmen of what their colleagues are doing, of how they have succeeded and where they have failed, of trends in population and of new methods and new products—is to create "progressive discontent," the feeling that, however successful a salesman may be, improvement is possible and necessary. Sometimes this method takes the shape of statements on the nature of selling, as in a quotation from a speech by William Benton: "Selling is at the very core of economic activity in a free enterprise society. A man who can sell is never long out of a job, in good times or bad. He can go to work each morning, confident that he is not only bettering himself but also bettering society, by satisfying wants that already exist and by creating further demand for products and services that mean, in at least a material way, a better way of life for all." Sometimes there are printed case studies of "hard sells" that were effective, or exhortations—"You Can't Sell EB by Remote Control, Radar, Crystal Gazing. To Sell EB you must get out in front of a prospect and make a presentation!"—or such sales slogans as "Wouldn't You Hate to Compete with *Britannica?*" or stories of men who have sold many sets by rote or improvisation. For salesmen seeking excuses for poor business, the *EB News* once printed a satirical "Alibi Almanac":

July—Everyone on the beach.
August—Too hot.
September—Too early in the season; people not back from the country. Those who are back are too busy preparing kiddies for school.
October—World Series is killing business. Unseasonable weather starts.
November—Political and business unrest due to elections. Football games absorbing great deal of interest.
December—Always bad. Everyone out Christmas shopping every evening.
January—No one has any money left after Christmas shopping. Only marketable item is do-it-yourself book on repairing electric trains.
February—Huge blizzards paralyze all transportation. Suburban towns hemmed in by gigantic snowdrifts. Car refuses to start in cold weather.

March—People are starting to worry about income tax due next month.
April—Everyone spending all their money on outfits for Easter Parade.
May—Daylight saving fouled up schedule. Unseasonable weather. Prospects cleaning up flooded basements.
June—Nice weather, everyone out driving in evenings. Also saving for vacations.

7

Although most of the salesmen work out their individual schedules in detail, there is always the possibility of making sales in odd places, at strange times, and under special circumstances. M. L. McClendon, of Houston, walked ten miles through swamps and the backwaters of a muddy river to find the commercial fisherman who had sent in a card; he finally hired a motorboat to take him down the slough where the fisherman's nets were spread, located his man, and came away with an order. Grant Pritchard found his Teaneck, New Jersey, customer exercising a trotting horse. Invited to sit alongside the prospect, Pritchard climbed aboard the carriage and held on tightly while the horse trotted along a bumpy road. Some hectic miles later he departed shakily but with a signed order card. Cy Kephart called on a colonel at Fort Leavenworth, Kansas, just as the officer and his wife were about to leave for a reception. Would Kephart be kind enough to watch the fifteen-month-old baby and the two older children? Kephart did, changing diapers and feeding milk to the infant. On their return, the grateful couple promptly signed up for a set.

A former shipping expert, C. B. Otto, has in his district of Washington, D.C., customers that include government officials, members of Congress and of the diplomatic corps, and staffs of foreign missions. Attempting to sell a set to the Soviet Embassy, Otto was interviewed by four secretaries before he was finally permitted to see the ambassador himself. A brief conversation followed about prices of respective bindings. "Thank you, you'll hear from us further," Otto was told. Two days later, he received a call from the embassy. Again he was interviewed by four secretaries, then led into the richly arrayed office of the ambassador and asked to make his presentation again. This time, however, the sale was completed for one of the expensively bound sets, with payment in cash.

Salesmen are advised against ever antagonizing a client or arguing, but Ken Hiatt, a former marine and one of four brothers engaged in selling the *Encyclopaedia Britannica,* won an order by doing both—and more. On a hot summer day, he spied a burly young man dressed in army tans working with hammer in hand on a half-completed house near Long Beach, California. In a spirit of serviceman camaraderie, Hiatt asked, "Hi, you building a house?" The young man glared, wiped sweat from his brow, and roared, "What the hell do you think it is, a chicken coop?" Hiatt responded, "Well, Buster, after looking at you, it could be most anything, a barn, a pigpen, or even a chicken coop." At this, the other man threw his hammer to the ground, strode over to Hiatt, and began waving his fists. In a second, both men were rolling in combat on the dusty soil. Hiatt soon bested his opponent and helped him to his feet. The two men glared at each other, then broke into laughter. The house builder explained that Hiatt's question could not have come at a less appropriate time, for he had been struggling for months with his house and had just hit himself on the hand with his hammer. More conversation followed, and, Hiatt later reported to his district manager, "Needless to say, this ex-G.I. became a buyer."

In contrast, Merritt M. Wood, Jr., as a beginning salesman in Hobbs, New Mexico, made a presentation to a family whose head was a stolid, silent man. Although the wife and children seemed eager to have the set, the man sat and stared. Wood recalled what his trainer had told him about the "five-second pause" after the presentation. He waited; there was no response. He repeated his closing statements about the set's value and the terms of payment. Still no reply. His pauses grew longer and longer. Finally, the wife and children left for a movie, and the man continued to crack his knuckles, rub his chin, and stare at the display material, and he did so for two hours, during which Wood smoked an entire pack of cigarettes. At the end of this period of silence, the man whispered hoarsely, "I'll take it."

Presentations before physically handicapped prospects require special techniques. Noel L. Boydston, a Chicago representative for *Britannica Junior,* used up a pad of notepaper in dealing with the deaf-mute parents of two small children. There were many times when he was not certain his points were being understood. Deaf-mute friends arrived and interrupted the presentation, and Boydston waited patiently while all four conversed in sign language. After the visitors left, the presentation was resumed, and another pad of paper was used up. The woman wrote: "How can this set be a good investment for children one and three years old?" "One picture is worth 10,000 words," wrote Boydston. The answer satisfied the parents. "If just one of our children benefits from this program it will be worth the price of the investment," wrote the mother. "How much is the down payment?"

There are salesmen who, even when their goals for the day or week have been reached, cannot seem to resist selling. James Wilson had put in eight days of hard work in Denver, securing nine solid orders. He had run out of immediate prospects and was sitting in a restaurant having breakfast when he met a dentist to whom he had sold a set a year earlier. In a five-minute chat with the dentist, he picked up the name of a prospect in a small town sixty miles away. He found where his prospect's home was by asking the first man he met on the main street. Just as the prospect was signing his order card, the man who had given Wilson his directions telephoned and asked him to call at his house. There he sold another set. In nine days, Wilson's earnings came to some $800.

Even on his Florida honeymoon, Ralph Sonneman, nicknamed "Supersonic," continued to sell. When he came back to his Houston district, he kept to his customarily furious pace, selling, on one particular weekend, nine sets. Sonneman has made presentations in French, Spanish, and German. He also plays the piano for his customers—"but only after they've signed the order card."

Ralph C. A. Gilbert, who came into EB salesmanship after careers as reporter, professional dancer, manufacturers' agent, and Canadian army officer, once gained nineteen orders in a single week in the British Columbia area, traveling by automobile, plane, water taxi, jeep, logging railroad, and on foot.

An advocate of the sales-are-where-you-find-them school, too, is Ernest V. Stolen, Alaska's district manager, who travels by snowshoe and by plane. He has sold as many as twenty-two sets in a single week for commissions of $1,750, and his monthly record of $4,617 in commissions in 1951 is considered the top mark of recent years. Once, seated in a plane next to the owner of a chain of radio stations in Alaska, he sold him a set, then alighted, got into his car, and picked up a hitchhiker. Before the hitchhiker left, he, too, had signed up to become an *Encyclopaedia Britannica* owner.

8

For many of these salesmen there exist values and satisfactions beyond earned commissions. In their ranks are professionals who undoubtedly could earn as much money or more selling other books or other products. But those who have often been spurred to reflect on the deeper nature of their activities speak of "an identification with greatness" that they feel is theirs; of the encyclopaedia as "the finest set of culture in twenty-four volumes anywhere"; of "a service motive" in trying to persuade potential customers, and of an awareness that to sell the *Encyclopaedia Britannica* is to spread education and information and provide a means by which each reader of the volumes may be spurred to learn more than he already knows.

This *Encyclopaedia Britannica* they seek to sell in the United States and in many lands—for there are *EB* representatives in Canada, Mexico, Central America, South America, England, Scotland, Ireland, the Philippines, Japan, South Africa, Alaska, the Hawaiian Islands, Australia, New Zealand, and other countries—thrives as the leader in the realm of encyclopaedias. It has endured throughout a long and intellectually adventurous life and has met and overcome formidable difficulties in its years as a commercial publishing enterprise.

Since 1768, the *Encyclopaedia Britannica* has served the cause of education and enlightenment in placid times and in periods of tumult, recording the changes and advances in man's and the world's development. In all that time, its principles have withstood change, although to meet shifting demands the techniques and mechanics of editing and publishing it have repeatedly been revised. These principles are basic:

To convey knowledge and information in a system as comprehensive as its physical limits will permit.

To insist on the authenticity and reliability of its contents.

To present, with each successive edition, inventories of man's ideas and accomplishments up to the time of publication.

To secure as contributors men and women who are the acclaimed and acknowledged authorities in their fields of endeavor.

These are all qualities of substance. They form the foundation of the *Encyclopaedia Britannica* and give it its strength and its influence.

Those who produce and those who sell this encyclopaedia speak of its past with interest and pride. But they are also conscious of the importance of the present. "My perhaps narrow way of viewing it," Walter Yust once wrote, "is that there has been no edition of the *Encyclopaedia Britannica* greater than the current one." The salesman declares, "When you acquire the present edition, sir, you are getting the very best there is."

And they and their colleagues have the confidence that for future generations, as for those of the past and the present, the *Encyclopaedia Britannica* will continue to serve as a register—authoritative and valuable and respected—of the progress of human knowledge.

Acknowledgments and Bibliography

Besides the persons cited earlier, many others assisted with interviews, letters, unpublished memoirs, court records, and assorted research materials, suggestions, and ideas.

Those affiliated with the *Encyclopaedia Britannica*—to whose files and records I was allowed unlimited access—include J. R. Bradley, Miss Felicité Buhl, James E. Colvin, Robert E. Conger, Miss Daphne Daume, Holman Faust, A. M. Gilbert, Thomas Goetz, Harry Houghton, John Howe, Harry Joy, Howard Kasch, Paul Kruse, Mrs. Mae MacKay, Len Meyer, Mrs. Harriet L. Milburn, Maurice B. Mitchell, Warren Preece, Paul E. Seaman, Carleton Smith, Miss Virginia Stenberg, and Don E. Walter. In London's *Encyclopaedia Britannica* headquarters additional aid was given by S. D. Keetch and by the late Hector McNeil.

Among the officials, past and present, of Sears, Roebuck and Company who helped were General Robert E. Wood, Lessing Rosenwald, and Emil J. Pollock. William J. Cox, former president of Encyclopaedia Britannica, Inc., his son, Warren Cox, and Fred Davis furnished important background information. Horace E. Hooper, Jr., and Nathaniel L. Hooper, sons of one of the two Americans who revolutionized the history of the *Encyclopaedia Britannica*, and W. Montgomery Jackson, son of the other American, were highly considerate in supplying data about their fathers' business and personal lives. Miss Margaret Schneider of New York contributed anecdotal material about her former employer, William Montgomery Jackson.

Appreciation for varied aid ranging from information on specific subjects to guidance in research problems must be expressed to Laird Bell, of Chicago; Manchester Boddy, of San Diego County, California; Mrs. Lavinia Dudley, editor-in-chief of the *Encyclopaedia Americana;* Philip Gee, of London and Edinburgh; Sir Louis Gluckstein, of London; Paul G. Hoffman, of Los Angeles; Barry Holloway and H. B. Kinneally, vice-presidents of the Grolier Society; Robert Whyte Mason, British consul in Chicago; Frederic G. Melcher, editor of *Publishers' Weekly;* William V. Morgenstern, of the University of Chicago; J. D. Newth, managing director of A. & C. Black, London; John Nuveen, of Chicago; S. C. Roberts, master of Pembroke College, Cambridge, England; Harold H. Swift, of Chicago; and R. D. Williamson, of Berkshire, England. Invaluably helpful were Benjamin Bowman, of Newberry Library, Chicago; Herbert Hewitt, chief of the reference division of the Chicago Public Library; Chester Lewis, head of the *New York Times* reference library; Miss Virginia McEachern, chief of the *Chicago Sun-Times* reference department; Miss Virginia Smucker, chief of *Time* magazine's reference library, and members of the reference library staff of the British Museum in London. For important counsel, my gratitude is due such newspaper colleagues as William Stoneman, chief of the Paris bureau of the Chicago *Daily News;* Arthur Veysey, chief of the London bureau of the *Chicago Tribune;* and Lloyd Wendt, assistant Sunday editor of the *Chicago Tribune.* The transcripts of William Montgomery Jackson's suit against Horace Hooper in August, 1911, and the subsequent trial in the Supreme Court of New York County in January, 1912, were obtained with the co-operation of Attorney A. M. Gilbert, of New York. I. Grant Scott, clerk of the Superior Court of New Jersey, supplied records relating to other phases of the Jackson-Hooper litigation.

Herbert P. Zimmerman, former president of R. R. Donnelley and

Sons Company, graciously permitted the use of his private and informative memoir of the relationship of his concern to the *Encyclopaedia Britannica*. For special technical help and advice, I offer warm acknowledgement to Professor Bernard Kogan, of the University of Illinois at Chicago, and to Gifford Ernest, scholar and journalist; and for certain vital assistance, to Marshall Field, Jr., editor and publisher of the *Chicago Sun-Times*, and to Milburn P. Akers, its executive editor.

Following is a partial list of bibliographical materials used.

BOOKS

ALTICK, RICHARD D. *The English Common Reader*. Chicago: University of Chicago Press, 1957.

BELL, E. H. C. *The Life and Letters of C. F. Moberly Bell*. London: Richards, 1927.

BLACK, JOHN SUTHERLAND, and CHRYSTAL, G. W. *The Life of William Robertson Smith*. London: A. & C. Black, 1912.

BOWMAN, WILLIAM DODGSON. *The Story of "The Times."* London: Dial Press, 1931.

BRIGGS, ASA. *Victorian People*. Chicago: University of Chicago Press, 1956.

BRYCE, JAMES. *Studies in Contemporary Biography*. New York: Macmillan Co., 1903.

CHAMBERS, ROBERT. *Lives of Illustrious and Distinguished Scotsmen From the Earliest Period to the Present Time*. Glasgow: Blackie & Son, 1836–37.

CHEW, SAMUEL. *Fruit among the Leaves: An Anniversary Anthology*. New York: Appleton-Century-Crofts, 1950.

CONSTABLE, THOMAS. *Archibald Constable and His Literary Correspondents*, esp. Vol. II. Edinburgh: Edmonston and Douglas, 1873.

COURTNEY, JANET E. *Recollected in Tranquillity*. London: Heinemann, 1926.

————. *An Oxford Portrait Gallery*. London: Chapman and Hall, 1931.

CROCKER, LESTER G. *The Embattled Philosopher: A Life of Denis Diderot*. East Lansing: Michigan State College Press, 1955.

CROXTON, ARTHUR. *Crowded Nights—and Days*. London: Sampson, Low and Marston, 1930.

DARK, SIDNEY. *The Life of Sir Arthur Pearson*. London: Hodder & Stoughton, 1930.

DORAN, GEORGE H. *Chronicles of Barabbas*. New York: Rinehart & Co., 1935.

DUFFUS, R. L. *Books: Their Place in a Democracy*. Boston: Houghton Mifflin Co., 1930.

EMMET, BORIS, and JEUCK, JOHN E. *Catalogues and Counters*. Chicago: University of Chicago Press, 1950.

Encyclopaedia Britannica. Readings in all editions from 1768–71 to date. Also numerous pirated editions, subsidiary publications, advertising booklets, study guides, compilations of articles, and yearbooks.

FIELD, EUGENE. *A Little Book of Profitable Tales.* New York: Scribner's Sons, 1895.

GOODING, LYDIA MARIAN. "The *Encyclopaedia Britannica:* A Critical and Historical Study." Unpublished Master's thesis, Columbia University, New York, 1929.

GOODSPEED, CHARLES E. *Yankee Bookseller.* Boston: Houghton Mifflin Co., 1937.

HAMMERTON, SIR JOHN A. *With Northcliffe in Fleet Street.* London: Hutchinson & Co., 1932.

————. *Books and Myself.* London: Macdonald & Co., 1944.

The History of the Book War. London: The Times, 1907.

The History of "The Times." 4 Vols. New York: Macmillan Co., 1935–52.

HYDE, WILLIAM H. "The *Encyclopaedia Britannica:* Study of the 14th Edition." Unpublished Master's thesis, Columbia University, New York, 1938.

JOHNSON, ROY W. and LYNCH, RUSSELL W. *The Sales Strategy of John H. Patterson.* Chicago: Dartnell Corp., 1932.

JONES, KENNEDY. *Fleet Street and Downing Street.* London: Hutchinson & Co., 1919.

JOYCE, MICHAEL. *Edinburgh: The Golden Age, 1769–1832.* London: Longmans, Green & Co., 1951.

KAY, JOHN. *A Series of Original Portraits and Caricature Etchings.* Edinburgh: Carver and Gidder, 1837–38.

KERR, ROBERT. *Memoirs of the Life, Writings and Correspondence of William Smellie.* 2 vols. Edinburgh: John Anderson, 1811.

KIRSCHNER, EDWIN J. *The Zeppelin in the Atomic Age.* Urbana: University of Illinois Press, 1957.

KITCHIN, F. HARCOURT. *Moberly Bell and His Times: An Unofficial Narrative.* London: Phillip Allan & Co., 1925.

LEGOUIS, EMILE, and CAZAMIAN, LOUIS. *A History of English Literature.* New York: Macmillan Co., 1935.

LEHMANN-HAUPT, HELLMUT, *et al. The Book in America.* New York: R. R. Bowker, 1939.

LUCAS, EDWARD VERRALL, and GRAVES, CHARLES LARCOM. *Wisdom on the Hire System.* London: Isbister, 1903.

————. *Wisdom While You Wait.* London: Britt, 1903.

————. *Signs of the Times; or, The Hustler's Almanac for 1907.* London: Alston Rivers, 1908.

LUNT, W. E. *A History of England.* New York: Harper & Bros., 1928.

MACMILLAN, SIR FREDERICK. *The Net Book Agreement.* Glasgow: University Press, 1924.

MEEK, ROBERT. *A Biographical Sketch of the Life of James Tytler.* Edinburgh: Denovan, 1805.

MEREDITH, F. M., "The *Encyclopaedia Britannica:* History and Comparison of the 7th and 8th Editions." Unpublished Master's thesis, Columbia University, New York, 1931.

MORGAN, CHARLES. *The House of Macmillan, 1843–1943.* New York: Macmillan Co., 1944.

MORTIMER, J. H. *Confessions of a Book Agent; or, Twenty Years by Stage and Rail.* Chicago: Cooperative, 1906.

NAPIER, MACVEY. *Selection from the Correspondence of the Late Macvey Napier.* London: Macmillan & Co., 1879.

NICHOLSON, ALEXANDER. *Memoirs of Adam Black.* Edinburgh: A. & C. Black, 1885.

OGLESBY, THADDEUS K. *Some Truths of History: A Vindication of the South against the Encyclopaedia Britannica and Other Maligners.* Atlanta, Ga.: Byrd, 1903.

OWEN, W. (ed.). *New and Complete Dictionary of Arts and Sciences.* London, 1754–63.

PEARSON, HESKETH. *Sir Walter Scott.* New York: Harper & Bros., 1954.

PHELPS, ROSE B. "The *Encyclopaedia Britannica:* 9th Edition." Unpublished Master's thesis, Columbia University, New York, 1930.

REED, DORIS M. "The *Encyclopaedia Britannica:* A Critical and Historical Study of the 11th Edition." Unpublished Master's thesis, Columbia University, New York, 1931.

RYAN, A. P. *Lord Northcliffe.* London: Collins Sons & Co., 1953.

SELIGMAN, E. R. A. *The Economics of Instalment Selling.* New York: Harper & Bros., 1927.

SHEEHAN, DONALD. *This Was Publishing.* Bloomington: Indiana University Press, 1952.

SHOVE, RAYMOND HOWARD. *Cheap Book Production in the United States, 1870–1891.* Urbana: University of Illinois Press, 1937.

SMILES, SAMUEL. *A Publisher and His Friends.* London: John Murray, 1911.

"The Times" and the Publishers. London: Publishers' Association, 1906.

TREDREY, F. D., *The House of Blackwood, 1804–1954.* Edinburgh: Blackwood & Sons, 1954.

TURNER, E. S. *The Shocking History of Advertising!* New York: E. P. Dutton & Co., 1953.

UNWIN, SIR STANLEY. *The Truth About Publishing.* London: Allen & Unwin, 1926.

WATT, FRANCIS. *The Book of Edinburgh Anecdote.* London: Foulis, 1912.

WELLS, DORIS M. "The Ownership and the Sales and Publication Policy of the *Encyclopaedia Britannica* since the Ninth Edition." Unpublished Master's thesis, Columbia University, New York, 1929.

WILSON, ARTHUR M. *Diderot: The Testing Years.* New York: Oxford University Press, 1957.

WRIGHT, WILLARD HUNTINGTON. *Misinforming a Nation.* New York: Huebsch, 1917.

Hundreds of articles in magazines and newspapers published in the United States and Great Britain were read. Because a full listing would be inordinately lengthy, the following is offered as representative of the scores of sources.

British:

Athenaeum, June 15, 1861, statistics on seventh and eighth editions of *Encyclopaedia Britannica;* Aug. 30, 1862, biography of Thomas Stewart Traill; June 7, Aug. 16, and Nov. 8, 1902, review of articles in tenth edition; Sept. 3, 1910, and Feb. 4, Feb. 25, Apr. 22, and Aug. 26, 1911, articles on controversy over *EB* affiliation with Cambridge University.

Blackwood's, April, 1817, review of supplement to fifth edition; March, 1927, "First English Encyclopaedia."

Connoisseur, March, 1911, review of eleventh edition.

Edinburgh Review, April, 1889, review of ninth edition.

Lancet, scattered editions from Feb. 25 through Nov. 25, 1911, especially on medical subjects in eleventh edition.

London Mercury, November, 1929, review of fourteenth edition.

Meliora, November, 1887, comments on eighth edition.

Nation, May 25 and Oct. 26, 1911, reviews and comment on eleventh edition.

Nature, scattered issues from Mar. 4 through Sept. 7, 1875, reviews and evaluations of scientific articles in early volumes of ninth edition; scattered issues from Feb. 2, 1911, through Jan. 11, 1912, comment on eleventh edition articles on scientific and technical subjects.

Publishers' Circular, scattered issues from Sept. 3, 1910, through Dec. 2, 1911, articles and comment in connection with Cambridge University and Hooper-Jackson litigation.

Review of Reviews, May, 1902, review of tenth edition; March, 1908, "Encyclopaedias, Past and Present" by Louis Windmuller.

Saturday Review, Apr. 4, 1903, on connection with the *Times.*

Tablet, scattered issues from Mar. 4, 1911, through Jan. 27, 1912, on music and architecture but mostly on Catholic criticism of eleventh edition.

The Month, August, 1882, "The *Encyclopaedia Britannica* on the Jesuits," by William Laughman; scattered issues from June through December, 1911, especially on Catholic criticism.

American:

America, scattered issues from July 8, through Sept. 9, 1911, criticism of Catholic articles in eleventh edition; Sept. 27, 1930, and Oct. 4, 1930, letters on Catholic articles.

American, May 22, 1896, article stressing need for more American contributors.

American Historical Review, October, 1911, historical summary by George L. Burr of development of encyclopaedias.

Annals of American Academy of Political and Social Science, 1911, "Encyclopaedia Britannica, 11th Edition," by Emory R. Johnson.

Bookman, January, 1927, "Hail, Columbia!" by Bartlett Cormack.

Business Week, Nov. 21, 1942, article on Sears, Roebuck ownership; May 14, 1953, a good summary of *EB*'s business history.

Independent, Aug. 24, 1911, "Trials of an Encyclopedist," by C. M. Francis; Jan. 4, 1912, "The *Encyclopaedia Britannica* and Catholicism," by Carlton J. H. Hayes.

Literary Digest, Feb. 21, 1914, "The King of All Encyclopaedias," article on the history of Chinese encyclopaedias; May 29, 1926, article about J. L. Garvin as editor.

Nation, May 25 and Oct. 26, 1911, "The New Britannica," by Louis Heilperin; Oct. 27, 1926, "Peace in the Encyclopaedia"; Oct. 23, 1929, "The World of Men and Things," by William Macdonald.

New Yorker, Nov. 29, 1952, Dwight Macdonald's review of *Great Books of the Western World*.

Outlook, Jan. 24, 1917, on "Americanization" of *EB*.

Philosophical Review, January, 1915, "Dilemma of Diderot" by Carl Becker.

Publishers' Weekly, Nov. 10, 1906, on the Book War; June 5, 1909, on Hooper-Jackson litigation; scattered editions from Oct. 22, 1910, through Jan. 7, 1911, on Cambridge affiliation; Sept. 2, 1911, and Mar. 30, 1912, Hooper-Jackson litigation; June 24, 1922, Hooper obituary; Mar. 31, 1923, "Romance of Book Publishing," account of life of Jackson; Jan. 30, 1943, transfer of *EB* to University of Chicago.

Reedy's Mirror, scattered issues from Jan. 14 through Nov. 24, 1916, anti-*EB* articles by William Marion Reedy; scattered issues from Nov. 24 through Dec. 29, 1916, "Culture in the *Encyclopaedia Britannica*," critical articles by Willard Huntington Wright later collected in his book, *Misinforming a Nation*.

Saturday Review of Literature, Oct. 23, 1926, "The New Britannica," by C. K. Ogden; Oct. 12, 1929, "Hail, Britannica!" by Allan Nevins, review of fourteenth edition; Oct. 19, 1929, "A History of Culture," further comment on fourteenth edition; Nov. 9, 1929, "Science in the Britannica," by James R. Angell; May 2, 1942, "Thirty-two Million Word Classic" by W. A. Lydgate; May 11, 1946, on errors in *EB*.

Saturday Evening Post, July 21–28, 1945, "160 Miles of Words" by Warren Olivier.

Time, Feb. 1, 1943, "Cachet without Cash"; Apr. 16, 1945, on art collection; Jan. 15, 1951, "From A to Zygote."

Newspapers most widely used—yet with varying frequency—were the *Times* of London, including scattered editions of its *Literary Supplement*, from 1885 to date; *New York Evening Post*, 1890–1900; *New York Herald-Tribune*, 1929 to date; *New York Times*, 1900 to date; *Chicago Daily News*, 1915 to date; *Chicago Record-Herald*, 1910; *Chicago Sun* and *Chicago Sun-Times*, 1943 to date; *Chicago Times*, 1935–36; *Chicago Tribune*, 1900 to date.

Index

Index

St. Andrews University, 52
St. Cyres, Viscount; *see* Northcote, Stafford Henry
St. James's Gazette, 89, 90, 144
St. John's College, 263
Salpeter, Harry, 265
Sandow, Eugene, 104, 112, 165
Saturday Review (British), 102
  on fourteenth edition, 229
Saturday Review (New York), on educational films, 263
  see also *Saturday Review of Literature*
Saturday Review of Literature (New York)
  on thirteenth edition, 217
  on fourteenth edition, 230
  see also *Saturday Review* (New York)
Saunders, George, 205
Savidge, Irene, 225–26
Savile Club, 202
Savoy Hotel, 96, 105, 135, 167
Scheer, Admiral Reinhard, 214
Schneider, Margaret, 189
Schoenewald, Louis G., 239–40, 242, 244, 260, 271–72
Schuster, M. Lincoln, 261
Scot, eighteenth-century engraver, 25
Scot's Journal, 9
Scot's Observer, 61
Scotsman, 39
Scott, Henry (Duke of Buccleuch), 14
Scott, Dr. James Brown, 213
Scott, Robert Falcon, 131
Scott, Sir Walter, 27
  contributions to fifth edition supplement, 32–35
  break with Constable, 39–41, 46
  mentioned, 49, 50, 68, 95
Scott's Miscellany, 41
Scribner's Sons, Charles, 63, 64, 65, 67, 185, 186
Seaborg, Glenn T., 290
Seaman, Paul E., 272, 301, 303, 304
Sears, Roebuck and Company, 196, 201, 204, 212, 222
  ownership of the *Encyclopaedia Britannica,* 228, 235–59
  later connections, 269–70, 276
Selfridge, Harry Gordon, 222
Servières, Jean Grolier de, 75
Seymour, eighteenth-century engraver, 25
Shadwell, Dr. Arthur, 123
Shakespeare, William, 19

Shattuck Military School, 250
Shaw, Flora, 80
Shaw, George Bernard, 123, 212–13, 289–90, 298
Shelley, Percy Bysshe, 55
Sheraton, Thomas, 43
Sherer, Albert W., 261
Shipman, Judge William D., 67–68
Shirk, A. Urban, 297
Shotwell, James T., 227
Sibley, Mrs. Clara Frances, 126
Sibley, Dr. Walter Knowsley, 126–27, 128
Sickert, Oswald, 106, 163, 165
Signs of the Times, or The Hustler's Almanac for 1907, 125
Simpkin, Marshall and Company, 115, 122
Simpson, Dr. W. D., 229–30
"$64,000 Question, The," 244
Skinner, Otis, 226
Smellie, Alexander, 9
Smellie, William, 8
  and first edition of *Encyclopaedia Britannica,* 9–14
  later writings, 14
  final years, 14–15
  mentioned, 16, 23, 42, 95
Smith, Alfred E., 226
Smith, Sydney, 27, 32
Smith, William Pirie, 55
Smith, William Robertson
  early life, 55–56
  articles for ninth edition of the *Encyclopaedia Britannica,* 56
  subsequent controversy, 57–61
  appointed co-editor of ninth edition, 60–61
  final years, 61
  mentioned, 62, 66, 173, 293
Smither, eighteenth-century engraver, 25
Society of Antiquarians of Scotland, 14
Society for the Checking of Abuses in Public Advertising, 73
Society of Writers to the Signet, 27
Some Truths of History, 64
Sonneman, Ralph, 312
Spanish-American War, 84
Spectator, on eleventh edition, 173–74
Spencer, Herbert, 55
Spiegel, Inc., 271
Stagg, Amos Alonzo, 217
Stalin, Joseph, 216
Standard, 133
Standard American Publishing Company, 91

Starr, Cecile, 263
Stead, William T., 139
Stedman, Edmund Clarence, 55
Steele, Richard, 10
Stefansson, Vilhjalmur, 275
Stevens, David, 253
Stevenson, Adlai E., 261
Stevenson, Kennedy, 261
Stevenson, Robert Louis, 54–55, 56
Stewart, Dugald, 31–32, 46, 48, 51
Stewart, Colonel Matthew, 48
Stimson, Henry L., 227
Stoddart, Joseph M., 64–65
Stoddart's Weekly, 65
Stolen, Ernest V., 312
Strand Magazine, 72
Strauss, Lewis L., 274
Stuart, Gilbert, 13–14
Stuart, John, 261
Studebaker Company, 261
Studies in Contemporary Biography,
61 n.
Subscription book selling
in the eighteenth century, 9–10
in the late-nineteenth century, 70–
71
in World War I, 201
Swift, Harold H., 256, 257, 259
Swift, Jonathan, 33
Swinburne, Algernon Charles, 55, 223,
234
Symonds, John Addington, 234
Syntopicon, 264
System of Chemistry, 26

Tables of Grammar, 10
Tablet, criticisms of eleventh edition,
174–75, 176, 177–78
Taft, William Howard, 162
T'ai P'ing Yu Tan, 6
Tatler, 170
Taunton, Rev. Ethelred, 174
Ten Eventful Years, 266–67, 271
Thackara, eighteenth-century engraver,
25
Thackeray, William Makepeace, 4, 68
Theiss, Earl E., 306
These Eventful Years, 212–15
Thomas, Albert, 213
Thomas, Isaiah, 70
Thompson, Abram, 43
Thompson, Sir Joseph, 203
Thomson, Dr. Thomas, 26, 42
Thomson, William (Lord Kelvin), 59
Thring, G. Herbert, 124
Time, 254

Times (London), 3–6, 47, 73, 76–77
history and crisis, 77–81
affiliation with *Encyclopaedia Britannica*, 81–83
ads for *Times* reprint, 83–84
and tenth edition, 96
"Tournament for Readers," 96–102
Norahcliffe acquires, 132–40
mentioned, 87, 88, 89, 107, 108, 109,
113, 114, 116, 117, 118, 119,
121, 122, 123, 124, 125, 126,
127, 128, 142, 143, 146, 150,
151, 164, 179, 187, 188, 191,
204, 205, 230
Times Beer Club, 126
Times Book Club, 114–31, 140–42, 168
Times Book Club Festival, 126
Times Cigar Club, 126
Times Cooperative Clothing Club, 125
Times Egg Club, 125
Times Furnishing Company, Ltd., 89
Times Gazetteer, 4, 81, 89, 108
Times Literary Supplement, 80, 120,
122, 129–30, 229–30,
Times Meat Club, 125
Times Private Motoring Track, 126
Times Royal Academy, 125–26
Tirpitz, Admiral Alfred von, 214
Tit-Bits, 72
Tolstoy, Leo, 264
Torrington (Conn.) *Register*, 237
Tovey, Donald Francis, 172, 234, 290
Tower of Babel, 19
Trafalgar Hotel, 51
Traill, Thomas, 49
Traill, Dr. Thomas Stewart, 49
Trenchard, eighteenth-century en-
graver, 25
Trevelyan, George, 123
Trinity College (Dublin), 174
Trotsky, Leon, 216
Truman, Harry S., 270, 286
Tunney, Gene, 226, 230
Twain, Mark; *see* Clemens, Samuel
Langhorne
"Twenty-one," 244
Tyler, Ralph, 261
Tytler, John, 17–23
on "Flying," 20–21
his *System of Surgery*, 22
"The Rising of the Sun in the West,"
22
death of, 22–23

Union of Soviet Socialist Republics,
274, 293

United States Rubber Company, 302
Universal Encyclopaedia, 65
Universal History, 17
University Club (New York), 243
University of Chicago, 221–22, 238, 245, 249, 251, 252
  affiliation with the *Encyclopaedia Britannica,* 253–59, 260, 261, 263, 265, 269, 271, 275, 278, 283, 294
University of Chicago Federated Theological Faculty, 294
University of Chicago Press, 253
"University of Chicago Round Table," 252–53
University of Chicago's Public Relations, The, 251
University of Dublin, 202
University of Ghent, 205
University of Illinois, 272
University of London, 221, 277, 283
University of Pennsylvania, 235
Untermeyer, Louis, 216
Untermyer, Irwin, 197
Untermyer, Samuel, 183–88, 197, 228
Ussher, Archbishop James, 19
Utilitarianism, 35, 36

Van Dine, S. S.; *see* Wright, Willard Huntington
Van Doren, Carl, 216
Van Doren, Mark, 263
Vassar College, 230–31
Victoria, Queen, 129, 131, 140, 190
Vincent of Beauvais, 6
Virgil, 10
Voltaire, 7
Voroshilov, Klementi, 293
Voyage of the Discovery, 131
Vvedensky, B. A., 293

Walgreen, Charles R., 251–52
Wallace, Donald MacKenzie, 80, 89–91, 93, 95
Walter, Arthur Fraser, 5, 79–80, 111, 115–16, 126, 127, 128, 132–40
Walter, Don E., 274
Walter, Godfrey, 126, 132–33
Walter, John, 3, 78, 126
Walter, John II, 78–79
Walter, John III, 79, 81
Wanamaker, John, 67, 103
War of 1812, 33
Wardle, Thomas, 38
Warrington, Justice, 128, 139
Washington, George, 25, 51, 294
Washington, Martha, 297

Watson, Dr. John B., 227
Watt, James, 293
Waugh, Frederic, 265
Weedon's Modern Encyclopaedia, 242
Weekly Journal, 9
Weir, Robin, 297
Wellhausen, Julius, 60
Wells, H. G., 104, 214, 223
Western Book and Stationery Company, 71, 91
Western Electric Company, 261
Westminster Catholic Federation, 225
Westminster Review, 36
Whately, Archbishop Richard, 51
Whinery, Charles Crawford, 143, 147, 148, 149, 154, 201–2
Whipple, Sherman, 184
White, Joseph Blanco, 46
Whitney, Dr. William D., 69
Wight, Alexander, 43
Wilkinson, Clennell, 231, 233
William Shakespeare, 263
Wills, Helen, 226
Wilson, James, 312
Wilson, P. W., 243
Wilson, Woodrow, 168, 201, 205
Wisdom on the Hire System, 104–5
Wisdom While You Wait: Being a Foretaste of the Glories of the Inside-completuar Britanniaware, 102–4
Wolf, Dr. Abraham, 221
Wollken, Charles, 198–99
Wollman, Henry, 152, 154
Wood, Sir Evelyn, 131
Wood, Grant, 265
Wood, Merritt M., Jr., 311
Wood, General Robert E., 236–37, 238, 245, 253
  negotiations to transfer ownership of the *Encyclopaedia Britannica* to the University of Chicago, 254–59
  later connections with *Encyclopaedia Britannica,* 269–70, 278
Worcester Spy, 70
World Book Encyclopaedia, 273
World Language Dictionary, 274, 292, 300, 305
World War I, 193–94, 201, 266
World War II, 254, 269
World's Columbian Exposition, 69
Wright, Richard T., 157–58
Wright, Thomas, 123
Wright, Willard Huntington (S. S. Van Dine), 200–201, 217, 293
Wynne, Rev. John S., 175, 176

PRINTED IN THE U.S.A.